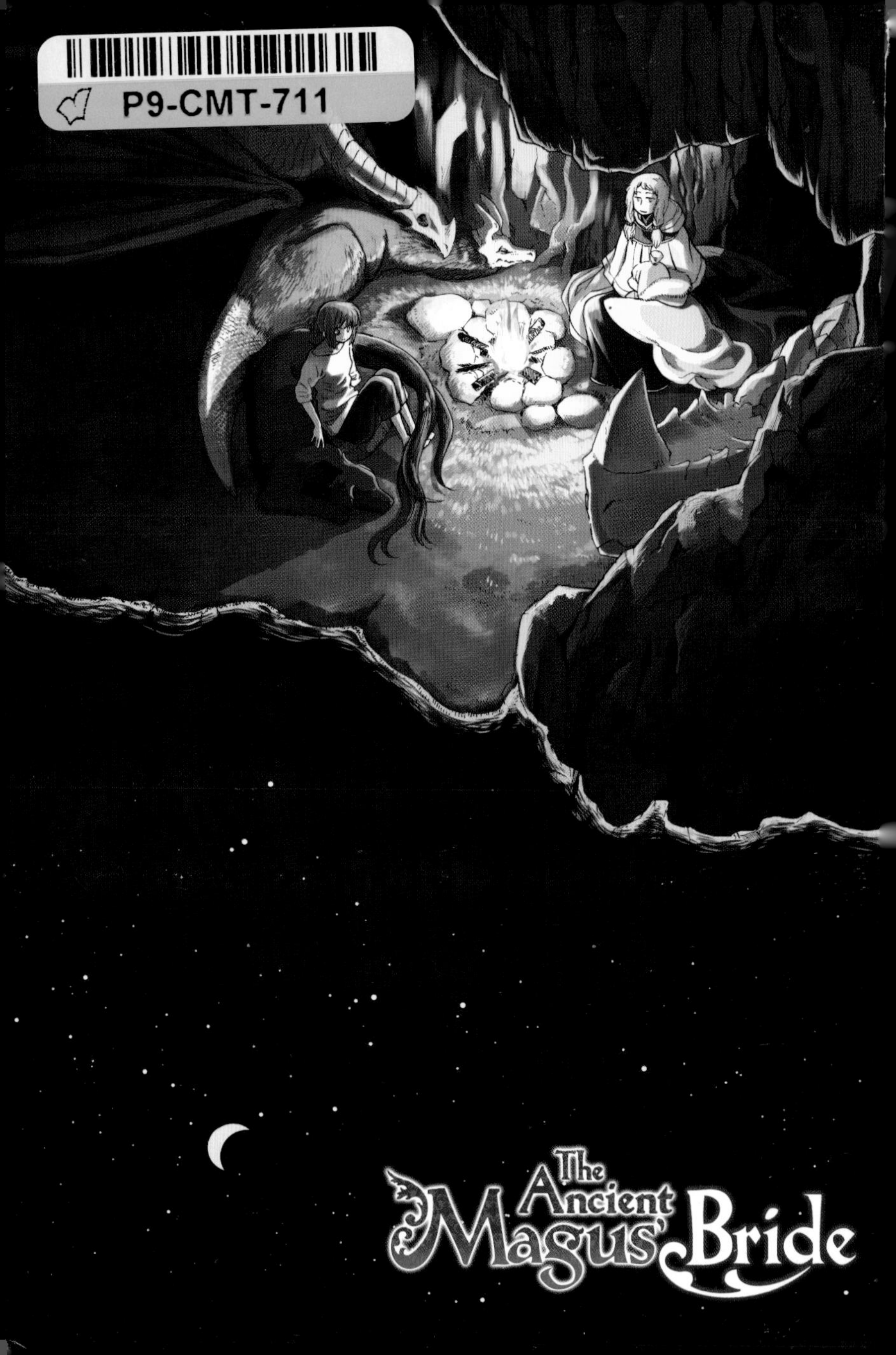
The Ancient Magus' Bride

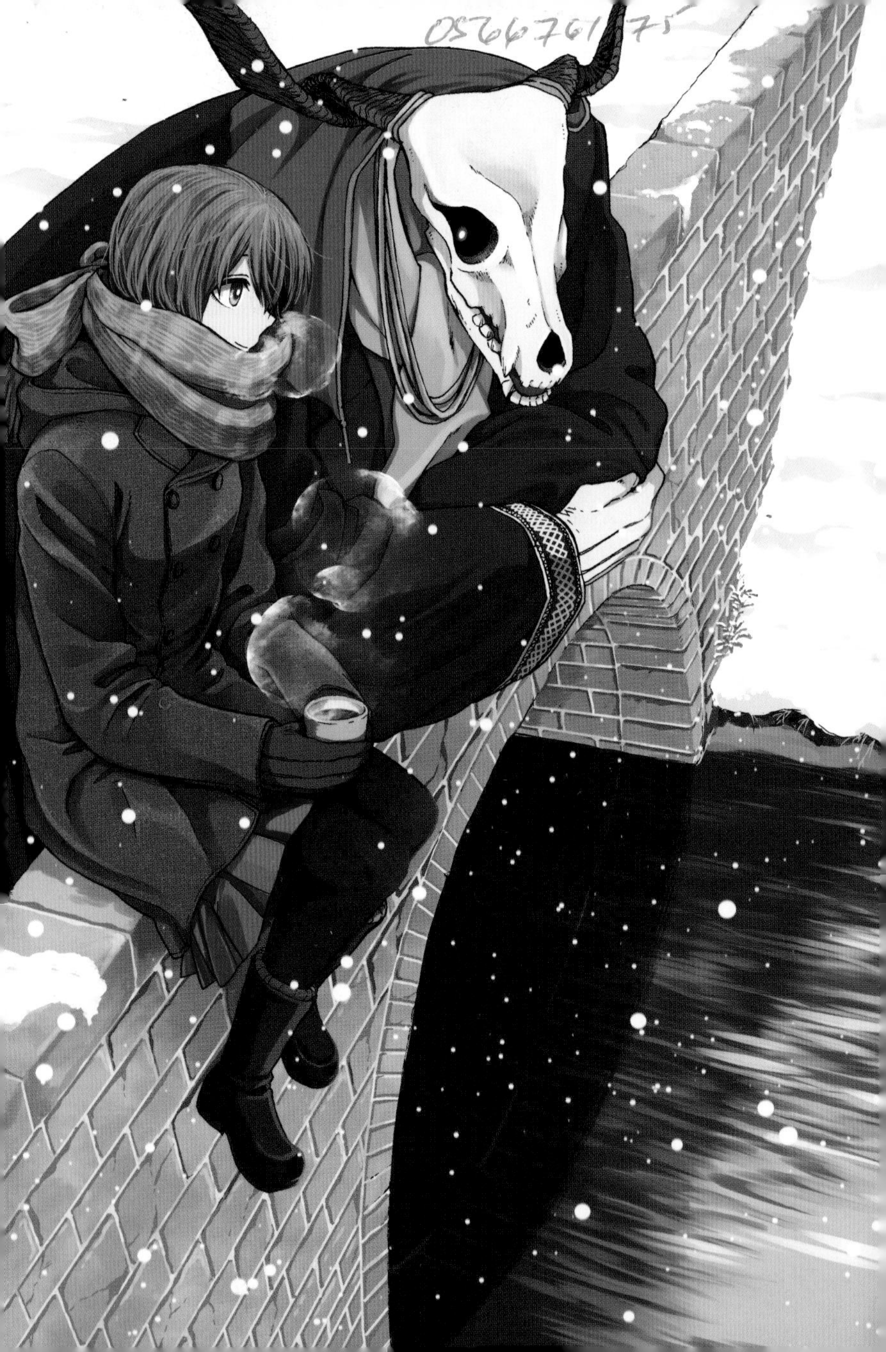

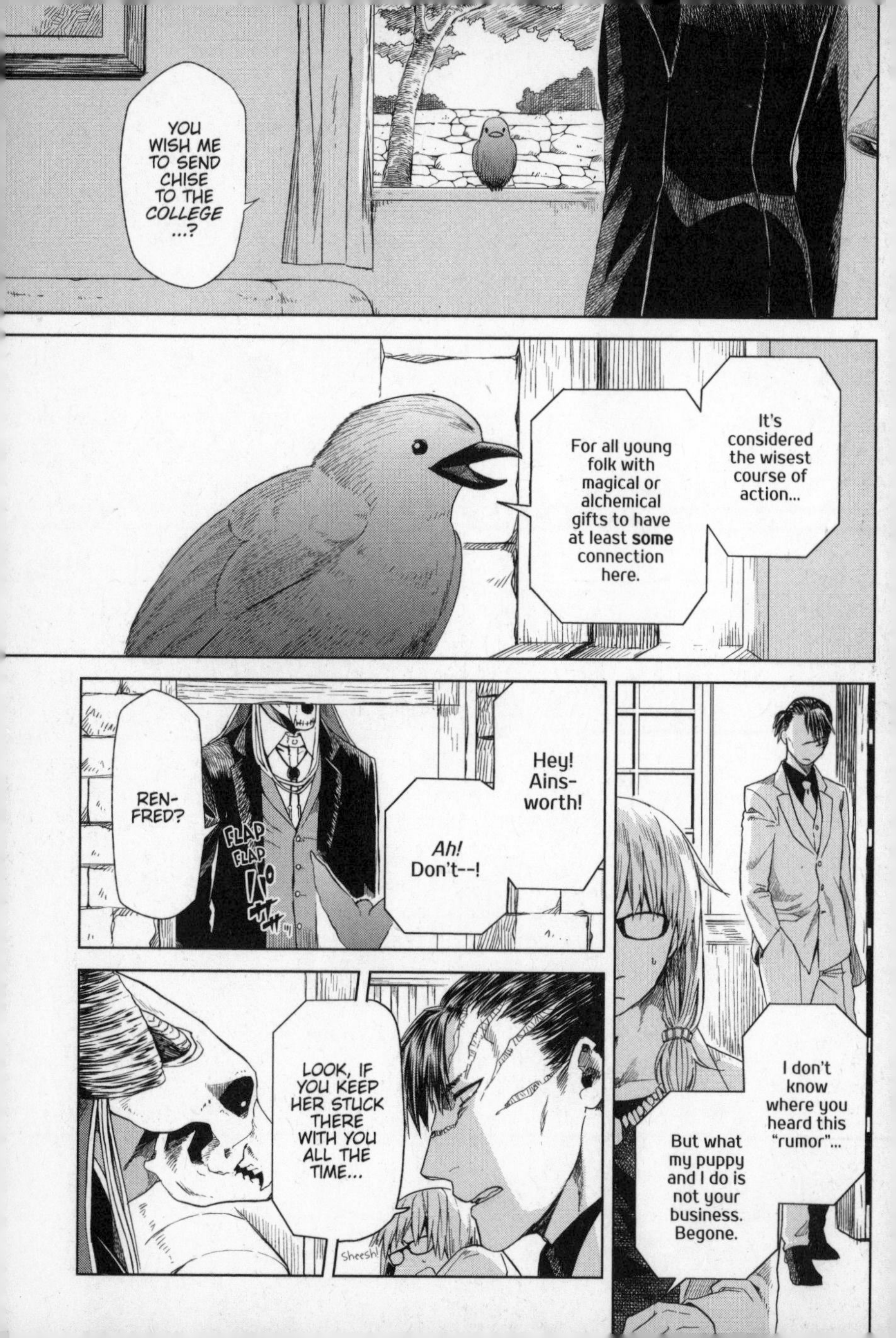
YOU WISH ME TO SEND CHISE TO THE COLLEGE ...?
It's considered the wisest course of action...
For all young folk with magical or alchemical gifts to have at least **some** connection here.
I don't know where you heard this "rumor"...
But what my puppy and I do is not your business. Begone.
Hey! Ainsworth!
Ah! Don't--!
REN-FRED?
FLAP FLAP
LOOK, IF YOU KEEP HER STUCK THERE WITH YOU ALL THE TIME...
Sheesh!

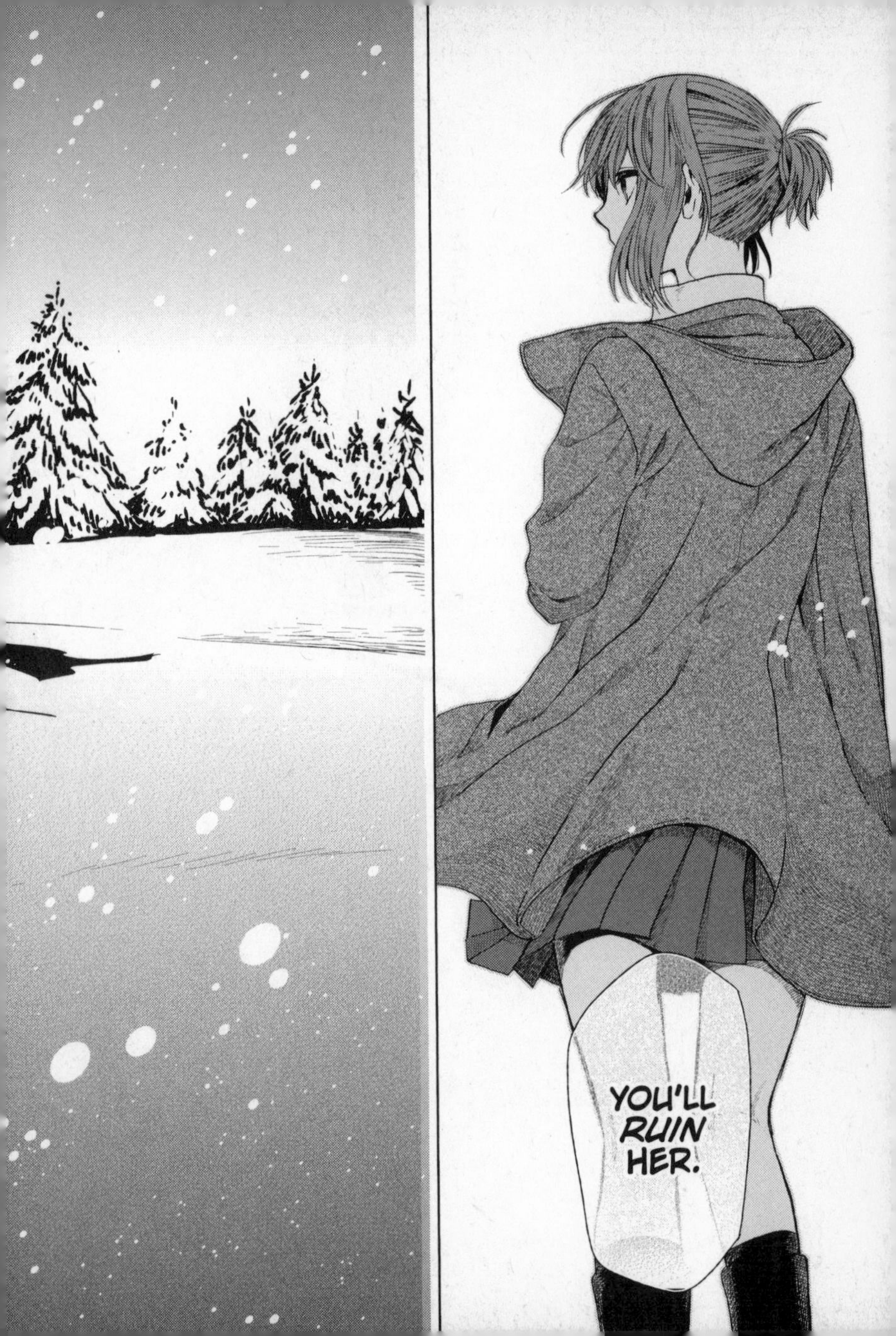
YOU'LL RUIN HER.

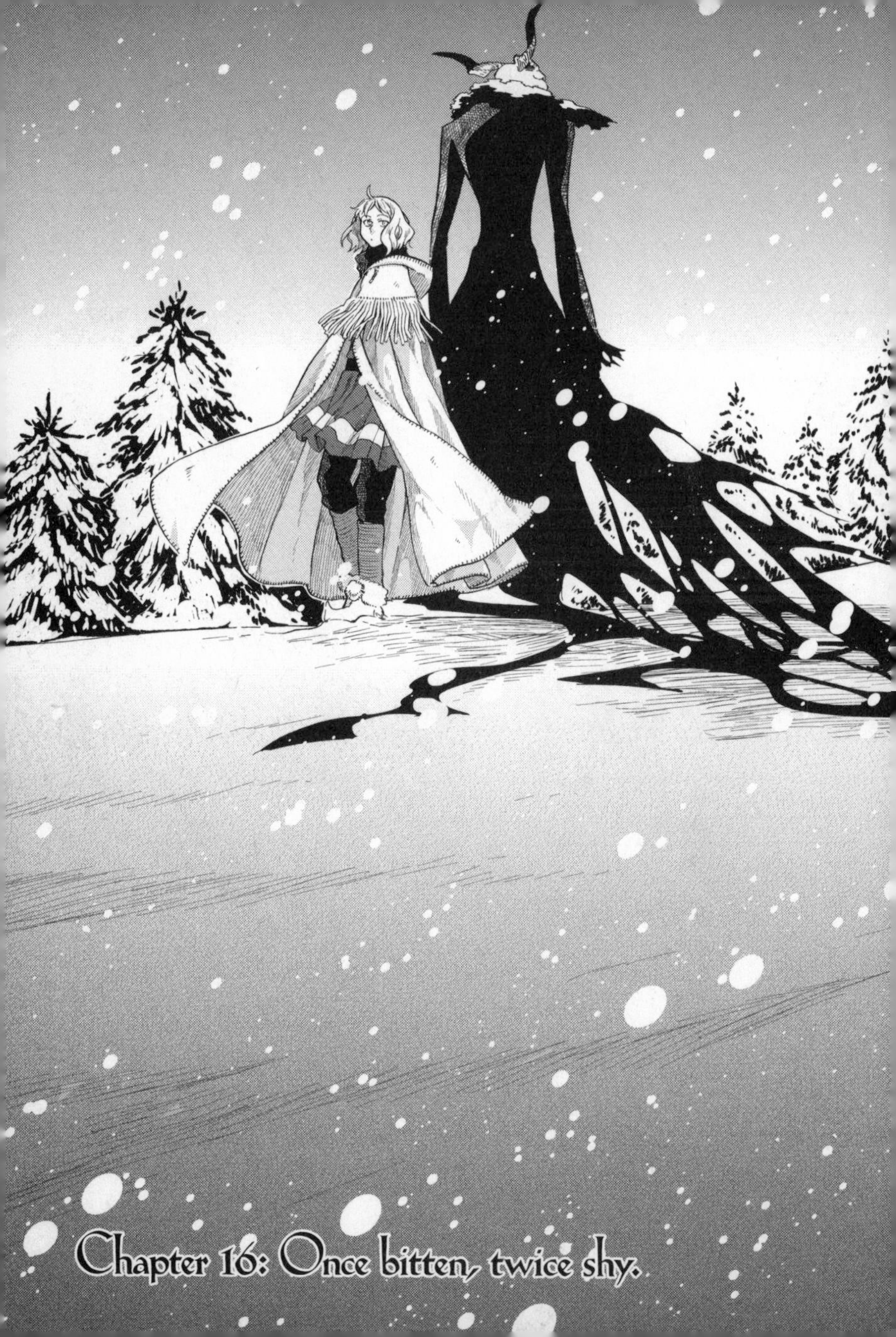

Chapter 16: Once bitten, twice shy.

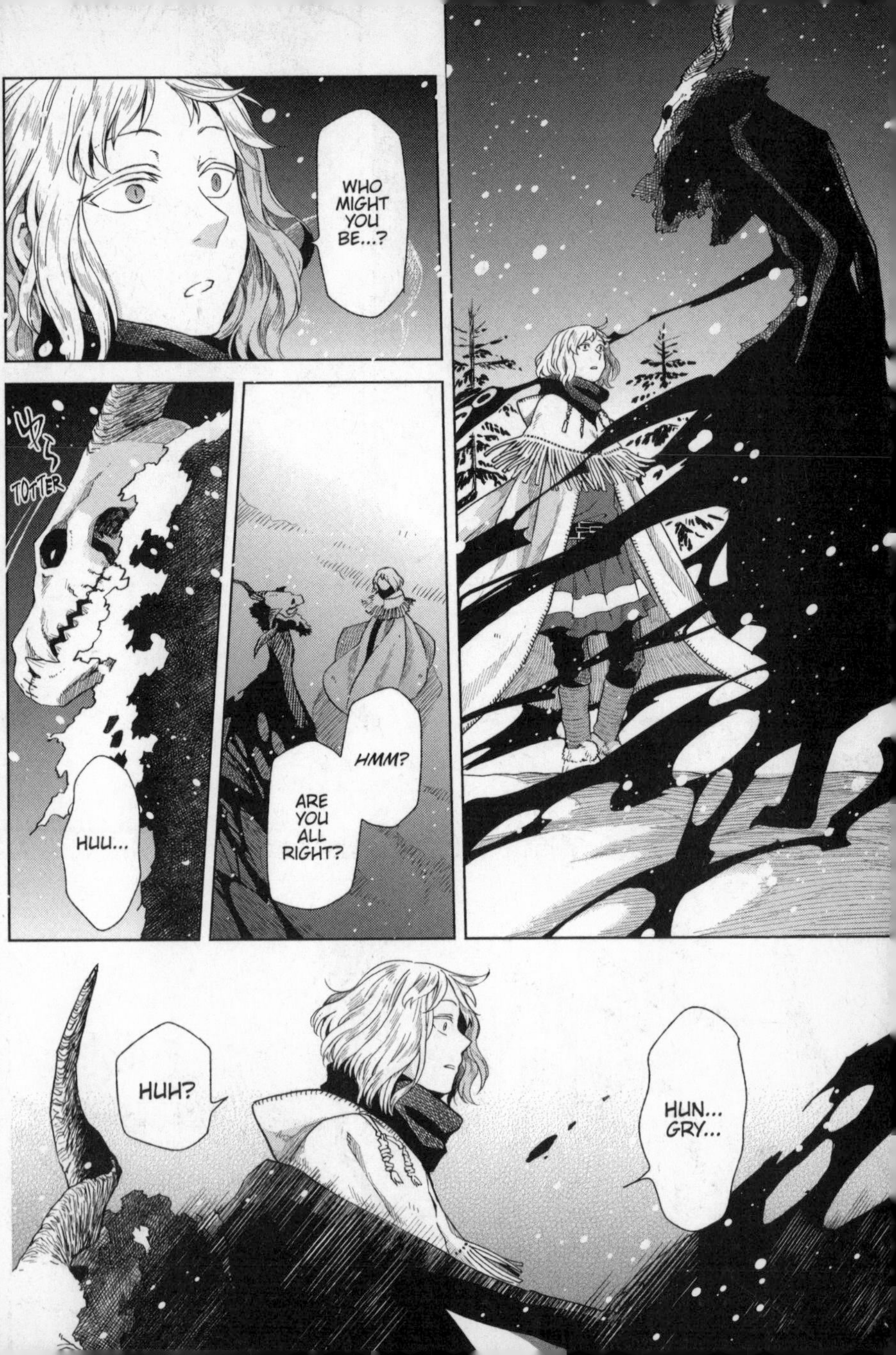
WHO MIGHT YOU BE...?
HMM?
ARE YOU ALL RIGHT?
TOTTER
HUU...
HUN... GRY...
HUH?

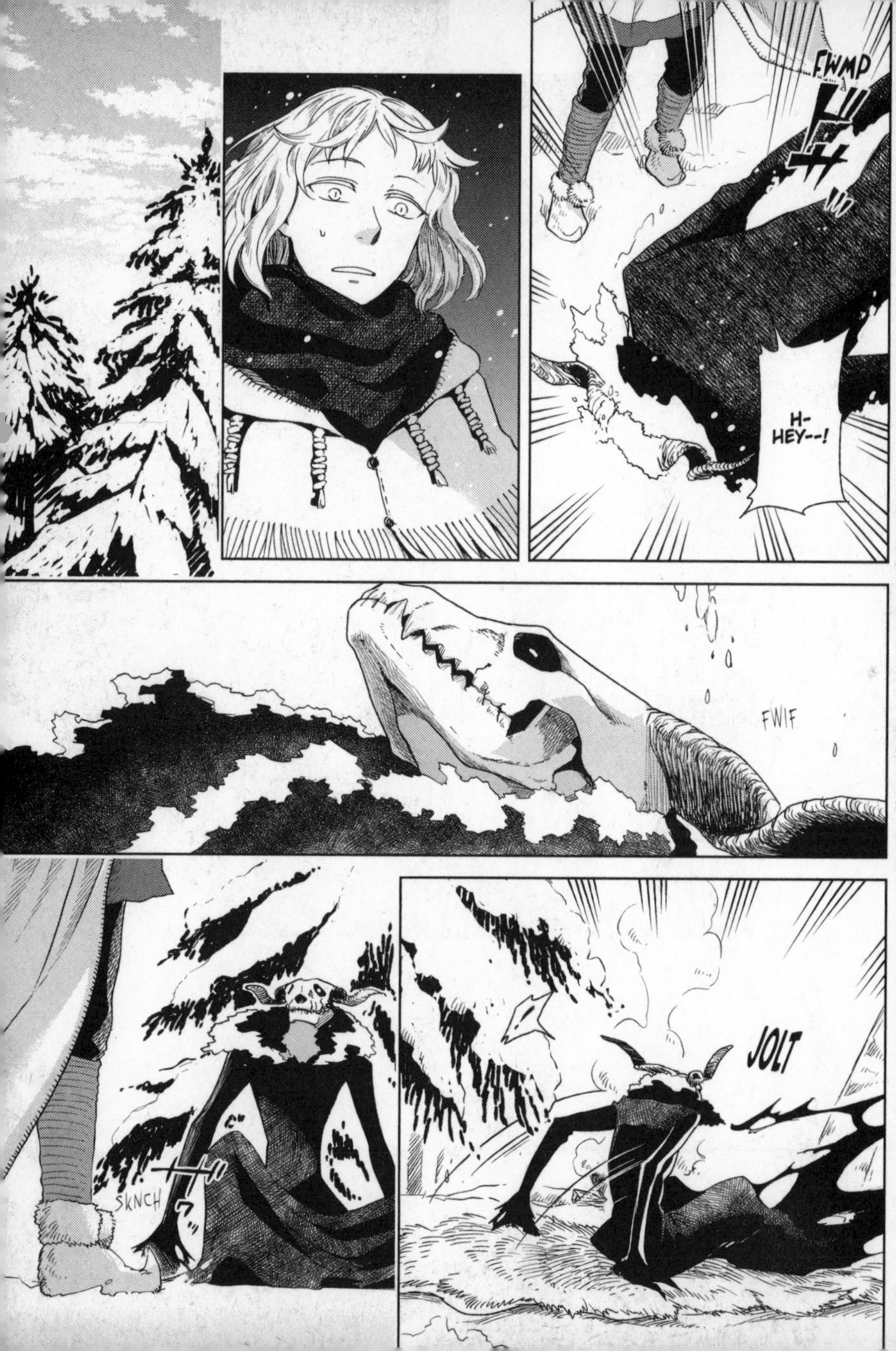
FWMP
H-
HEY--!
FWIF
JOLT
SKNCH

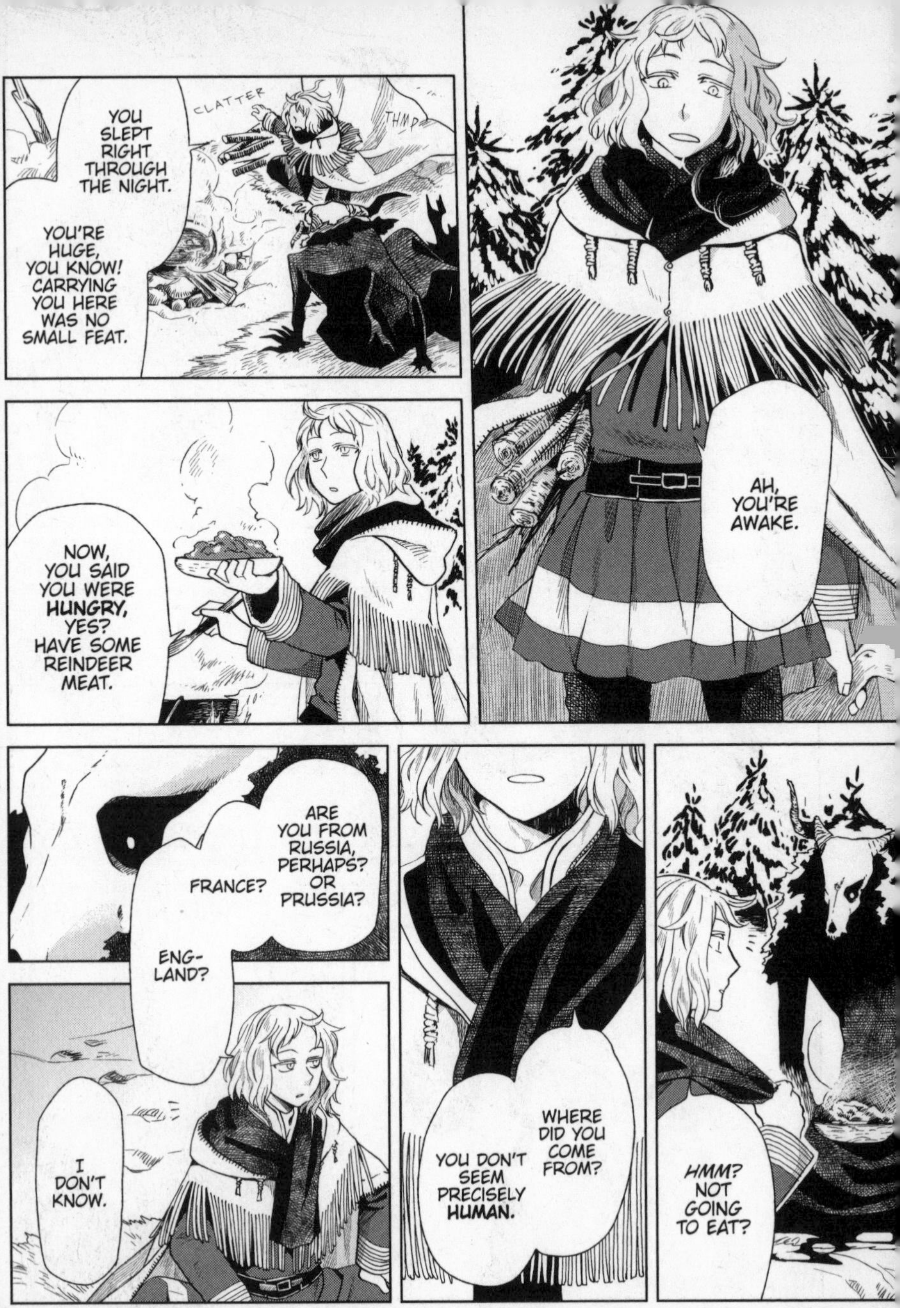
AH, YOU'RE AWAKE.
CLATTER
THMP
YOU SLEPT RIGHT THROUGH THE NIGHT.
YOU'RE HUGE, YOU KNOW! CARRYING YOU HERE WAS NO SMALL FEAT.
NOW, YOU SAID YOU WERE **HUNGRY,** YES? HAVE SOME REINDEER MEAT.
HMM? NOT GOING TO EAT?
WHERE DID YOU COME FROM?
YOU DON'T SEEM PRECISELY **HUMAN.**
ARE YOU FROM RUSSIA, PERHAPS? OR PRUSSIA?
FRANCE?
ENG-LAND?
I DON'T KNOW.

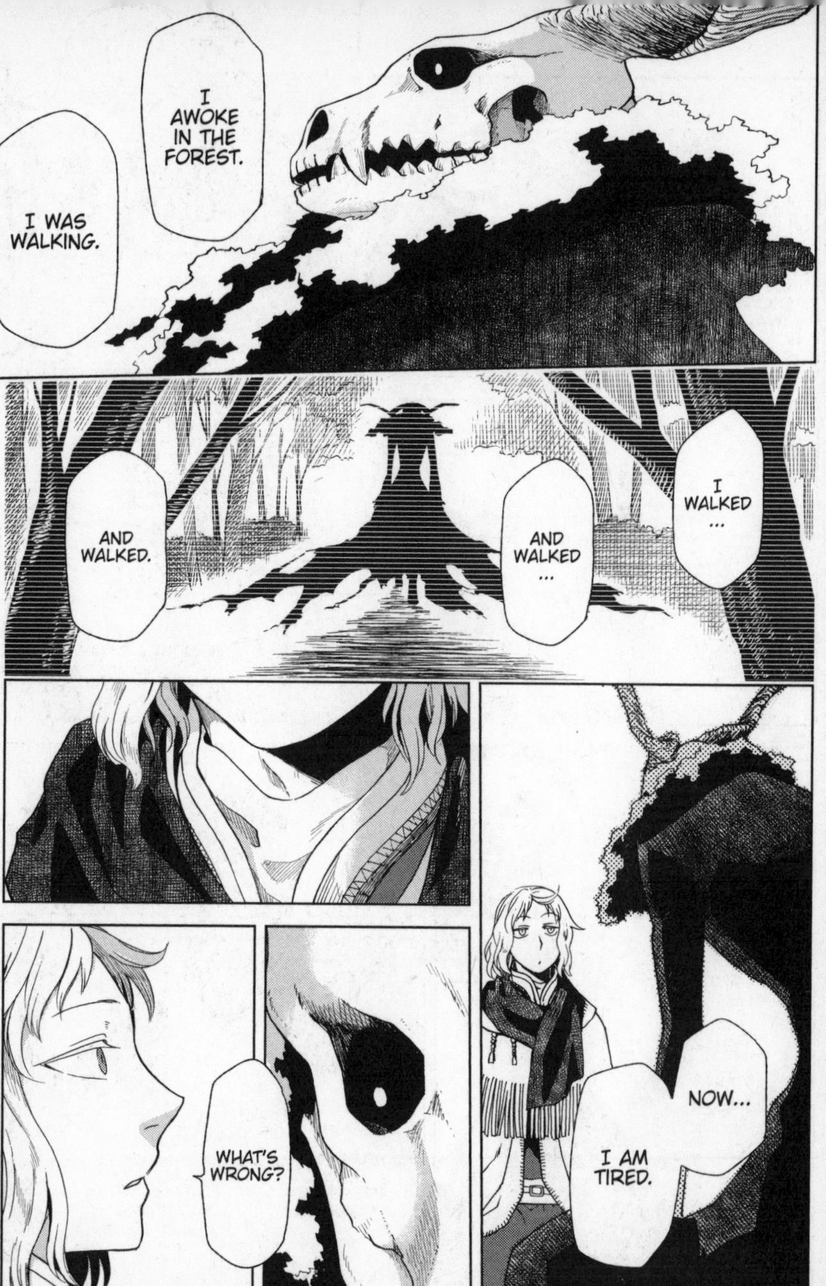
I AWOKE IN THE FOREST.
I WAS WALKING.
I WALKED ...
AND WALKED ...
AND WALKED.
NOW...
I AM TIRED.
WHAT'S WRONG?

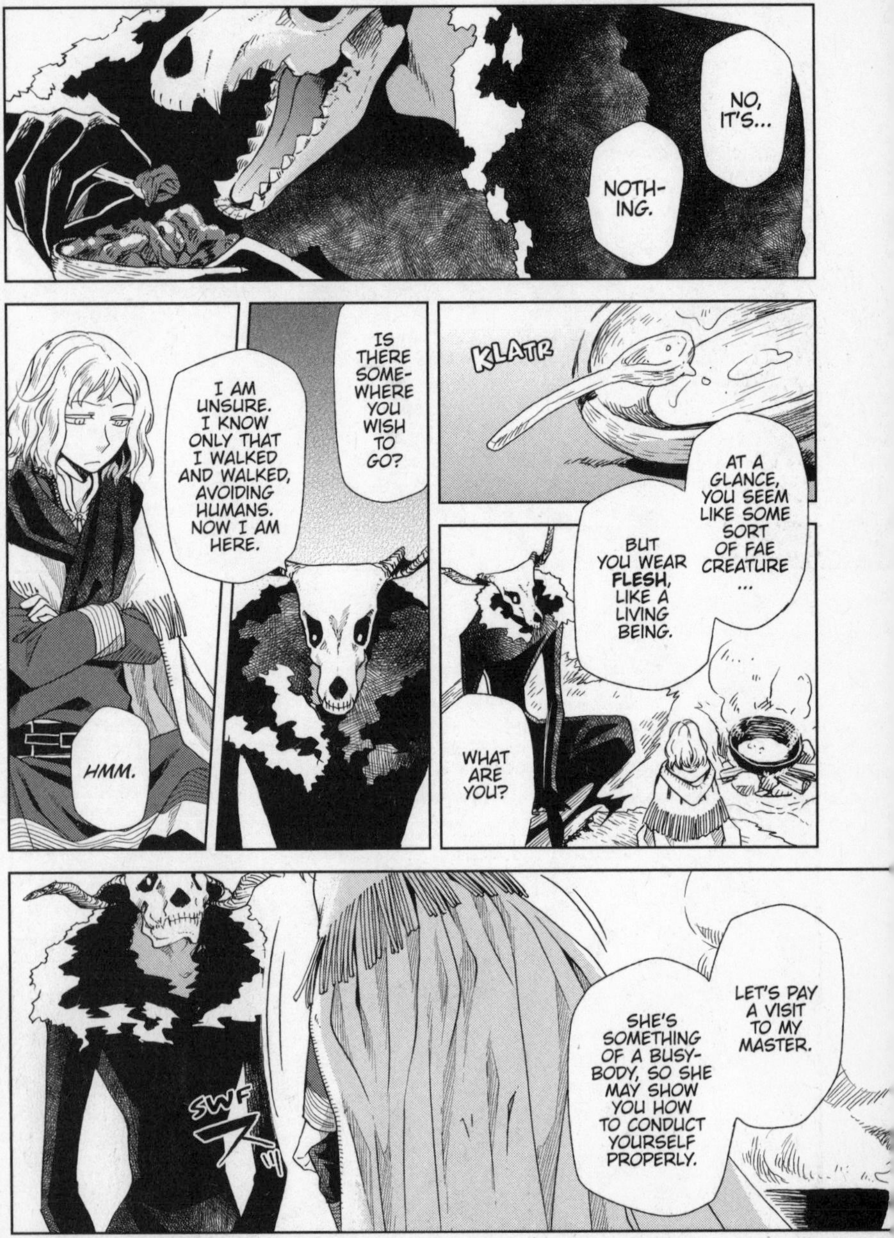
NO, IT'S...
NOTH-ING.
KLATR
AT A GLANCE, YOU SEEM LIKE SOME SORT OF FAE CREATURE ...
BUT YOU WEAR **FLESH**, LIKE A LIVING BEING.
...
WHAT ARE YOU?
IS THERE SOMEWHERE YOU WISH TO GO?
I AM UNSURE. I KNOW ONLY THAT I WALKED AND WALKED, AVOIDING HUMANS. NOW I AM HERE.
HMM.
LET'S PAY A VISIT TO MY MASTER.
SHE'S SOMETHING OF A BUSY-BODY, SO SHE MAY SHOW YOU HOW TO CONDUCT YOURSELF PROPERLY.
SWF

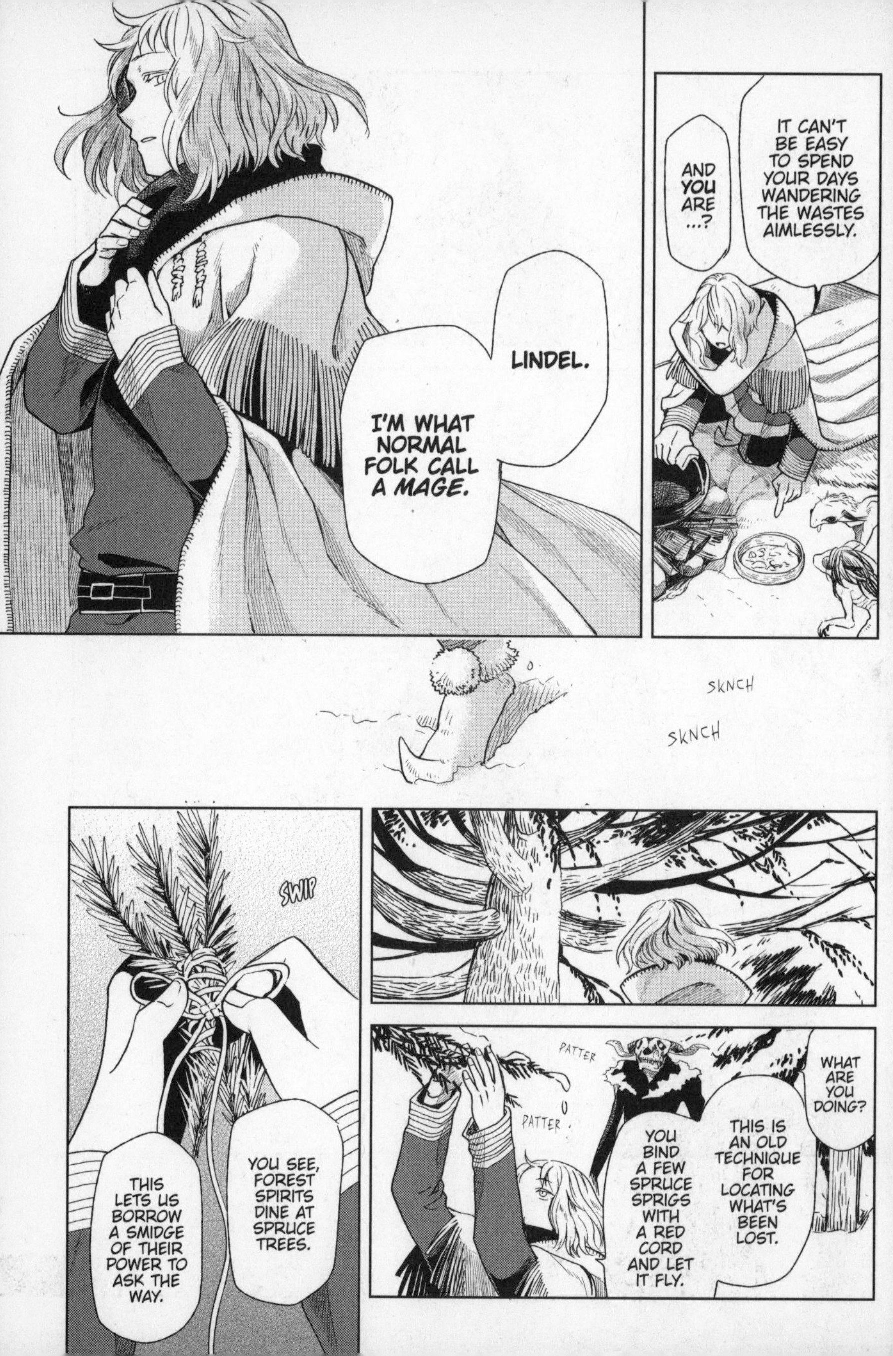
IT CAN'T BE EASY TO SPEND YOUR DAYS WANDERING THE WASTES AIMLESSLY.
AND YOU ARE ...?
LINDEL.
I'M WHAT NORMAL FOLK CALL A *MAGE.*
SKNCH
SKNCH
WHAT ARE YOU DOING?
THIS IS AN OLD TECHNIQUE FOR LOCATING WHAT'S BEEN LOST.
YOU BIND A FEW SPRUCE SPRIGS WITH A RED CORD AND LET IT FLY.
PATTER
PATTER
SWIP
YOU SEE, FOREST SPIRITS DINE AT SPRUCE TREES.
THIS LETS US BORROW A SMIDGE OF THEIR POWER TO ASK THE WAY.

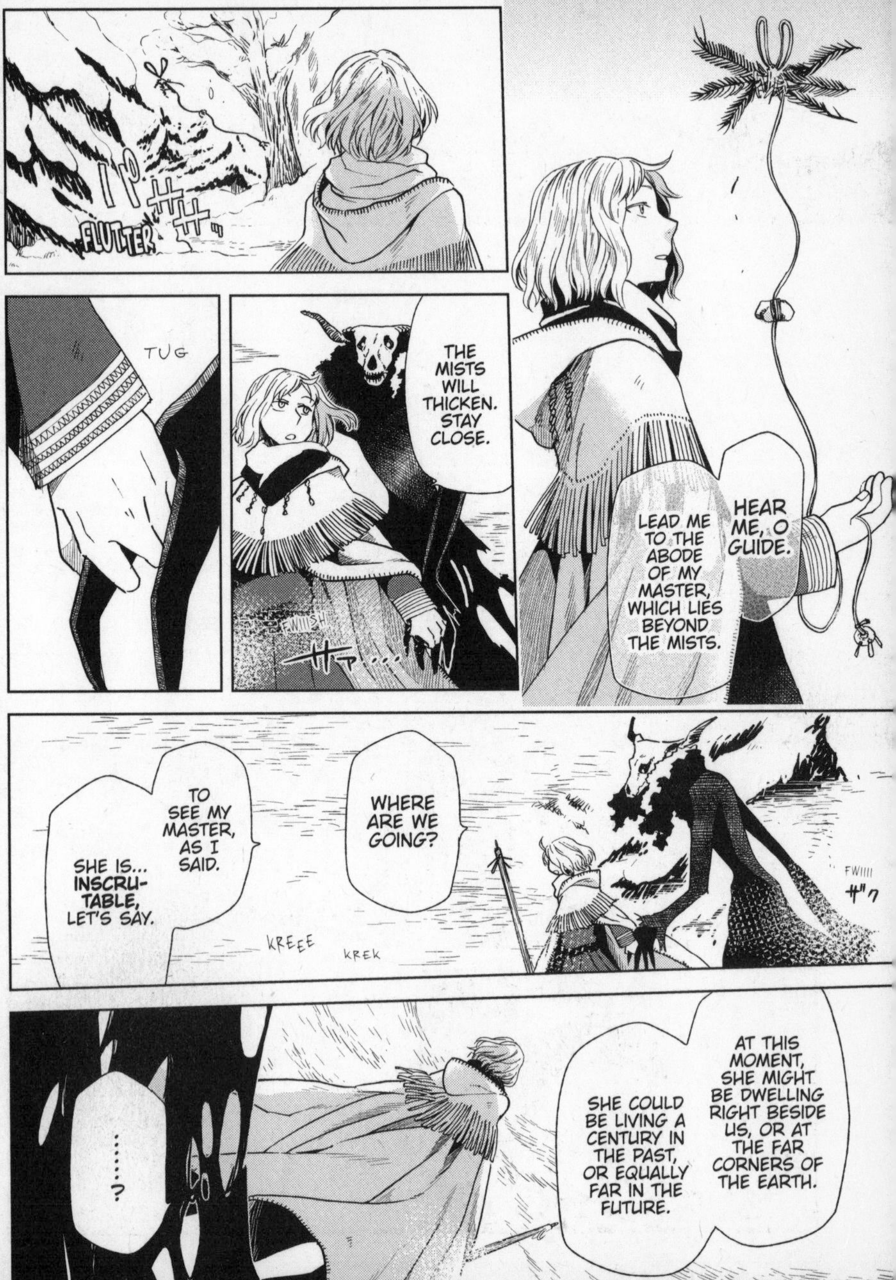
HEAR ME, O GUIDE.
LEAD ME TO THE ABODE OF MY MASTER, WHICH LIES BEYOND THE MISTS.
FLUTTER
THE MISTS WILL THICKEN. STAY CLOSE.
FWIISH
TUG
FWIIII
WHERE ARE WE GOING?
TO SEE MY MASTER, AS I SAID.
SHE IS... INSCRUTABLE, LET'S SAY.
KREEE
KREK
AT THIS MOMENT, SHE MIGHT BE DWELLING RIGHT BESIDE US, OR AT THE FAR CORNERS OF THE EARTH.
SHE COULD BE LIVING A CENTURY IN THE PAST, OR EQUALLY FAR IN THE FUTURE.
......?

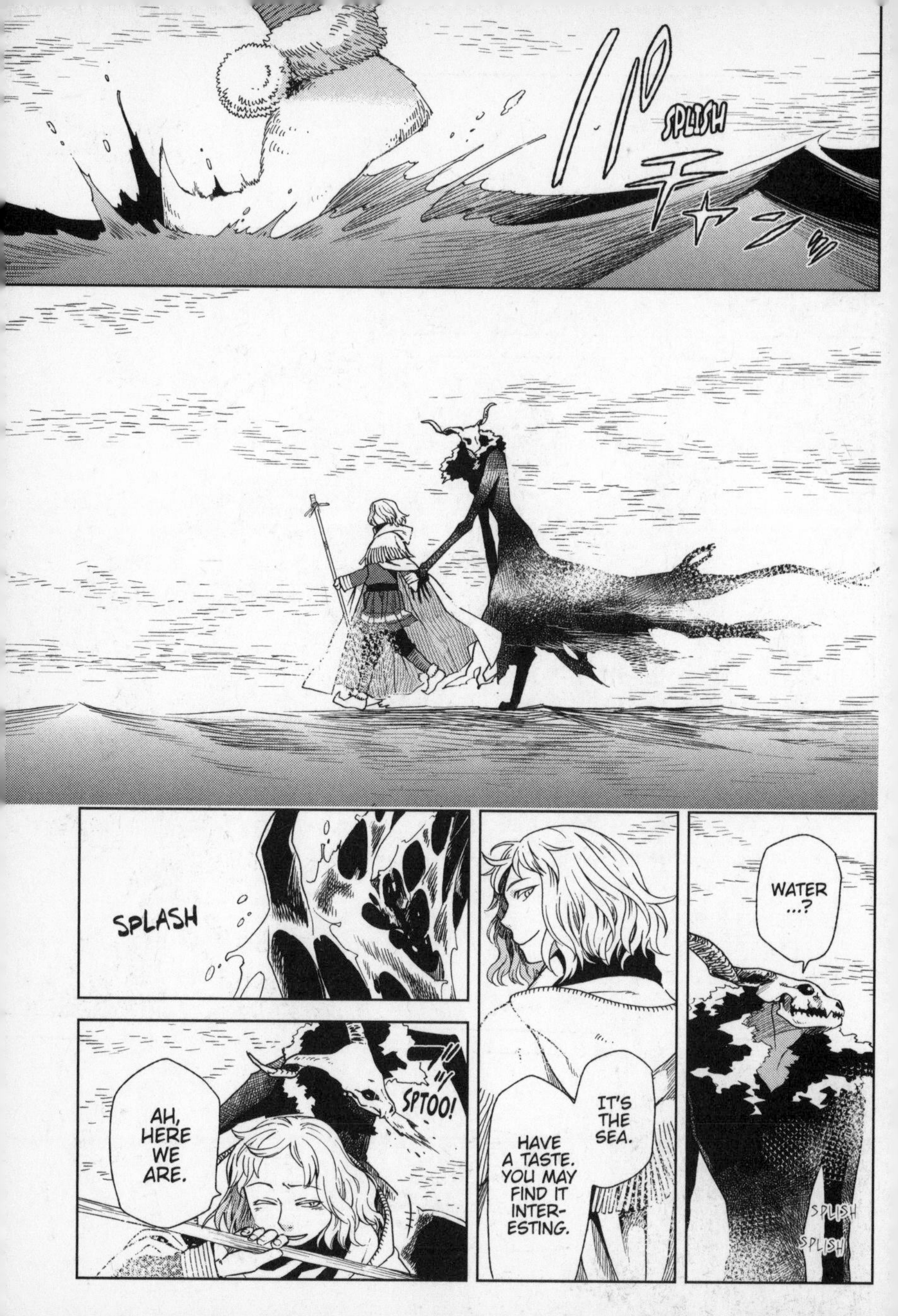
SPLISH
パチャンッ
WATER ...?
SPLISH
SPLISH
IT'S THE SEA.
HAVE A TASTE. YOU MAY FIND IT INTER-ESTING.
SPLASH
SPTOO!
AH, HERE WE ARE.

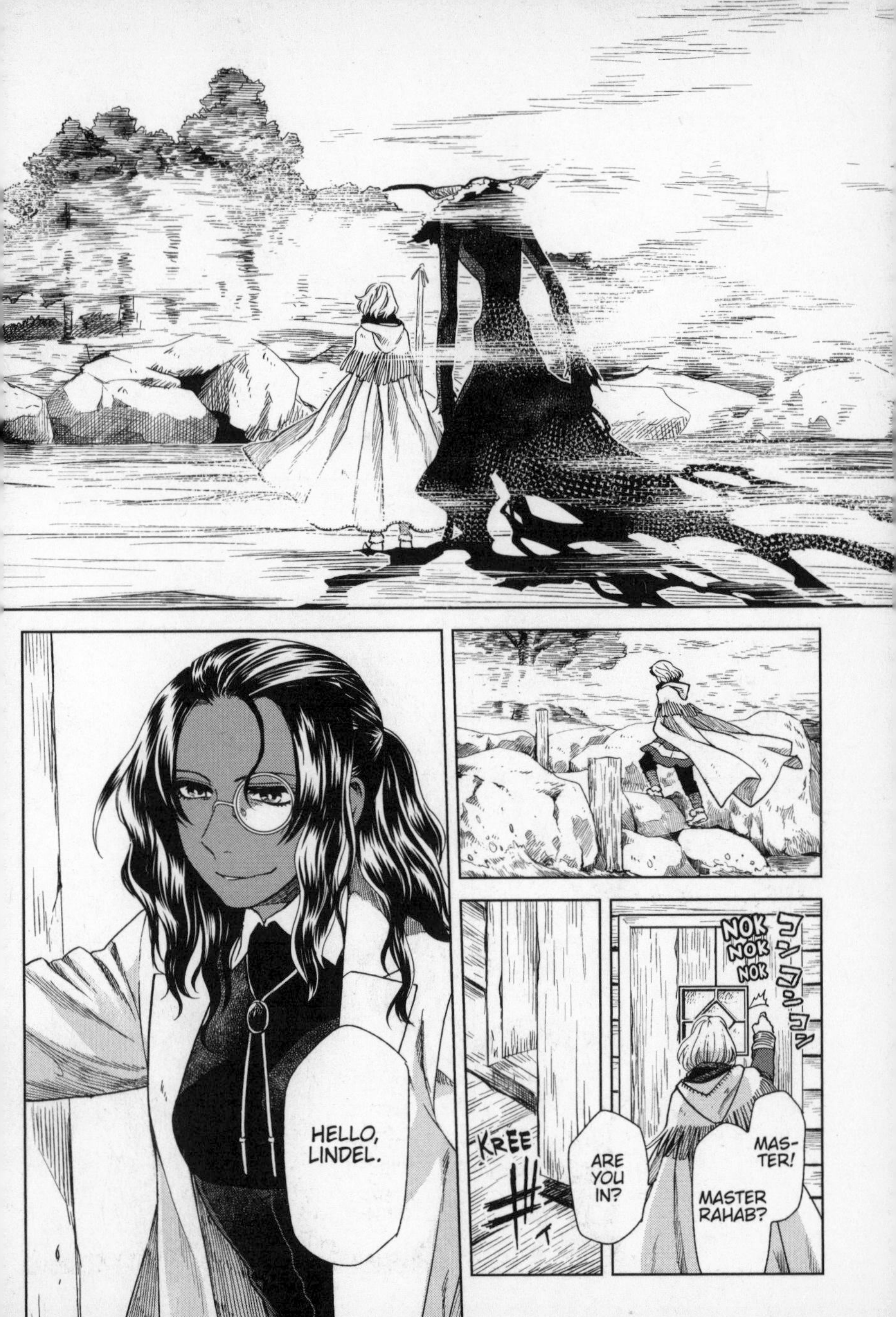
NOK NOK NOK
コンコンコン
MAS-TER!
MASTER RAHAB?
ARE YOU IN?
KREE
HELLO, LINDEL.

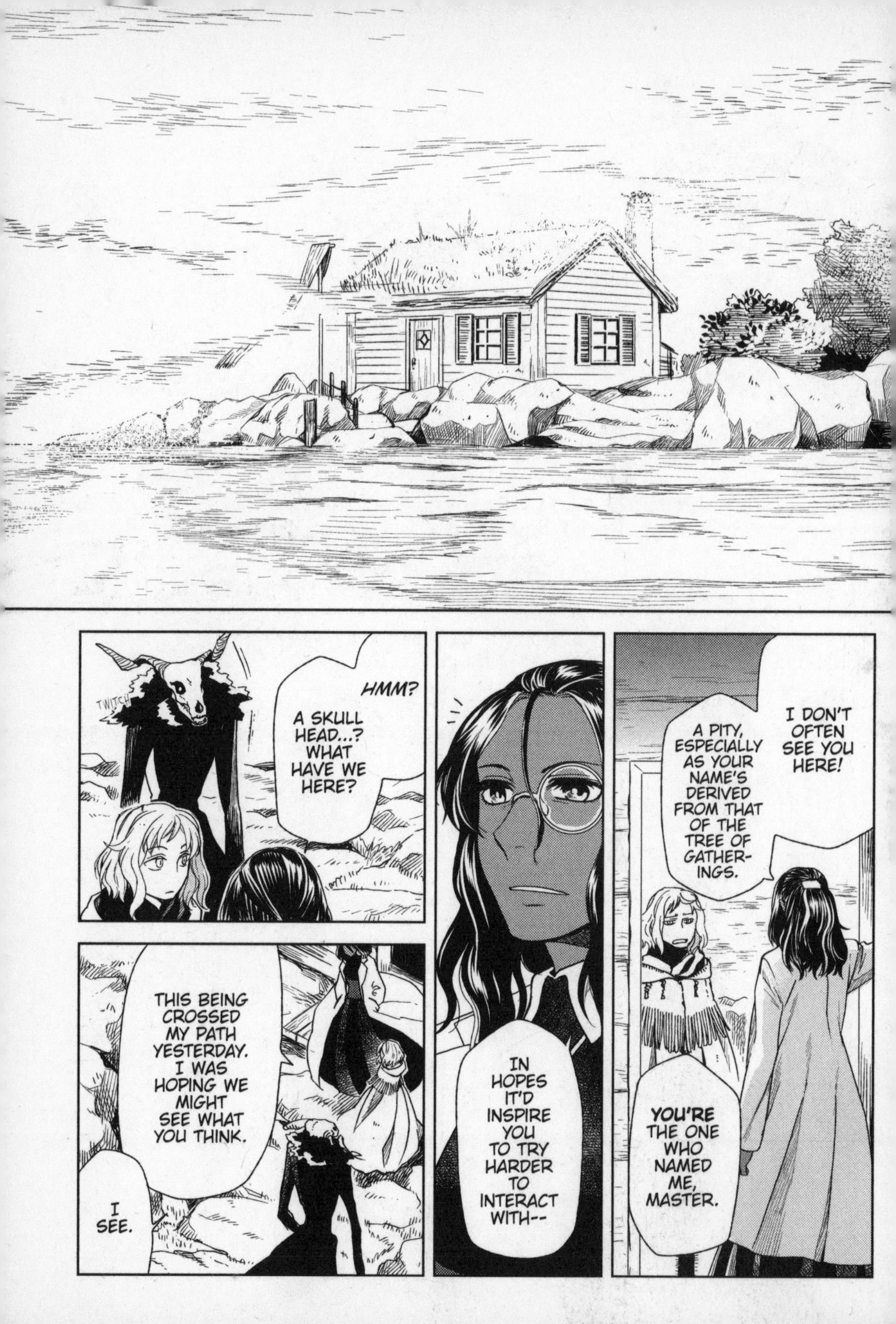
I DON'T OFTEN SEE YOU HERE!
A PITY, ESPECIALLY AS YOUR NAME'S DERIVED FROM THAT OF THE TREE OF GATHER-INGS.
YOU'RE THE ONE WHO NAMED ME, MASTER.
IN HOPES IT'D INSPIRE YOU TO TRY HARDER TO INTERACT WITH--
HMM?
A SKULL HEAD...? WHAT HAVE WE HERE?
TWITCH
THIS BEING CROSSED MY PATH YESTERDAY. I WAS HOPING WE MIGHT SEE WHAT YOU THINK.
I SEE.

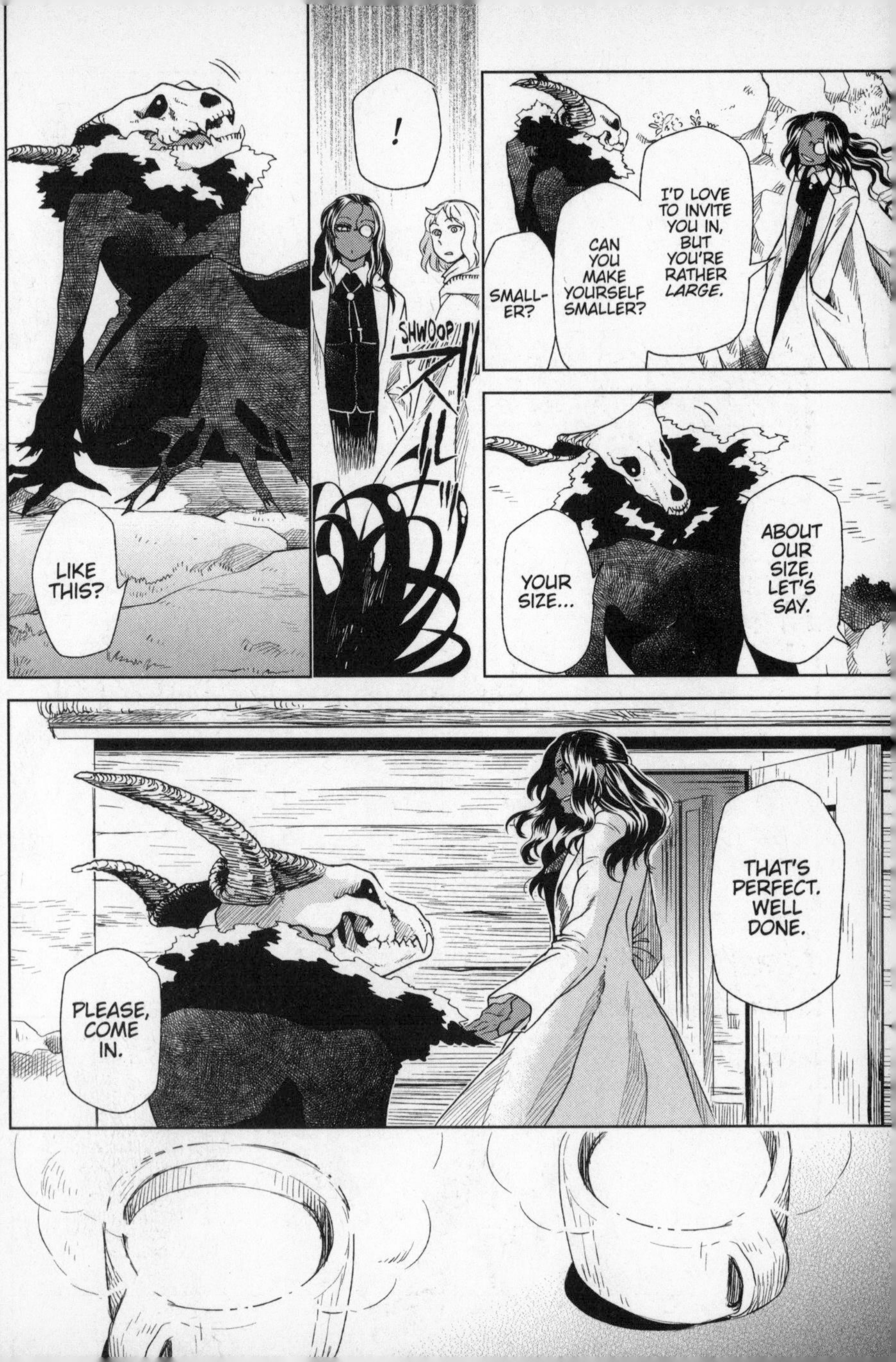
I'D LOVE TO INVITE YOU IN, BUT YOU'RE RATHER LARGE.
CAN YOU MAKE YOURSELF SMALLER?
SMALL-ER?
ABOUT OUR SIZE, LET'S SAY.
YOUR SIZE...
!
SHWOOP
LIKE THIS?
THAT'S PERFECT. WELL DONE.
PLEASE, COME IN.

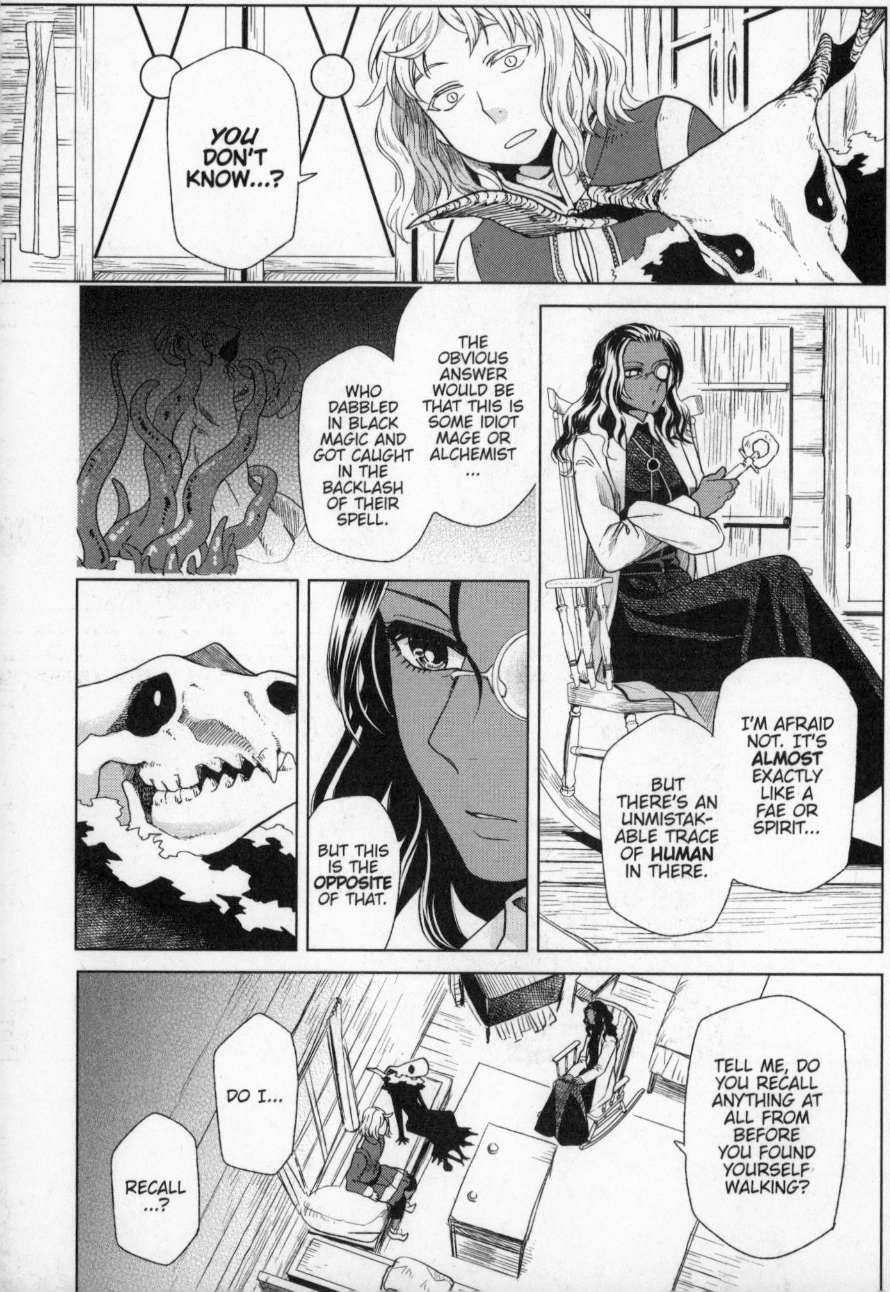
YOU DON'T KNOW...?
I'M AFRAID NOT. IT'S ALMOST EXACTLY LIKE A FAE OR SPIRIT...
BUT THERE'S AN UNMISTAKABLE TRACE OF HUMAN IN THERE.
THE OBVIOUS ANSWER WOULD BE THAT THIS IS SOME IDIOT MAGE OR ALCHEMIST ...
WHO DABBLED IN BLACK MAGIC AND GOT CAUGHT IN THE BACKLASH OF THEIR SPELL.
BUT THIS IS THE OPPOSITE OF THAT.
TELL ME, DO YOU RECALL ANYTHING AT ALL FROM BEFORE YOU FOUND YOURSELF WALKING?
DO I...
RECALL ...?

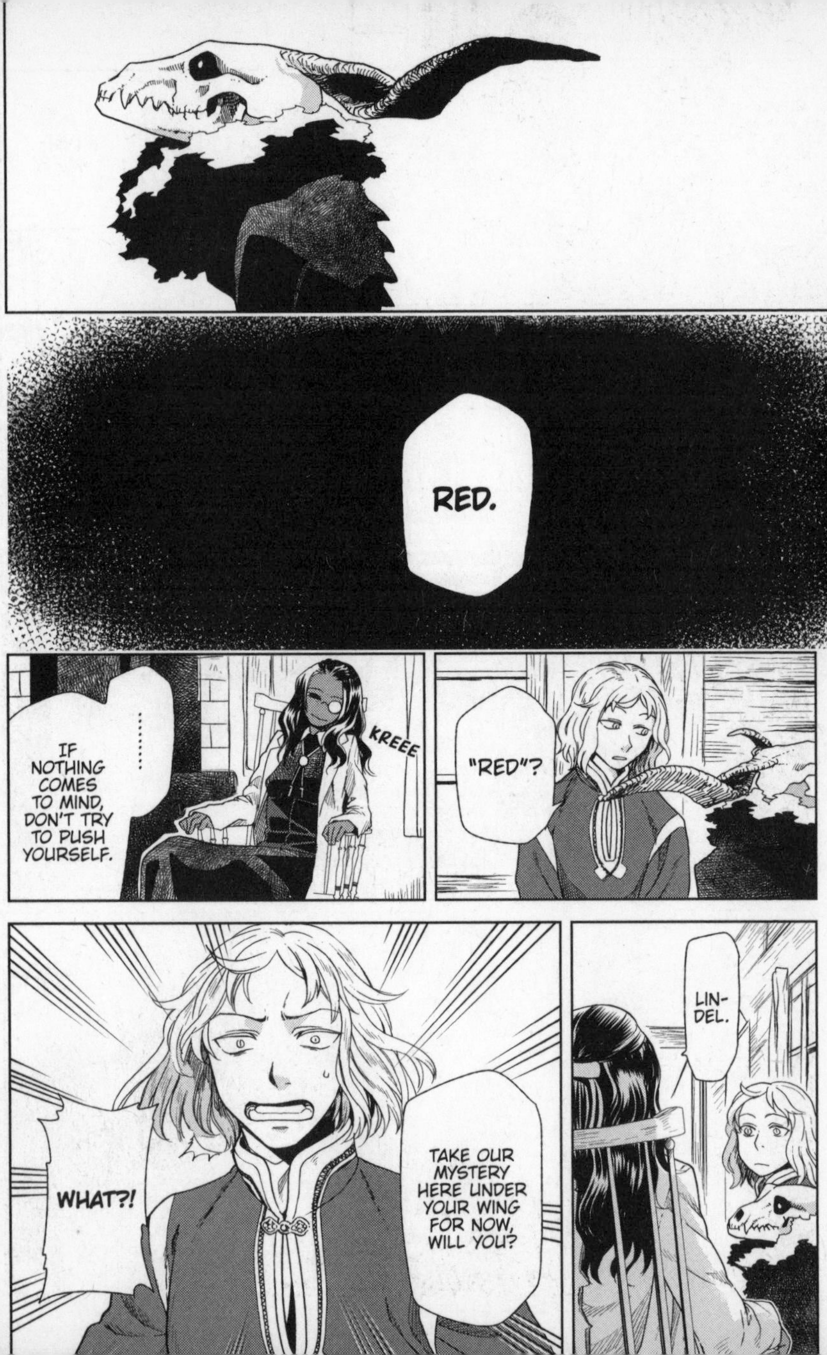
RED.
"RED"?
KREEE
......
IF NOTHING COMES TO MIND, DON'T TRY TO PUSH YOURSELF.
LIN-DEL.
TAKE OUR MYSTERY HERE UNDER YOUR WING FOR NOW, WILL YOU?
WHAT?!

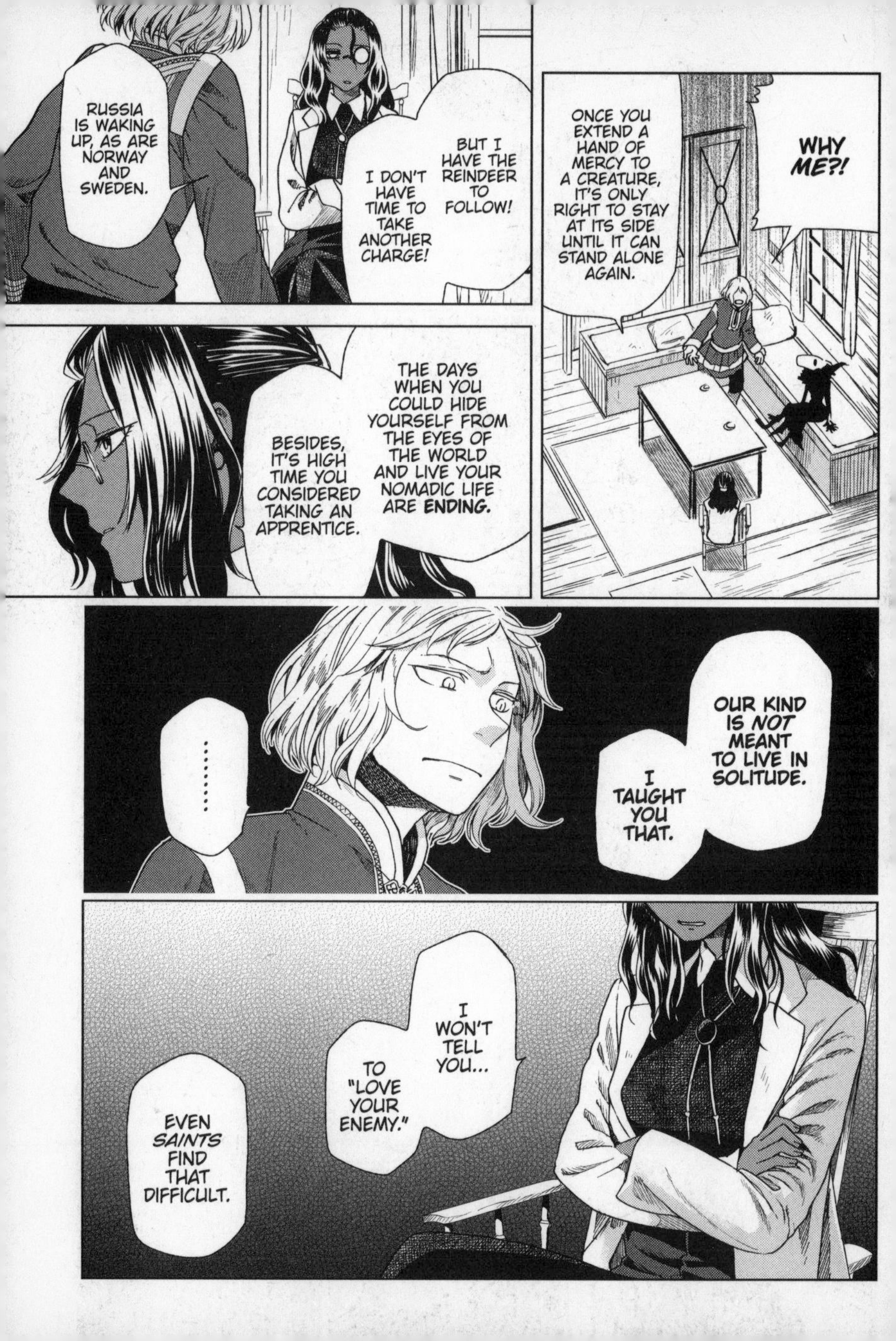
WHY *ME?!*
ONCE YOU EXTEND A HAND OF MERCY TO A CREATURE, IT'S ONLY RIGHT TO STAY AT ITS SIDE UNTIL IT CAN STAND ALONE AGAIN.
BUT I HAVE THE REINDEER TO FOLLOW!
I DON'T HAVE TIME TO TAKE ANOTHER CHARGE!
RUSSIA IS WAKING UP, AS ARE NORWAY AND SWEDEN.
THE DAYS WHEN YOU COULD HIDE YOURSELF FROM THE EYES OF THE WORLD AND LIVE YOUR NOMADIC LIFE ARE **ENDING.**
BESIDES, IT'S HIGH TIME YOU CONSIDERED TAKING AN APPRENTICE.
OUR KIND IS *NOT* MEANT TO LIVE IN SOLITUDE.
I TAUGHT YOU THAT.
......
I WON'T TELL YOU...
TO "LOVE YOUR ENEMY."
EVEN *SAINTS* FIND THAT DIFFICULT.

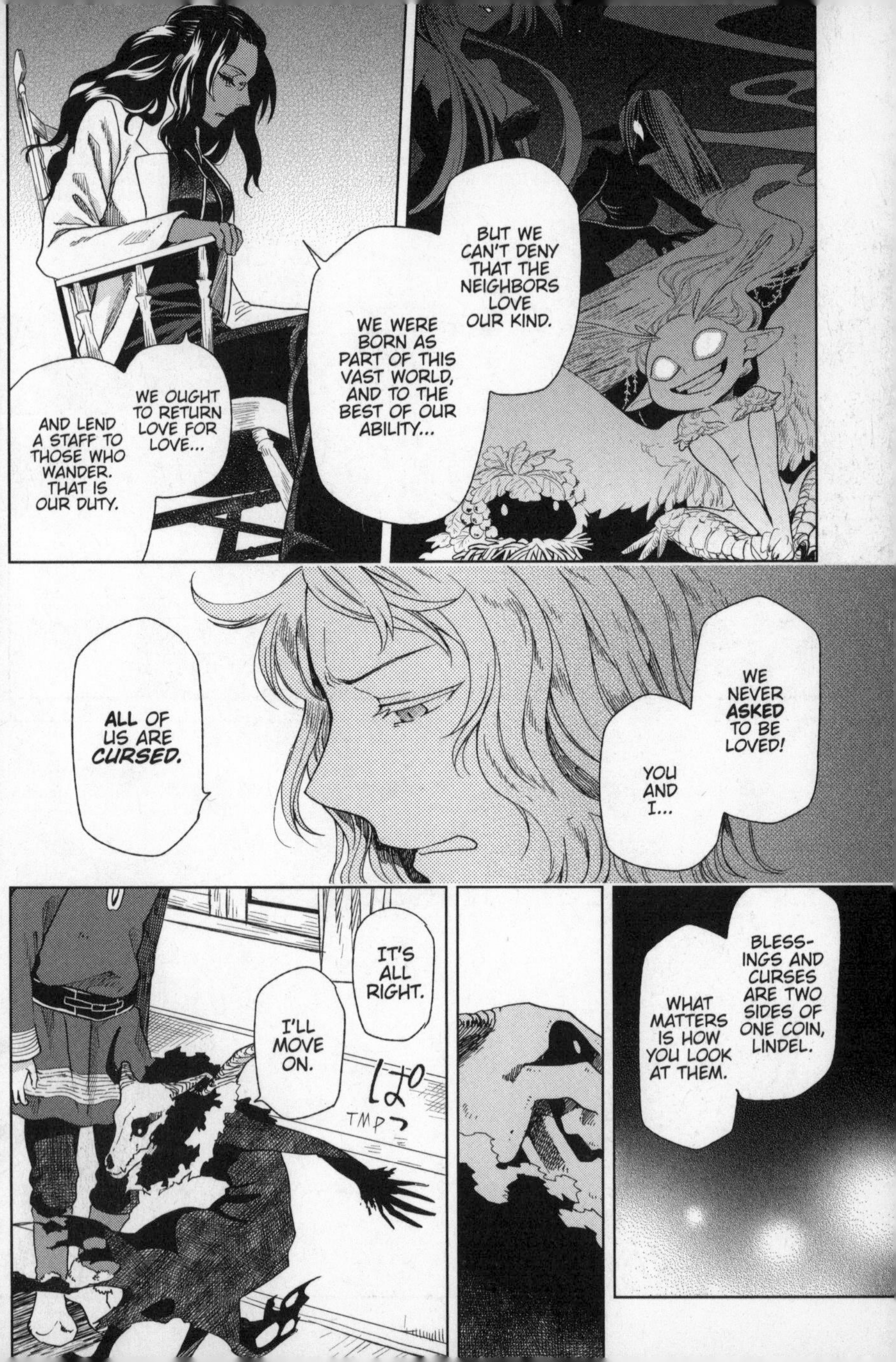

BUT WE CAN'T DENY THAT THE NEIGHBORS LOVE OUR KIND.
WE WERE BORN AS PART OF THIS VAST WORLD, AND TO THE BEST OF OUR ABILITY...
WE OUGHT TO RETURN LOVE FOR LOVE...
AND LEND A STAFF TO THOSE WHO WANDER. THAT IS OUR DUTY.
WE NEVER ASKED TO BE LOVED!
YOU AND I...
ALL OF US ARE CURSED.
BLESSINGS AND CURSES ARE TWO SIDES OF ONE COIN, LINDEL.
WHAT MATTERS IS HOW YOU LOOK AT THEM.
IT'S ALL RIGHT.
I'LL MOVE ON.
TMP

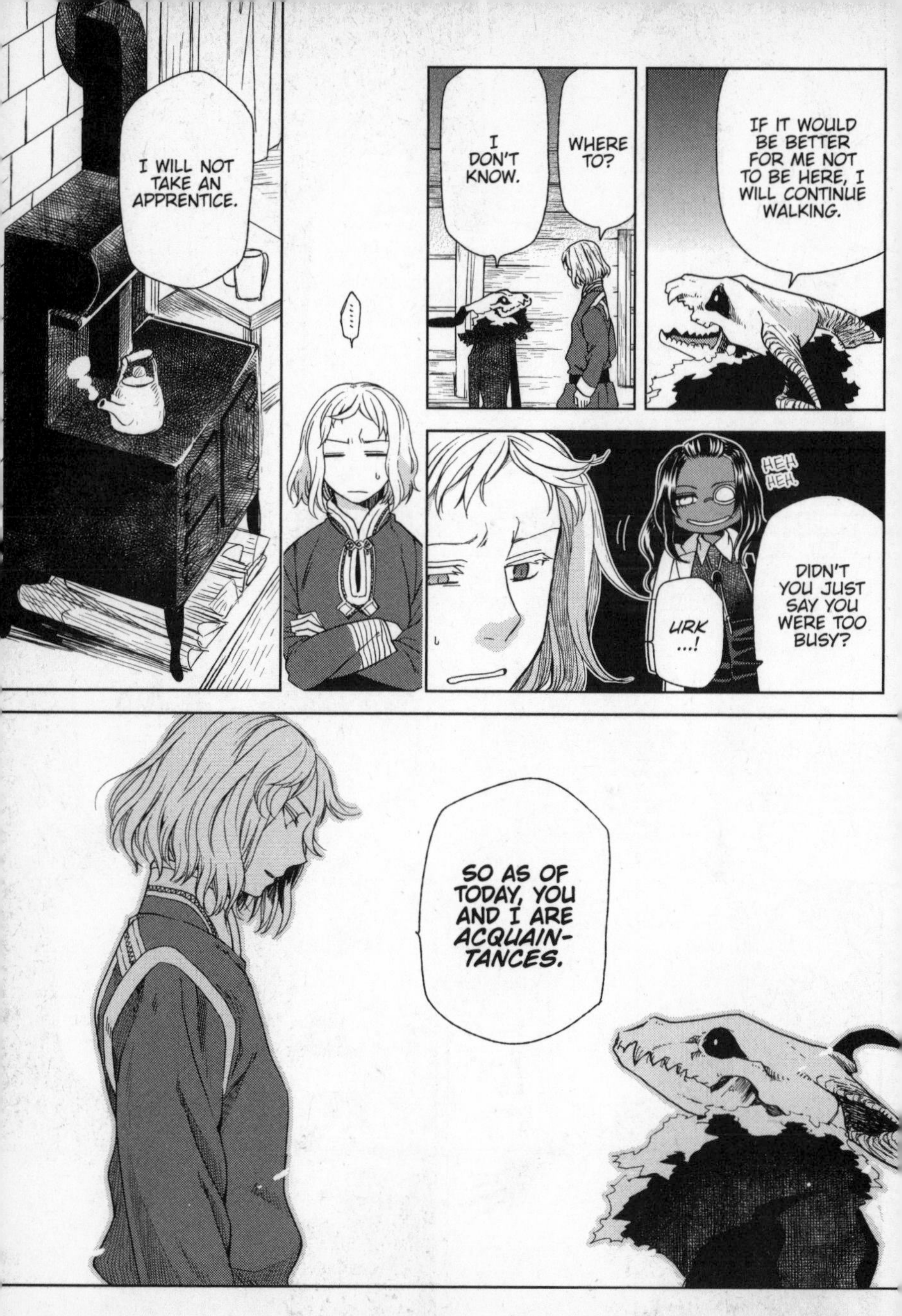
IF IT WOULD BE BETTER FOR ME NOT TO BE HERE, I WILL CONTINUE WALKING.
WHERE TO?
I DON'T KNOW.
HEH HEH.
DIDN'T YOU JUST SAY YOU WERE TOO BUSY?
URK ...!
......
I WILL NOT TAKE AN APPRENTICE.
SO AS OF TODAY, YOU AND I ARE ACQUAIN-TANCES.

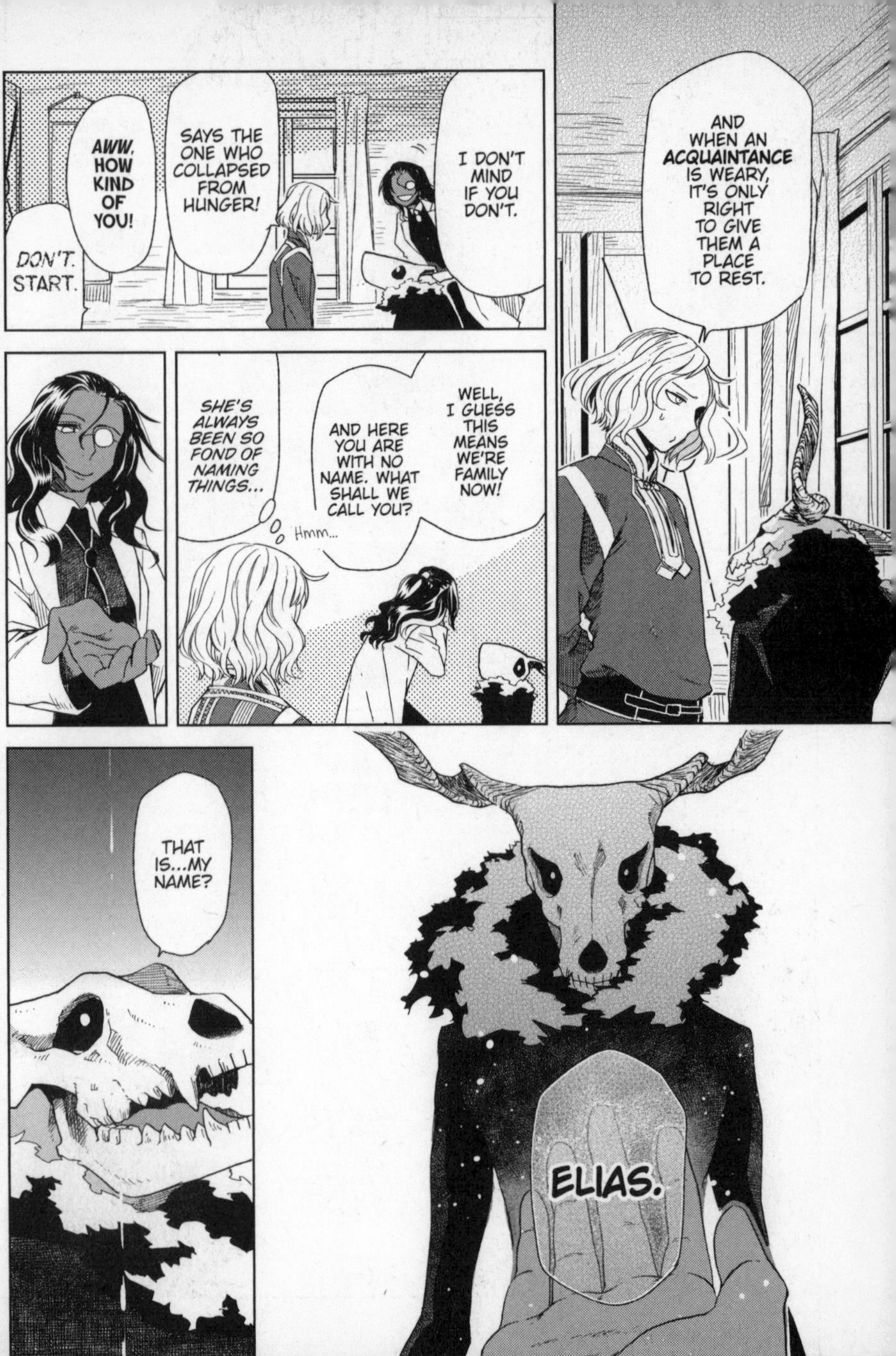
AND WHEN AN ACQUAINTANCE IS WEARY, IT'S ONLY RIGHT TO GIVE THEM A PLACE TO REST.
I DON'T MIND IF YOU DON'T.
SAYS THE ONE WHO COLLAPSED FROM HUNGER!
AWW, HOW KIND OF YOU!
DON'T. START.
WELL, I GUESS THIS MEANS WE'RE FAMILY NOW!
AND HERE YOU ARE WITH NO NAME. WHAT SHALL WE CALL YOU?
SHE'S ALWAYS BEEN SO FOND OF NAMING THINGS...
Hmm...
ELIAS.
THAT IS...MY NAME?

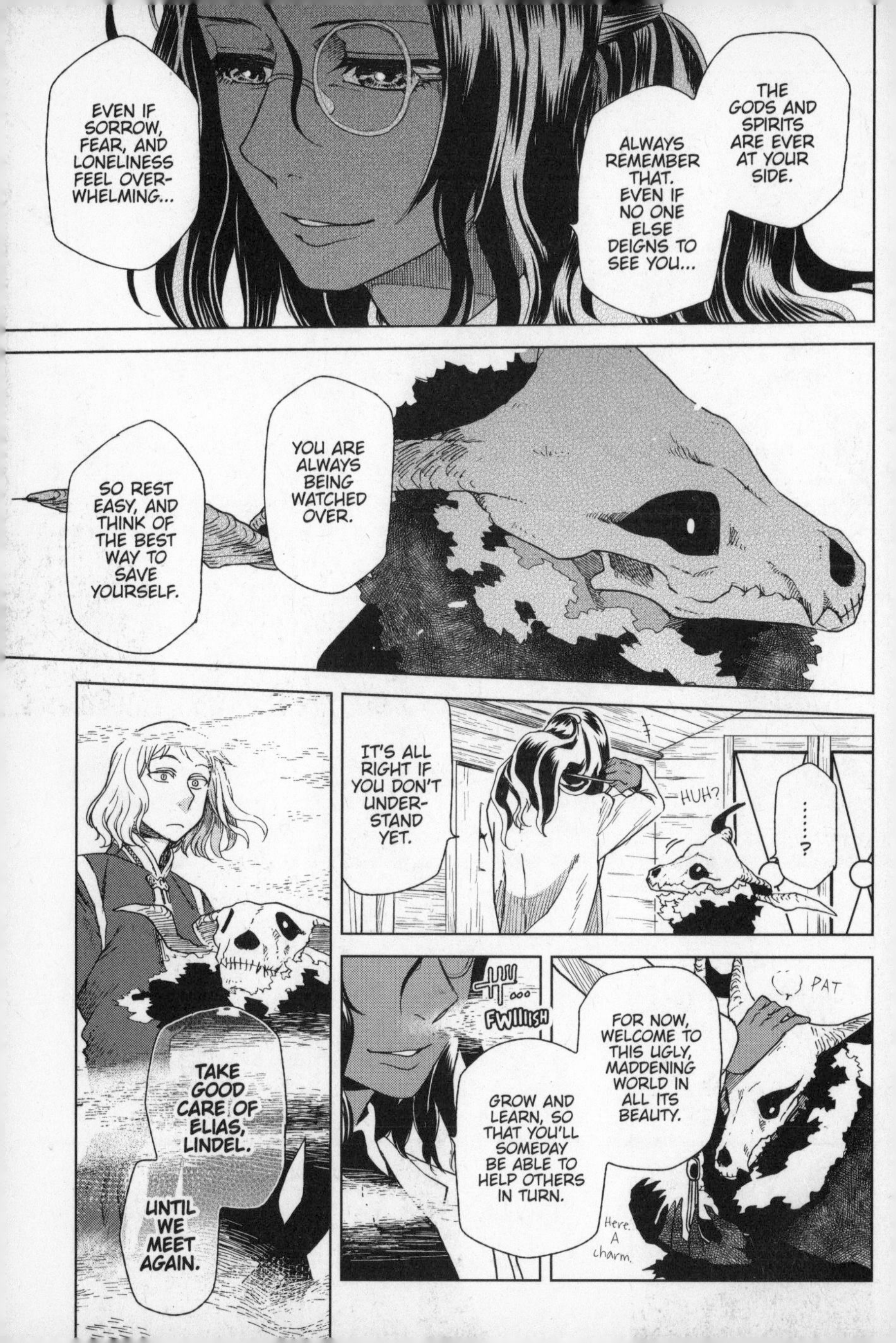
THE GODS AND SPIRITS ARE EVER AT YOUR SIDE.
ALWAYS REMEMBER THAT. EVEN IF NO ONE ELSE DEIGNS TO SEE YOU...
EVEN IF SORROW, FEAR, AND LONELINESS FEEL OVER-WHELMING...
YOU ARE ALWAYS BEING WATCHED OVER.
SO REST EASY, AND THINK OF THE BEST WAY TO SAVE YOURSELF.
......?
HUH?
IT'S ALL RIGHT IF YOU DON'T UNDER-STAND YET.
PAT
FOR NOW, WELCOME TO THIS UGLY, MADDENING WORLD IN ALL ITS BEAUTY.
Here. A charm.
FWIIIISH
GROW AND LEARN, SO THAT YOU'LL SOMEDAY BE ABLE TO HELP OTHERS IN TURN.
TAKE GOOD CARE OF ELIAS, LINDEL.
UNTIL WE MEET AGAIN.

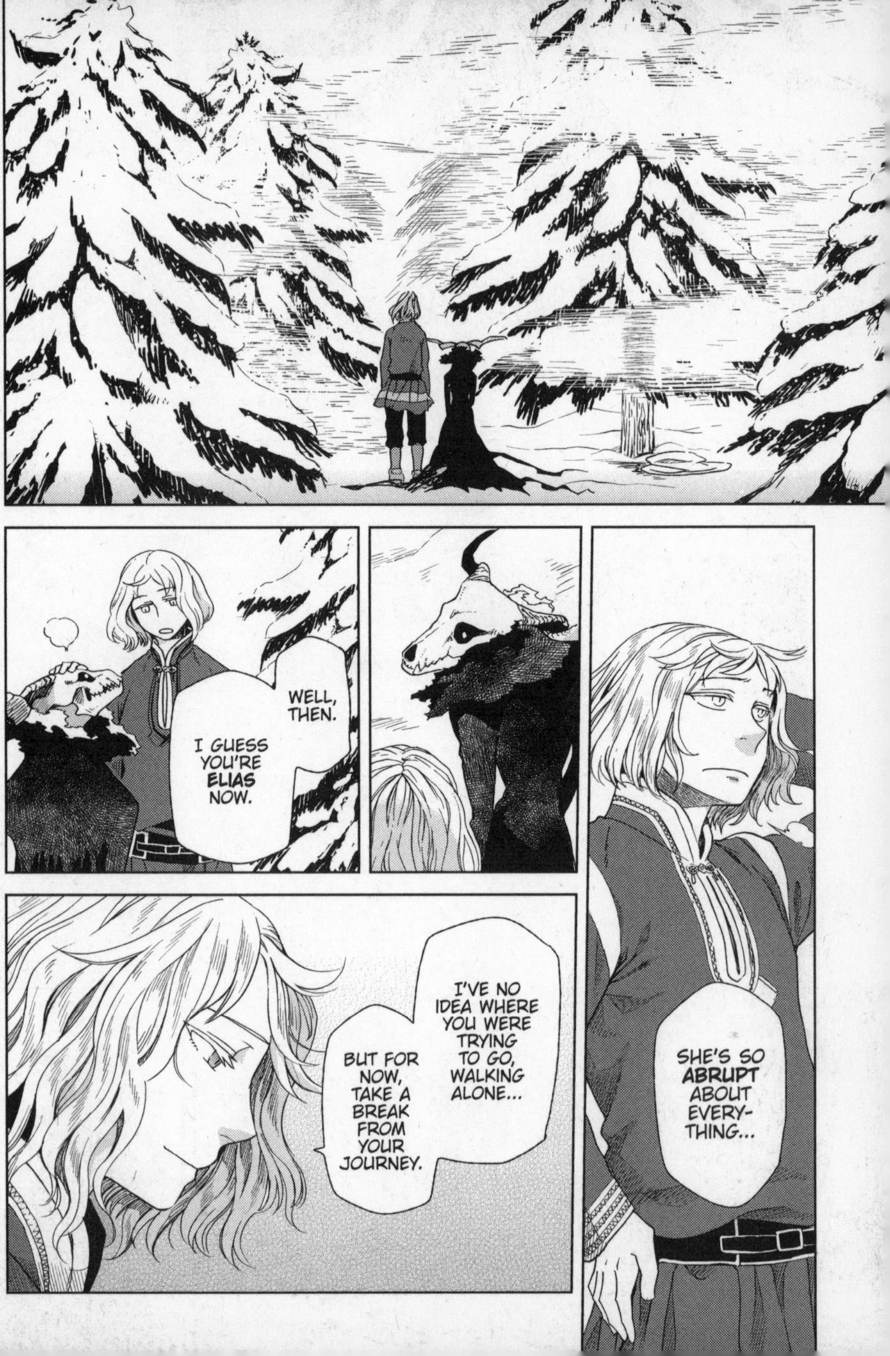
SHE'S SO ABRUPT ABOUT EVERYTHING...
WELL, THEN.
I GUESS YOU'RE ELIAS NOW.
I'VE NO IDEA WHERE YOU WERE TRYING TO GO, WALKING ALONE...
BUT FOR NOW, TAKE A BREAK FROM YOUR JOURNEY.

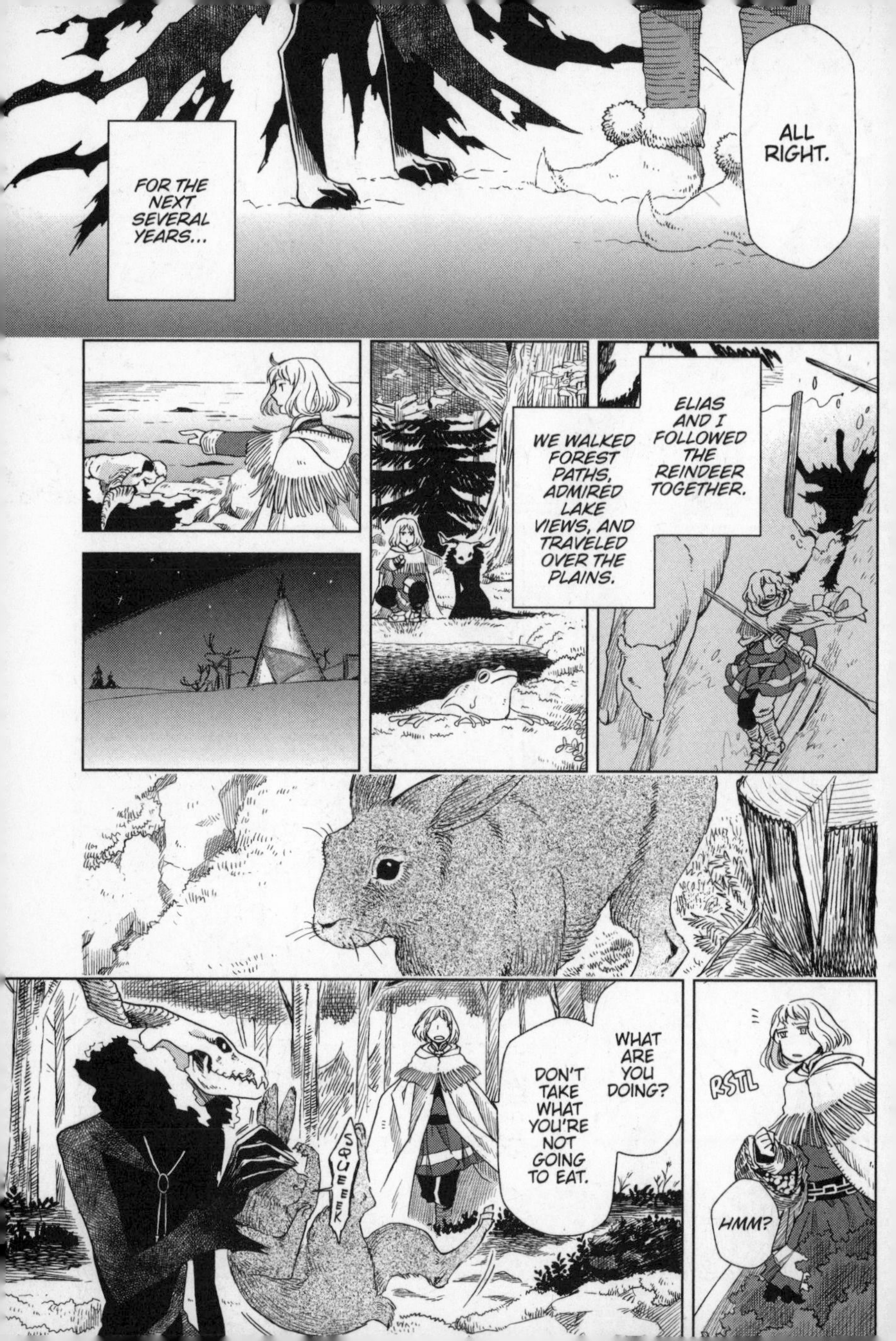

ALL RIGHT.
FOR THE NEXT SEVERAL YEARS...
ELIAS AND I FOLLOWED THE REINDEER TOGETHER.
WE WALKED FOREST PATHS, ADMIRED LAKE VIEWS, AND TRAVELED OVER THE PLAINS.
RSTL
HMM?
WHAT ARE YOU DOING?
DON'T TAKE WHAT YOU'RE NOT GOING TO EAT.
SQUEEEK

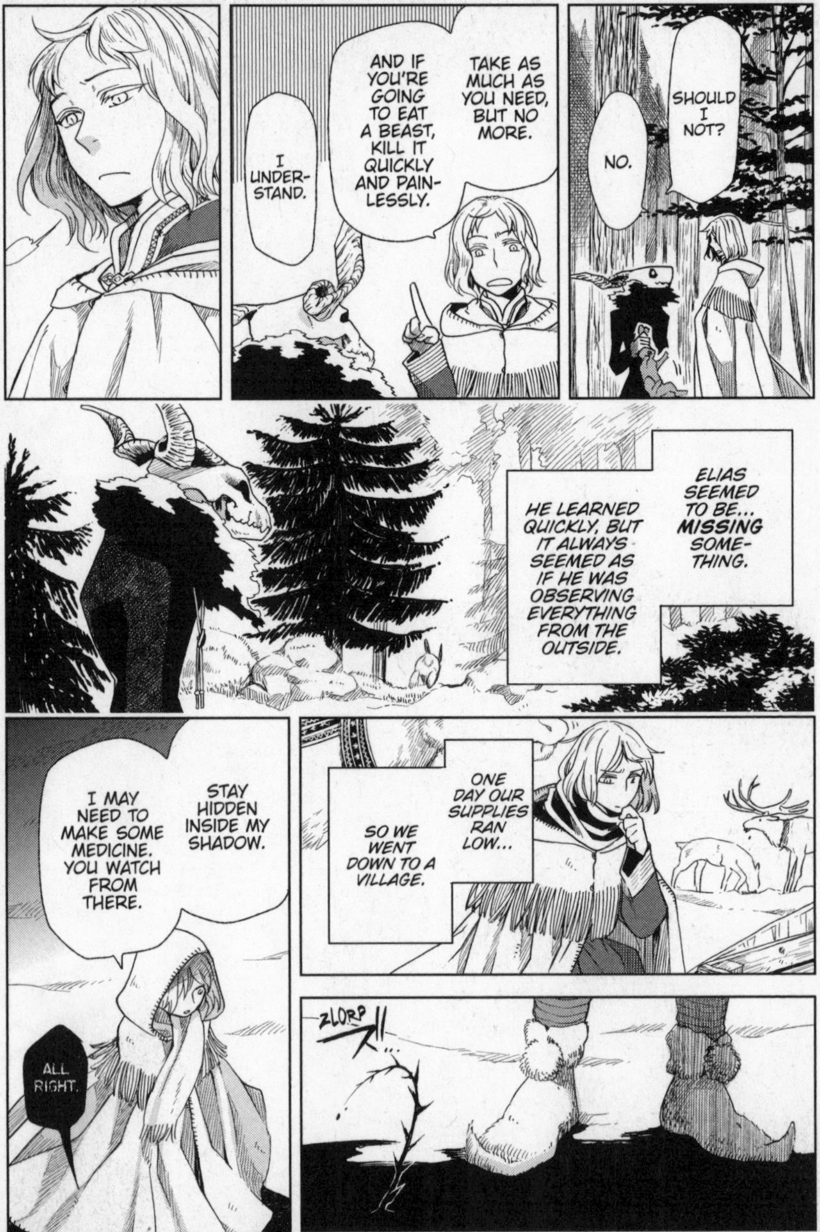
SHOULD I NOT?
NO.
TAKE AS MUCH AS YOU NEED, BUT NO MORE.
AND IF YOU'RE GOING TO EAT A BEAST, KILL IT QUICKLY AND PAINLESSLY.
I UNDERSTAND.
ELIAS SEEMED TO BE... MISSING SOMETHING.
HE LEARNED QUICKLY, BUT IT ALWAYS SEEMED AS IF HE WAS OBSERVING EVERYTHING FROM THE OUTSIDE.
ONE DAY OUR SUPPLIES RAN LOW...
SO WE WENT DOWN TO A VILLAGE.
ZLORP
STAY HIDDEN INSIDE MY SHADOW.
I MAY NEED TO MAKE SOME MEDICINE. YOU WATCH FROM THERE.
ALL RIGHT.

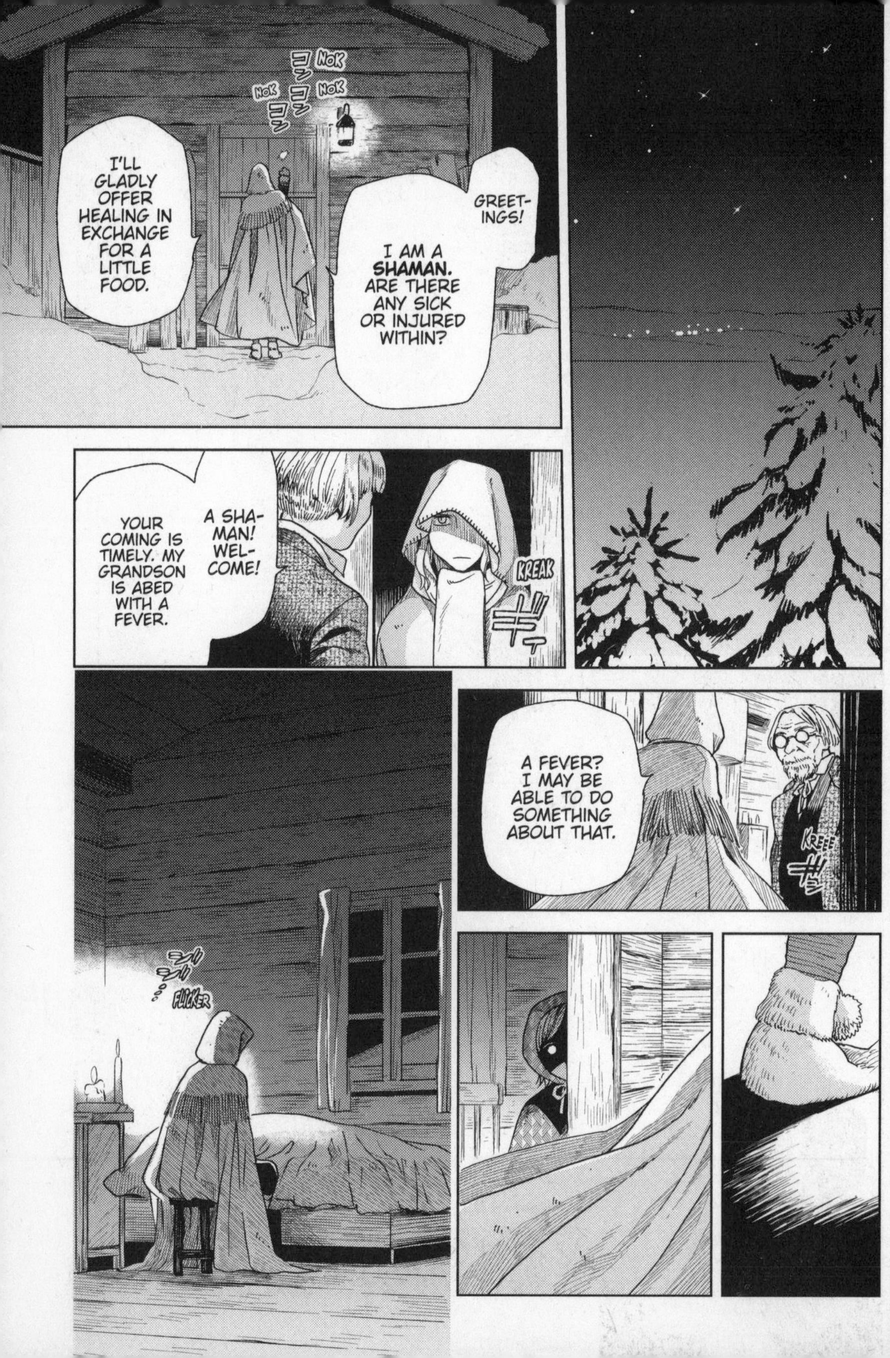
NOK NOK NOK
GREETINGS!
I AM A SHAMAN. ARE THERE ANY SICK OR INJURED WITHIN?
I'LL GLADLY OFFER HEALING IN EXCHANGE FOR A LITTLE FOOD.
KREAK
A SHAMAN! WELCOME!
YOUR COMING IS TIMELY. MY GRANDSON IS ABED WITH A FEVER.
A FEVER? I MAY BE ABLE TO DO SOMETHING ABOUT THAT.
KREEE
FLICKER

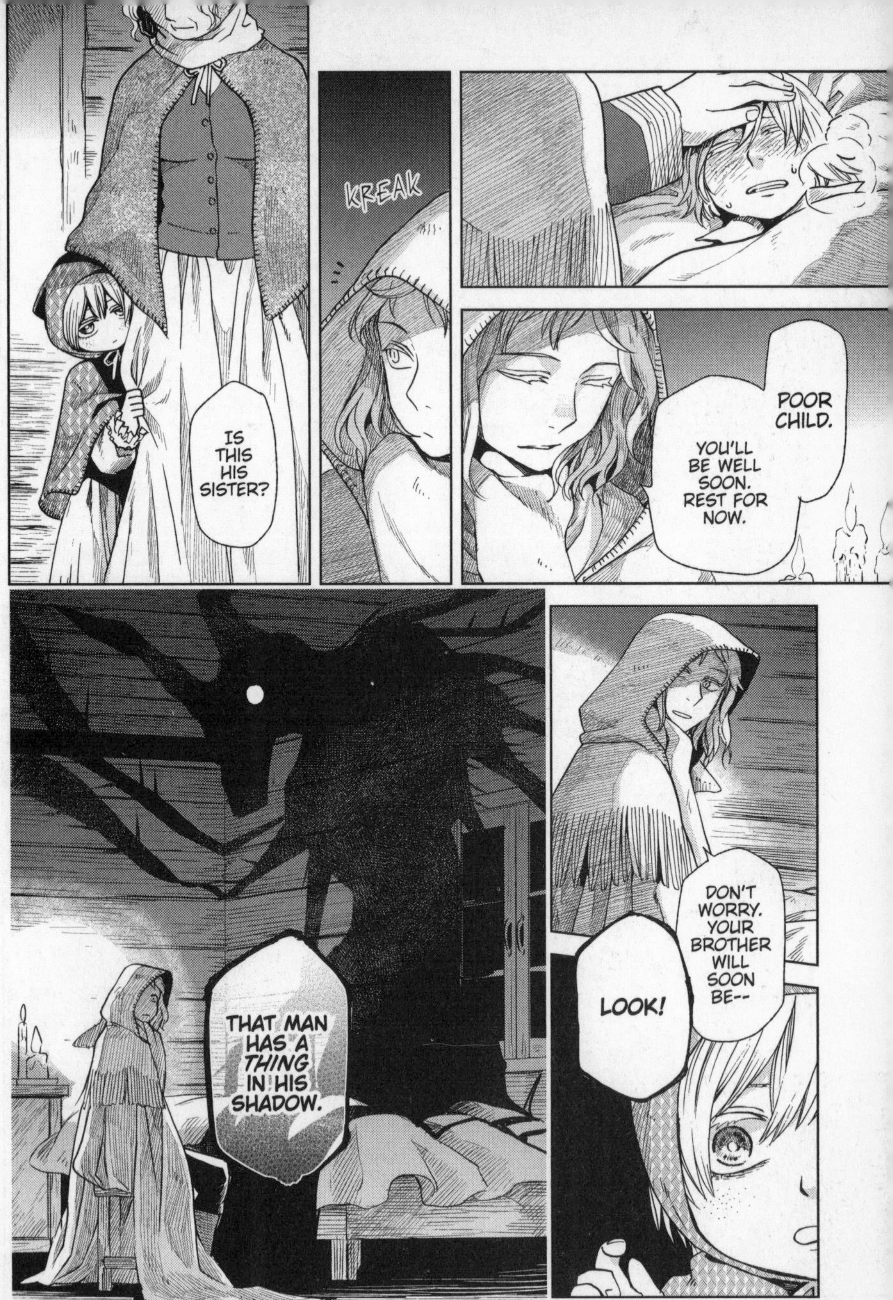
POOR CHILD.
YOU'LL BE WELL SOON. REST FOR NOW.
KREAK
IS THIS HIS SISTER?
DON'T WORRY. YOUR BROTHER WILL SOON BE--
LOOK!
THAT MAN HAS A *THING* IN HIS SHADOW.

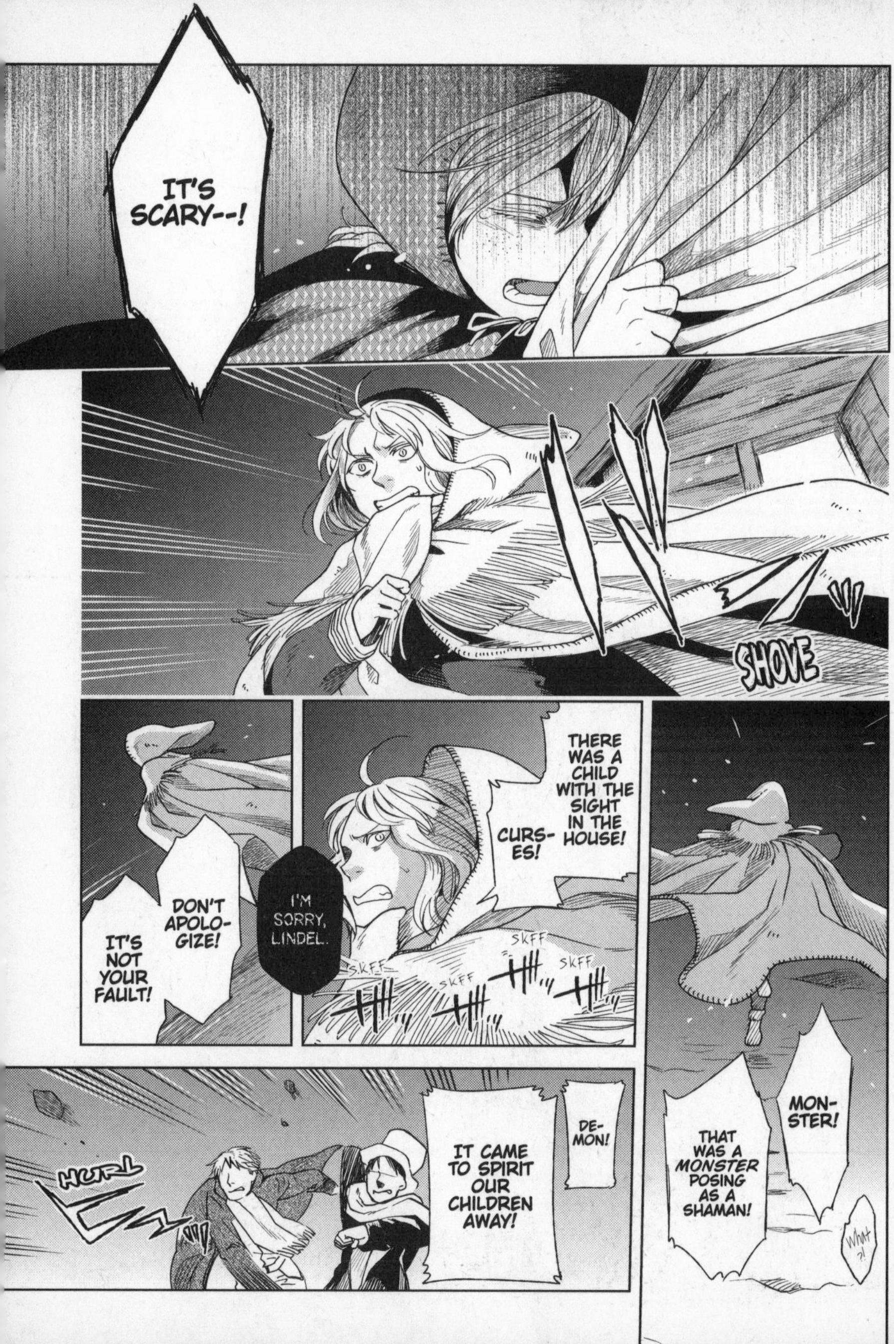
IT'S SCARY--!
SHOVE
MON-STER!
THAT WAS A MONSTER POSING AS A SHAMAN!
WHAT ?!
THERE WAS A CHILD WITH THE SIGHT IN THE HOUSE!
CURS-ES!
I'M SORRY, LINDEL.
SKFF
SKFF
SKFF
SKFF
DON'T APOLO-GIZE!
IT'S NOT YOUR FAULT!
DE-MON!
IT CAME TO SPIRIT OUR CHILDREN AWAY!
HURL

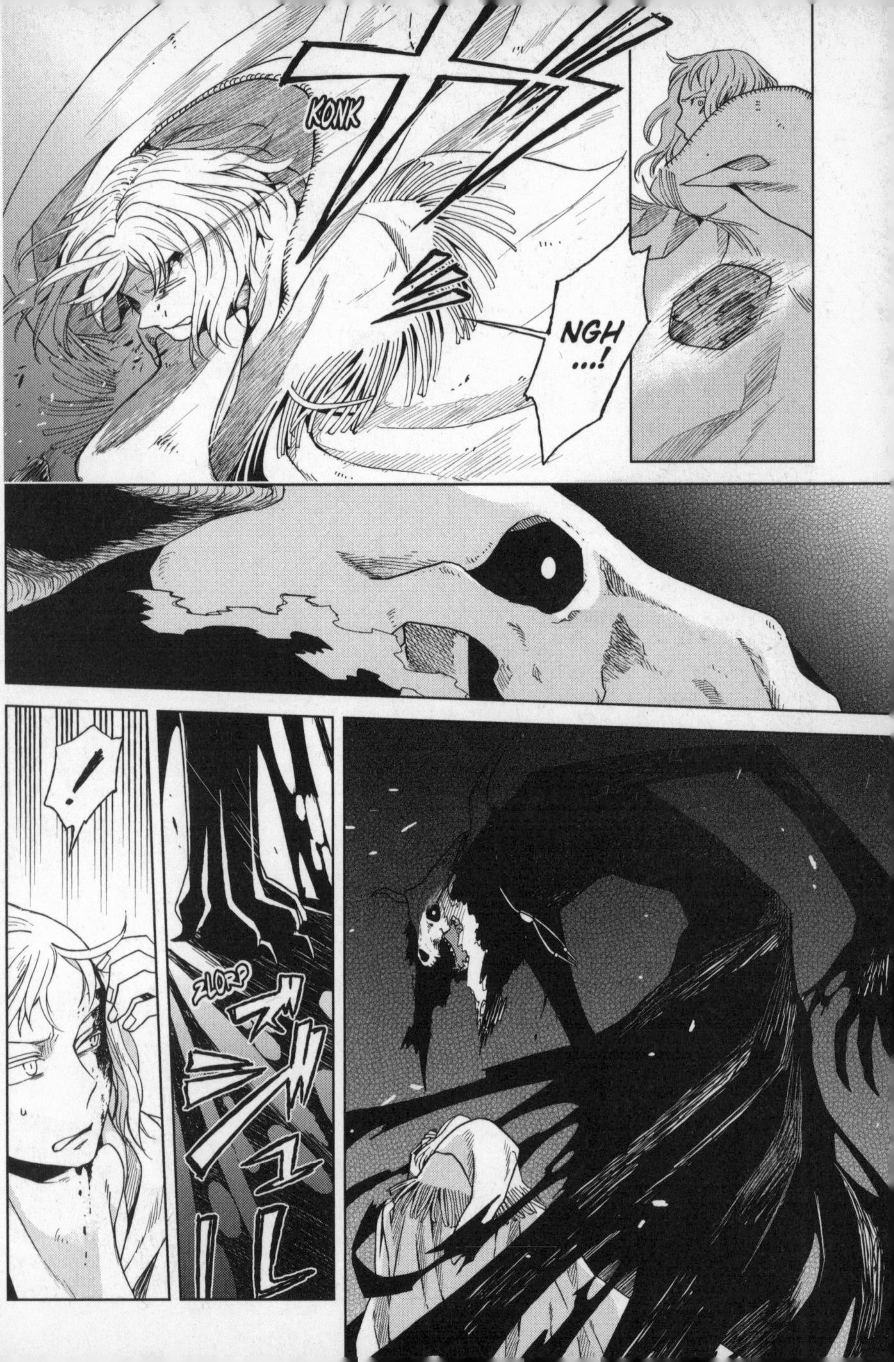
KONK
NGH ...!
ZLORP
!

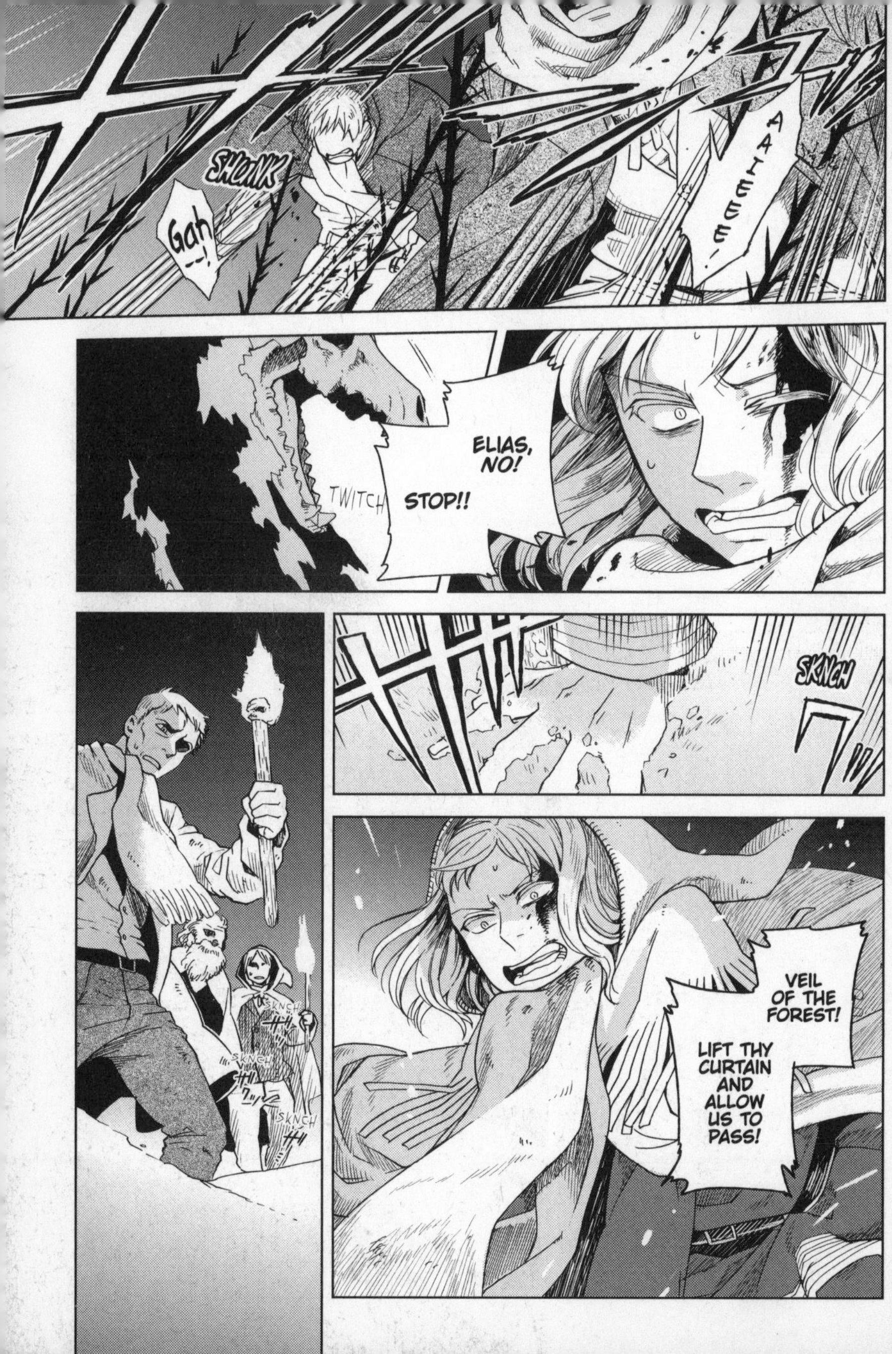
AAIEEEE!
SHUNK
Gah--!
ELIAS, NO!
STOP!!
TWITCH
SKNCH
VEIL OF THE FOREST!
LIFT THY CURTAIN AND ALLOW US TO PASS!
SKNCH
SKNCH
SKNCH

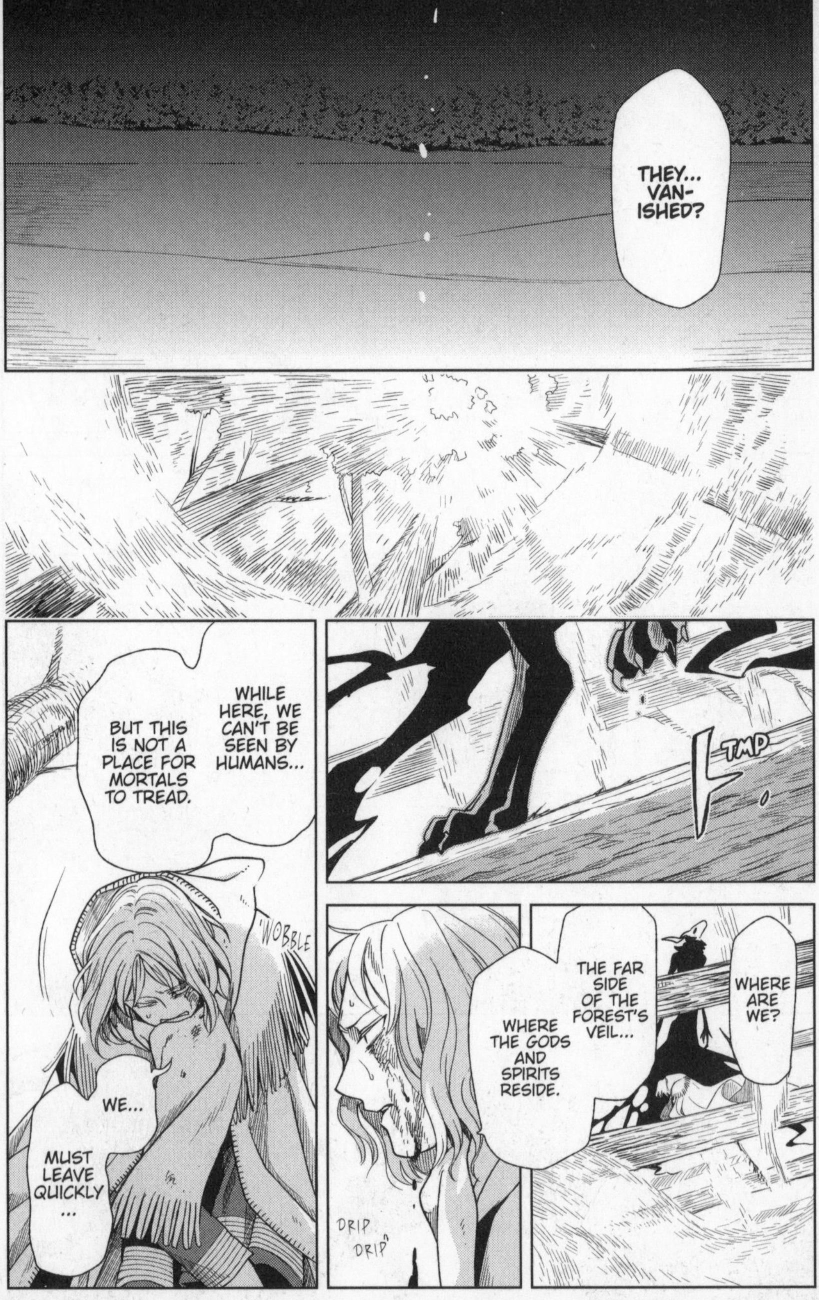
THEY... VAN-ISHED?
TMP
WHERE ARE WE?
THE FAR SIDE OF THE FOREST'S VEIL...
WHERE THE GODS AND SPIRITS RESIDE.
DRIP DRIP
WHILE HERE, WE CAN'T BE SEEN BY HUMANS...
BUT THIS IS NOT A PLACE FOR MORTALS TO TREAD.
WOBBLE
WE...
MUST LEAVE QUICKLY ...

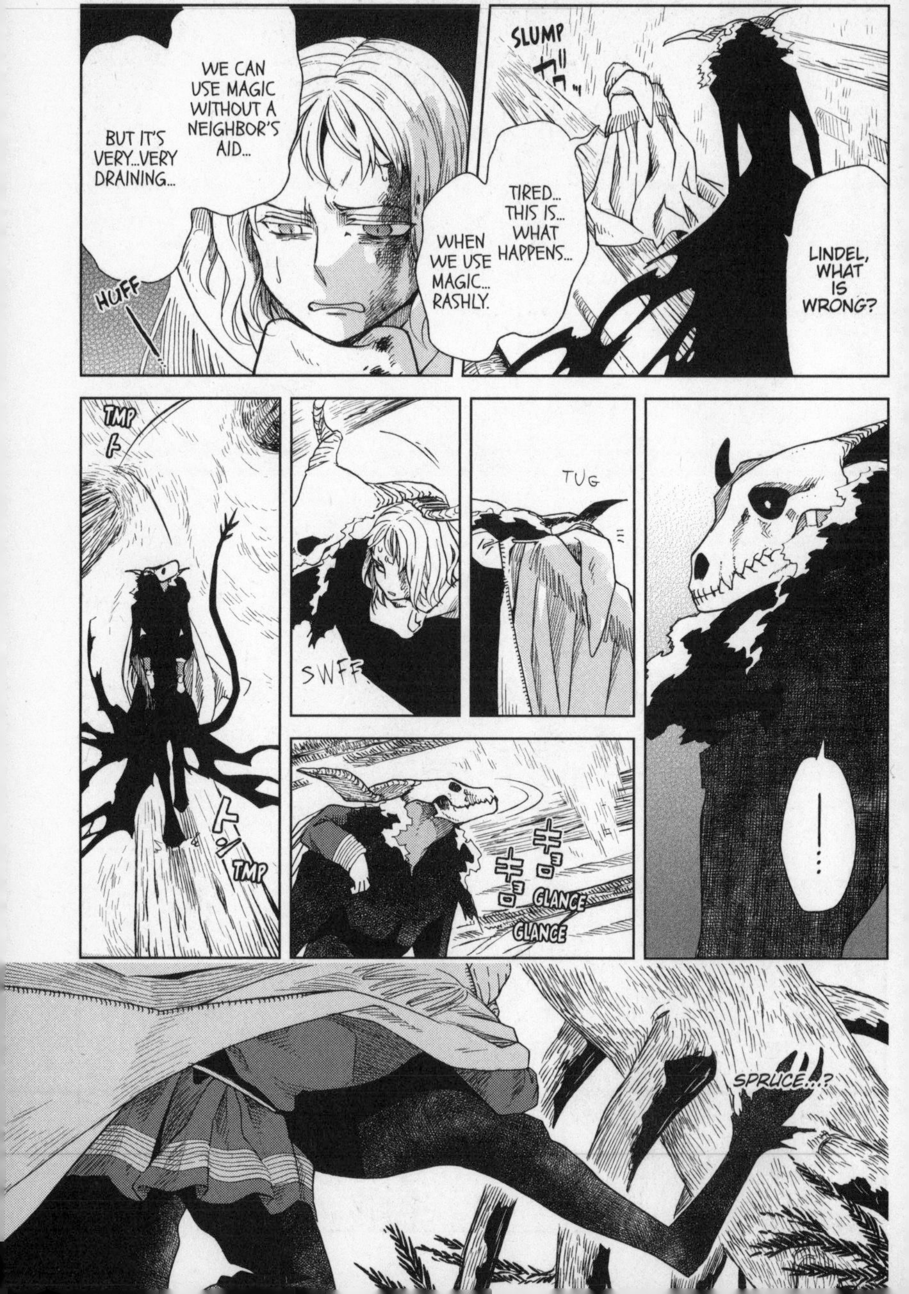
SLUMP
LINDEL, WHAT IS WRONG?
TIRED... THIS IS... WHAT HAPPENS...
WHEN WE USE MAGIC... RASHLY.
WE CAN USE MAGIC WITHOUT A NEIGHBOR'S AID...
BUT IT'S VERY...VERY DRAINING...
HUFF
!...
TUG
SWFF
GLANCE
GLANCE
TMP
TMP
SPRUCE...?

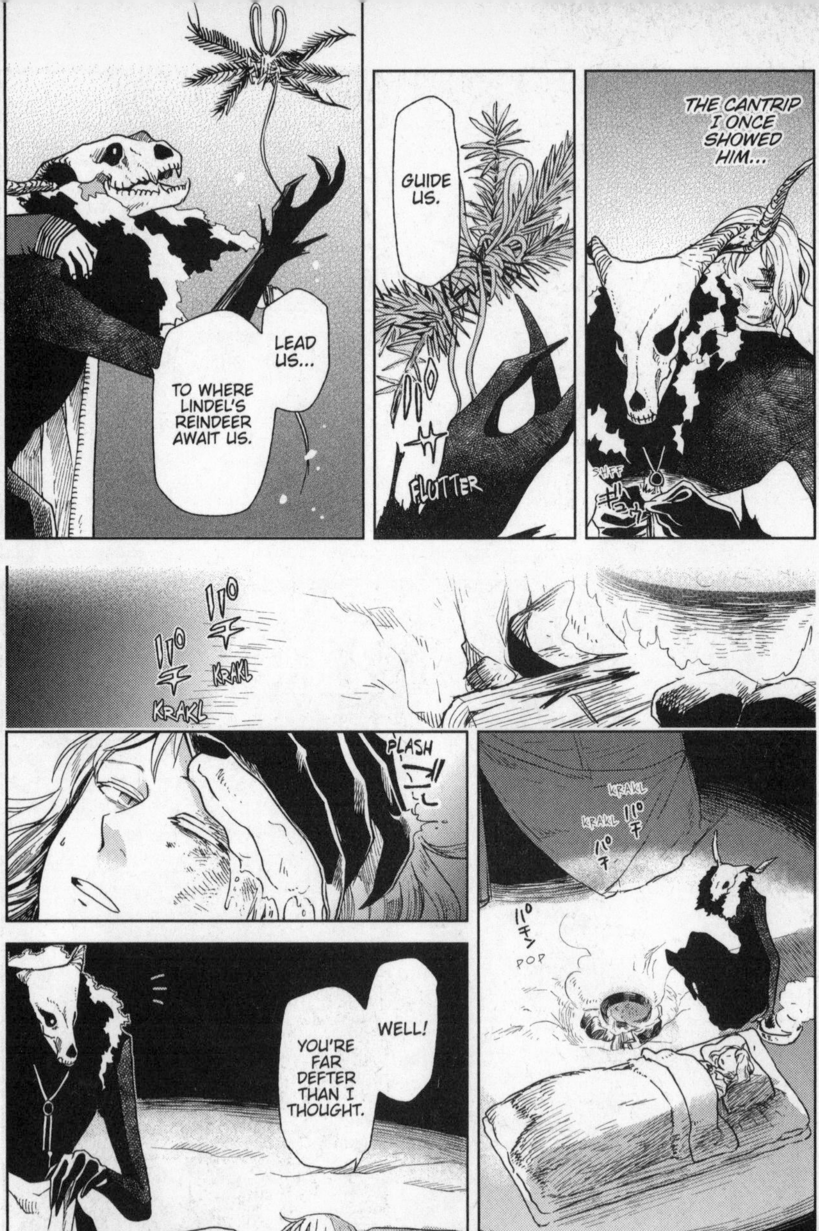
THE CANTRIP I ONCE SHOWED HIM...
SHUFF
GUIDE US.
FLUTTER
LEAD US...
TO WHERE LINDEL'S REINDEER AWAIT US.
KRAKL
KRAKL
KRAKL
KRAKL
POP
PLASH
WELL!
YOU'RE FAR DEFTER THAN I THOUGHT.

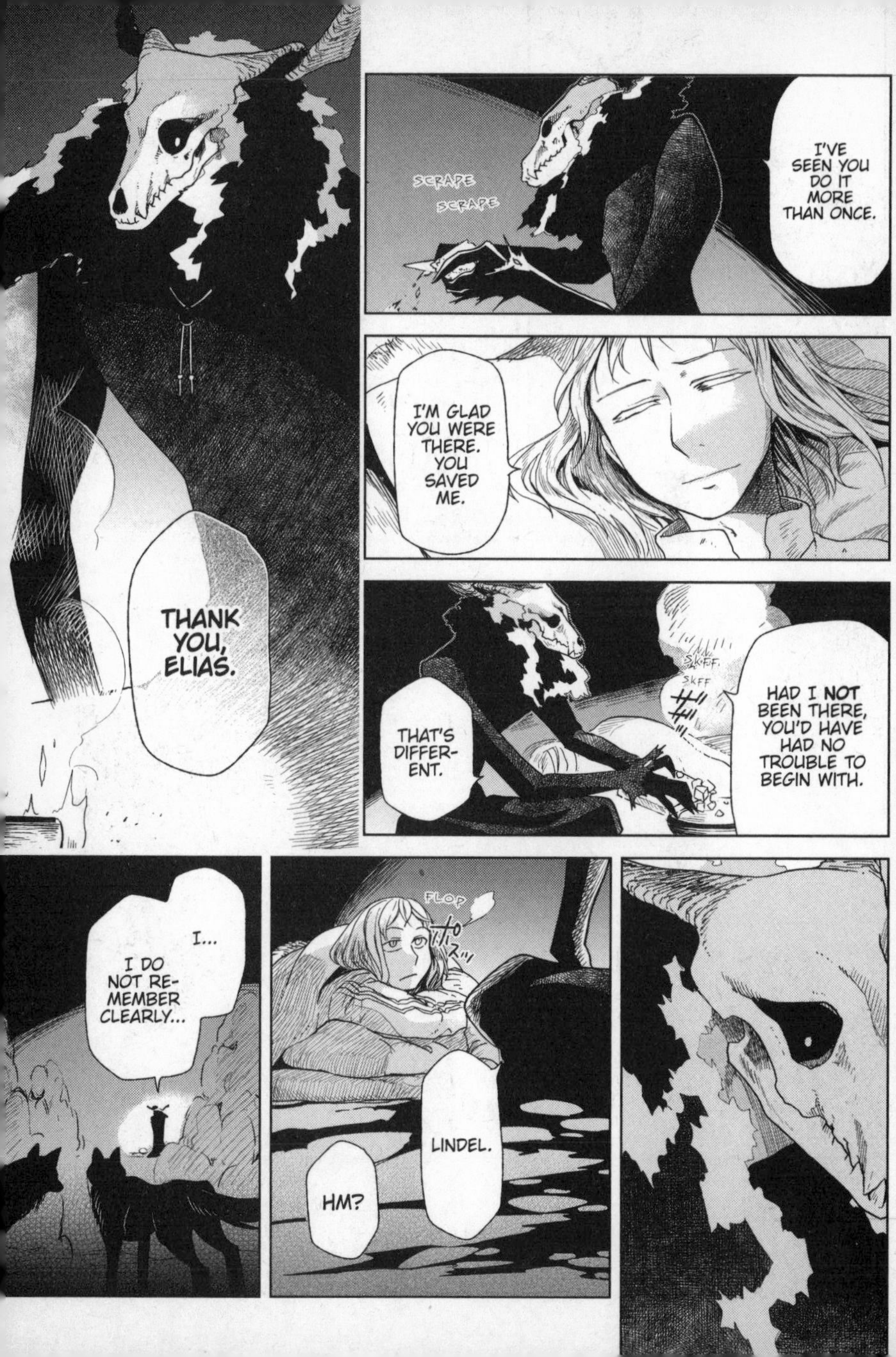

I'VE SEEN YOU DO IT MORE THAN ONCE.
SCRAPE
SCRAPE
I'M GLAD YOU WERE THERE. YOU SAVED ME.
HAD I NOT BEEN THERE, YOU'D HAVE HAD NO TROUBLE TO BEGIN WITH.
SKFF
SKFF
THAT'S DIFFER-ENT.
THANK YOU, ELIAS.
FLOP
LINDEL.
HM?
I...
I DO NOT RE-MEMBER CLEARLY...

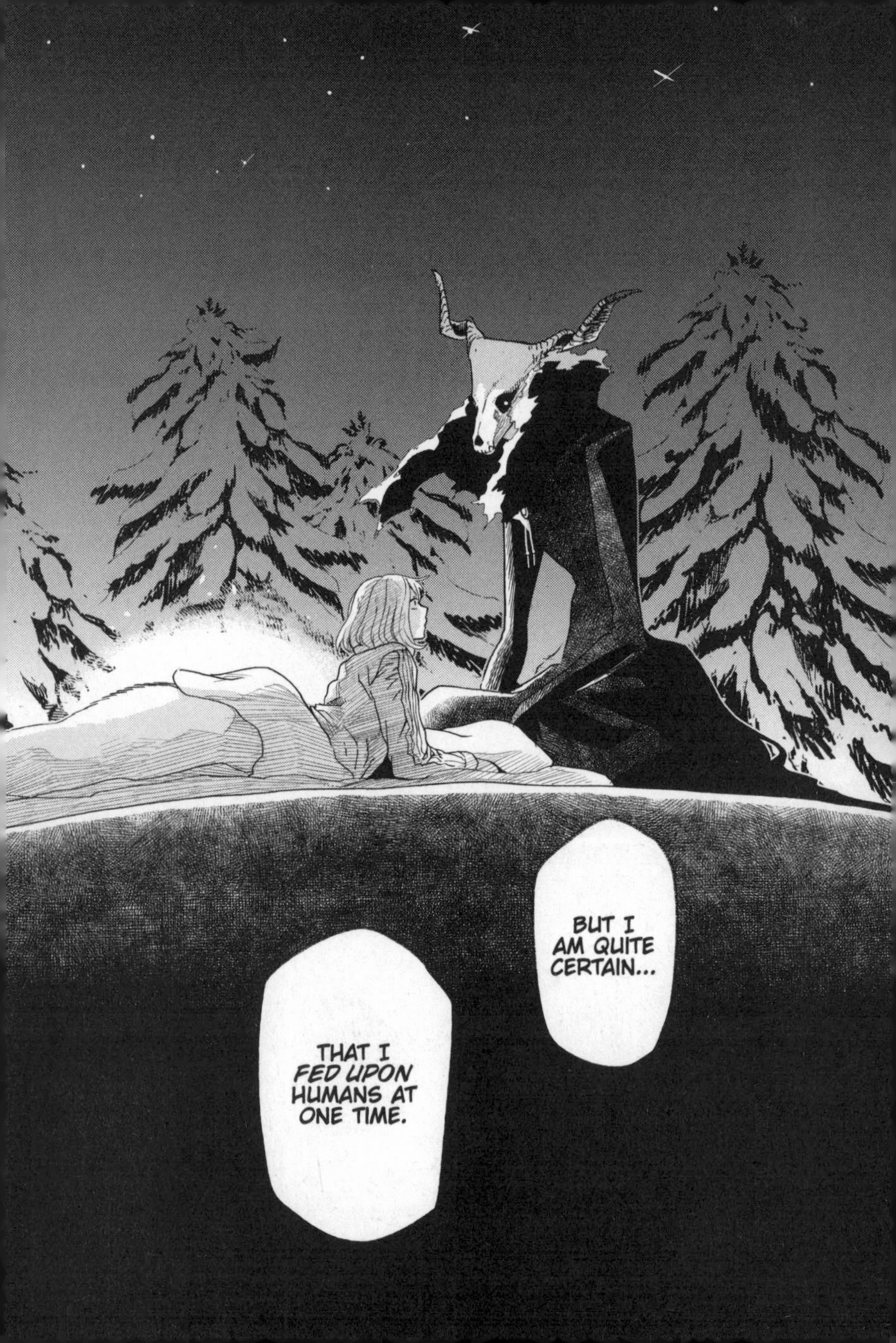
BUT I AM QUITE CERTAIN...
THAT I FED UPON HUMANS AT ONE TIME.

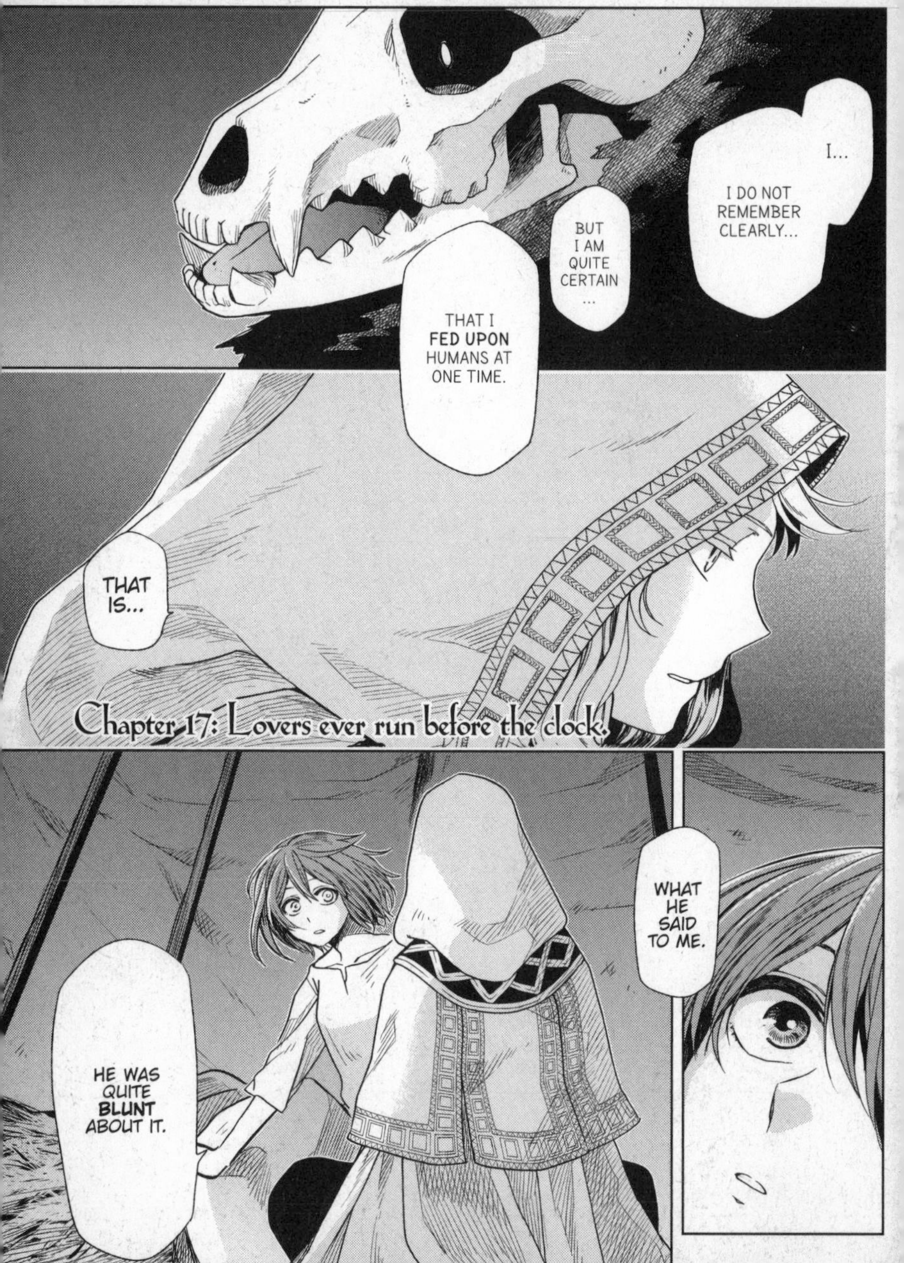
I...
I DO NOT REMEMBER CLEARLY...
BUT I AM QUITE CERTAIN ...
THAT I FED UPON HUMANS AT ONE TIME.
THAT IS...
Chapter 17: Lovers ever run before the clock.
WHAT HE SAID TO ME.
HE WAS QUITE BLUNT ABOUT IT.

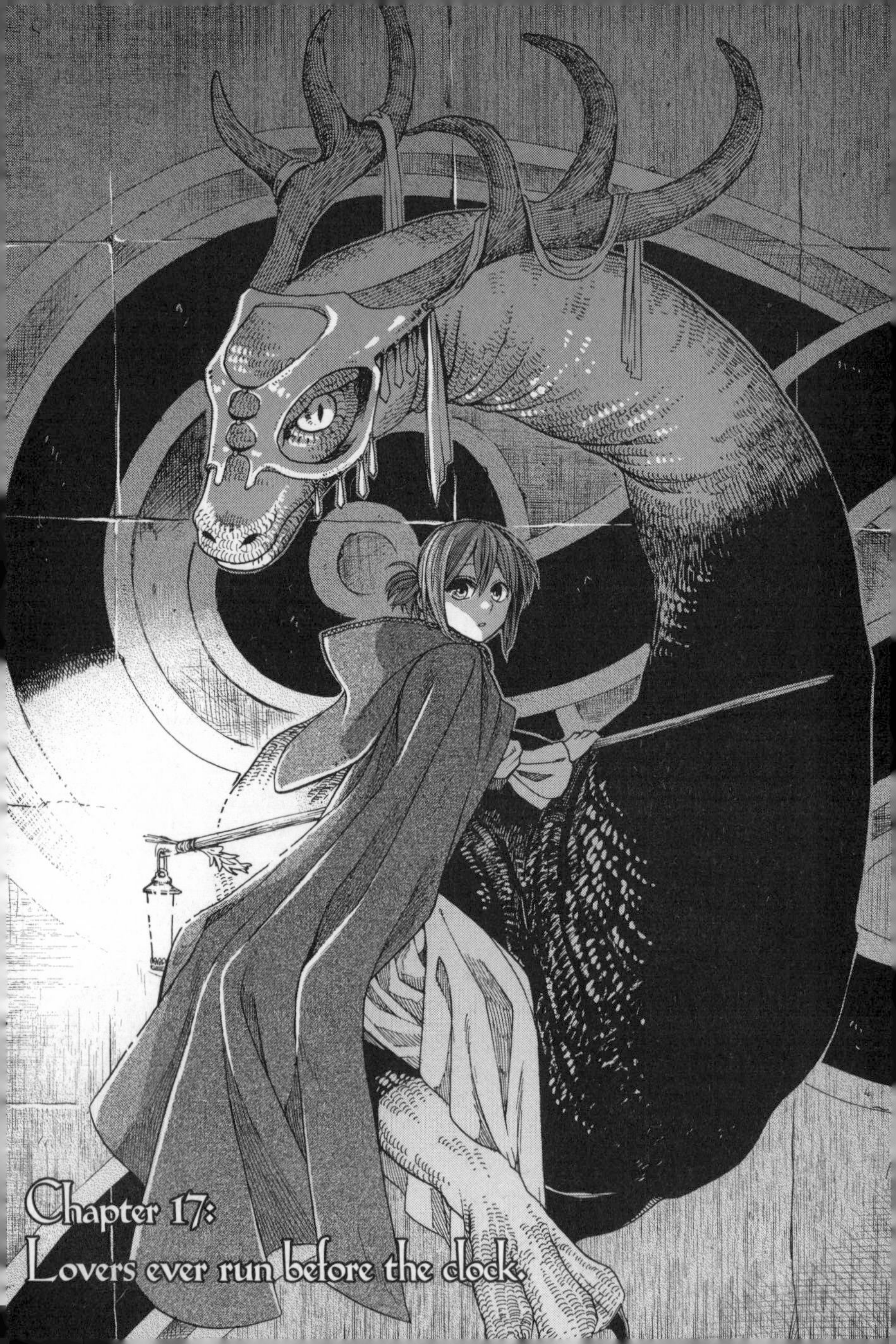
Chapter 17:
Lovers ever run before the clock.

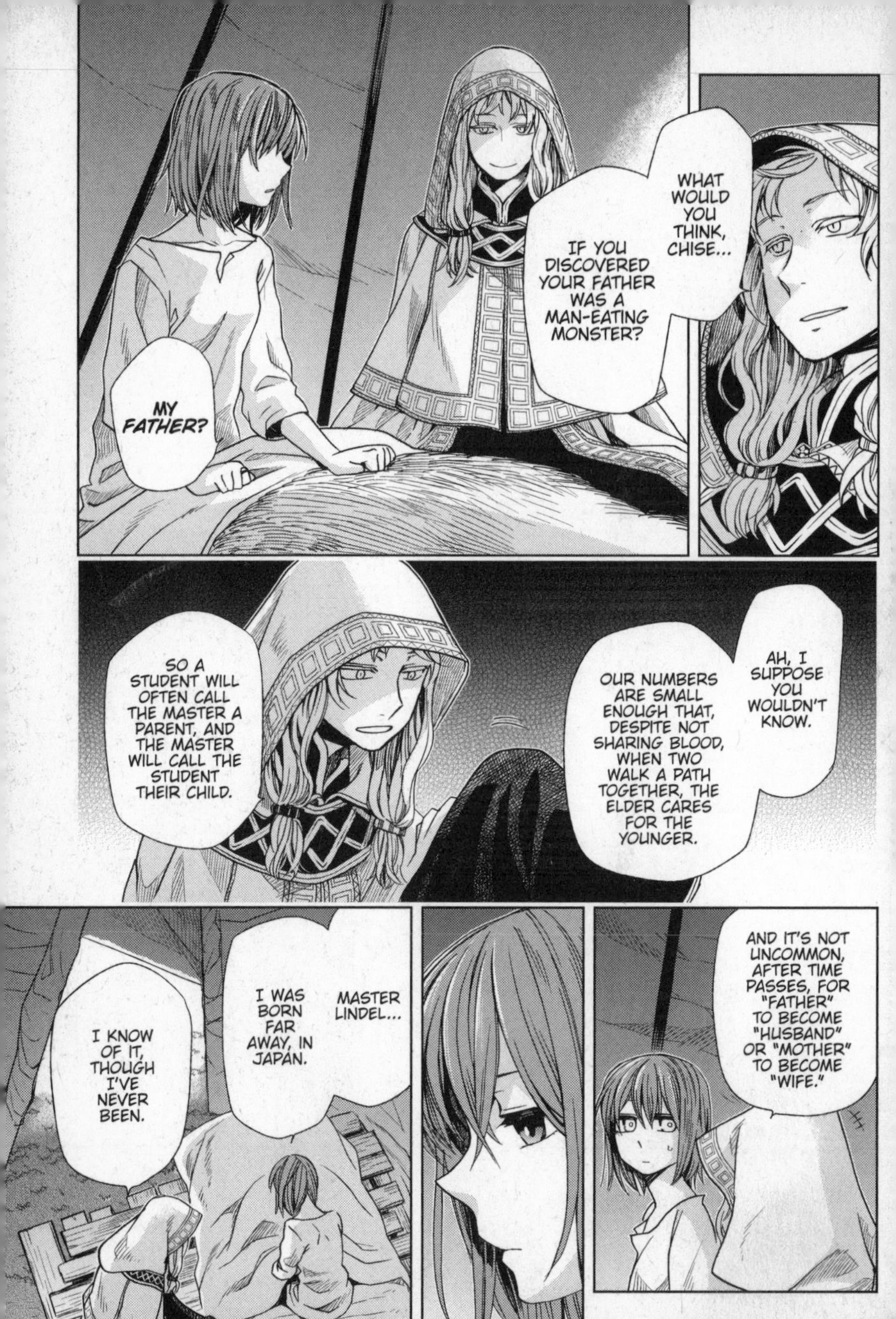
WHAT WOULD YOU THINK, CHISE...
IF YOU DISCOVERED YOUR FATHER WAS A MAN-EATING MONSTER?
MY FATHER?
AH, I SUPPOSE YOU WOULDN'T KNOW.
OUR NUMBERS ARE SMALL ENOUGH THAT, DESPITE NOT SHARING BLOOD, WHEN TWO WALK A PATH TOGETHER, THE ELDER CARES FOR THE YOUNGER.
SO A STUDENT WILL OFTEN CALL THE MASTER A PARENT, AND THE MASTER WILL CALL THE STUDENT THEIR CHILD.
AND IT'S NOT UNCOMMON, AFTER TIME PASSES, FOR "FATHER" TO BECOME "HUSBAND" OR "MOTHER" TO BECOME "WIFE."
MASTER LINDEL...
I WAS BORN FAR AWAY, IN JAPAN.
I KNOW OF IT, THOUGH I'VE NEVER BEEN.

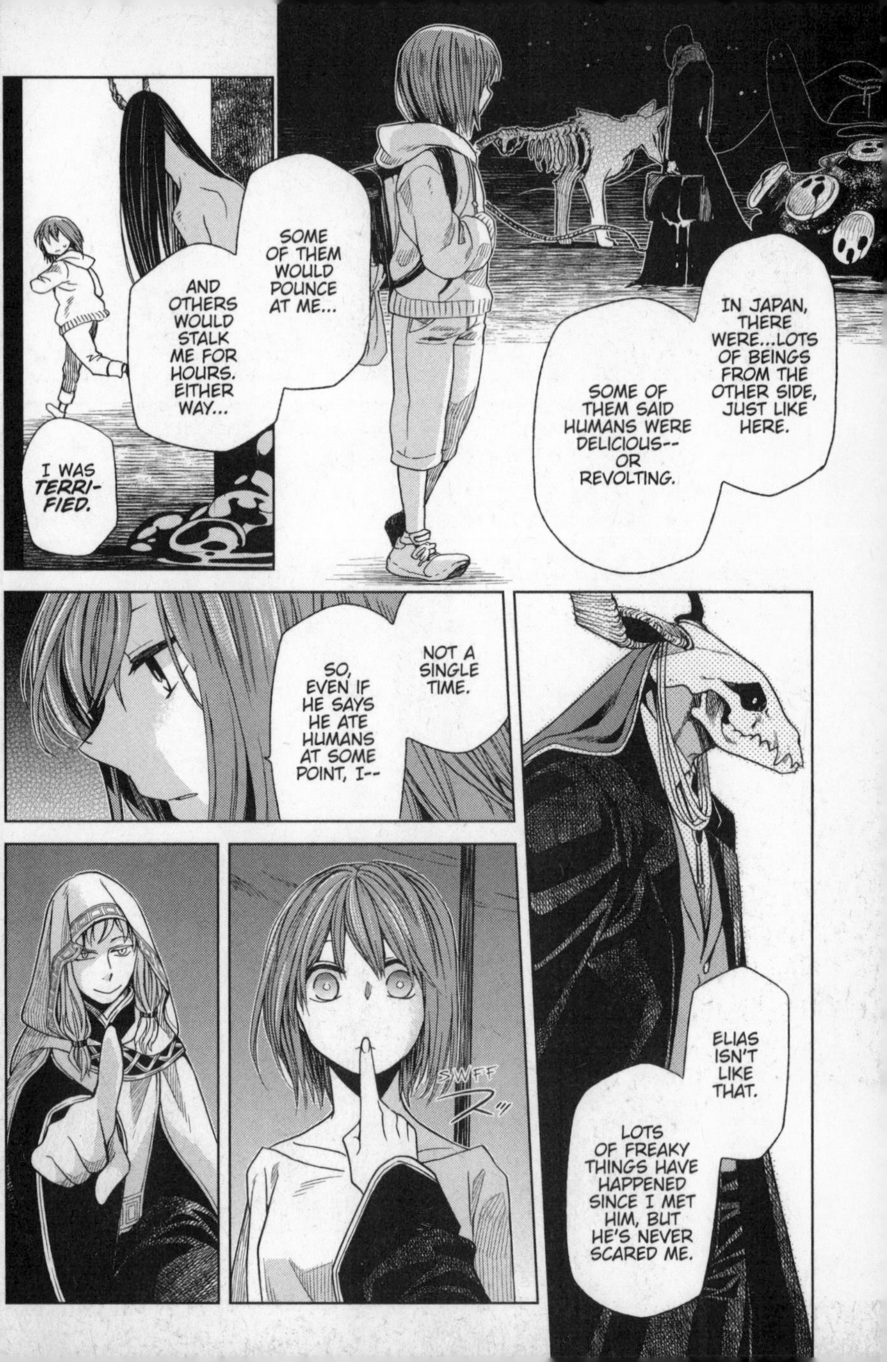
IN JAPAN, THERE WERE...LOTS OF BEINGS FROM THE OTHER SIDE, JUST LIKE HERE.
SOME OF THEM SAID HUMANS WERE DELICIOUS-- OR REVOLTING.
SOME OF THEM WOULD POUNCE AT ME...
AND OTHERS WOULD STALK ME FOR HOURS. EITHER WAY...
I WAS *TERRIFIED.*
ELIAS ISN'T LIKE THAT.
LOTS OF FREAKY THINGS HAVE HAPPENED SINCE I MET HIM, BUT HE'S NEVER SCARED ME.
NOT A SINGLE TIME.
SO, EVEN IF HE SAYS HE ATE HUMANS AT SOME POINT, I--
SWFF

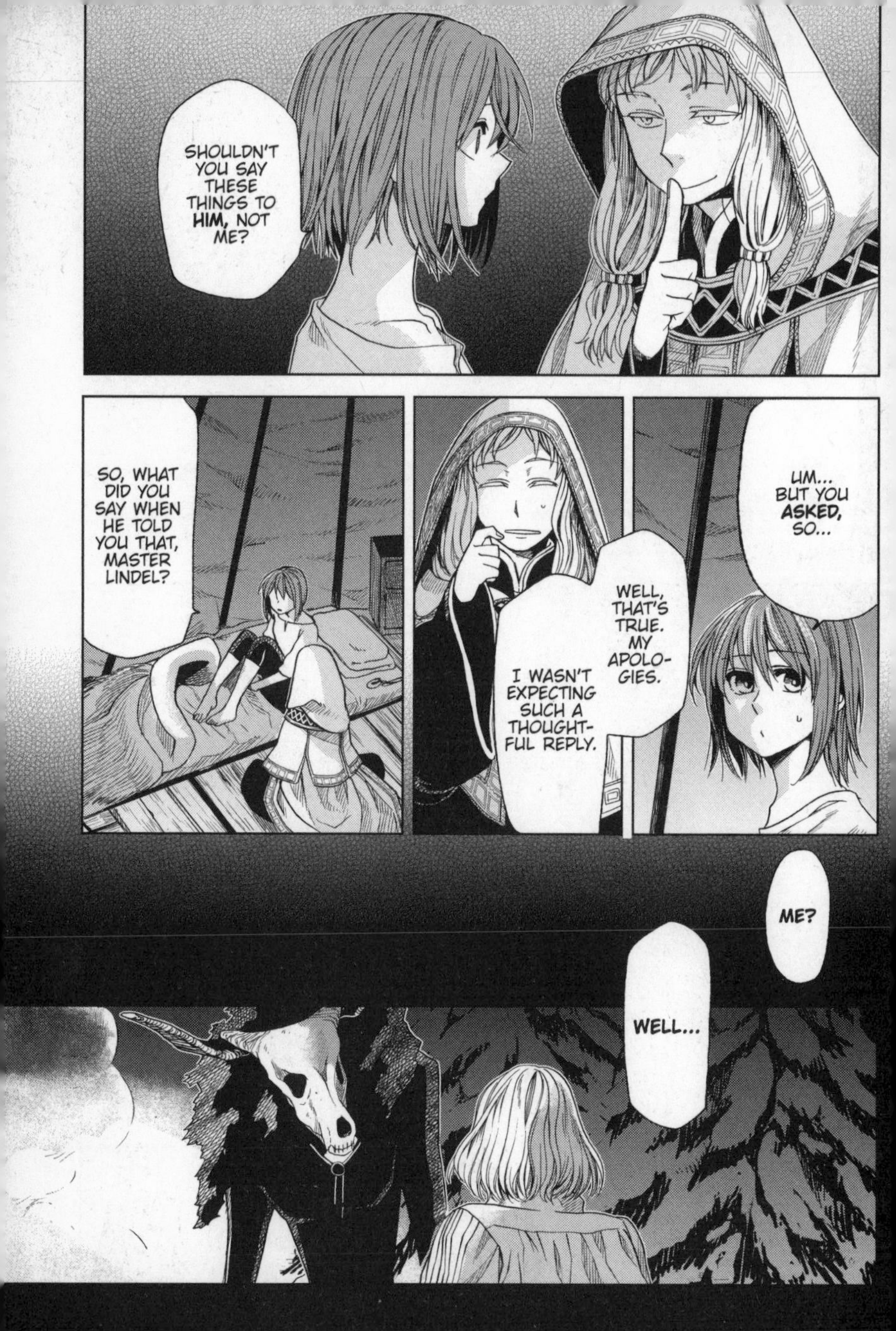
SHOULDN'T YOU SAY THESE THINGS TO **HIM,** NOT ME?
UM... BUT YOU **ASKED,** SO...
WELL, THAT'S TRUE. MY APOLOGIES.
I WASN'T EXPECTING SUCH A THOUGHTFUL REPLY.
SO, WHAT DID YOU SAY WHEN HE TOLD YOU THAT, MASTER LINDEL?
ME?
WELL...

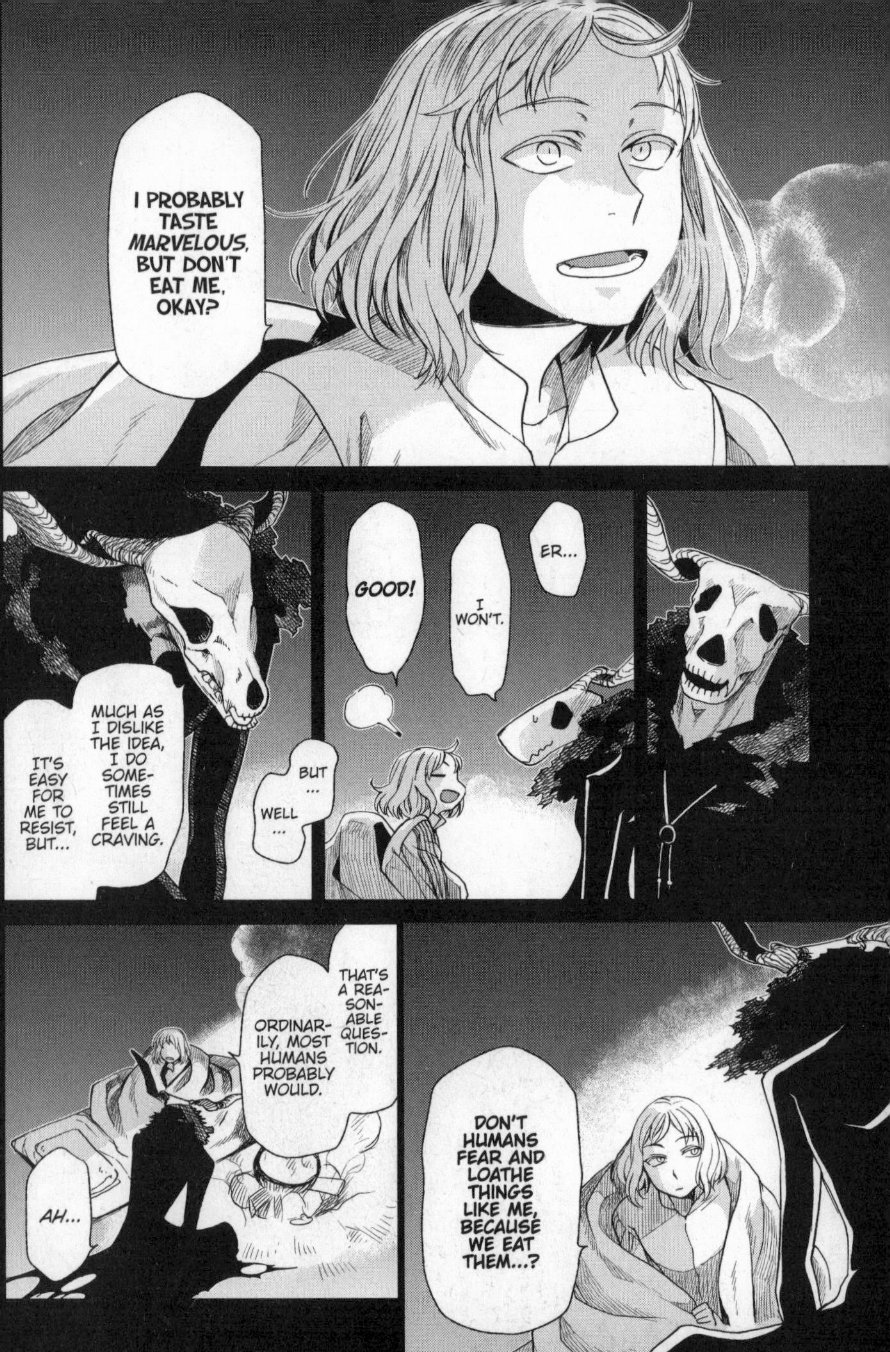
I PROBABLY TASTE *MARVELOUS*, BUT DON'T EAT ME, OKAY?
ER...
I WON'T.
GOOD!
BUT...
WELL...
MUCH AS I DISLIKE THE IDEA, I DO SOME-TIMES STILL FEEL A CRAVING.
IT'S EASY FOR ME TO RESIST, BUT...
DON'T HUMANS FEAR AND LOATHE THINGS LIKE ME, BECAUSE WE EAT THEM...?
THAT'S A REA-SON-ABLE QUES-TION.
ORDINAR-ILY, MOST HUMANS PROBABLY WOULD.
AH...

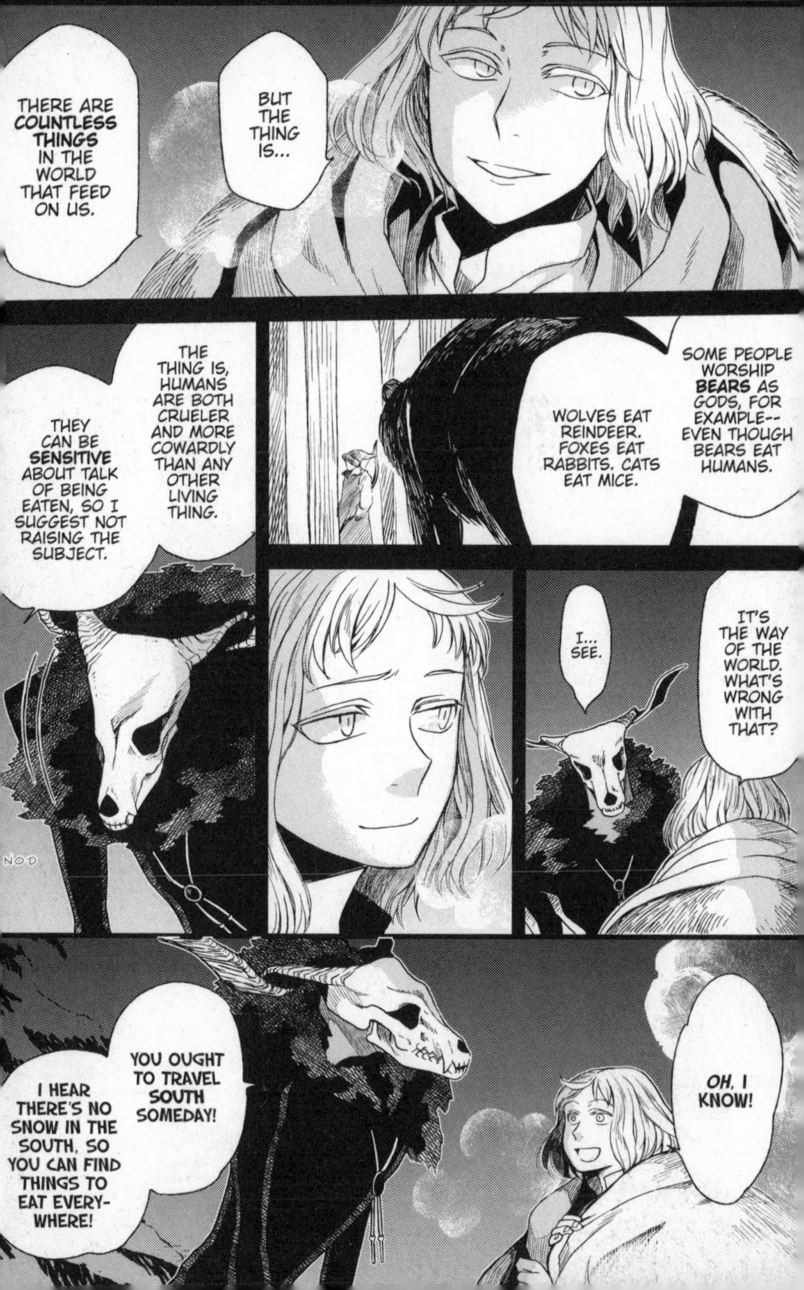
BUT THE THING IS...
THERE ARE COUNTLESS THINGS IN THE WORLD THAT FEED ON US.
SOME PEOPLE WORSHIP BEARS AS GODS, FOR EXAMPLE-- EVEN THOUGH BEARS EAT HUMANS.
WOLVES EAT REINDEER. FOXES EAT RABBITS. CATS EAT MICE.
IT'S THE WAY OF THE WORLD. WHAT'S WRONG WITH THAT?
I... SEE.
THE THING IS, HUMANS ARE BOTH CRUELER AND MORE COWARDLY THAN ANY OTHER LIVING THING.
THEY CAN BE SENSITIVE ABOUT TALK OF BEING EATEN, SO I SUGGEST NOT RAISING THE SUBJECT.
NOD
OH, I KNOW!
YOU OUGHT TO TRAVEL SOUTH SOMEDAY!
I HEAR THERE'S NO SNOW IN THE SOUTH, SO YOU CAN FIND THINGS TO EAT EVERY-WHERE!

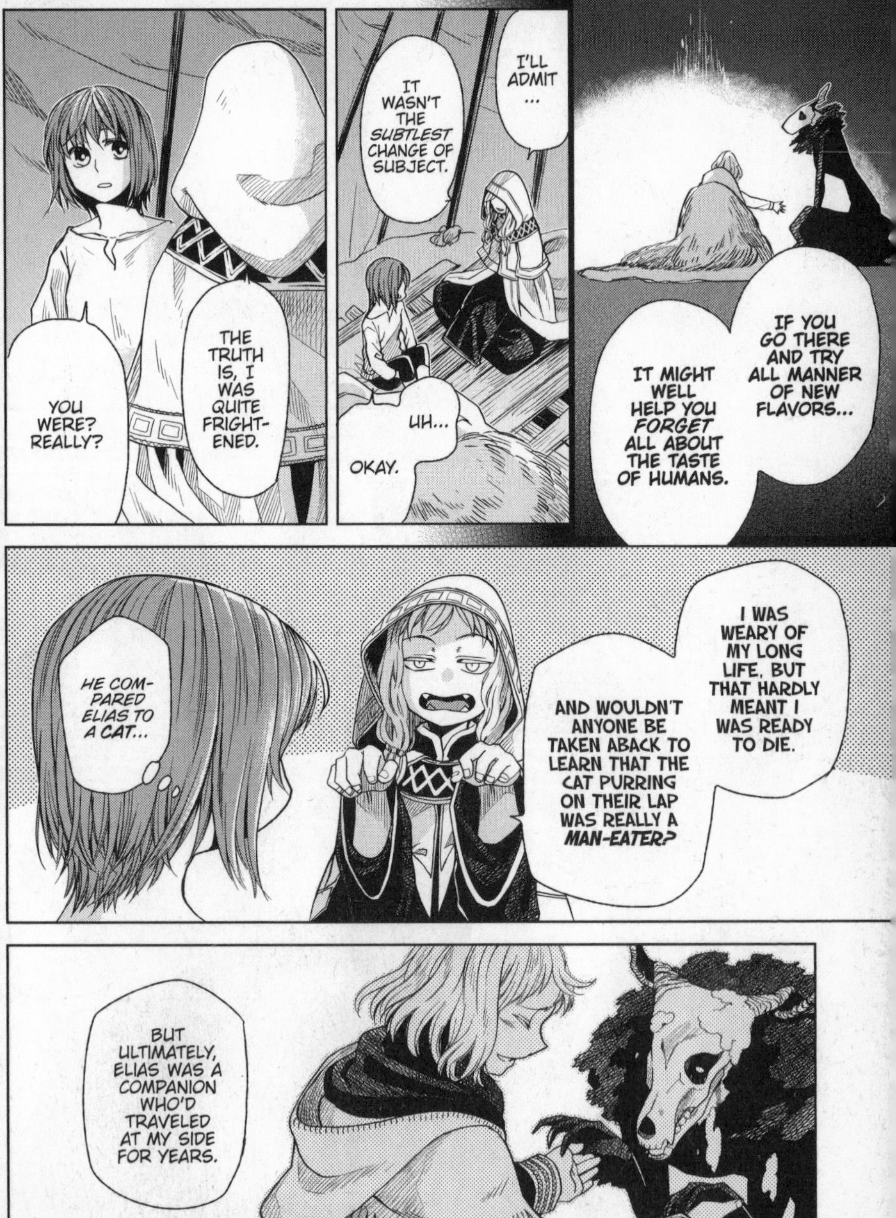
IF YOU GO THERE AND TRY ALL MANNER OF NEW FLAVORS...
IT MIGHT WELL HELP YOU FORGET ALL ABOUT THE TASTE OF HUMANS.
I'LL ADMIT...
IT WASN'T THE SUBTLEST CHANGE OF SUBJECT.
UH...
OKAY.
THE TRUTH IS, I WAS QUITE FRIGHTENED.
YOU WERE? REALLY?
I WAS WEARY OF MY LONG LIFE, BUT THAT HARDLY MEANT I WAS READY TO DIE.
AND WOULDN'T ANYONE BE TAKEN ABACK TO LEARN THAT THE CAT PURRING ON THEIR LAP WAS REALLY A MAN-EATER?
HE COMPARED ELIAS TO A CAT...
BUT ULTIMATELY, ELIAS WAS A COMPANION WHO'D TRAVELED AT MY SIDE FOR YEARS.

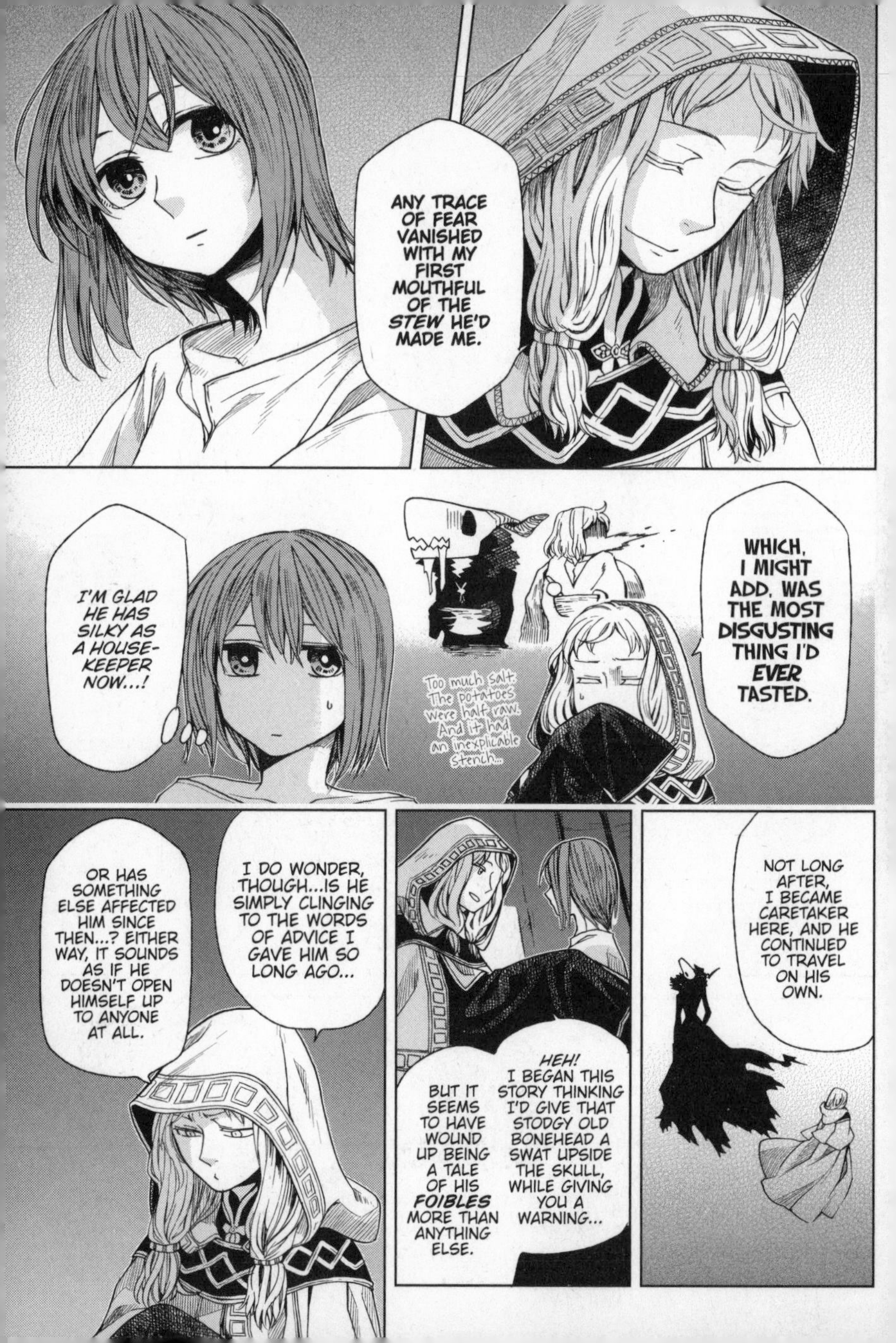
ANY TRACE OF FEAR VANISHED WITH MY FIRST MOUTHFUL OF THE STEW HE'D MADE ME.
WHICH, I MIGHT ADD, WAS THE MOST DISGUSTING THING I'D EVER TASTED.
Too much salt. The potatoes were half raw. And it had an inexplicable stench...
I'M GLAD HE HAS SILKY AS A HOUSEKEEPER NOW...!
NOT LONG AFTER, I BECAME CARETAKER HERE, AND HE CONTINUED TO TRAVEL ON HIS OWN.
HEH! I BEGAN THIS STORY THINKING I'D GIVE THAT STODGY OLD BONEHEAD A SWAT UPSIDE THE SKULL, WHILE GIVING YOU A WARNING...
BUT IT SEEMS TO HAVE WOUND UP BEING A TALE OF HIS FOIBLES MORE THAN ANYTHING ELSE.
I DO WONDER, THOUGH...IS HE SIMPLY CLINGING TO THE WORDS OF ADVICE I GAVE HIM SO LONG AGO...
OR HAS SOMETHING ELSE AFFECTED HIM SINCE THEN...? EITHER WAY, IT SOUNDS AS IF HE DOESN'T OPEN HIMSELF UP TO ANYONE AT ALL.

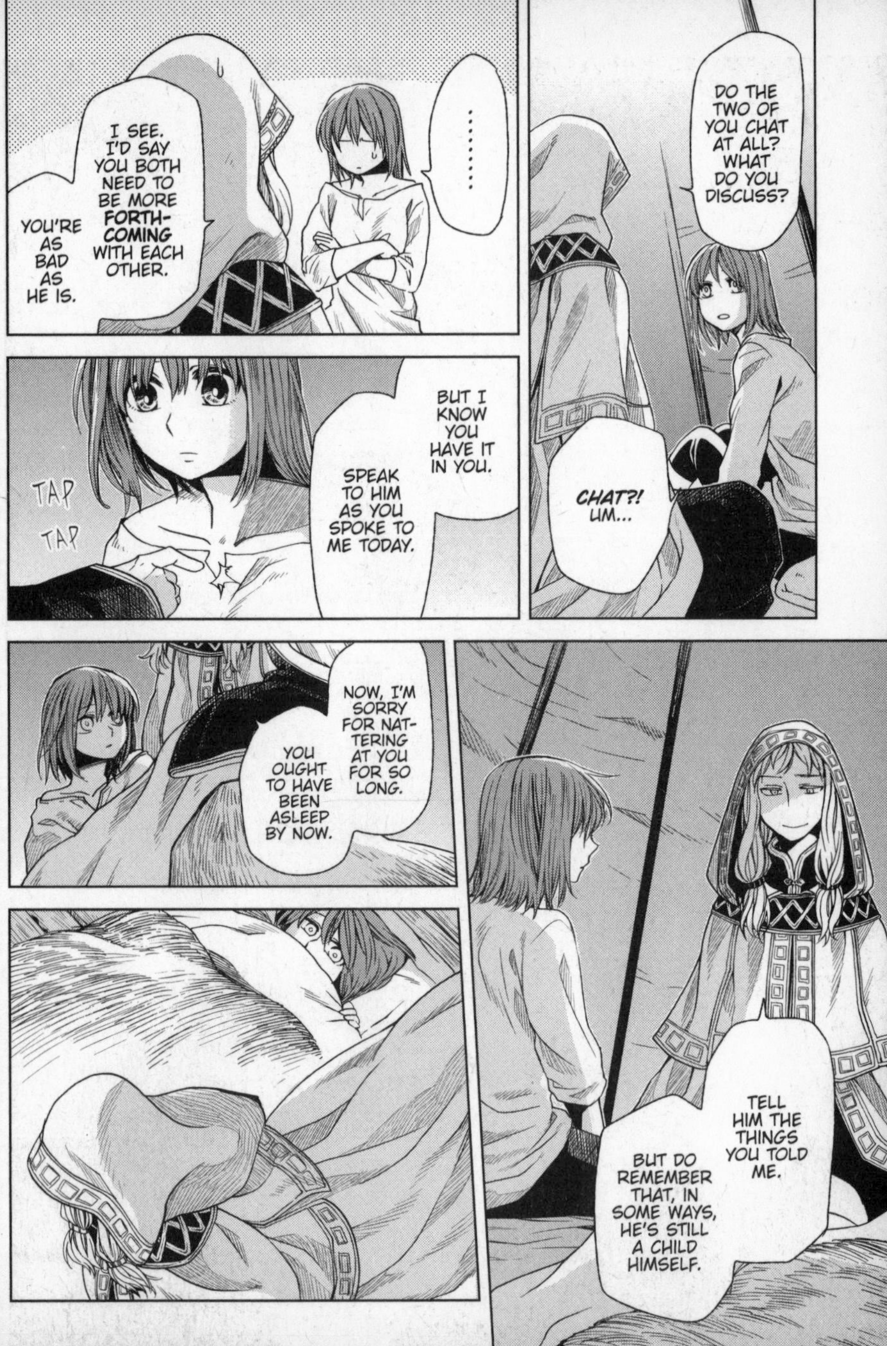
DO THE TWO OF YOU CHAT AT ALL? WHAT DO YOU DISCUSS?
CHAT?! UM...
......
I SEE. I'D SAY YOU BOTH NEED TO BE MORE **FORTH-COMING** WITH EACH OTHER.
YOU'RE AS BAD AS HE IS.
BUT I KNOW YOU HAVE IT IN YOU.
SPEAK TO HIM AS YOU SPOKE TO ME TODAY.
TAP
TAP
TELL HIM THE THINGS YOU TOLD ME.
BUT DO REMEMBER THAT, IN SOME WAYS, HE'S STILL A CHILD HIMSELF.
NOW, I'M SORRY FOR NAT-TERING AT YOU FOR SO LONG.
YOU OUGHT TO HAVE BEEN ASLEEP BY NOW.

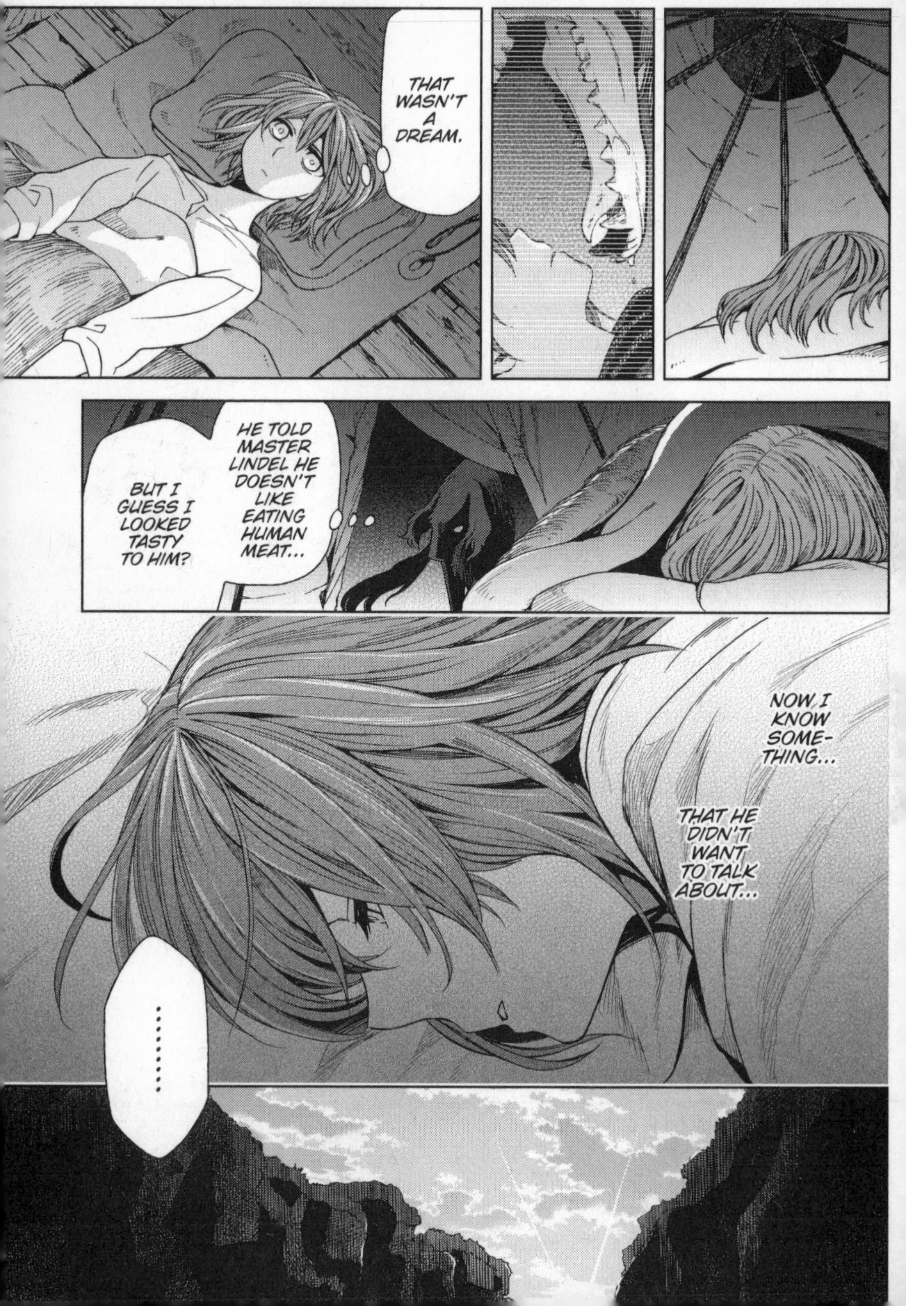
...
THAT WASN'T A DREAM.
HE TOLD MASTER LINDEL HE DOESN'T LIKE EATING HUMAN MEAT... BUT I GUESS I LOOKED TASTY TO HIM?
NOW I KNOW SOME-THING...
THAT HE DIDN'T WANT TO TALK ABOUT...
......

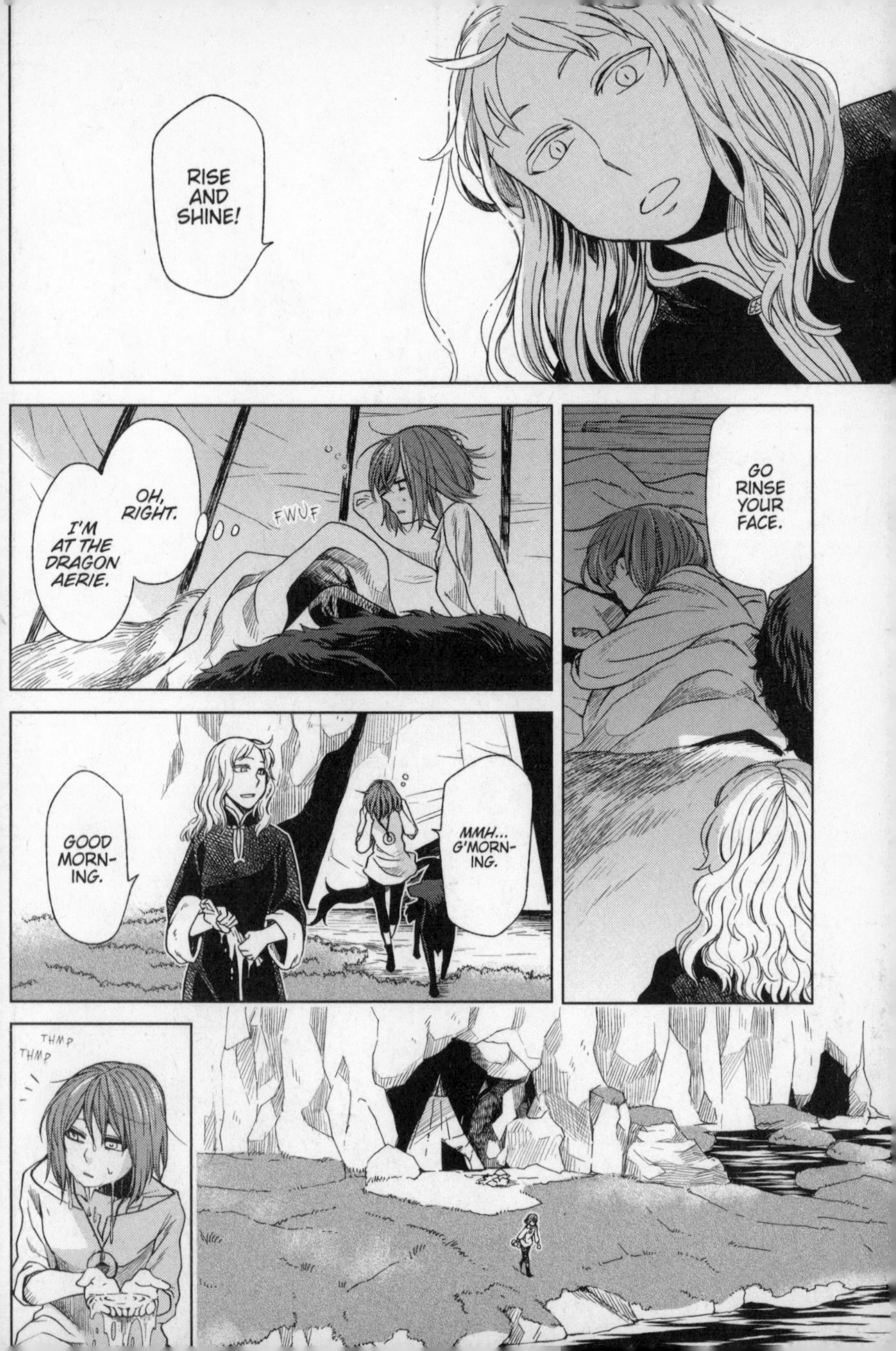
RISE AND SHINE!
GO RINSE YOUR FACE.
OH, RIGHT. I'M AT THE DRAGON AERIE.
FWUF
MMH... G'MORNING.
GOOD MORNING.
THMP THMP

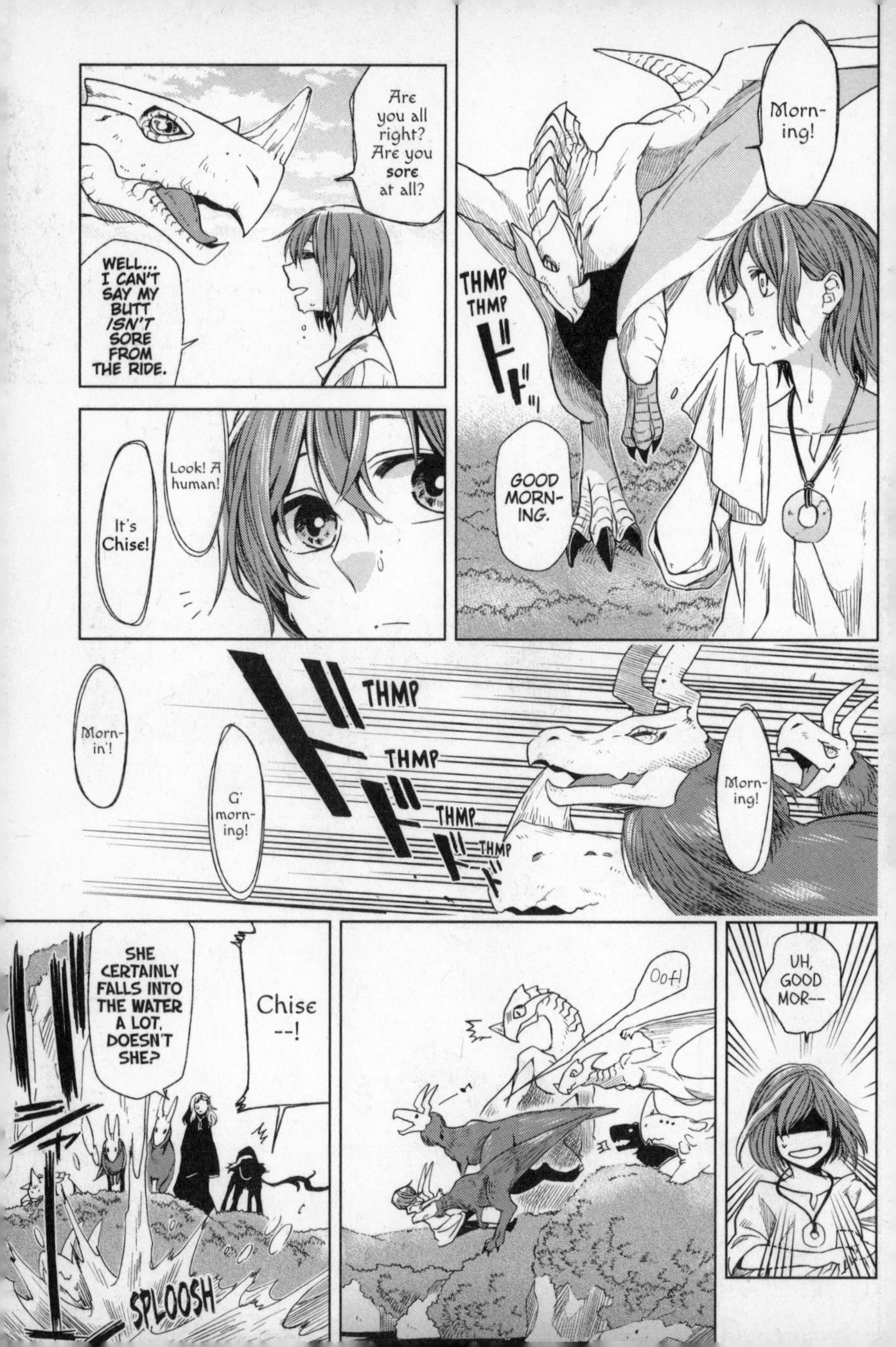
Morning!
THMP THMP
GOOD MORNING.
Are you all right? Are you sore at all?
WELL... I CAN'T SAY MY BUTT *ISN'T* SORE FROM THE RIDE.
Look! A human!
It's Chise!
Morning!
THMP
THMP
THMP
THMP
G' morning!
Morn-in'!
UH, GOOD MOR--
Oof!
Chise--!
SHE CERTAINLY FALLS INTO THE WATER A LOT, DOESN'T SHE?
SPLOOSH

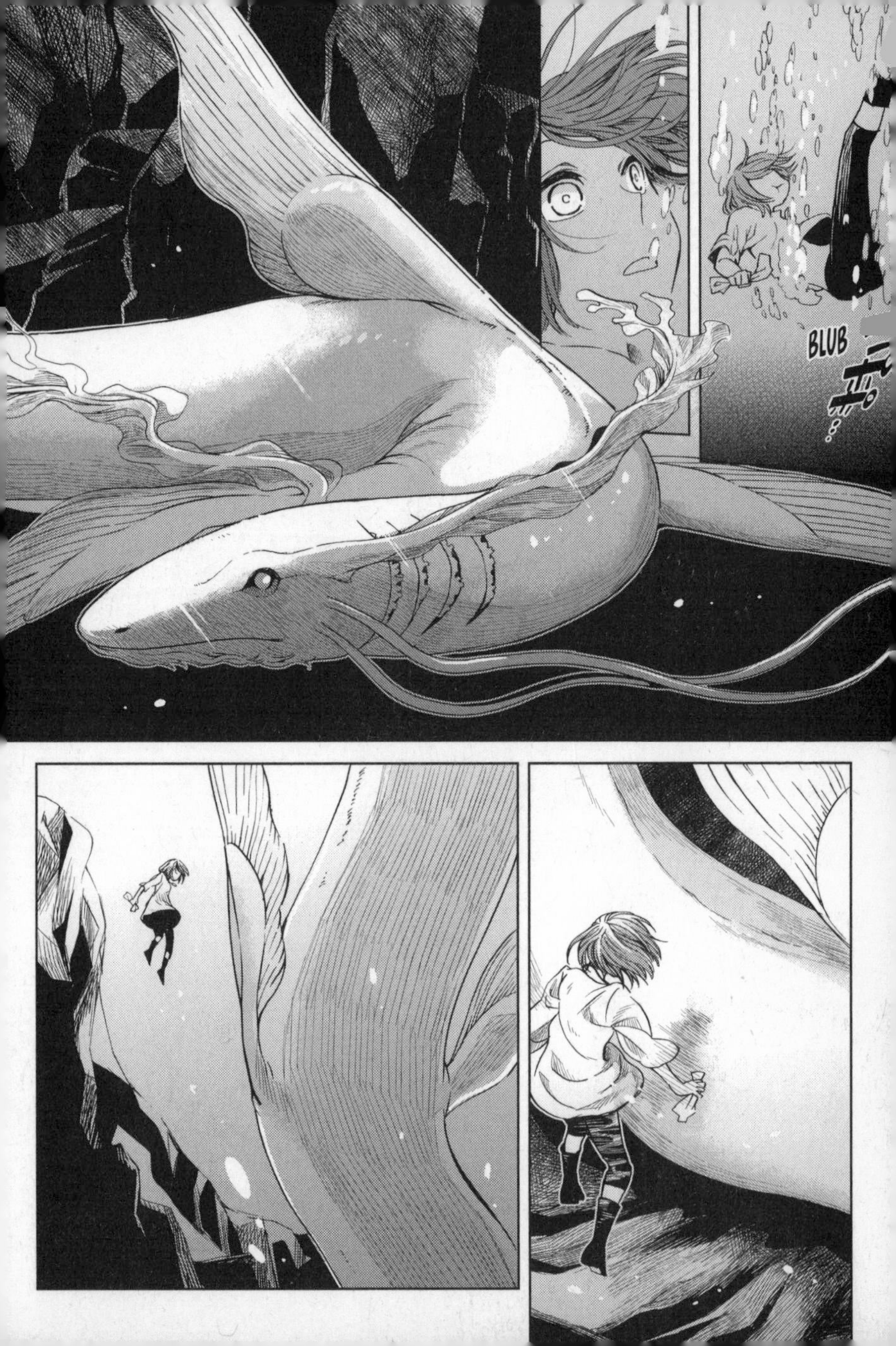
BLUB

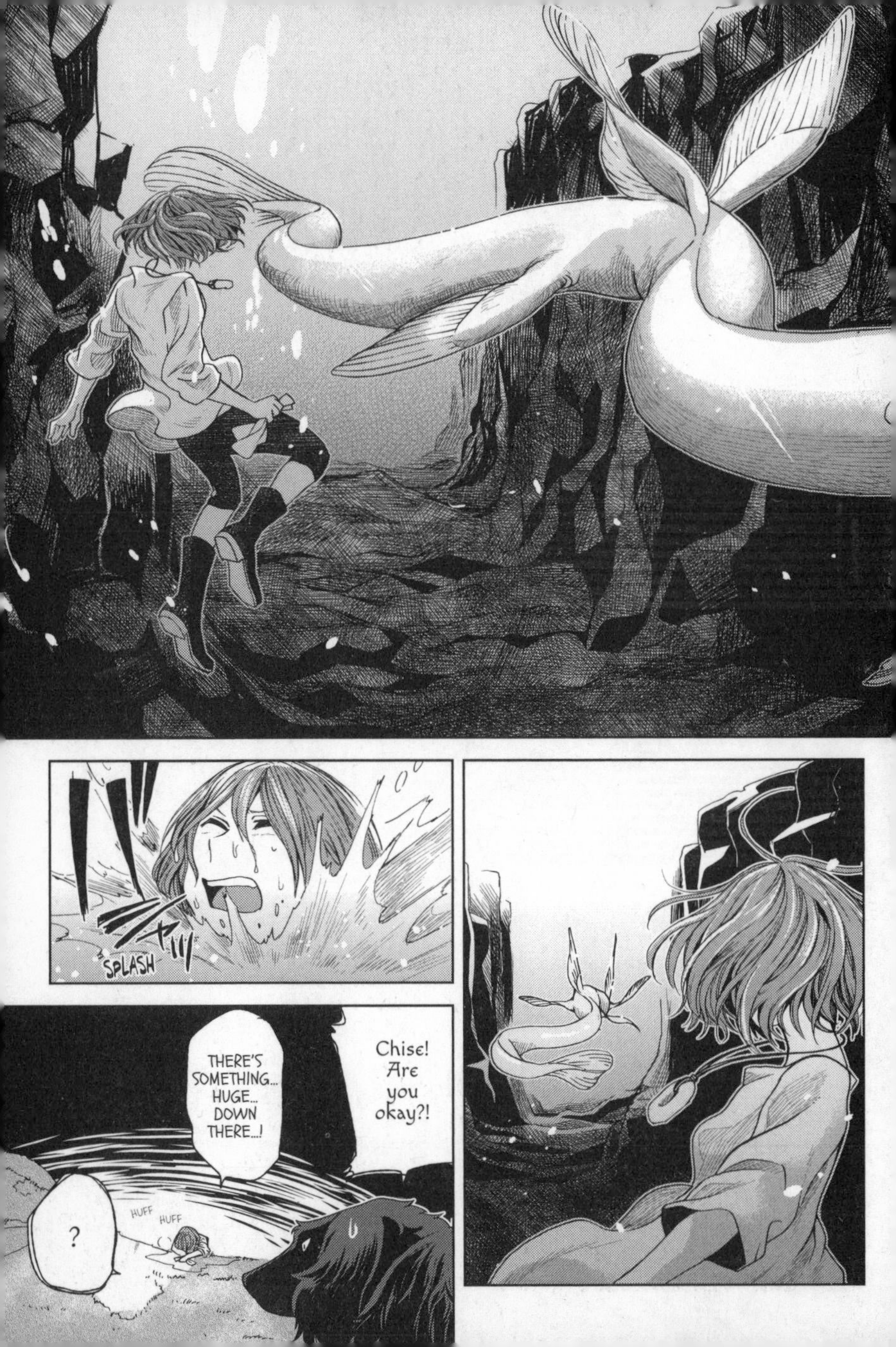
SPLASH
Chise! Are you okay?!
THERE'S SOMETHING... HUGE... DOWN THERE...!
HUFF HUFF
?

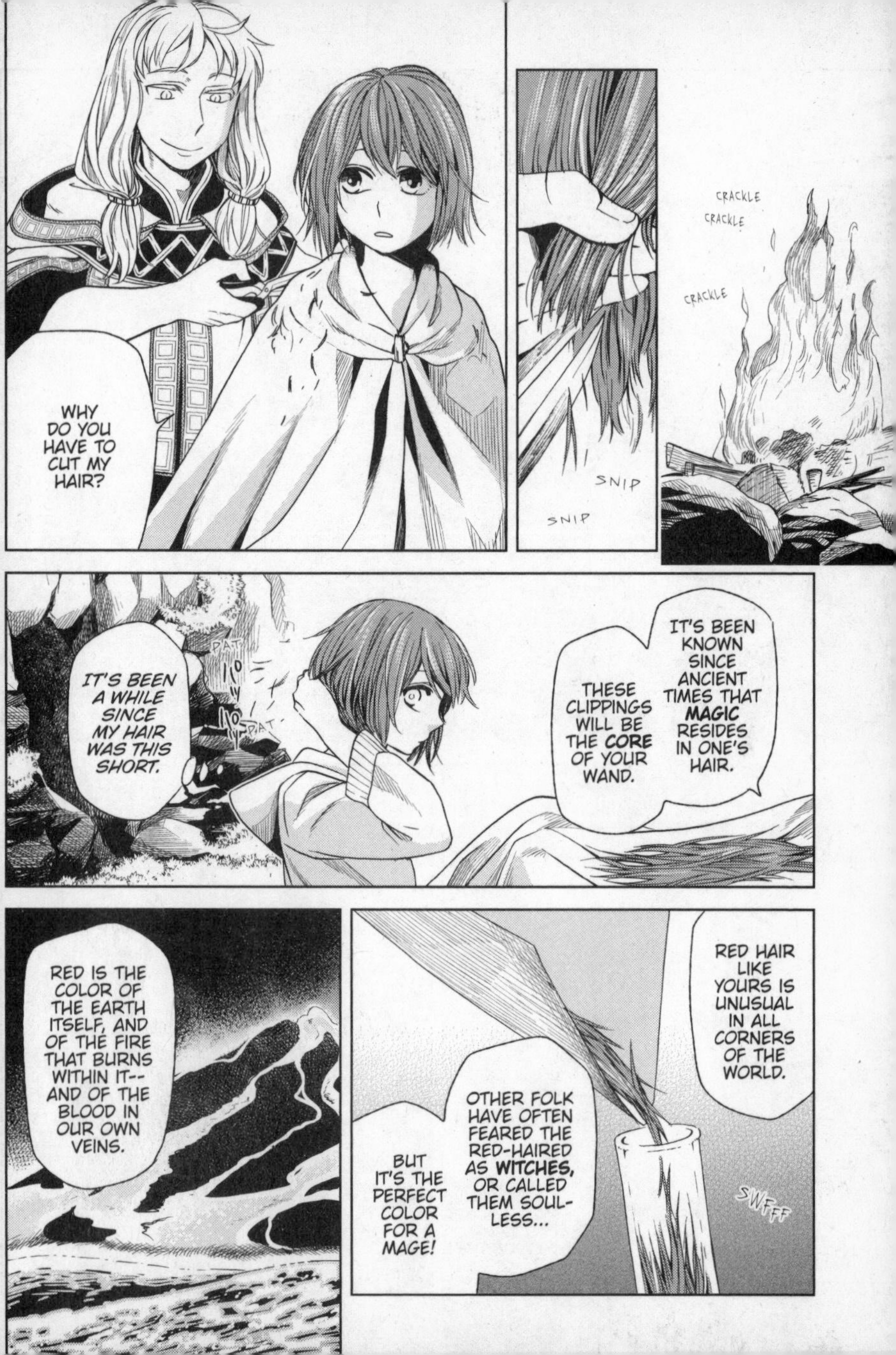
CRACKLE
CRACKLE
CRACKLE
SNIP
SNIP
WHY DO YOU HAVE TO CUT MY HAIR?
IT'S BEEN KNOWN SINCE ANCIENT TIMES THAT **MAGIC** RESIDES IN ONE'S HAIR.
THESE CLIPPINGS WILL BE THE **CORE** OF YOUR WAND.
PAT
PAT
IT'S BEEN A WHILE SINCE MY HAIR WAS THIS SHORT.
RED HAIR LIKE YOURS IS UNUSUAL IN ALL CORNERS OF THE WORLD.
OTHER FOLK HAVE OFTEN FEARED THE RED-HAIRED AS **WITCHES,** OR CALLED THEM SOUL-LESS...
BUT IT'S THE PERFECT COLOR FOR A MAGE!
SWFFF
RED IS THE COLOR OF THE EARTH ITSELF, AND OF THE FIRE THAT BURNS WITHIN IT-- AND OF THE BLOOD IN OUR OWN VEINS.

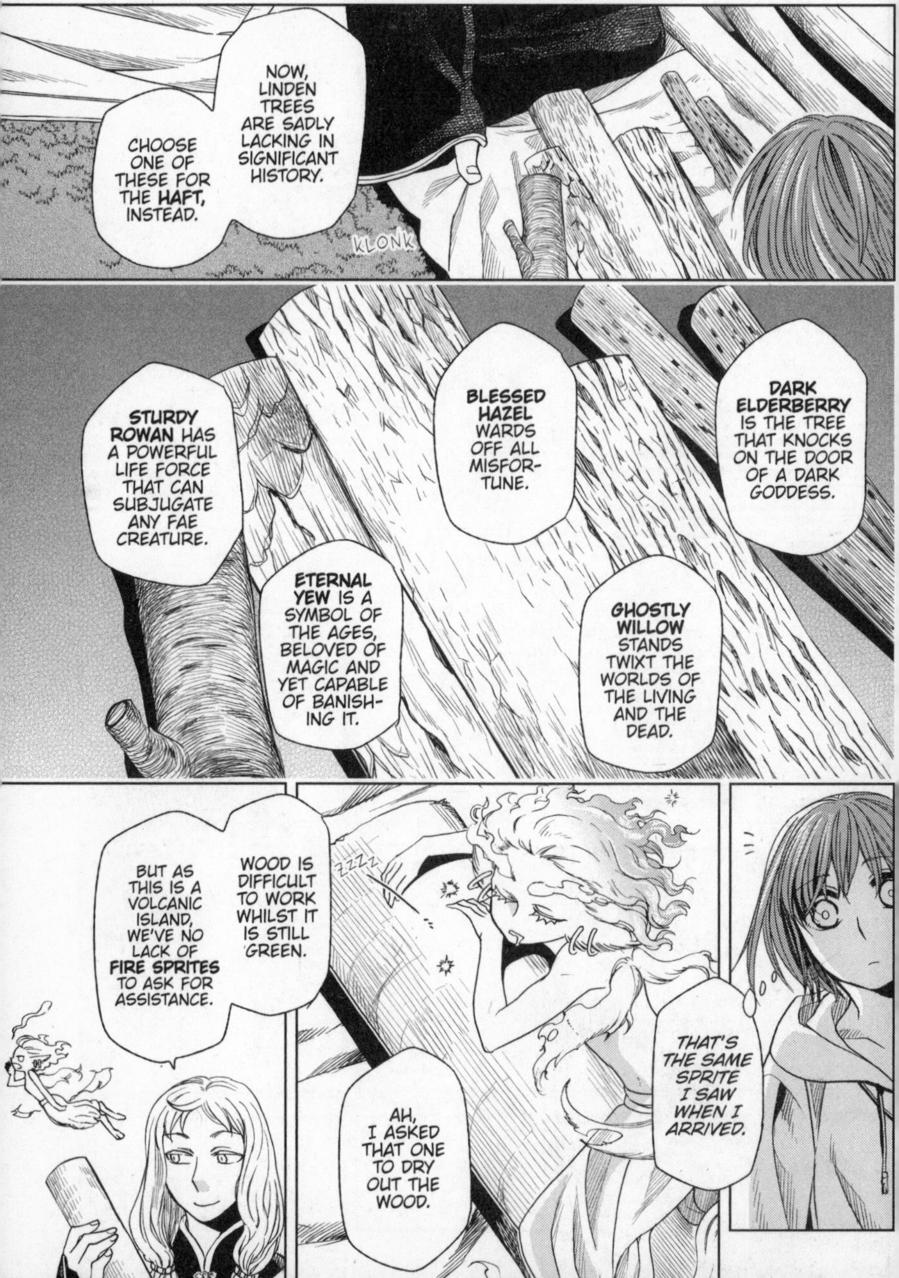
NOW, LINDEN TREES ARE SADLY LACKING IN SIGNIFICANT HISTORY.
CHOOSE ONE OF THESE FOR THE **HAFT,** INSTEAD.
KLONK
DARK ELDERBERRY IS THE TREE THAT KNOCKS ON THE DOOR OF A DARK GODDESS.
BLESSED HAZEL WARDS OFF ALL MISFOR-TUNE.
STURDY ROWAN HAS A POWERFUL LIFE FORCE THAT CAN SUBJUGATE ANY FAE CREATURE.
GHOSTLY WILLOW STANDS TWIXT THE WORLDS OF THE LIVING AND THE DEAD.
ETERNAL YEW IS A SYMBOL OF THE AGES, BELOVED OF MAGIC AND YET CAPABLE OF BANISH-ING IT.
THAT'S THE SAME SPRITE I SAW WHEN I ARRIVED.
ZZZZ
AH, I ASKED THAT ONE TO DRY OUT THE WOOD.
WOOD IS DIFFICULT TO WORK WHILST IT IS STILL GREEN.
BUT AS THIS IS A VOLCANIC ISLAND, WE'VE NO LACK OF **FIRE SPRITES** TO ASK FOR ASSISTANCE.

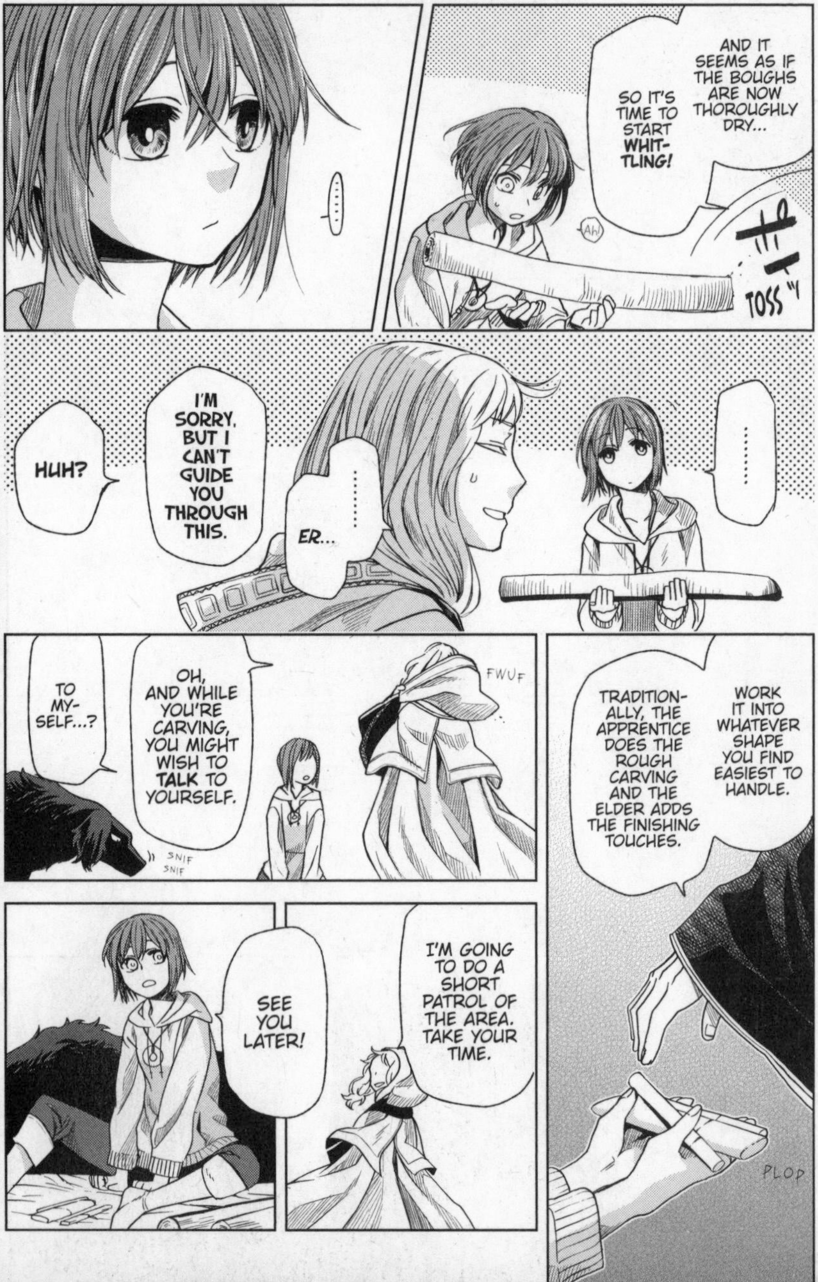
AND IT SEEMS AS IF THE BOUGHS ARE NOW THOROUGHLY DRY...
SO IT'S TIME TO START WHIT-TLING!
Ah!
TOSS
......
......
......
ER...
I'M SORRY, BUT I CAN'T GUIDE YOU THROUGH THIS.
HUH?
WORK IT INTO WHATEVER SHAPE YOU FIND EASIEST TO HANDLE.
TRADITION-ALLY, THE APPRENTICE DOES THE ROUGH CARVING AND THE ELDER ADDS THE FINISHING TOUCHES.
PLOP
FWUF
OH, AND WHILE YOU'RE CARVING, YOU MIGHT WISH TO TALK TO YOURSELF.
TO MY-SELF...?
SNIF SNIF
I'M GOING TO DO A SHORT PATROL OF THE AREA. TAKE YOUR TIME.
SEE YOU LATER!

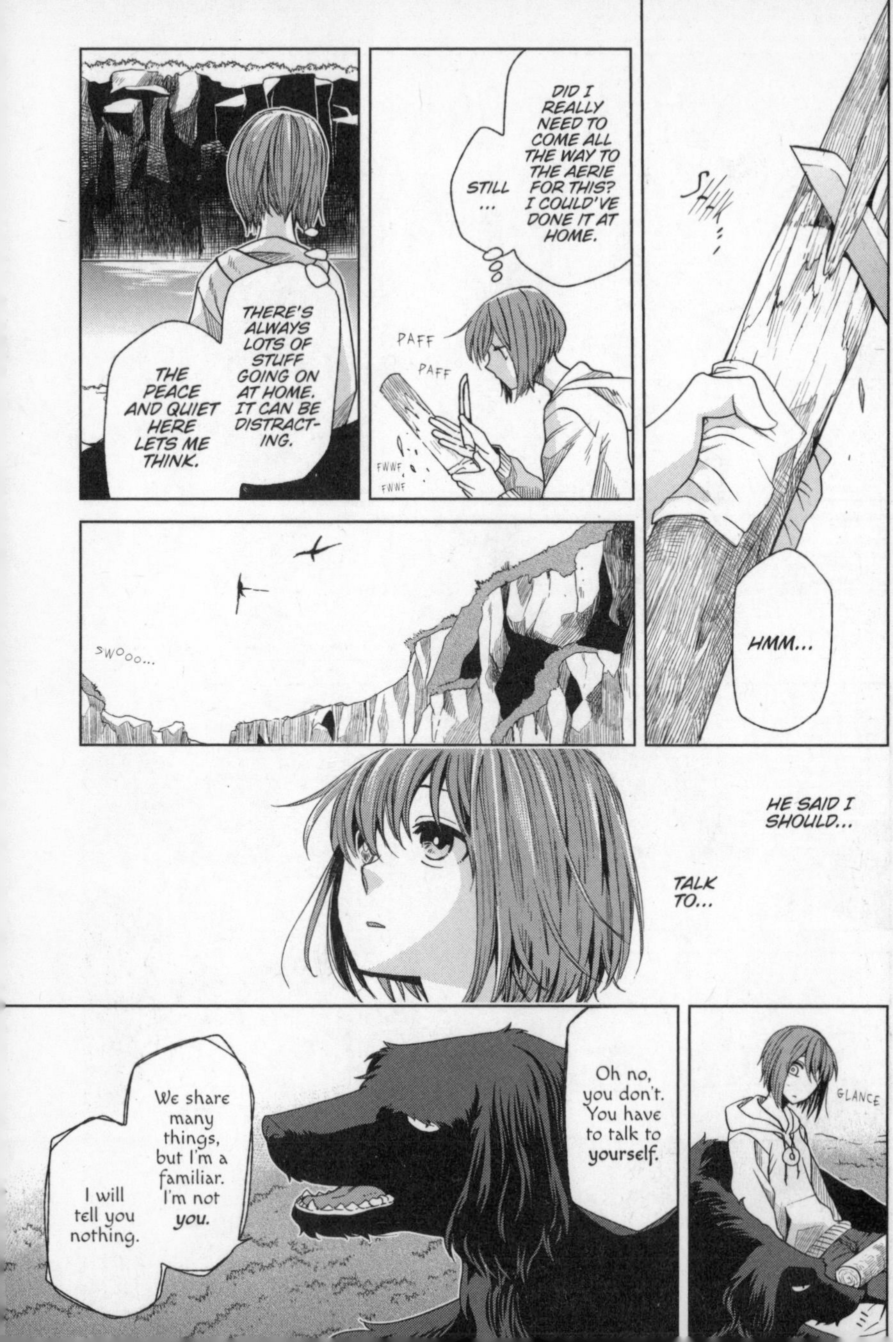
SHHK
HMM...
DID I REALLY NEED TO COME ALL THE WAY TO THE AERIE FOR THIS? I COULD'VE DONE IT AT HOME.
STILL...
PAFF
PAFF
FWWF
FWWF
THERE'S ALWAYS LOTS OF STUFF GOING ON AT HOME. IT CAN BE DISTRACTING.
THE PEACE AND QUIET HERE LETS ME THINK.
SWOOO...
HE SAID I SHOULD...
TALK TO...
GLANCE
Oh no, you don't. You have to talk to yourself.
We share many things, but I'm a familiar. I'm not you.
I will tell you nothing.

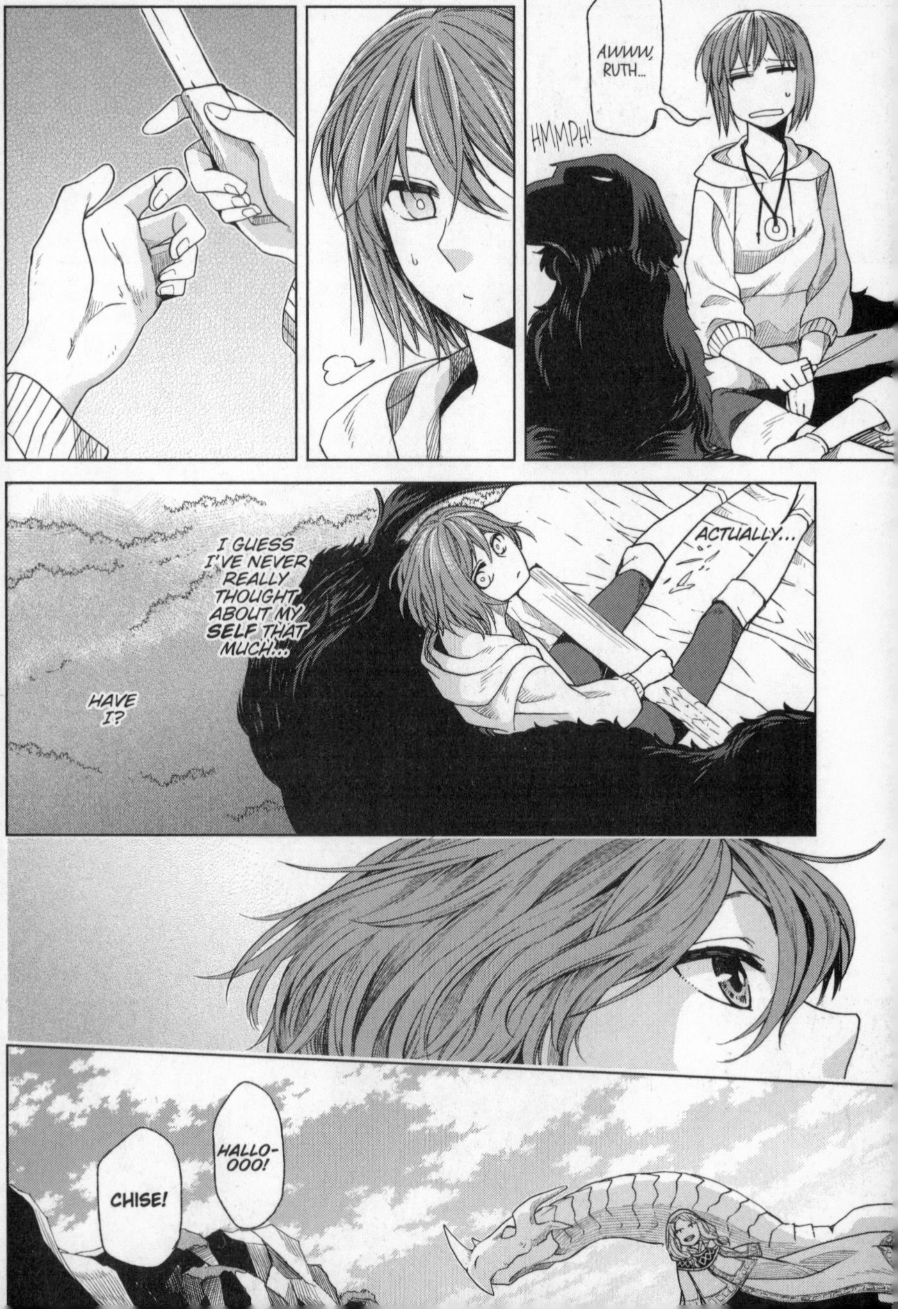
AWWW, RUTH...
HMMPH!
ACTUALLY...
I GUESS I'VE NEVER REALLY THOUGHT ABOUT MY **SELF** THAT MUCH...
HAVE I?
HALLO-OOO!
CHISE!

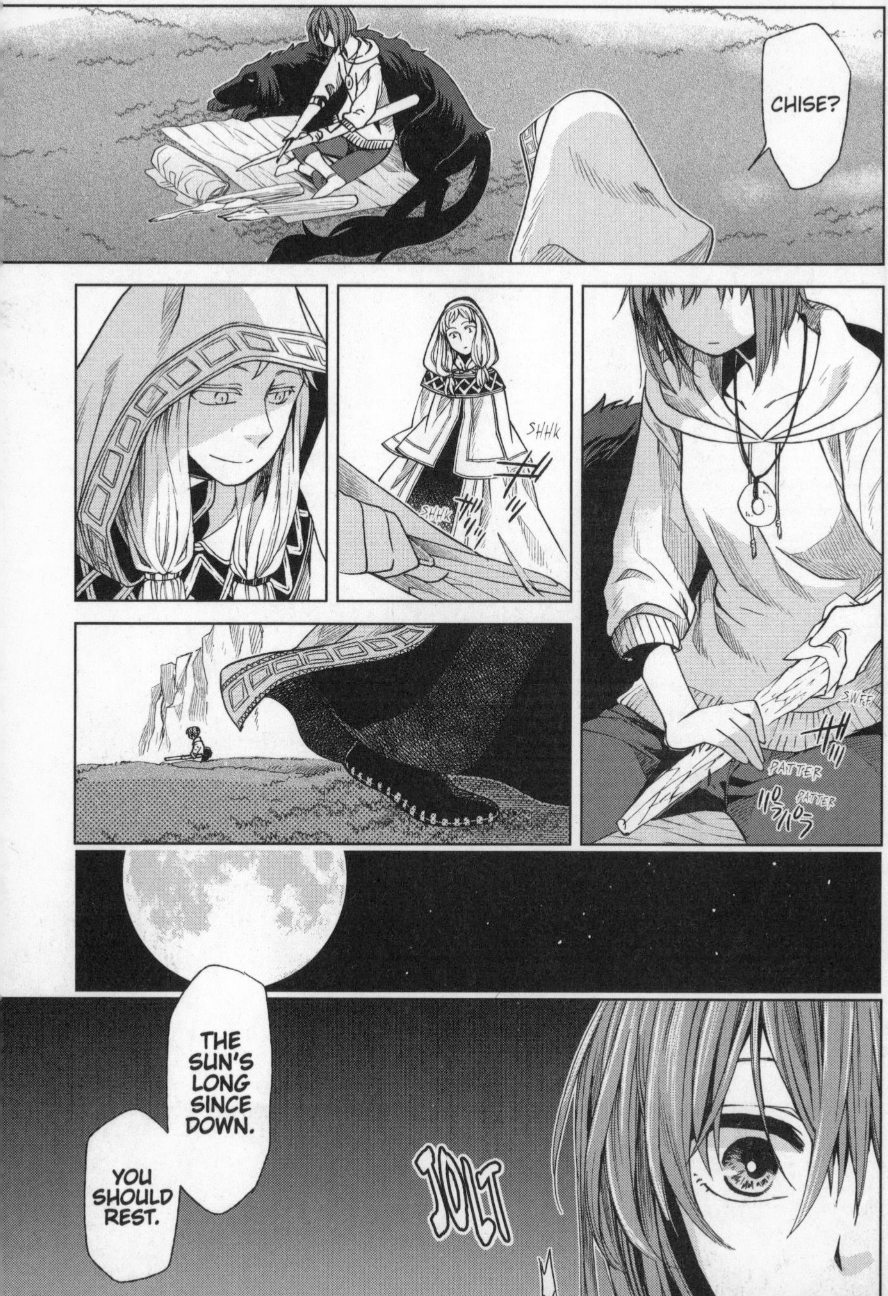
CHISE?
SWFF
PATTER
PATTER
SHHK
SHHK
THE SUN'S LONG SINCE DOWN.
YOU SHOULD REST.
JOLT

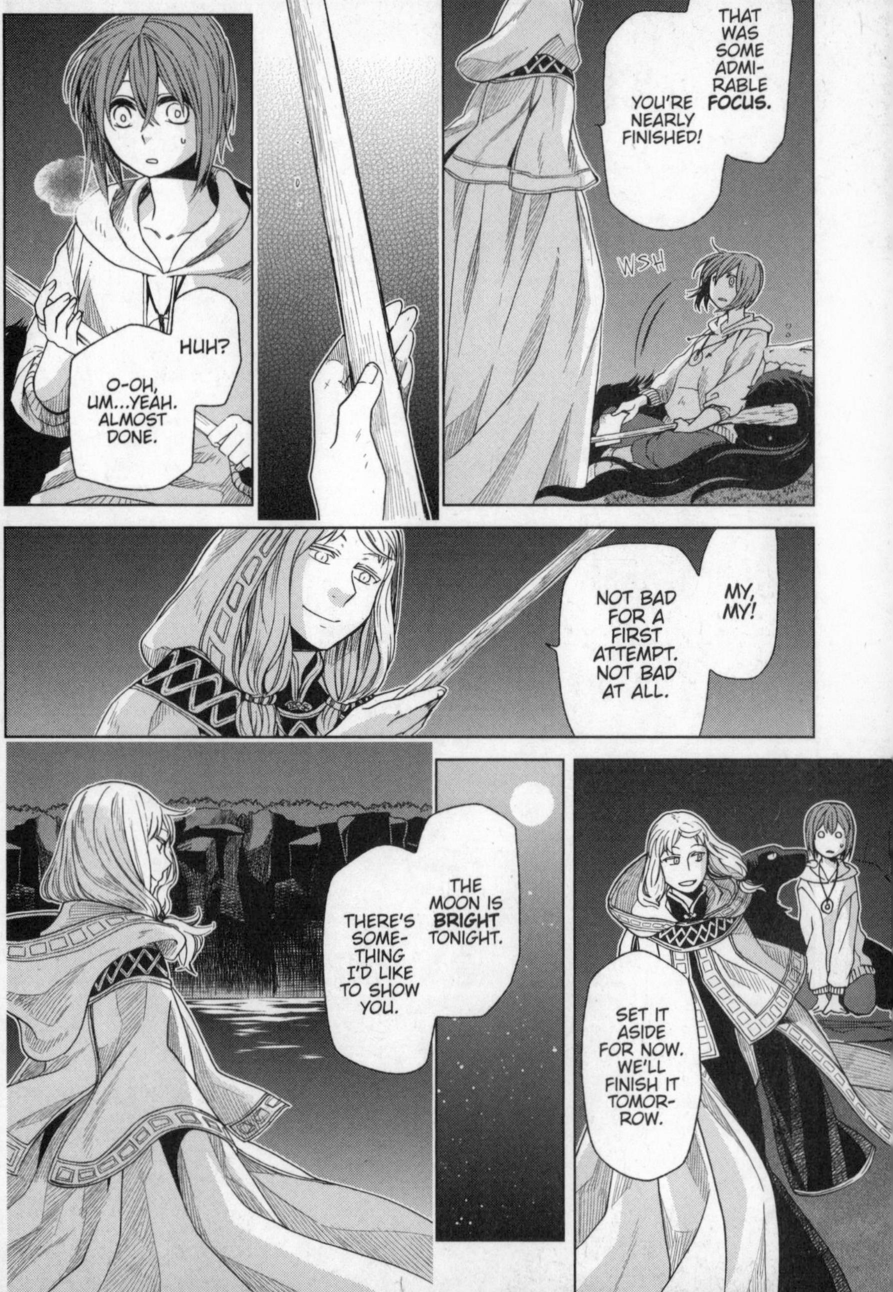
THAT WAS SOME ADMIRABLE FOCUS.
YOU'RE NEARLY FINISHED!
WSH
HUH?
O-OH, UM...YEAH. ALMOST DONE.
MY, MY!
NOT BAD FOR A FIRST ATTEMPT. NOT BAD AT ALL.
SET IT ASIDE FOR NOW. WE'LL FINISH IT TOMORROW.
THE MOON IS BRIGHT TONIGHT.
THERE'S SOMETHING I'D LIKE TO SHOW YOU.

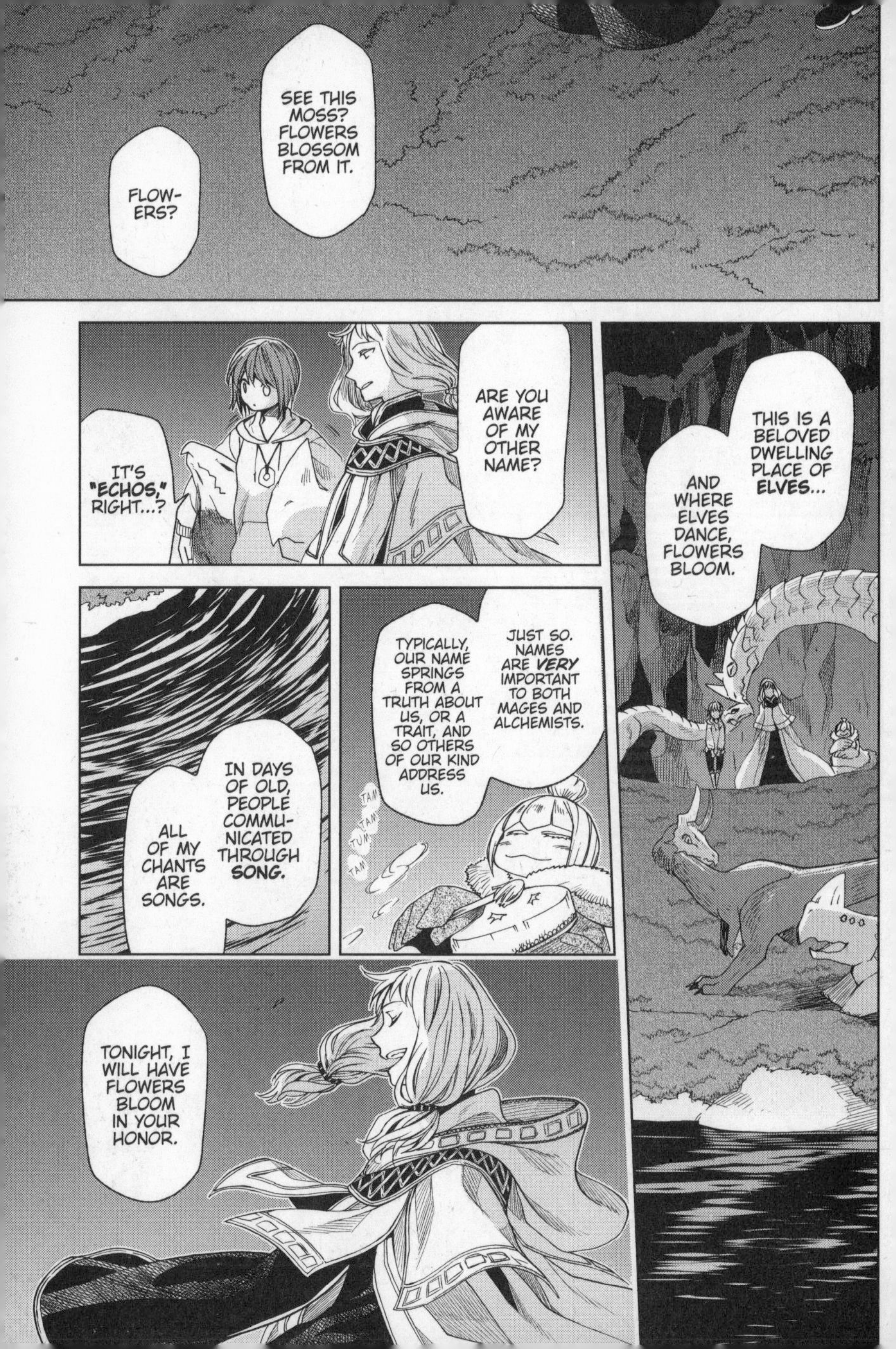
SEE THIS MOSS? FLOWERS BLOSSOM FROM IT.
FLOWERS?
THIS IS A BELOVED DWELLING PLACE OF ELVES...
AND WHERE ELVES DANCE, FLOWERS BLOOM.
ARE YOU AWARE OF MY OTHER NAME?
IT'S "ECHOS," RIGHT...?
JUST SO. NAMES ARE VERY IMPORTANT TO BOTH MAGES AND ALCHEMISTS.
TYPICALLY, OUR NAME SPRINGS FROM A TRUTH ABOUT US, OR A TRAIT, AND SO OTHERS OF OUR KIND ADDRESS US.
TAM TAM TUM TAM
IN DAYS OF OLD, PEOPLE COMMUNICATED THROUGH SONG.
ALL OF MY CHANTS ARE SONGS.
TONIGHT, I WILL HAVE FLOWERS BLOOM IN YOUR HONOR.

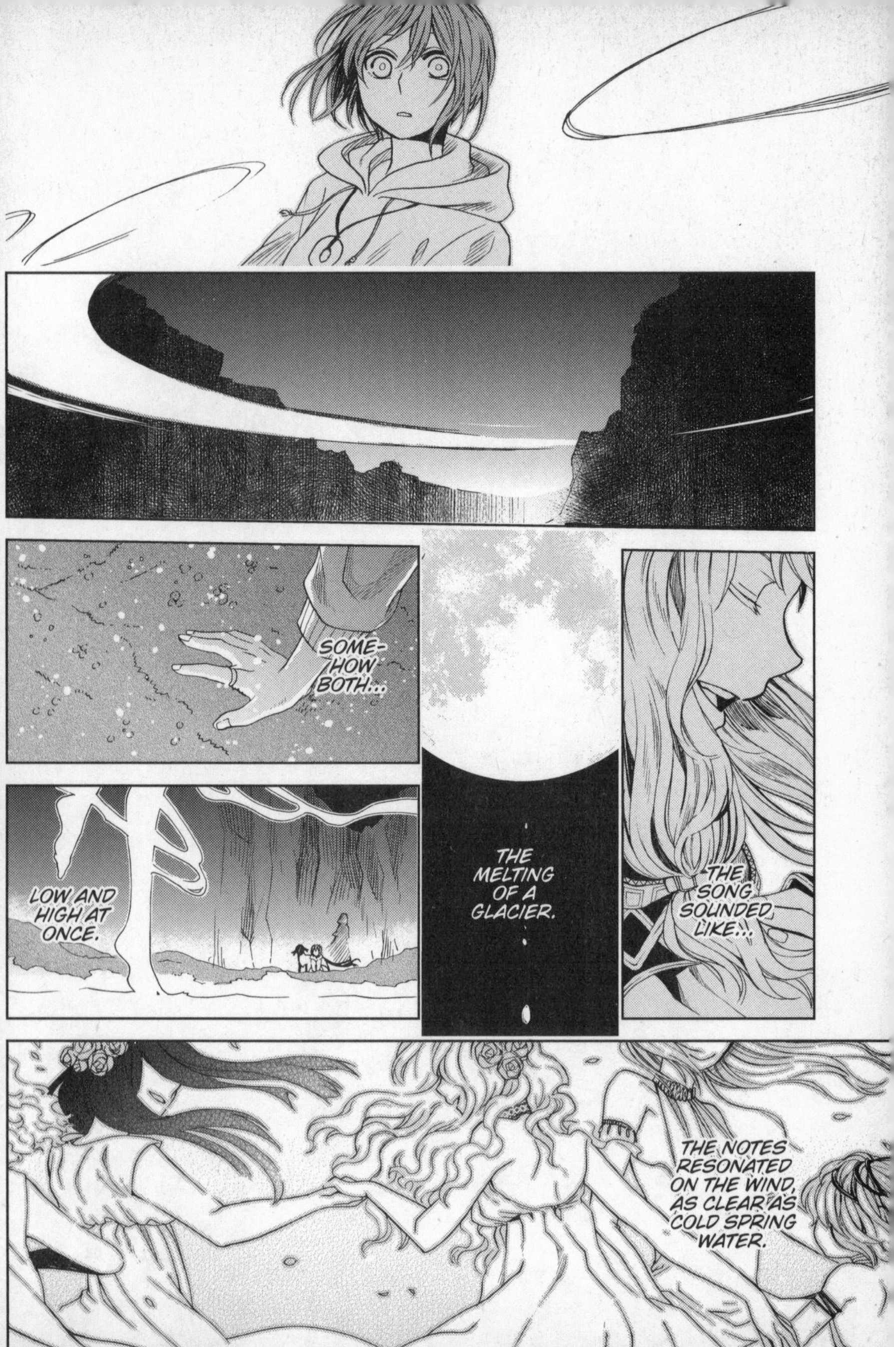
THE SONG SOUNDED LIKE...
THE MELTING OF A GLACIER.
SOME-HOW BOTH...
LOW AND HIGH AT ONCE.
THE NOTES RESONATED ON THE WIND, AS CLEAR AS COLD SPRING WATER.

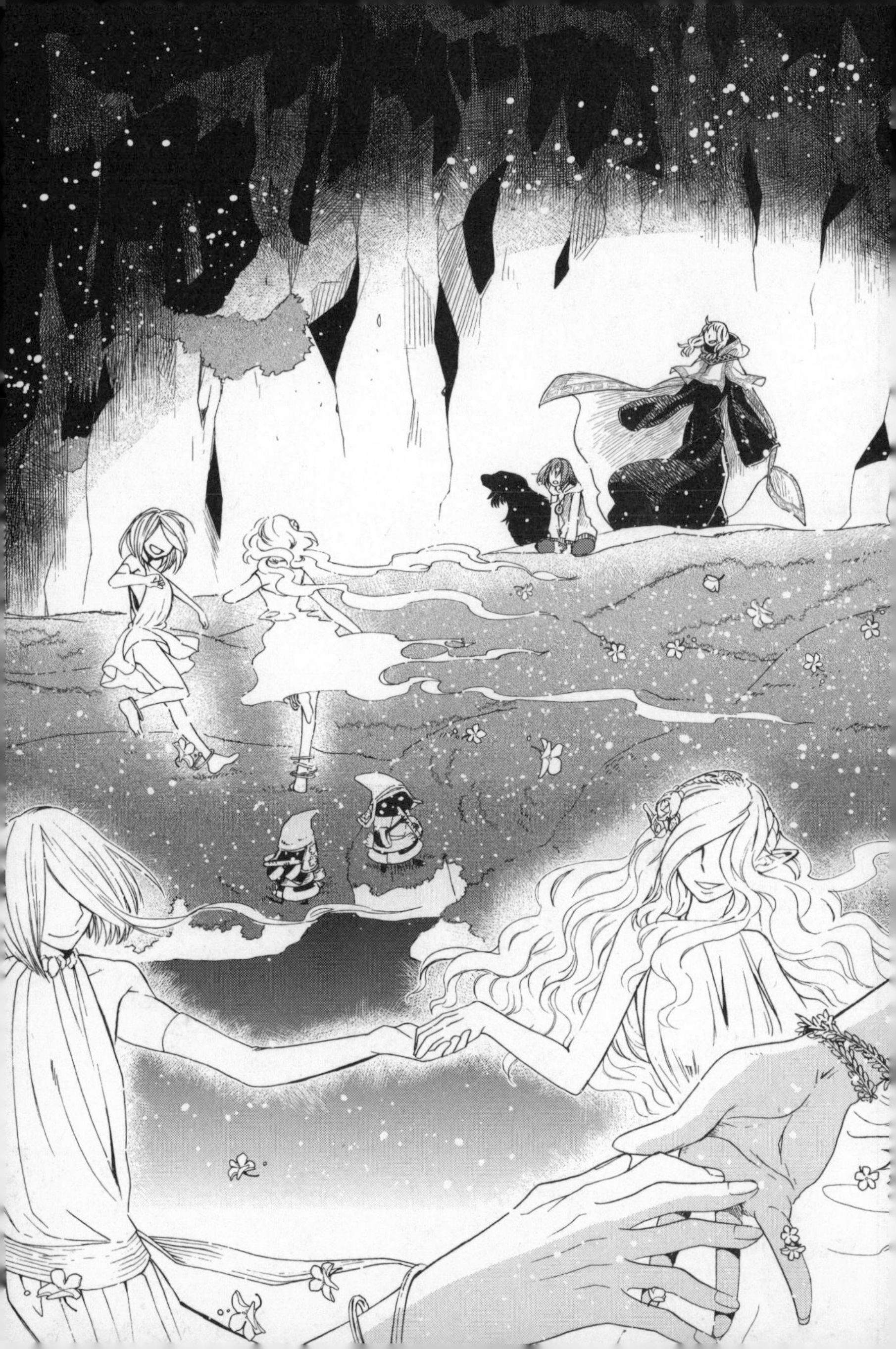

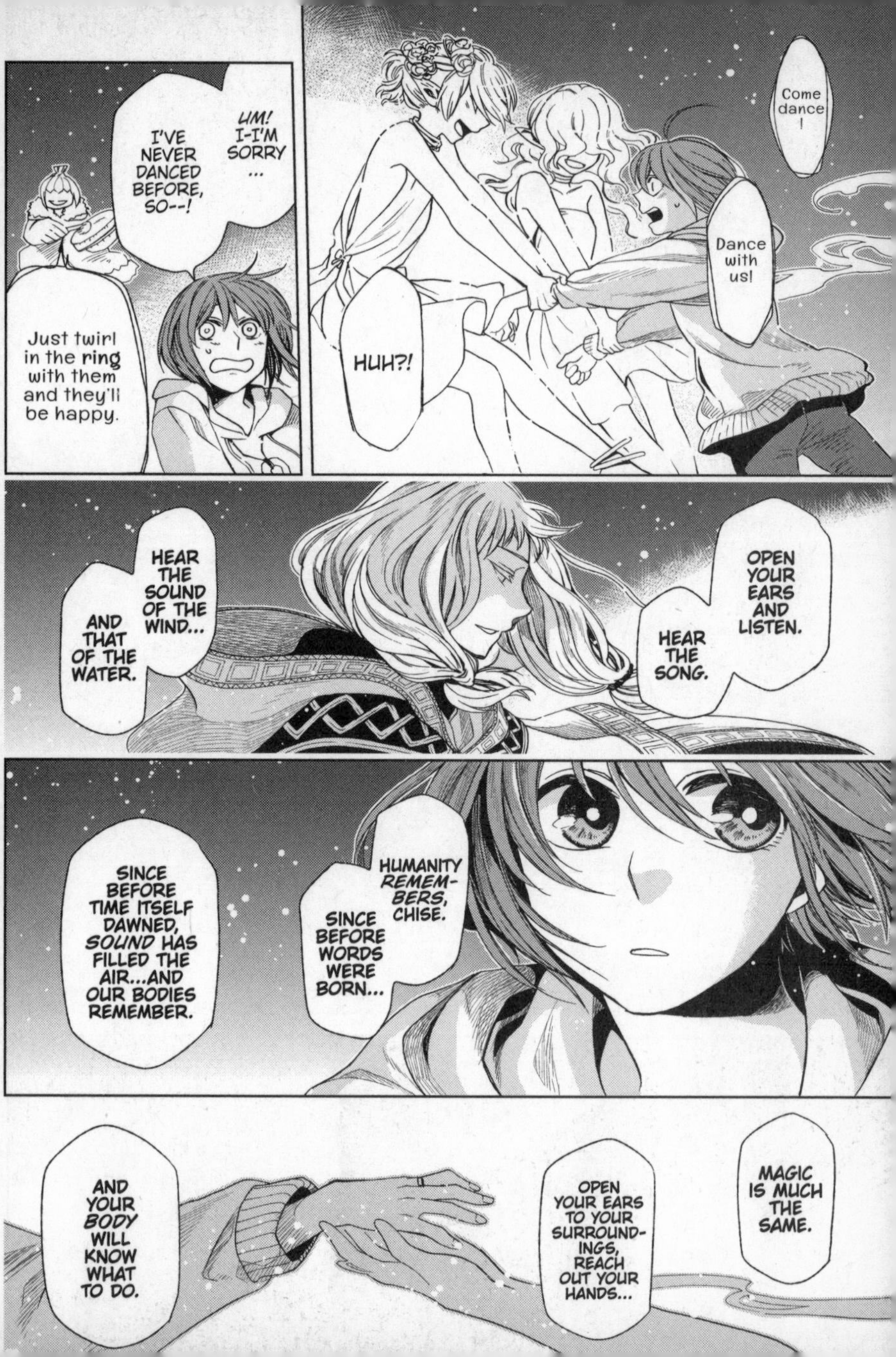
Come dance!
Dance with us!
HUH?!
UM! I-I'M SORRY...
I'VE NEVER DANCED BEFORE, SO--!
Just twirl in the ring with them and they'll be happy.
OPEN YOUR EARS AND LISTEN.
HEAR THE SONG.
HEAR THE SOUND OF THE WIND...
AND THAT OF THE WATER.
HUMANITY REMEMBERS, CHISE.
SINCE BEFORE WORDS WERE BORN...
SINCE BEFORE TIME ITSELF DAWNED, SOUND HAS FILLED THE AIR...AND OUR BODIES REMEMBER.
MAGIC IS MUCH THE SAME.
OPEN YOUR EARS TO YOUR SURROUNDINGS, REACH OUT YOUR HANDS...
AND YOUR BODY WILL KNOW WHAT TO DO.

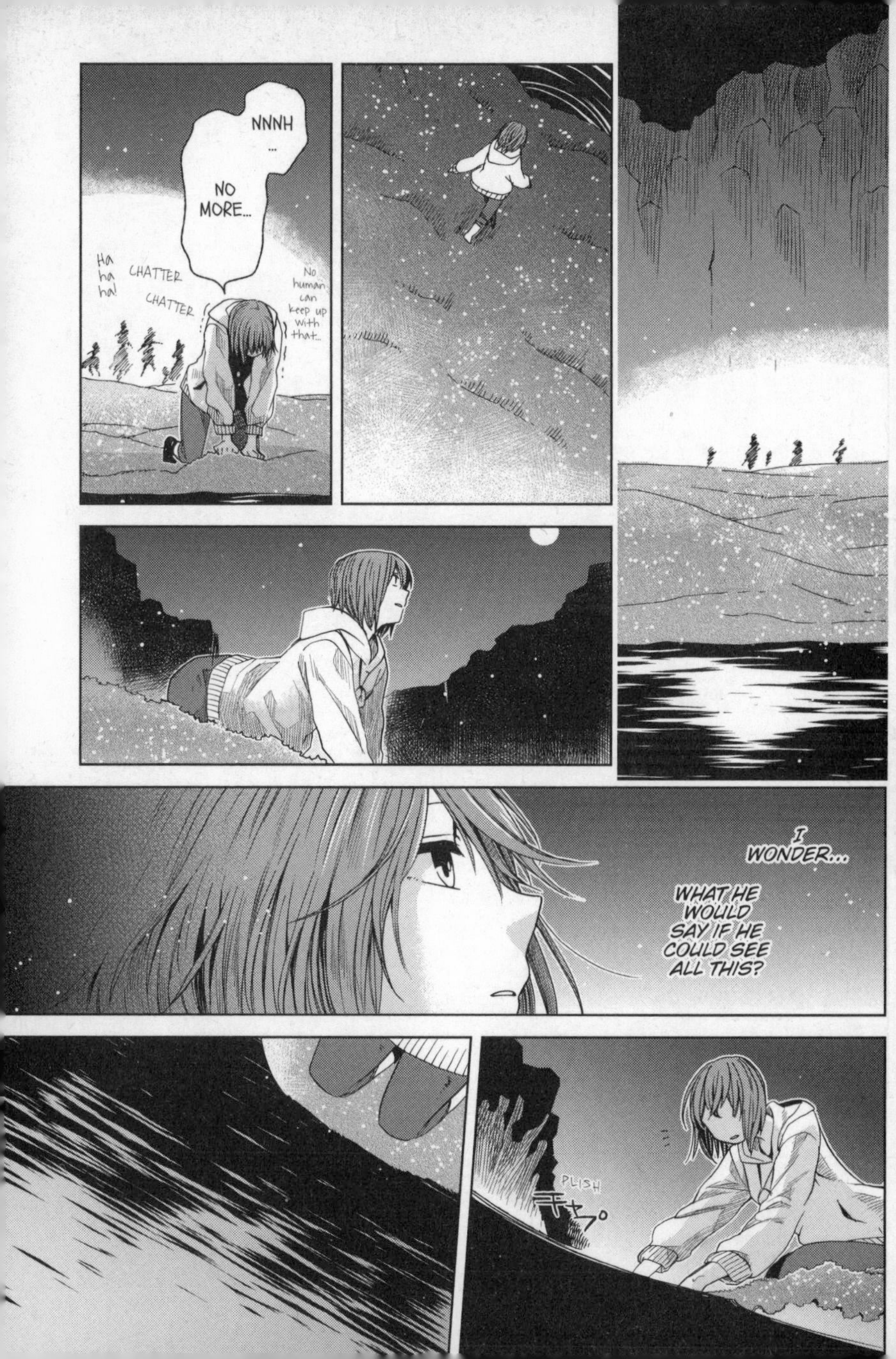
NNNH ... NO MORE...
No human can keep up with that...
Ha ha ha!
CHATTER
CHATTER
I WONDER...
WHAT HE WOULD SAY IF HE COULD SEE ALL THIS?
PLISH

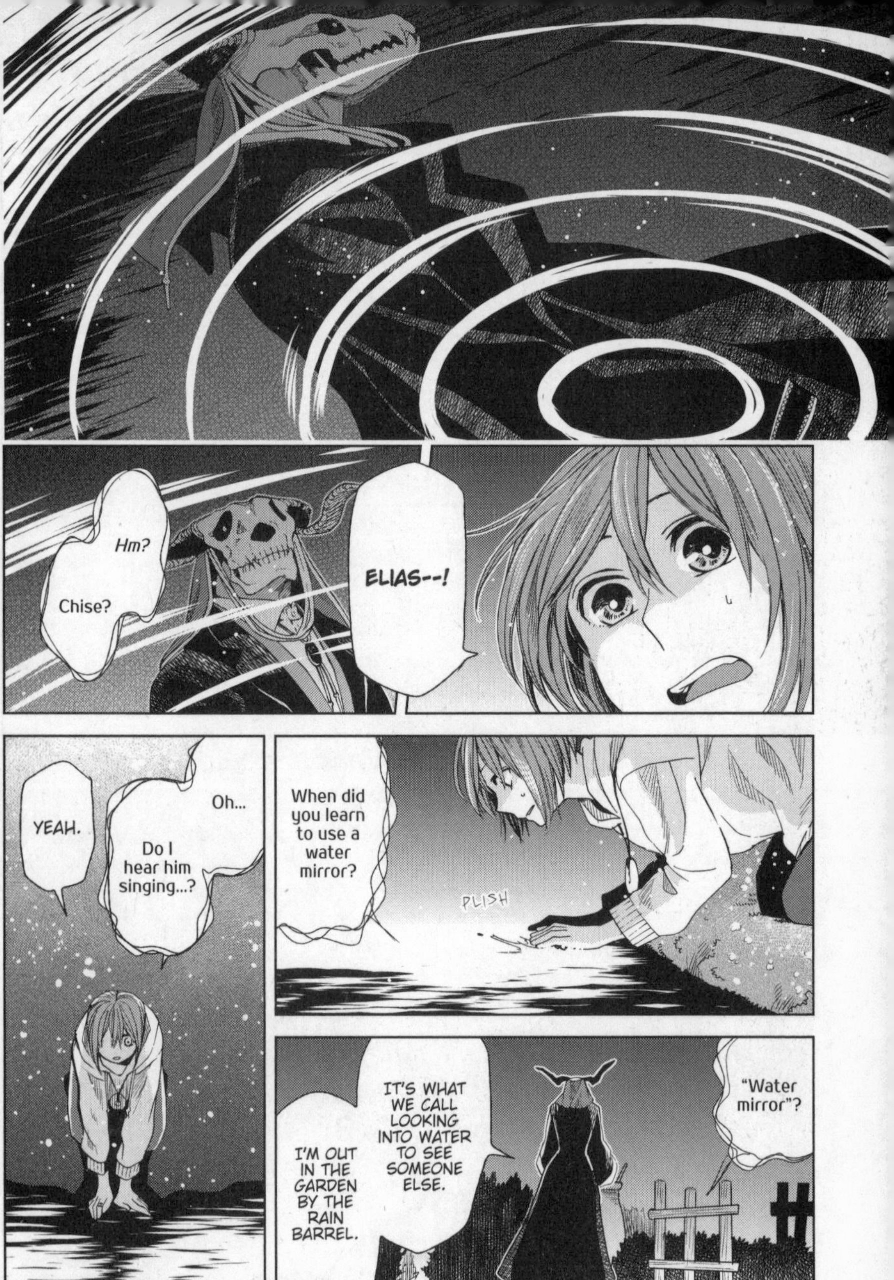
ELIAS--!
Hm?
Chise?
When did you learn to use a water mirror?
PLISH
"Water mirror"?
IT'S WHAT WE CALL LOOKING INTO WATER TO SEE SOMEONE ELSE.
I'M OUT IN THE GARDEN BY THE RAIN BARREL.
Oh...
Do I hear him singing...?
YEAH.

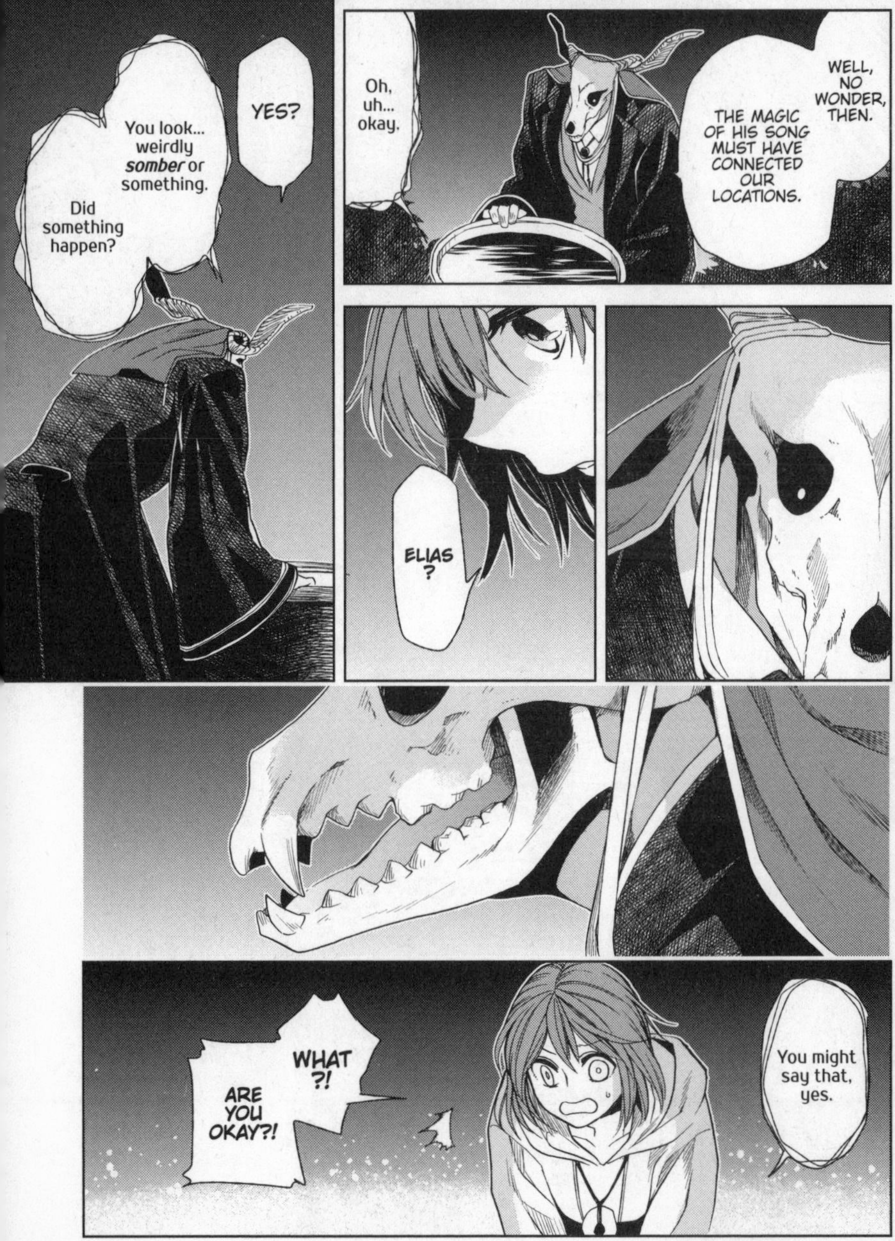
WELL, NO WONDER, THEN.
THE MAGIC OF HIS SONG MUST HAVE CONNECTED OUR LOCATIONS.
Oh, uh... okay.
ELIAS?
YES?
You look... weirdly *somber* or something.
Did something happen?
You might say that, yes.
WHAT?!
ARE YOU OKAY?!

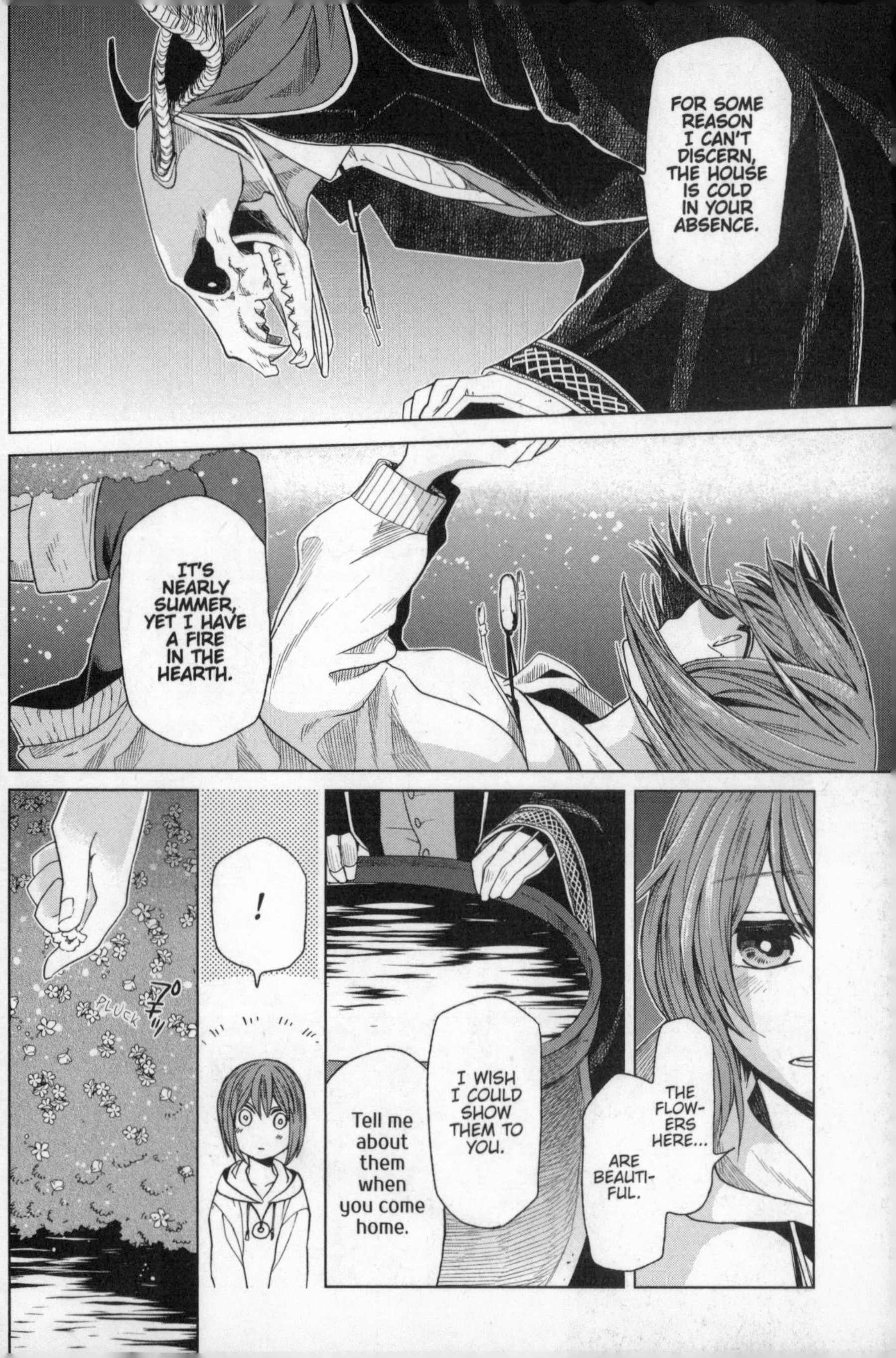
FOR SOME REASON I CAN'T DISCERN, THE HOUSE IS COLD IN YOUR ABSENCE.
IT'S NEARLY SUMMER, YET I HAVE A FIRE IN THE HEARTH.
THE FLOWERS HERE... ARE BEAUTIFUL.
I WISH I COULD SHOW THEM TO YOU.
!
Tell me about them when you come home.
PLUCK

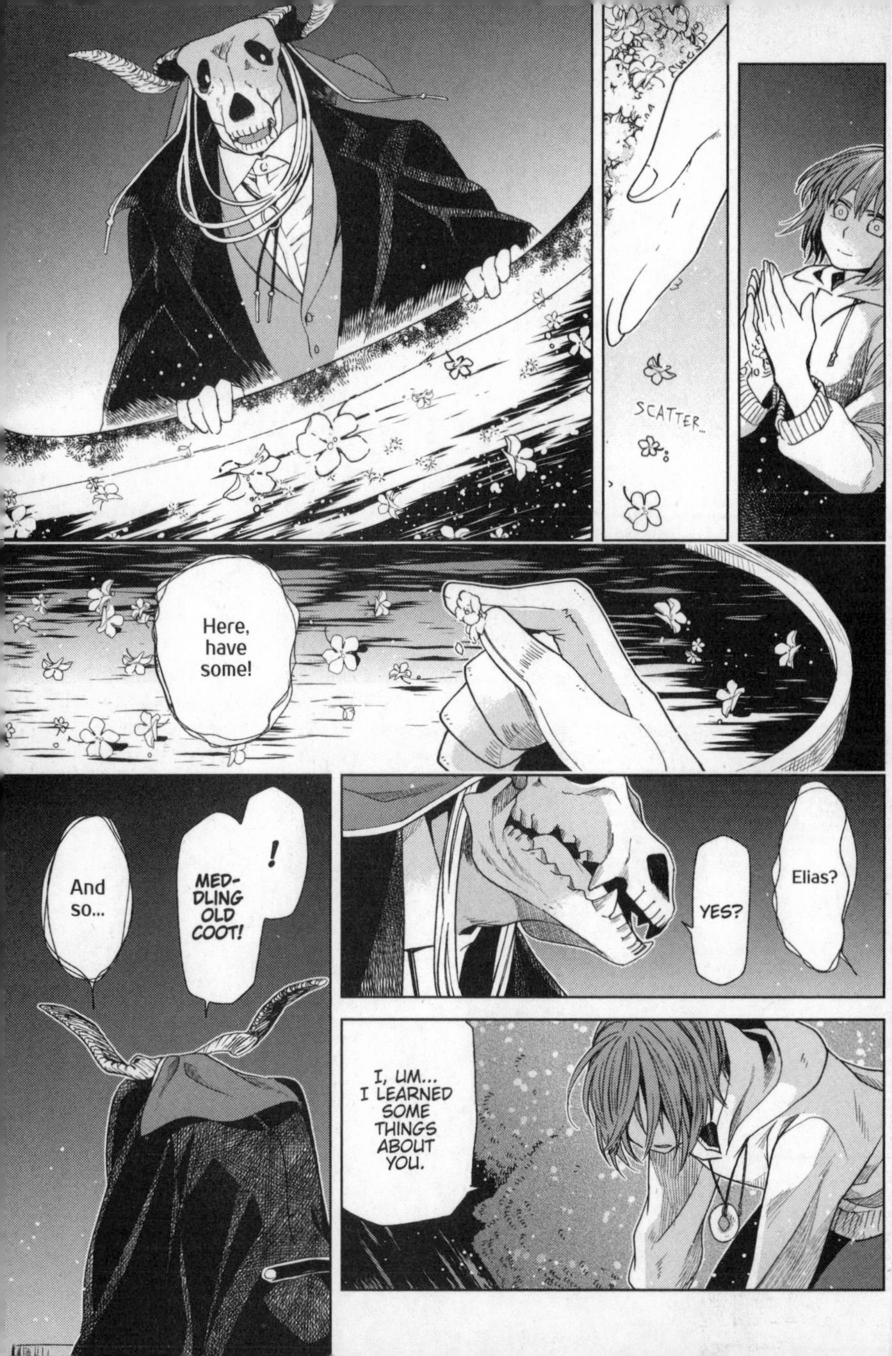
SCATTER...
Here, have some!
Elias?
YES?
I, UM... I LEARNED SOME THINGS ABOUT YOU.
!
MED-DLING OLD COOT!
And so...

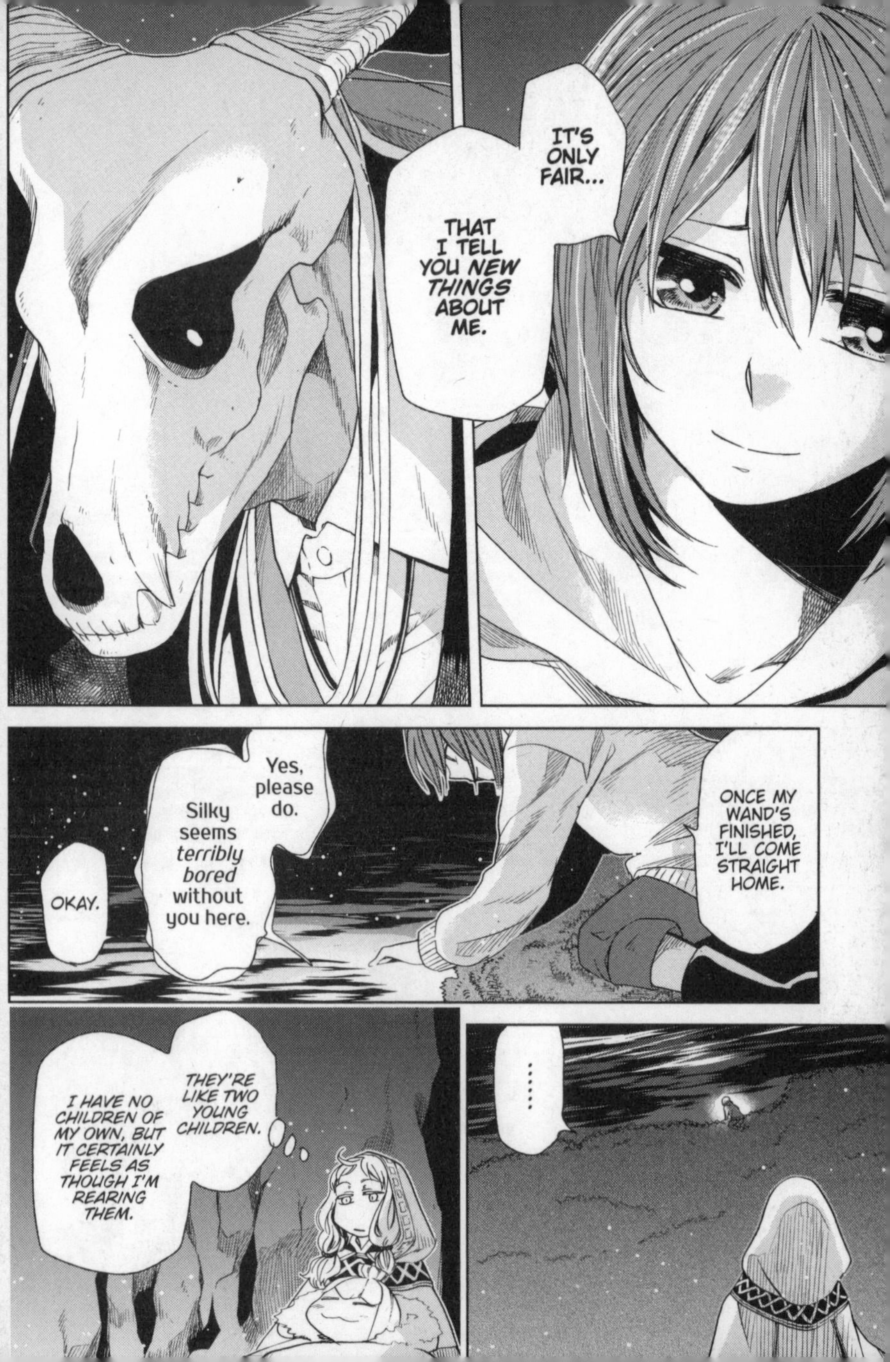

IT'S ONLY FAIR...
THAT I TELL YOU *NEW THINGS* ABOUT ME.
ONCE MY WAND'S FINISHED, I'LL COME STRAIGHT HOME.
Yes, please do.
Silky seems *terribly bored* without you here.
OKAY.
......
THEY'RE LIKE TWO YOUNG CHILDREN.
I HAVE NO CHILDREN OF MY OWN, BUT IT CERTAINLY FEELS AS THOUGH I'M REARING THEM.

Chapter 18: Better to ask the way than go astray.

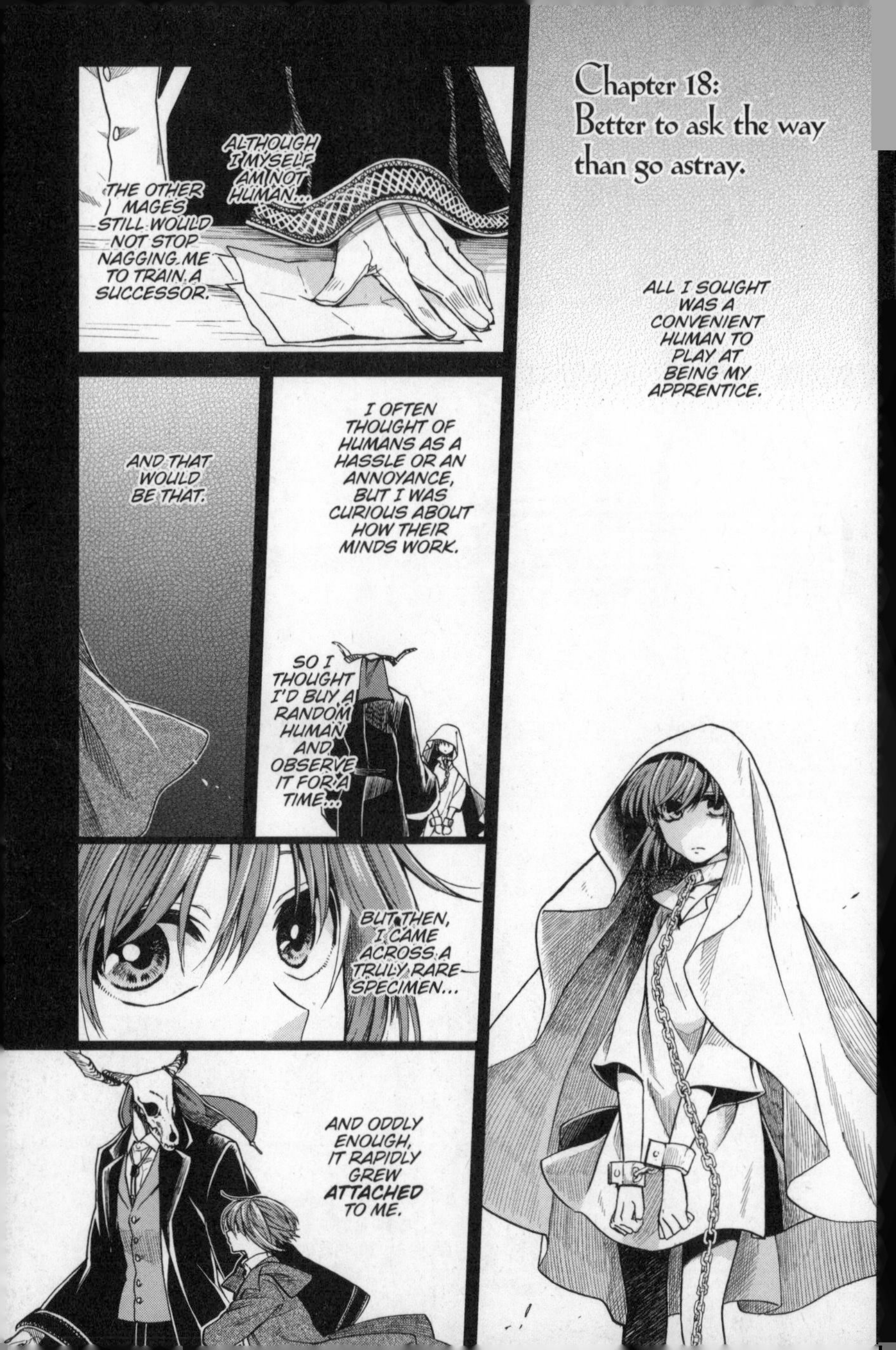
ALL I SOUGHT WAS A CONVENIENT HUMAN TO PLAY AT BEING MY APPRENTICE.
ALTHOUGH I MYSELF AM NOT HUMAN...
THE OTHER MAGES STILL WOULD NOT STOP NAGGING ME TO TRAIN A SUCCESSOR.
I OFTEN THOUGHT OF HUMANS AS A HASSLE OR AN ANNOYANCE, BUT I WAS CURIOUS ABOUT HOW THEIR MINDS WORK.
SO I THOUGHT I'D BUY A RANDOM HUMAN AND OBSERVE IT FOR A TIME...
AND THAT WOULD BE THAT.
BUT THEN, I CAME ACROSS A TRULY RARE SPECIMEN...
AND ODDLY ENOUGH, IT RAPIDLY GREW ATTACHED TO ME.

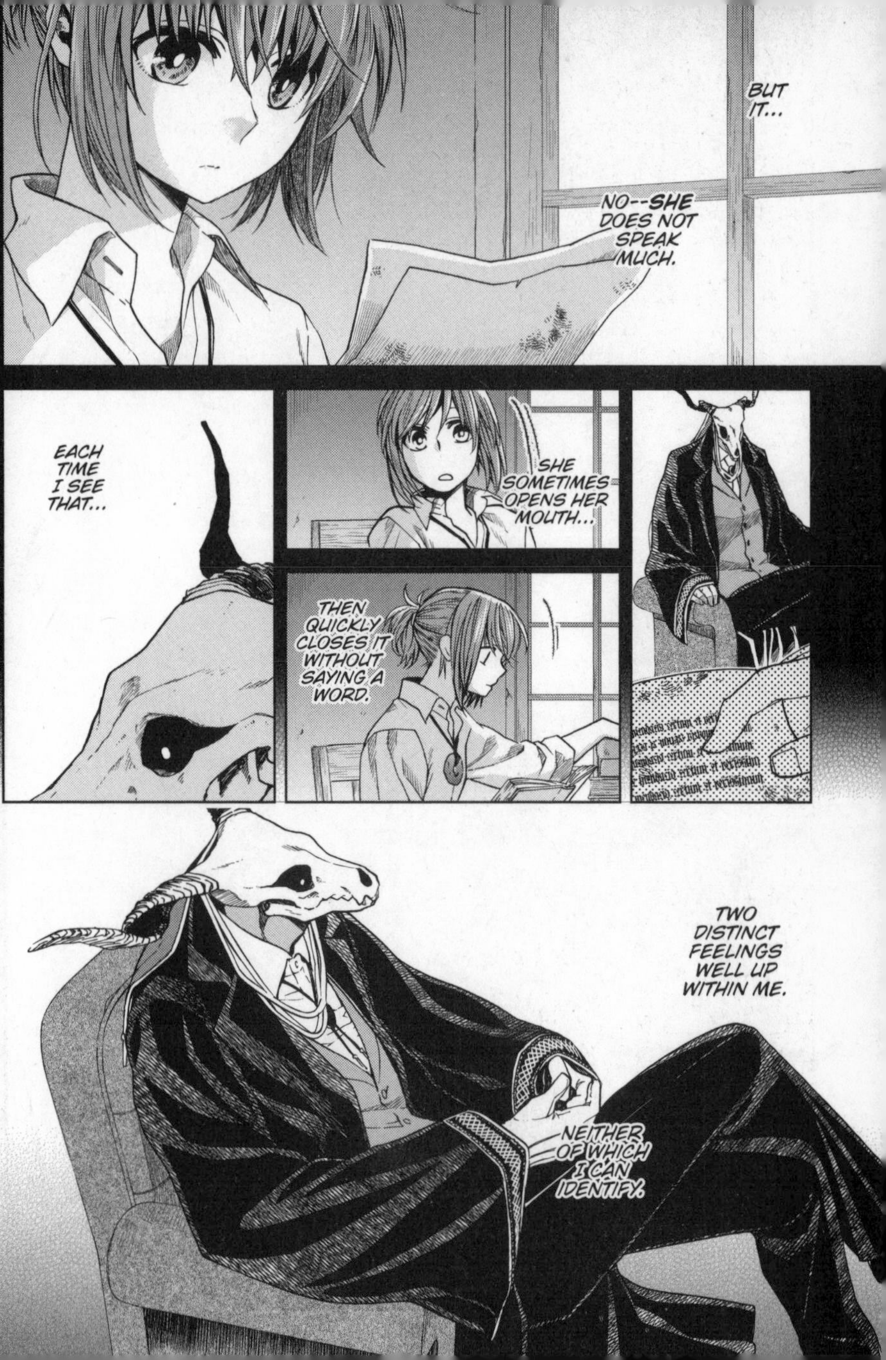
BUT IT...
NO--**SHE** DOES NOT SPEAK MUCH.
SHE SOMETIMES OPENS HER MOUTH...
THEN QUICKLY CLOSES IT WITHOUT SAYING A WORD.
EACH TIME I SEE THAT...
TWO DISTINCT FEELINGS WELL UP WITHIN ME.
NEITHER OF WHICH I CAN IDENTIFY.

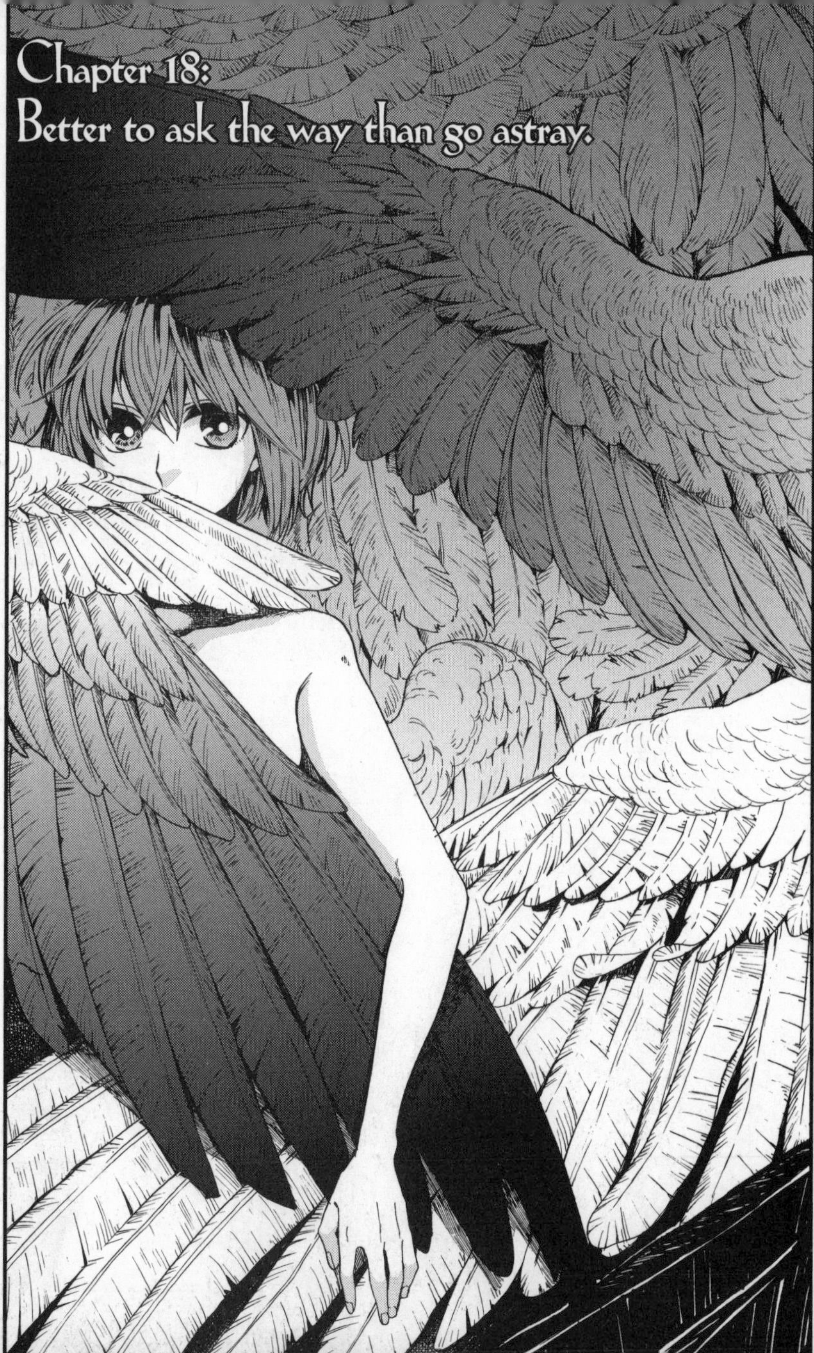
Chapter 18:
Better to ask the way than go astray.

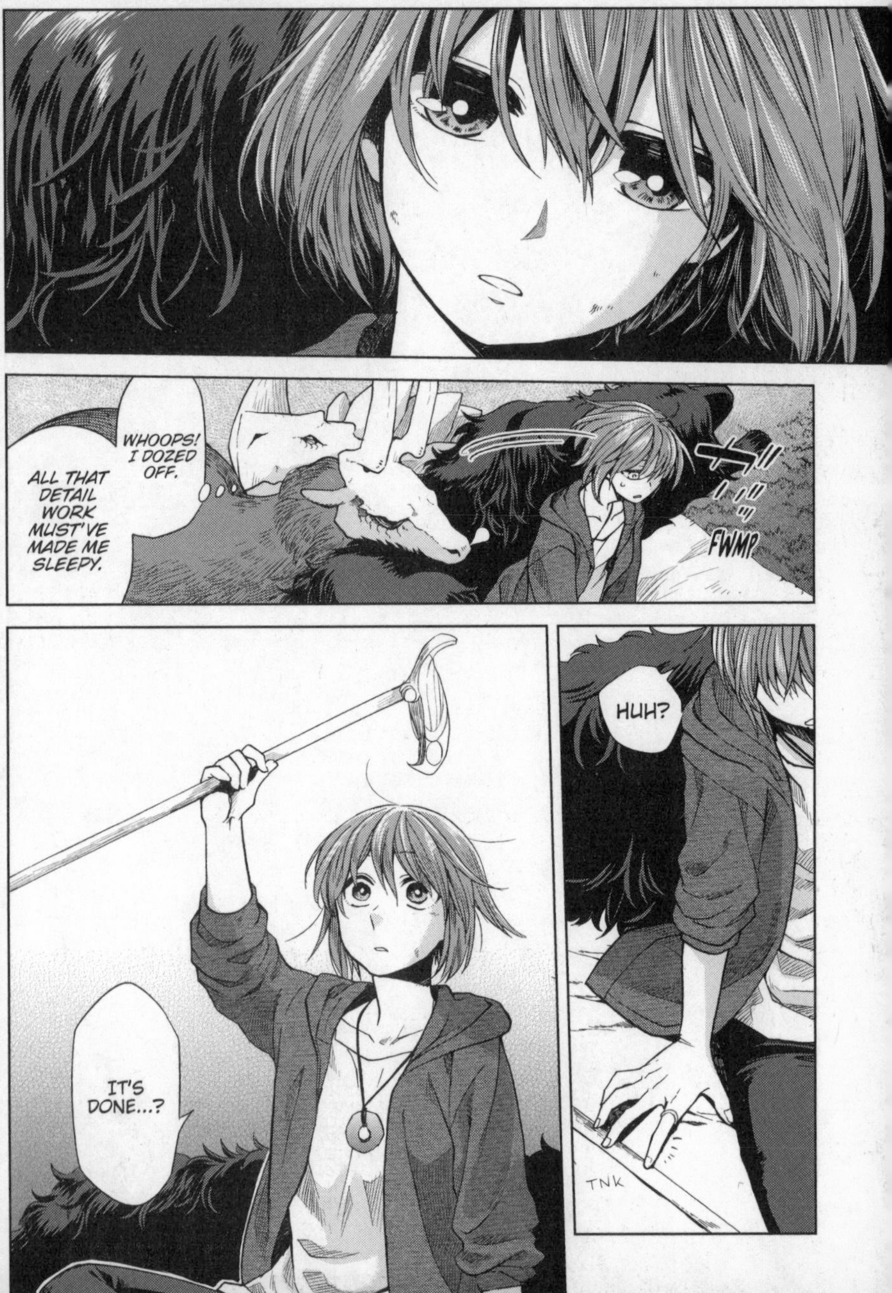
WHOOPS! I DOZED OFF.
ALL THAT DETAIL WORK MUST'VE MADE ME SLEEPY.
FWMP
HUH?
TNK
IT'S DONE...?

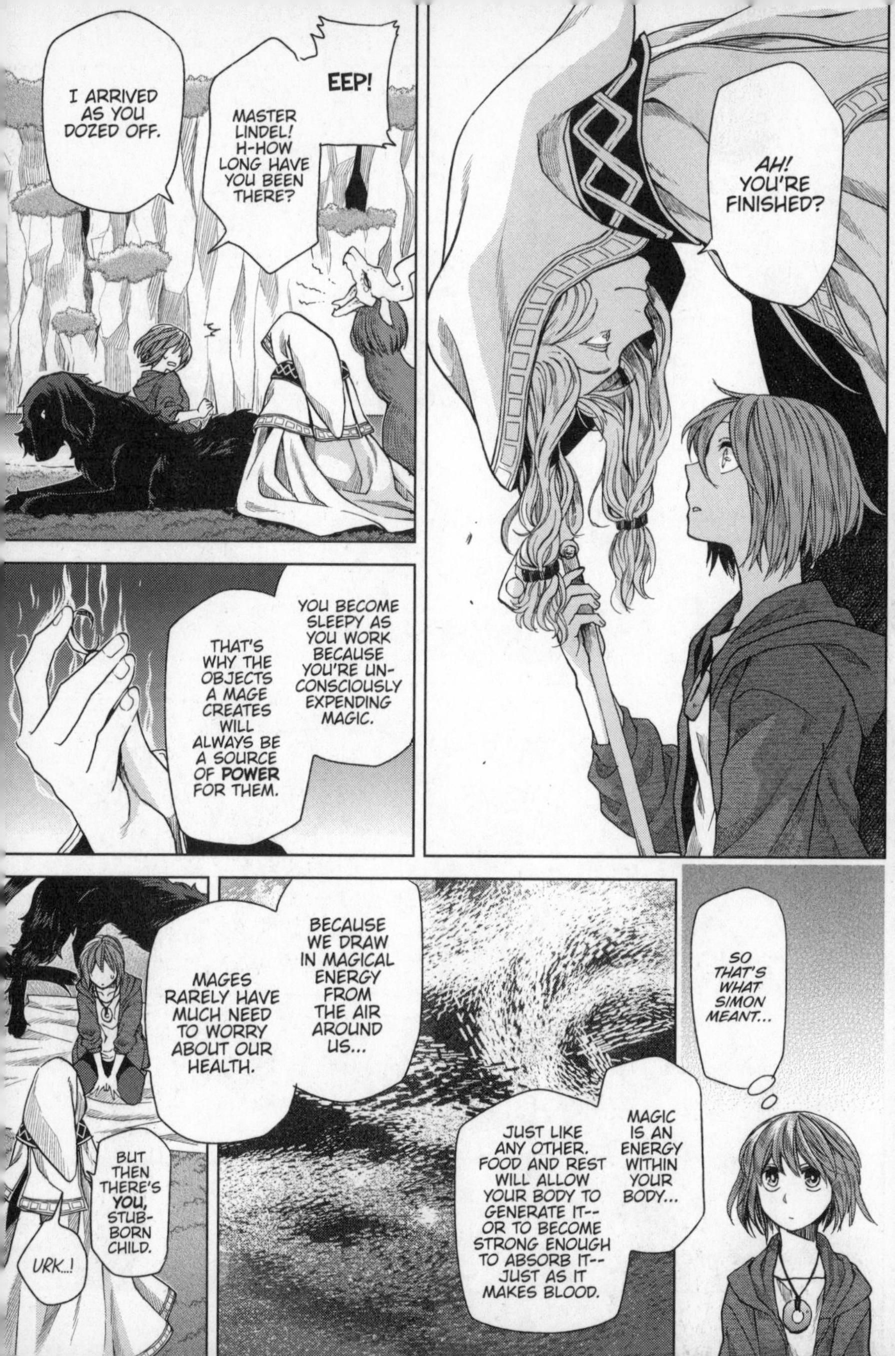
AH! YOU'RE FINISHED?
EEP!
MASTER LINDEL! H-HOW LONG HAVE YOU BEEN THERE?
I ARRIVED AS YOU DOZED OFF.
YOU BECOME SLEEPY AS YOU WORK BECAUSE YOU'RE UN-CONSCIOUSLY EXPENDING MAGIC.
THAT'S WHY THE OBJECTS A MAGE CREATES WILL ALWAYS BE A SOURCE OF **POWER** FOR THEM.
SO THAT'S WHAT SIMON MEANT...
MAGIC IS AN ENERGY WITHIN YOUR BODY...
JUST LIKE ANY OTHER. FOOD AND REST WILL ALLOW YOUR BODY TO GENERATE IT-- OR TO BECOME STRONG ENOUGH TO ABSORB IT-- JUST AS IT MAKES BLOOD.
BECAUSE WE DRAW IN MAGICAL ENERGY FROM THE AIR AROUND US...
MAGES RARELY HAVE MUCH NEED TO WORRY ABOUT OUR HEALTH.
BUT THEN THERE'S **YOU,** STUB-BORN CHILD.
URK..!

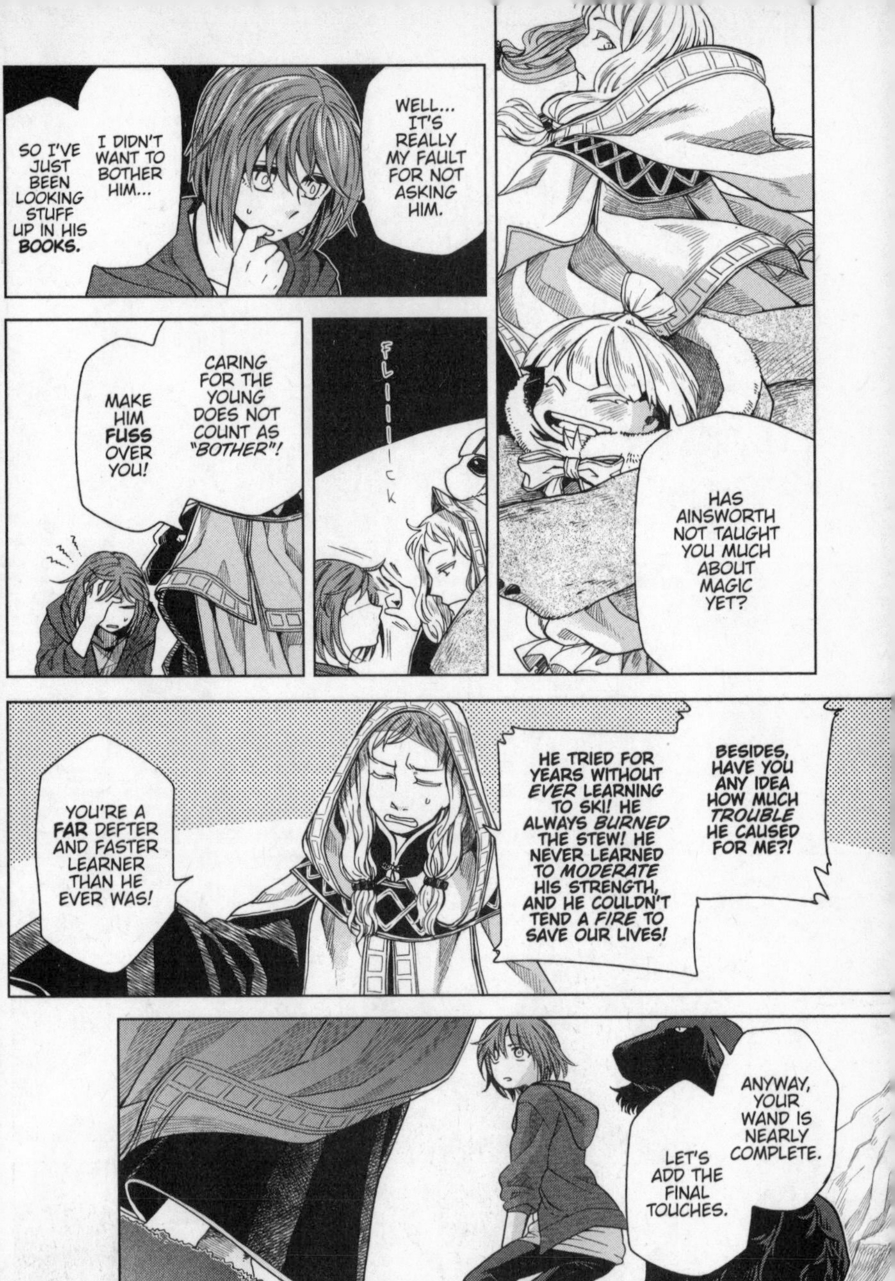

HAS AINSWORTH NOT TAUGHT YOU MUCH ABOUT MAGIC YET?
WELL... IT'S REALLY MY FAULT FOR NOT ASKING HIM.
I DIDN'T WANT TO BOTHER HIM...
SO I'VE JUST BEEN LOOKING STUFF UP IN HIS BOOKS.
FLIIIICK
CARING FOR THE YOUNG DOES NOT COUNT AS "BOTHER"!
MAKE HIM FUSS OVER YOU!
BESIDES, HAVE YOU ANY IDEA HOW MUCH TROUBLE HE CAUSED FOR ME?!
HE TRIED FOR YEARS WITHOUT EVER LEARNING TO SKI! HE ALWAYS BURNED THE STEW! HE NEVER LEARNED TO MODERATE HIS STRENGTH, AND HE COULDN'T TEND A FIRE TO SAVE OUR LIVES!
YOU'RE A FAR DEFTER AND FASTER LEARNER THAN HE EVER WAS!
ANYWAY, YOUR WAND IS NEARLY COMPLETE.
LET'S ADD THE FINAL TOUCHES.

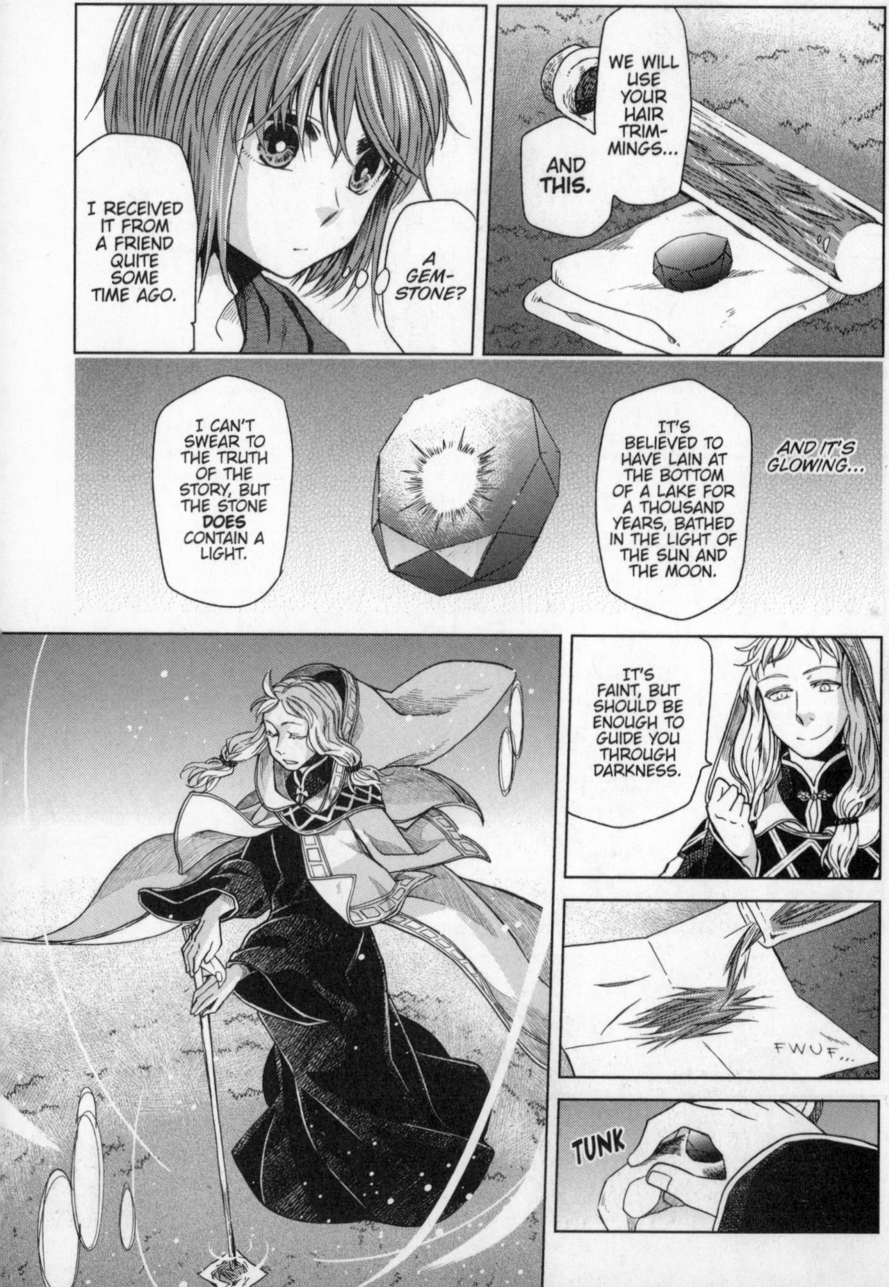
WE WILL USE YOUR HAIR TRIMMINGS...
AND THIS.
A GEMSTONE?
I RECEIVED IT FROM A FRIEND QUITE SOME TIME AGO.
AND IT'S GLOWING...
IT'S BELIEVED TO HAVE LAIN AT THE BOTTOM OF A LAKE FOR A THOUSAND YEARS, BATHED IN THE LIGHT OF THE SUN AND THE MOON.
I CAN'T SWEAR TO THE TRUTH OF THE STORY, BUT THE STONE DOES CONTAIN A LIGHT.
IT'S FAINT, BUT SHOULD BE ENOUGH TO GUIDE YOU THROUGH DARKNESS.
FWUF...
TUNK

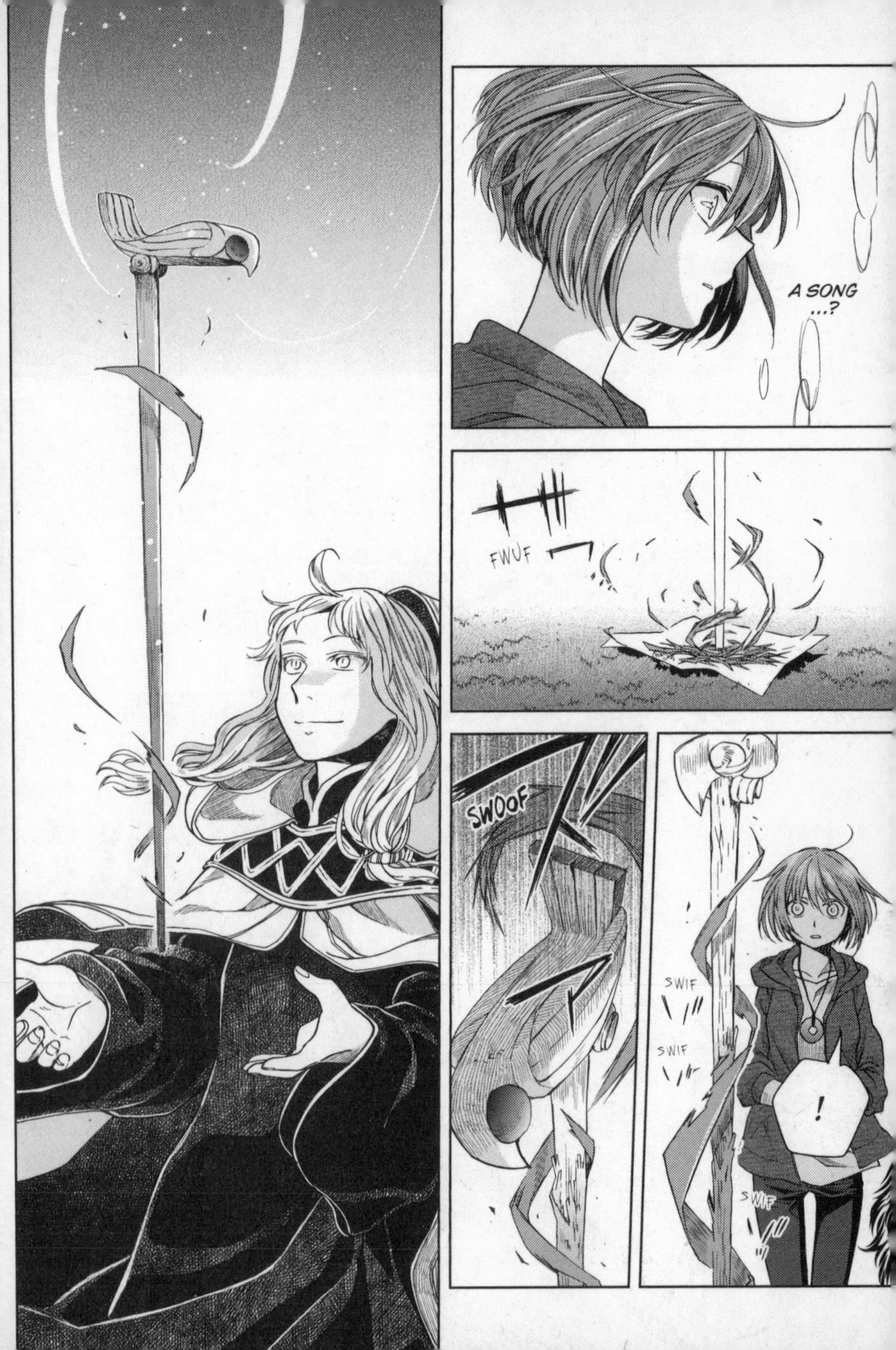
A SONG ...?
FWUF
SWIF
SWIF
!
SWIF
SWOOF

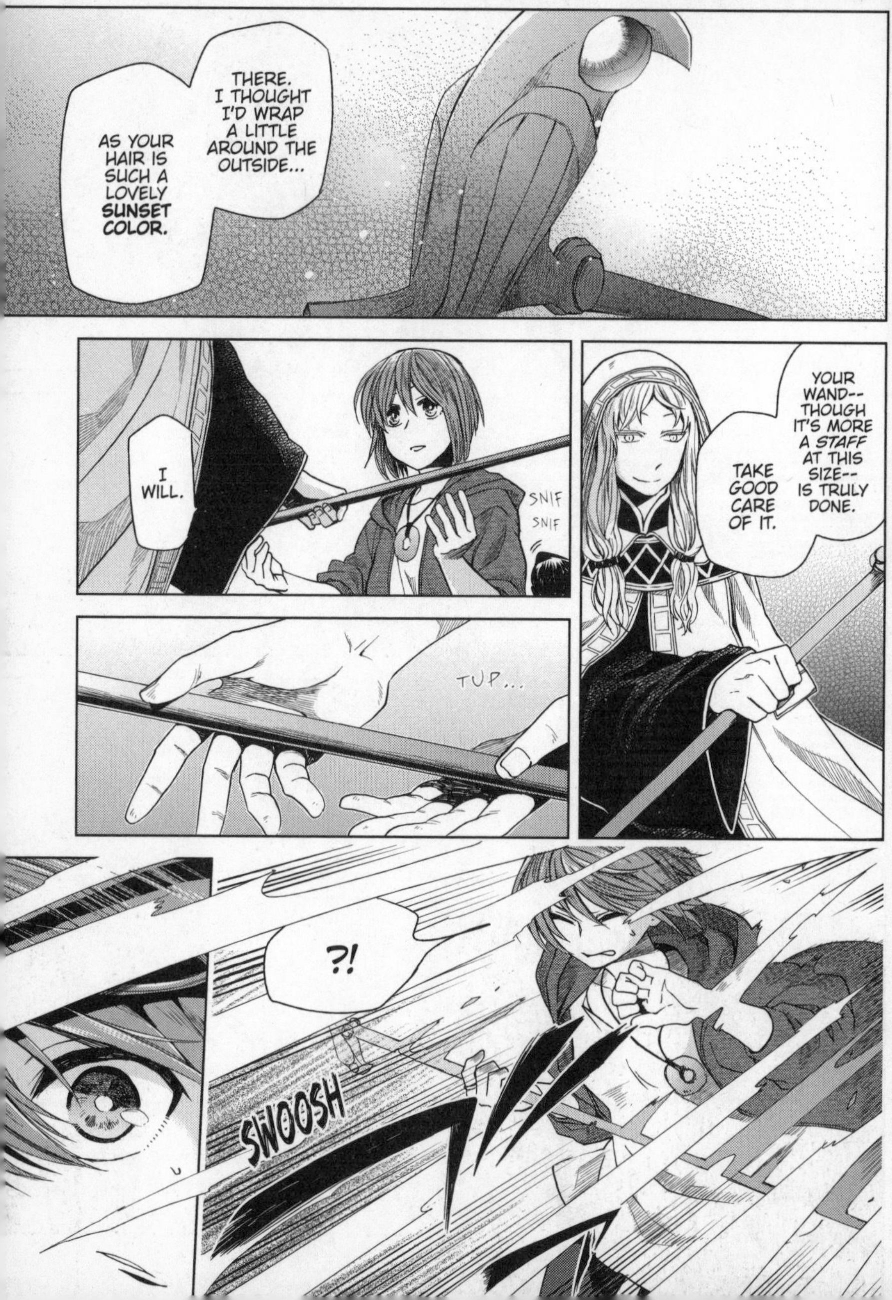
THERE. I THOUGHT I'D WRAP A LITTLE AROUND THE OUTSIDE...
AS YOUR HAIR IS SUCH A LOVELY **SUNSET** COLOR.
YOUR WAND-- THOUGH IT'S MORE A *STAFF* AT THIS SIZE-- IS TRULY DONE.
TAKE GOOD CARE OF IT.
SNIF SNIF
I WILL.
TUP...
?!
SWOOSH

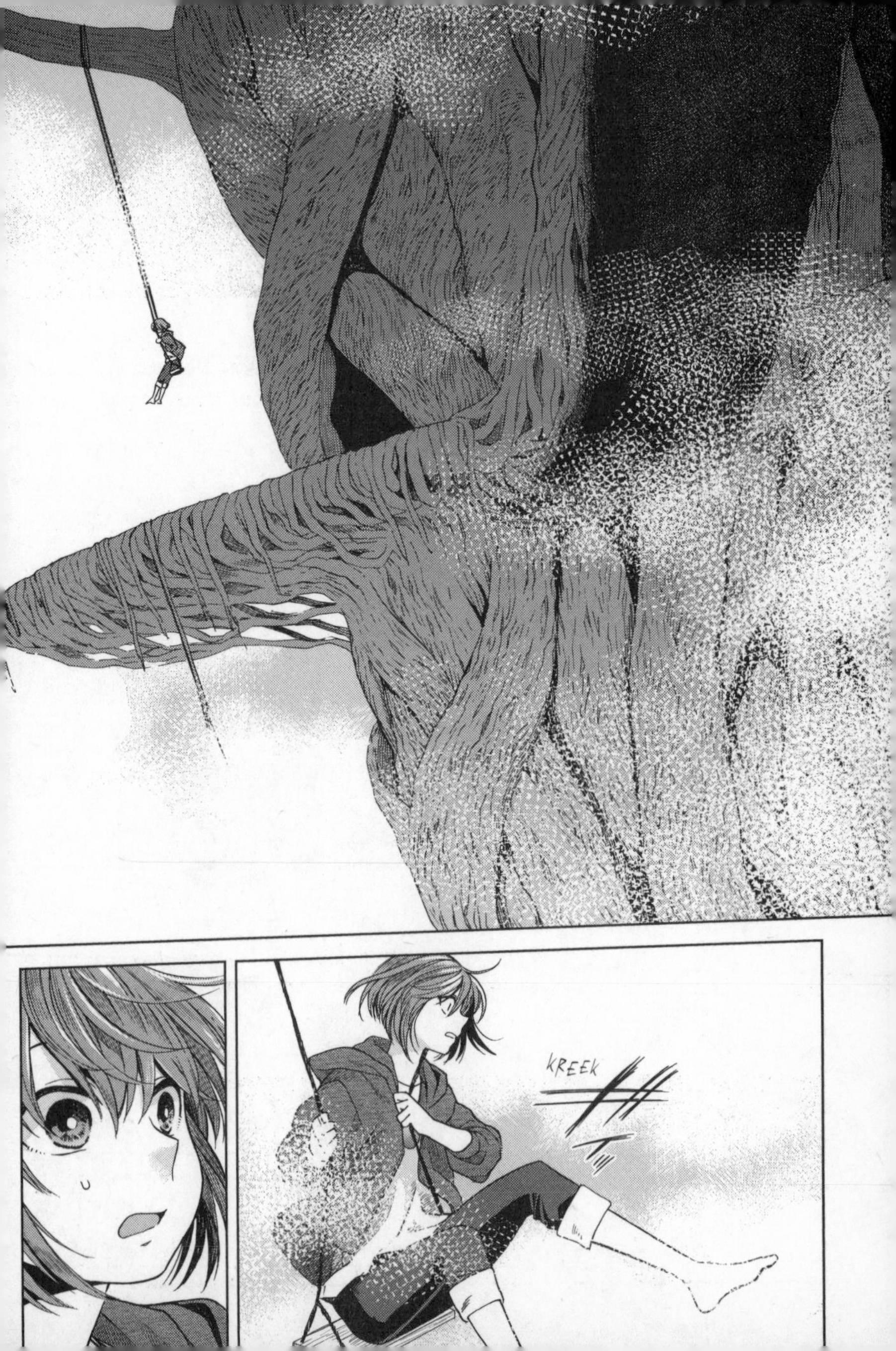
KREEK

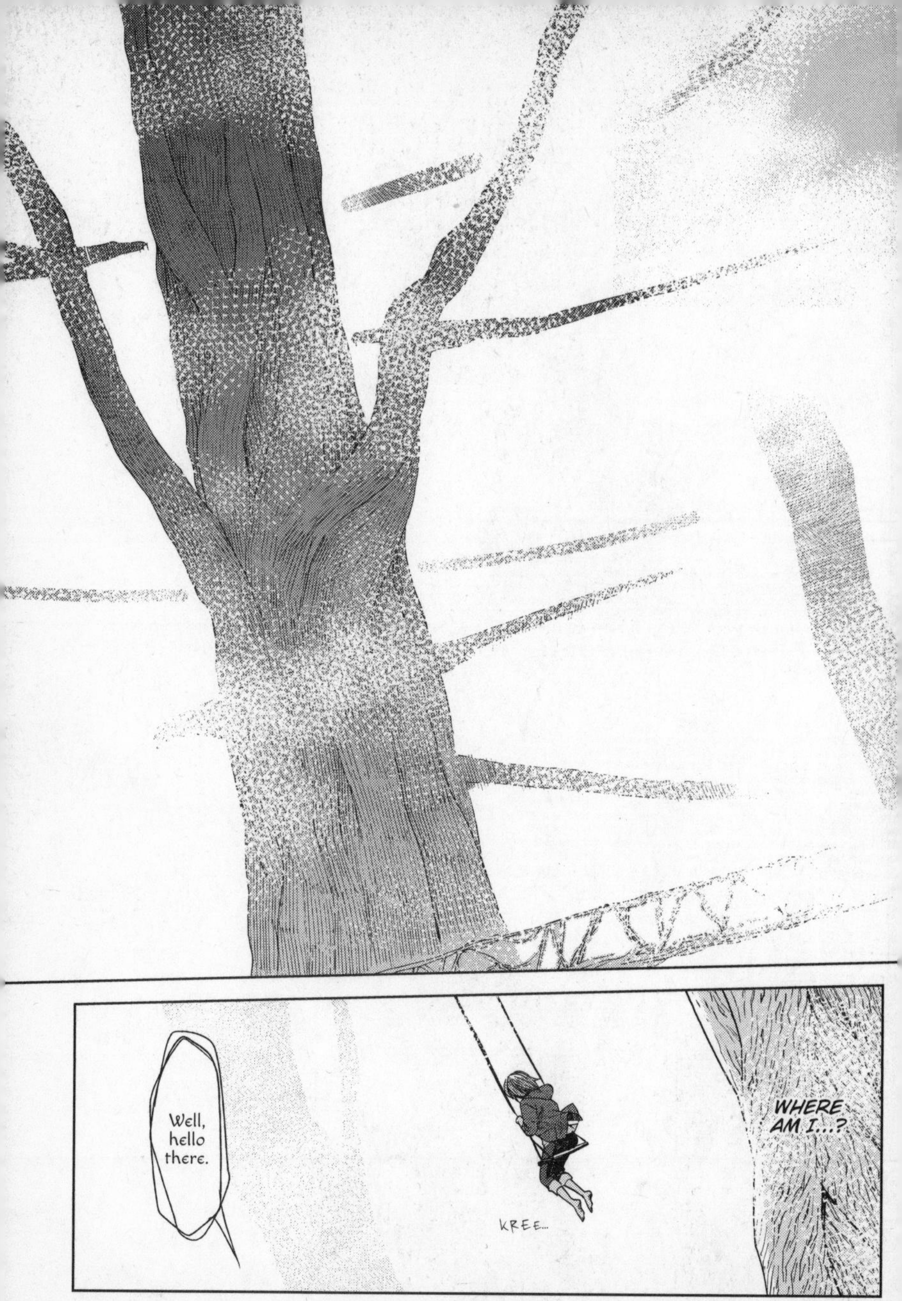
WHERE AM I...?
KREE...
Well, hello there.

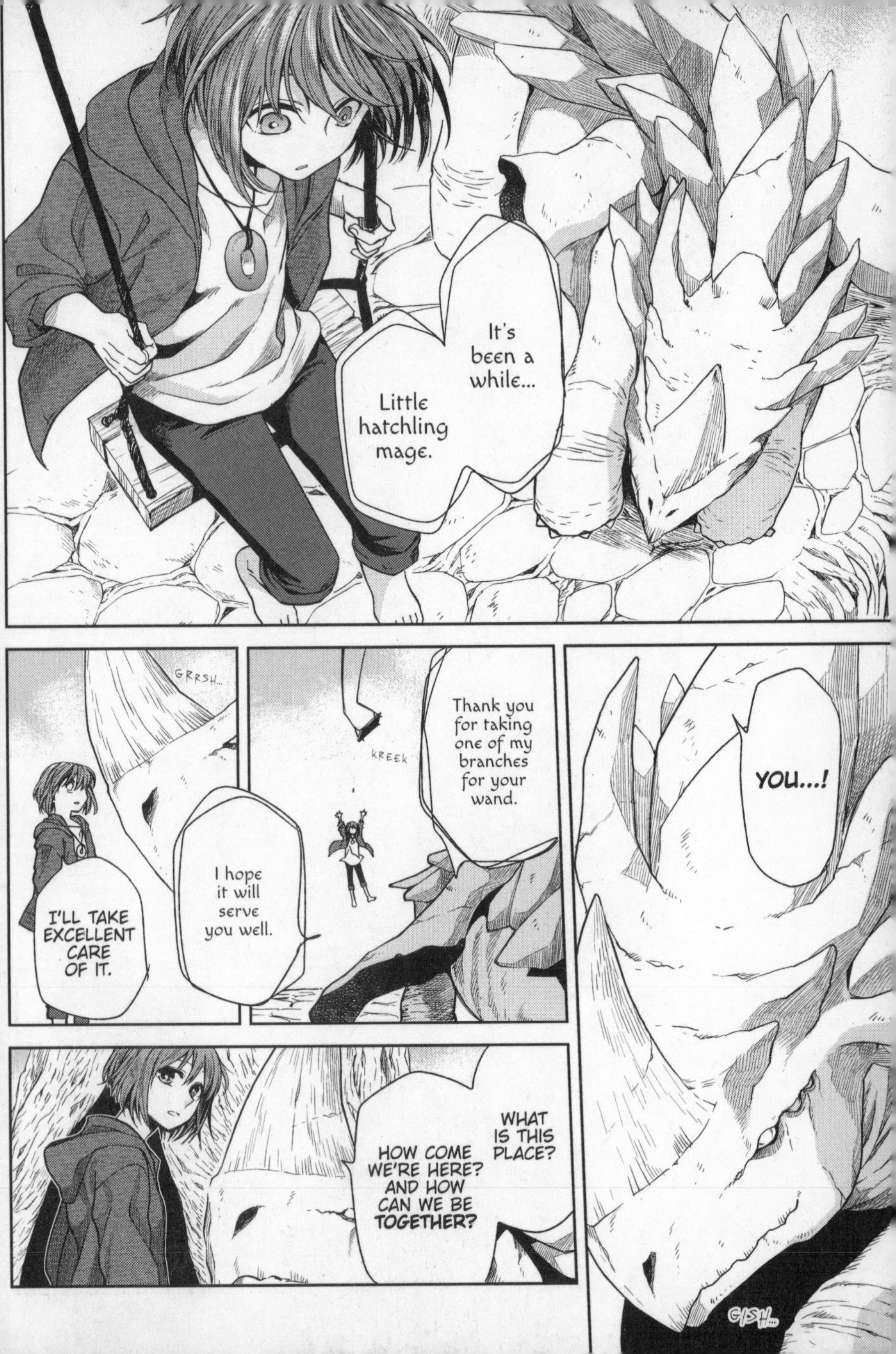
It's been a while...
Little hatchling mage.
YOU...!
Thank you for taking one of my branches for your wand.
KREEK
I hope it will serve you well.
GRRSH...
I'LL TAKE EXCELLENT CARE OF IT.
WHAT IS THIS PLACE?
HOW COME WE'RE HERE? AND HOW CAN WE BE TOGETHER?

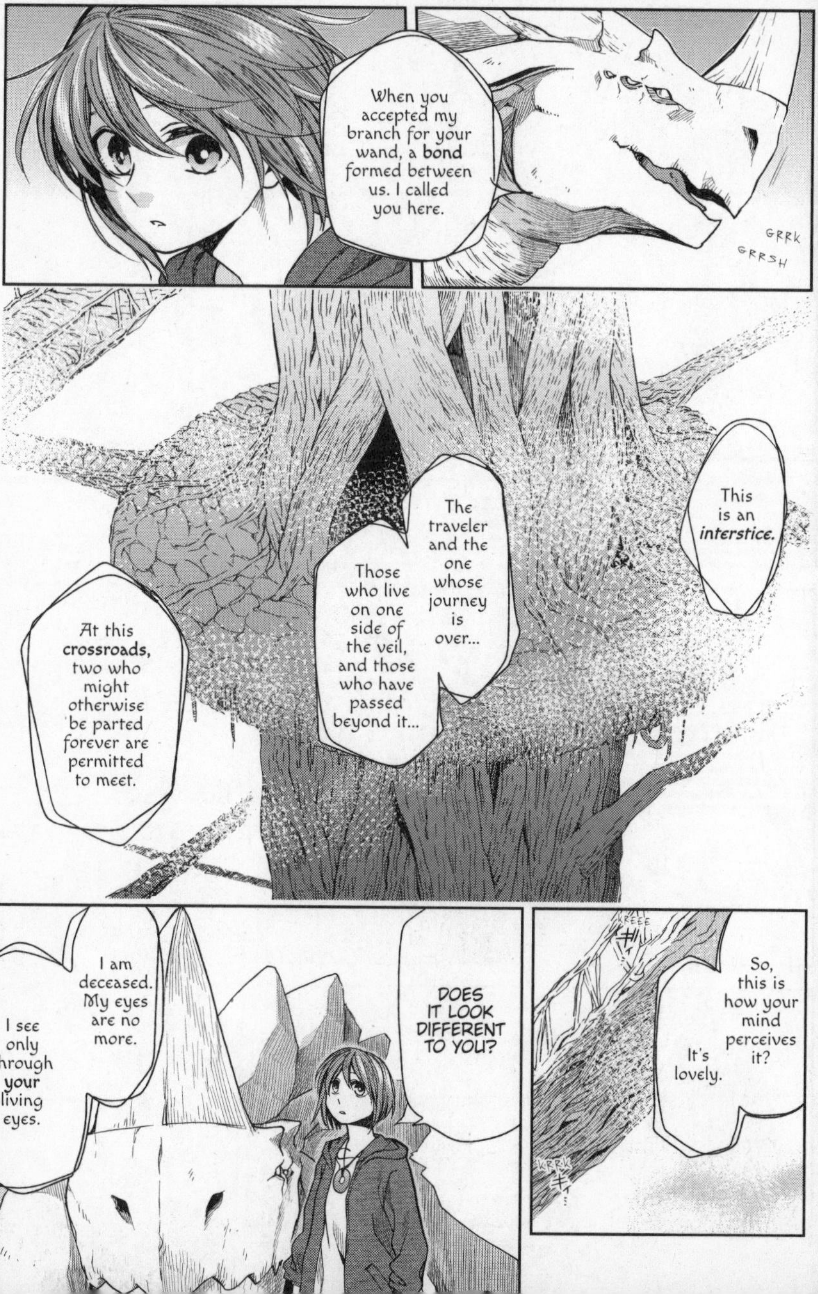
When you accepted my branch for your wand, a **bond** formed between us. I called you here.
GRRK
GRRSH
This is an ***interstice.***
The traveler and the one whose journey is over...
Those who live on one side of the veil, and those who have passed beyond it...
At this **crossroads,** two who might otherwise be parted forever are permitted to meet.
KREEE
So, this is how your mind perceives it?
It's lovely.
KRRK
DOES IT LOOK DIFFERENT TO YOU?
I am deceased. My eyes are no more.
I see only through **your** living eyes.

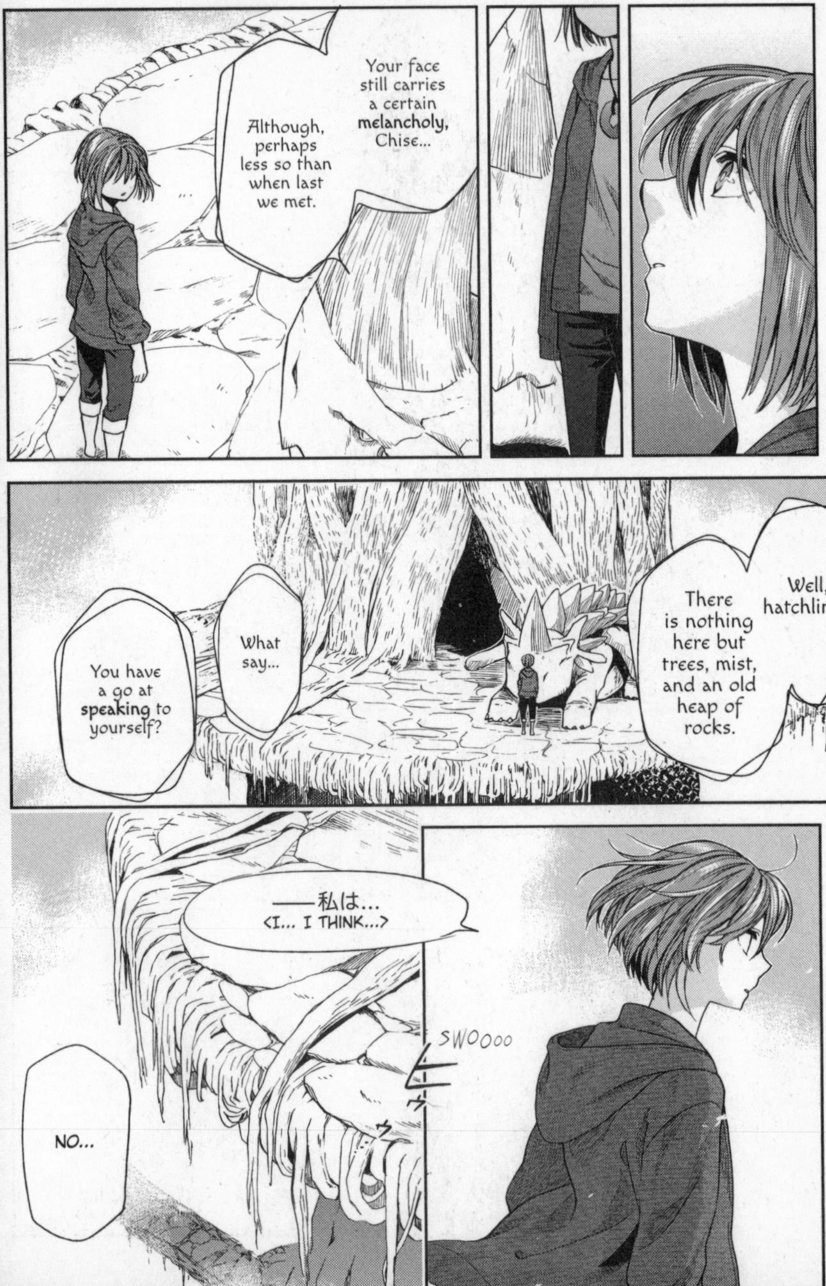
Your face still carries a certain melancholy, Chise...
Although, perhaps less so than when last we met.
...
Well, hatchling?
There is nothing here but trees, mist, and an old heap of rocks.
What say...
You have a go at speaking to yourself?
——私は…
<I... I THINK...>
SWOOOO
ヒュゥ
NO...

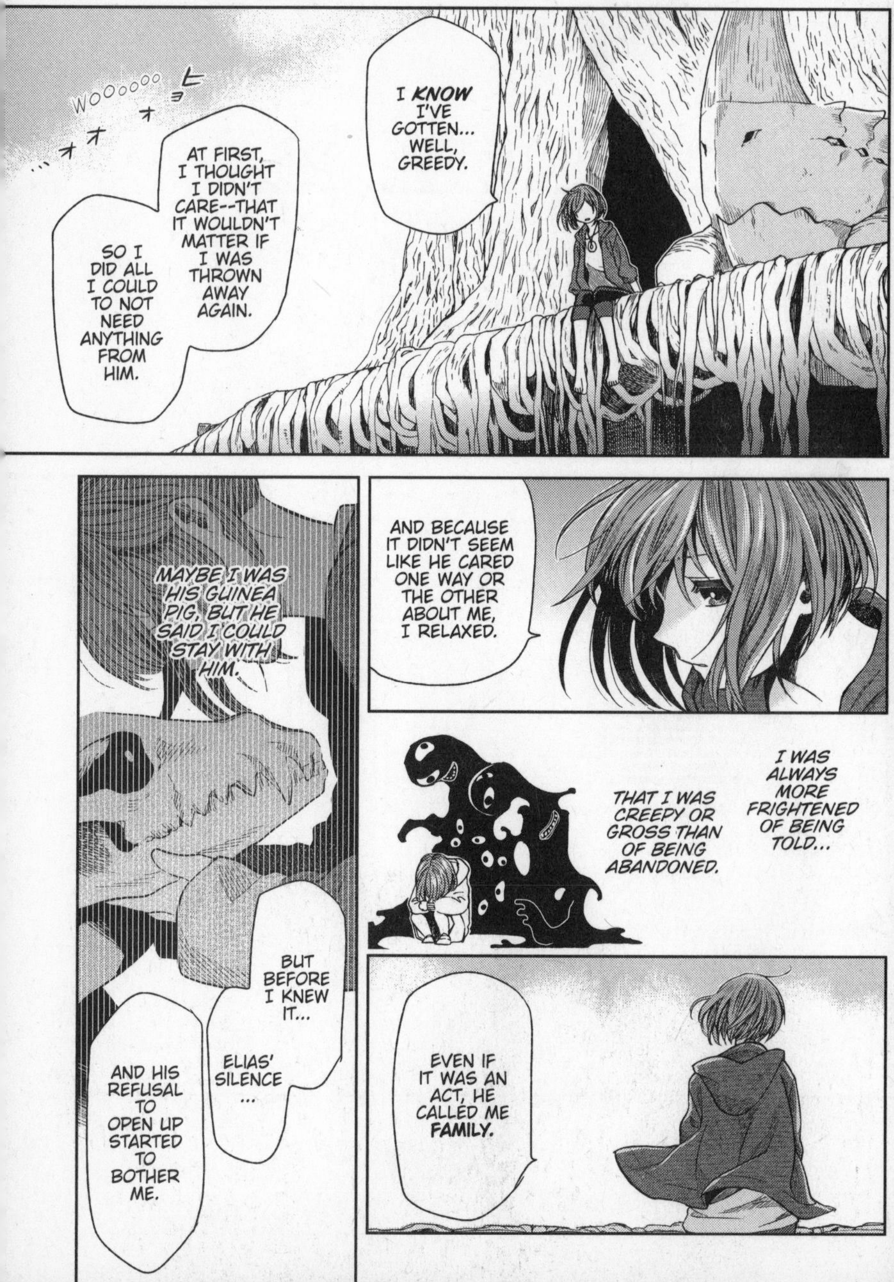

I *KNOW* I'VE GOTTEN... WELL, GREEDY.
WOOOOOO
ヒョオオオ…
AT FIRST, I THOUGHT I DIDN'T CARE--THAT IT WOULDN'T MATTER IF I WAS THROWN AWAY AGAIN.
SO I DID ALL I COULD TO NOT NEED ANYTHING FROM HIM.
AND BECAUSE IT DIDN'T SEEM LIKE HE CARED ONE WAY OR THE OTHER ABOUT ME, I RELAXED.
I WAS ALWAYS MORE FRIGHTENED OF BEING TOLD...
THAT I WAS CREEPY OR GROSS THAN OF BEING ABANDONED.
EVEN IF IT WAS AN ACT, HE CALLED ME **FAMILY.**
MAYBE I WAS HIS GUINEA PIG, BUT HE SAID I COULD STAY WITH HIM.
BUT BEFORE I KNEW IT...
ELIAS' SILENCE ...
AND HIS REFUSAL TO OPEN UP STARTED TO BOTHER ME.

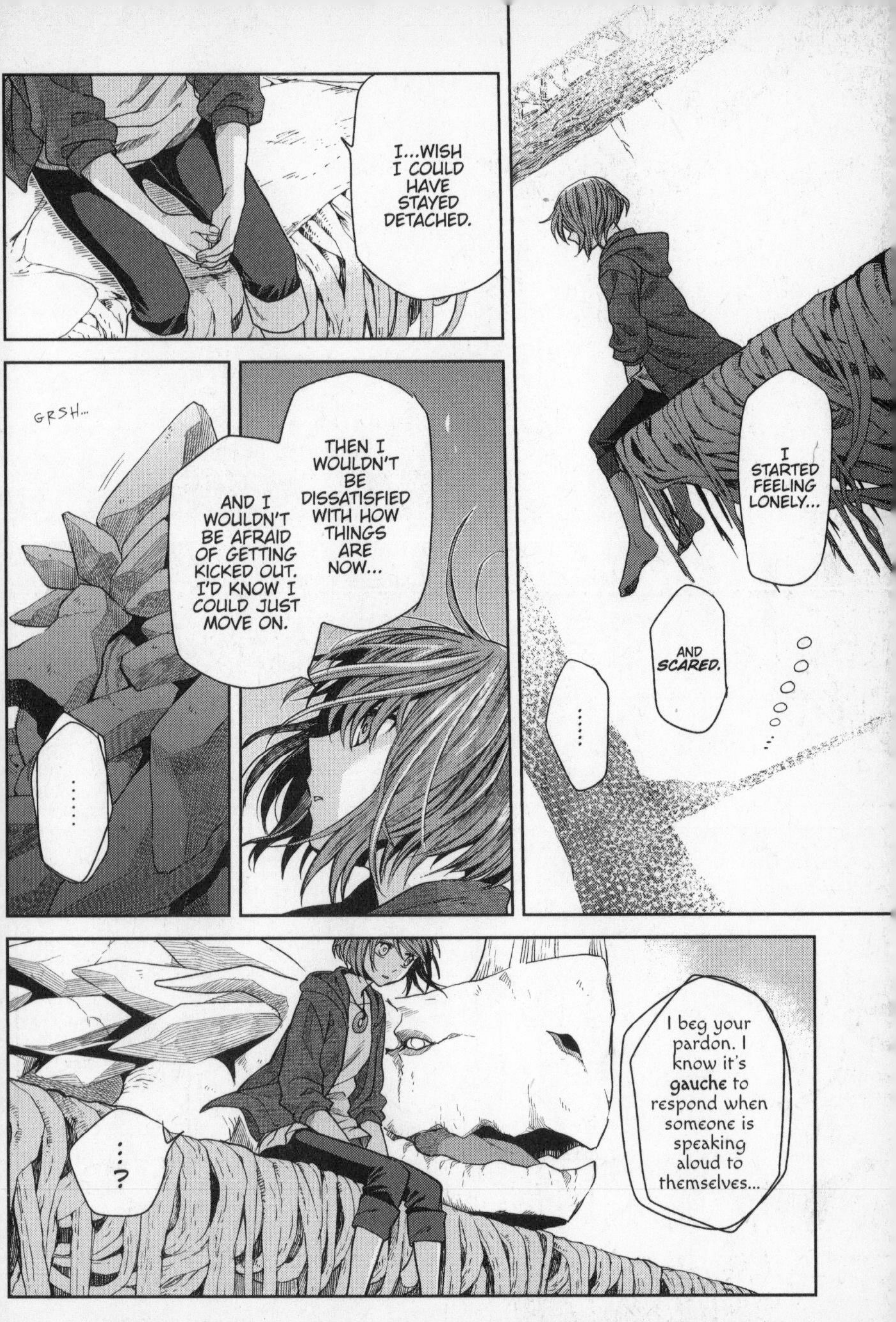
I STARTED FEELING LONELY...
AND SCARED.
......
I...WISH I COULD HAVE STAYED DETACHED.
THEN I WOULDN'T BE DISSATISFIED WITH HOW THINGS ARE NOW...
AND I WOULDN'T BE AFRAID OF GETTING KICKED OUT. I'D KNOW I COULD JUST MOVE ON.
GRSH...
......
I beg your pardon. I know it's gauche to respond when someone is speaking aloud to themselves...
...?

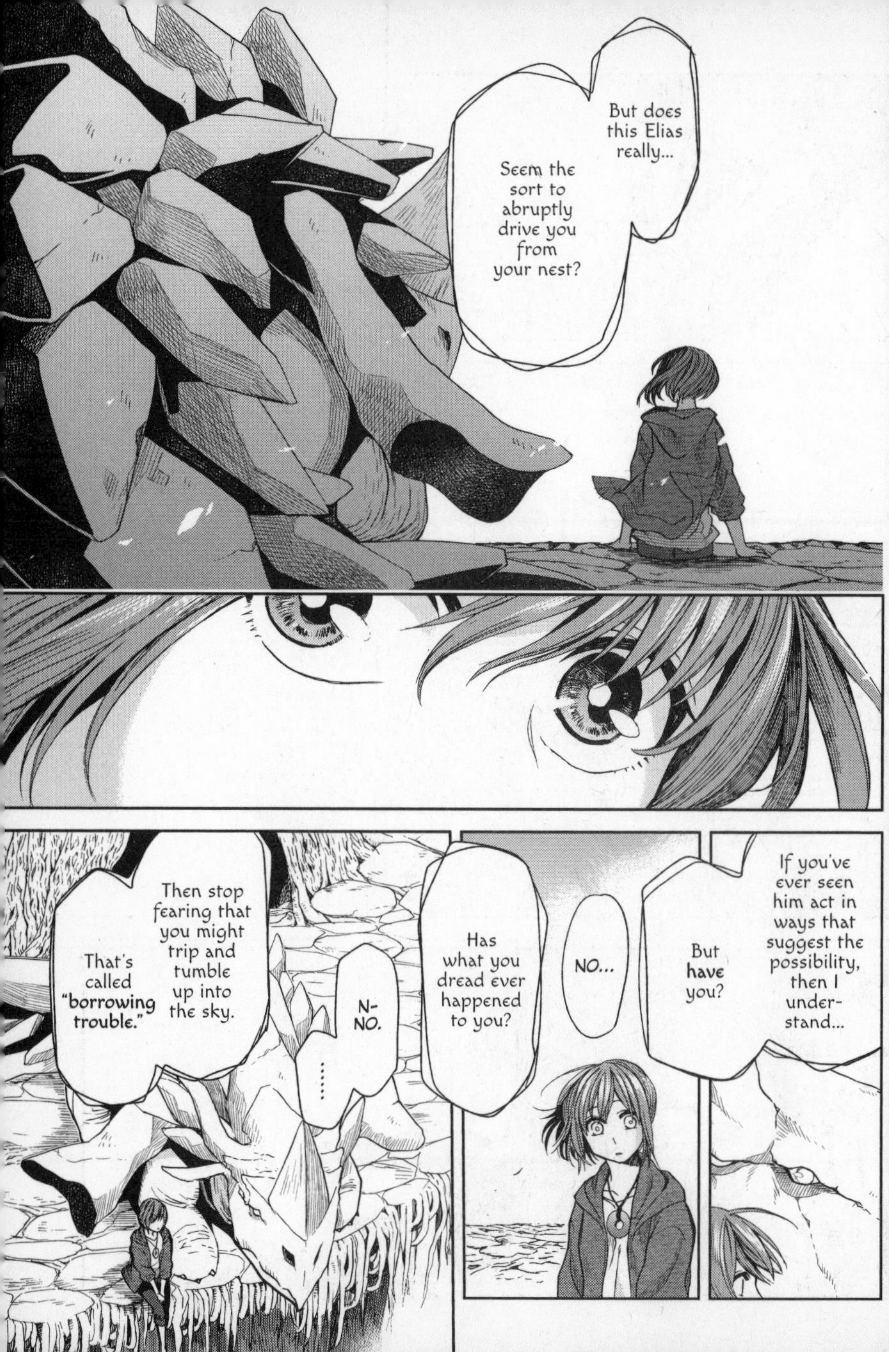
But does this Elias really...
Seem the sort to abruptly drive you from your nest?
If you've ever seen him act in ways that suggest the possibility, then I under-stand...
But **have** you?
NO...
Has what you dread ever happened to you?
N-NO.
......
Then stop fearing that you might trip and tumble up into the sky.
That's called **"borrowing trouble."**

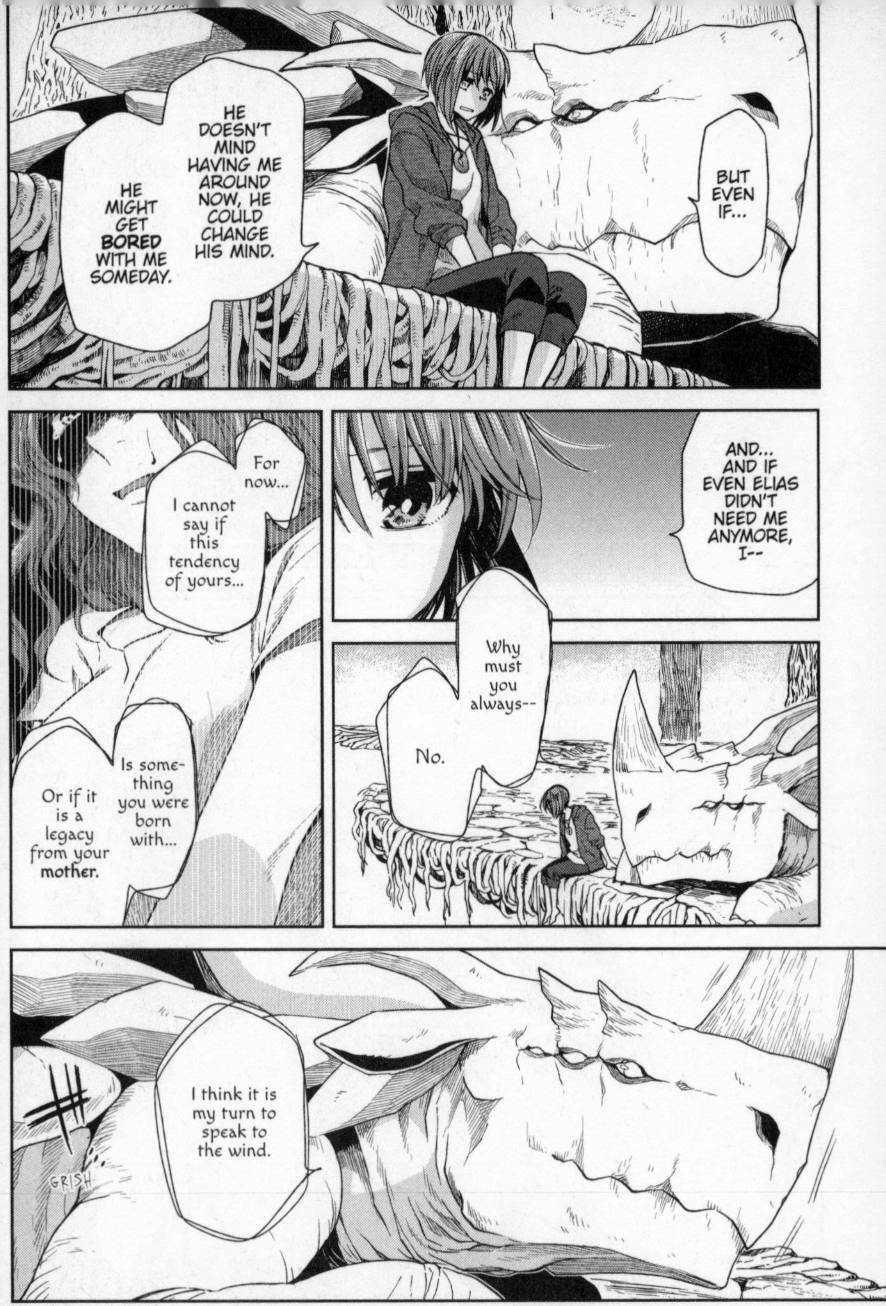
BUT EVEN IF...
HE DOESN'T MIND HAVING ME AROUND NOW, HE COULD CHANGE HIS MIND.
HE MIGHT GET **BORED** WITH ME SOMEDAY.
AND... AND IF EVEN ELIAS DIDN'T NEED ME ANYMORE, I--
Why must you always--
No.
For now...
I cannot say if this tendency of yours...
Is something you were born with...
Or if it is a legacy from your **mother.**
I think it is my turn to speak to the wind.
GRISH

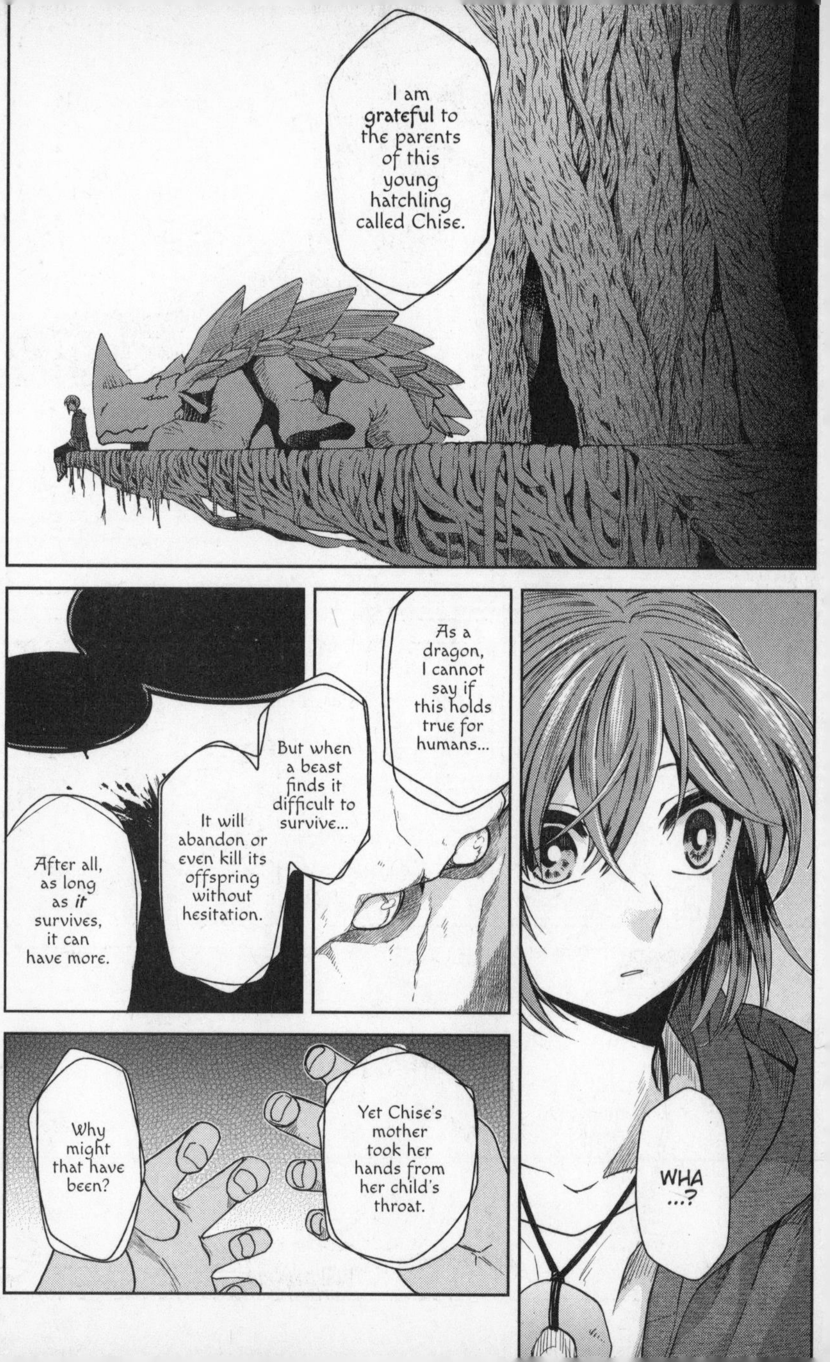

I am grateful to the parents of this young hatchling called Chise.
As a dragon, I cannot say if this holds true for humans...
But when a beast finds it difficult to survive...
It will abandon or even kill its offspring without hesitation.
After all, as long as *it* survives, it can have more.
Yet Chise's mother took her hands from her child's throat.
Why might that have been?
WHA ...?

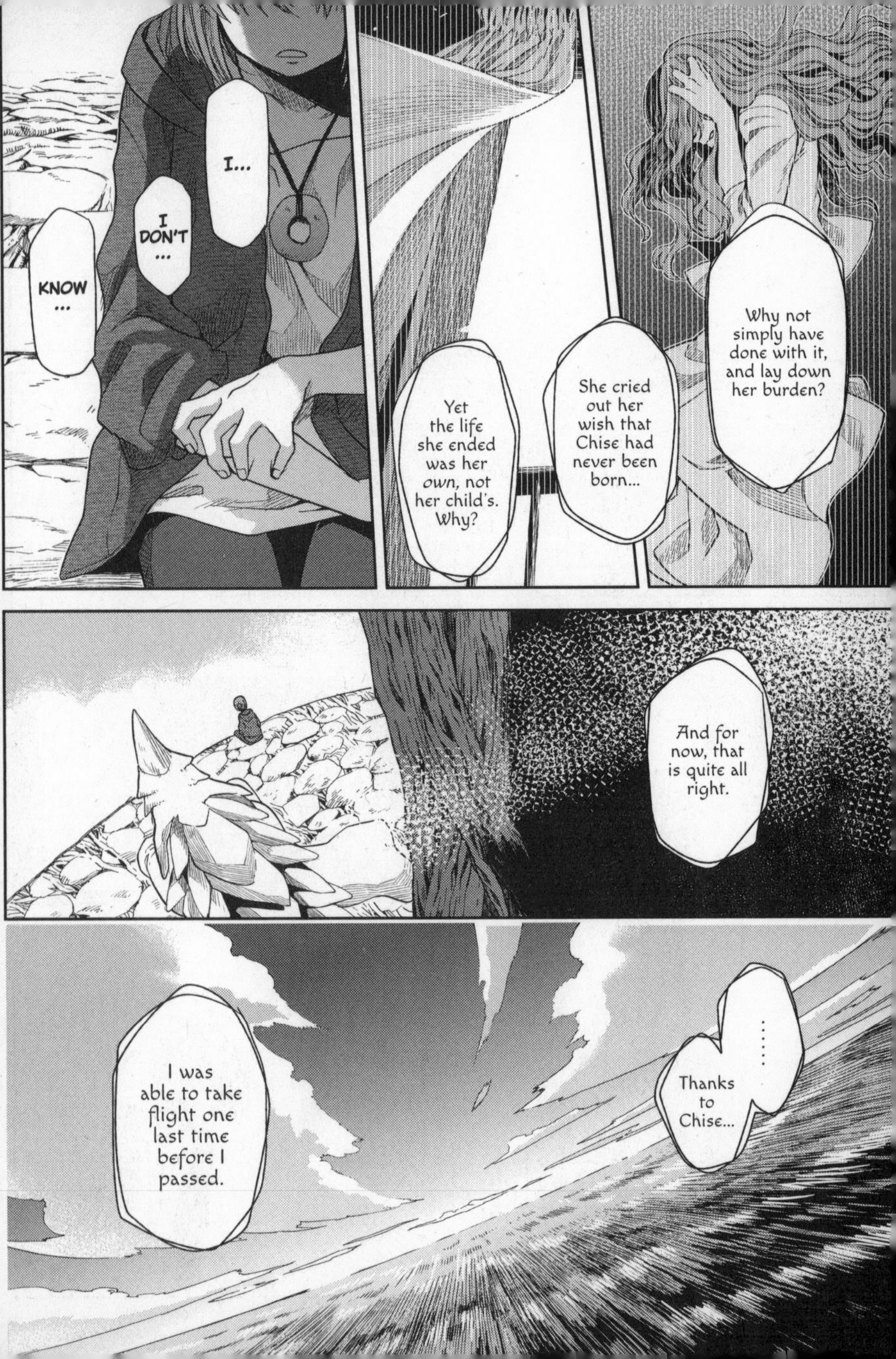
Why not simply have done with it, and lay down her burden?
She cried out her wish that Chise had never been born...
Yet the life she ended was her *own*, not her child's. Why?
I...
I DON'T ...
KNOW ...
And for now, that is quite all right.
......
Thanks to Chise...
I was able to take flight one last time before I passed.

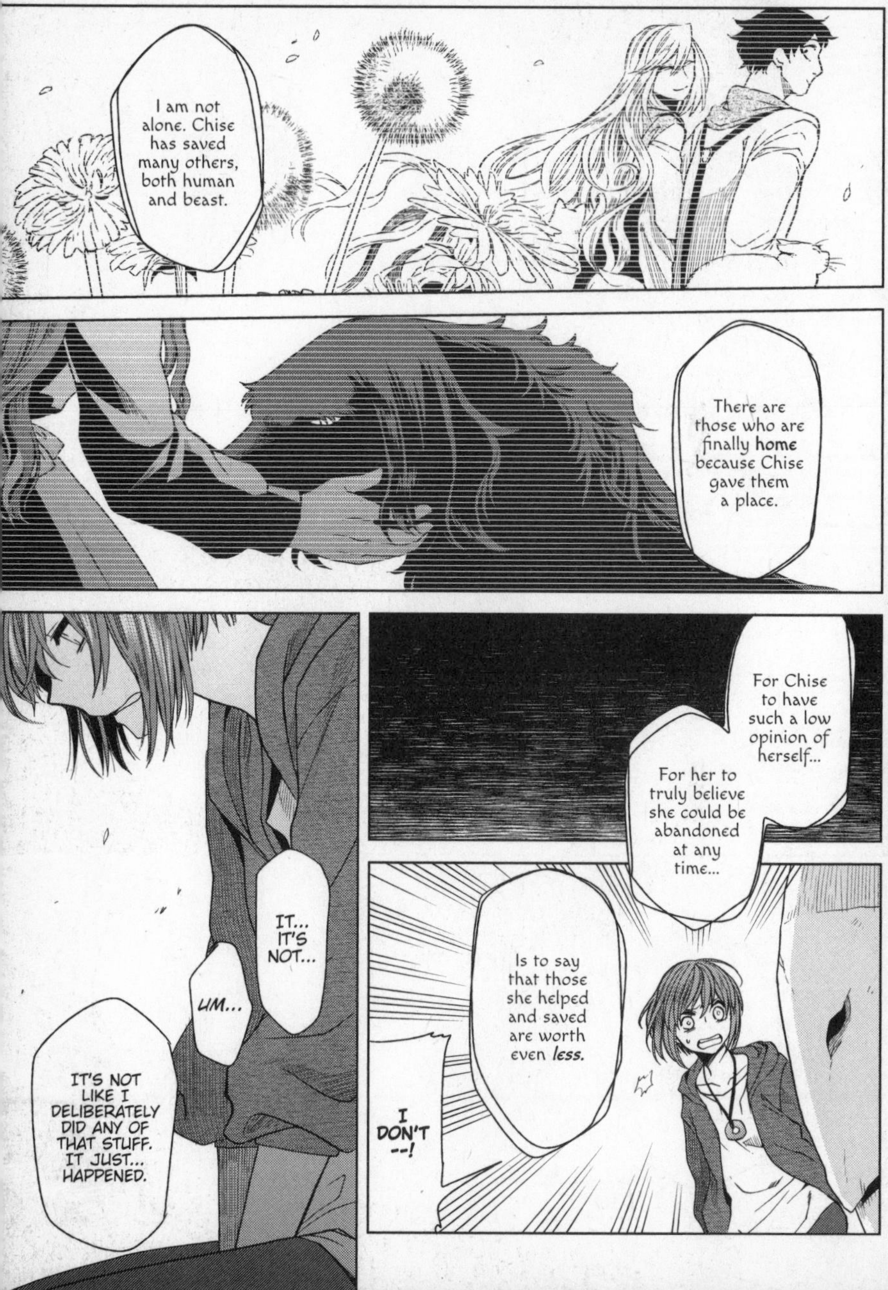
I am not alone. Chise has saved many others, both human and beast.
There are those who are finally **home** because Chise gave them a place.
For Chise to have such a low opinion of herself...
For her to truly believe she could be abandoned at any time...
Is to say that those she helped and saved are worth even *less.*
I DON'T --!
IT... IT'S NOT...
UM...
IT'S NOT LIKE I DELIBERATELY DID ANY OF THAT STUFF. IT JUST... HAPPENED.

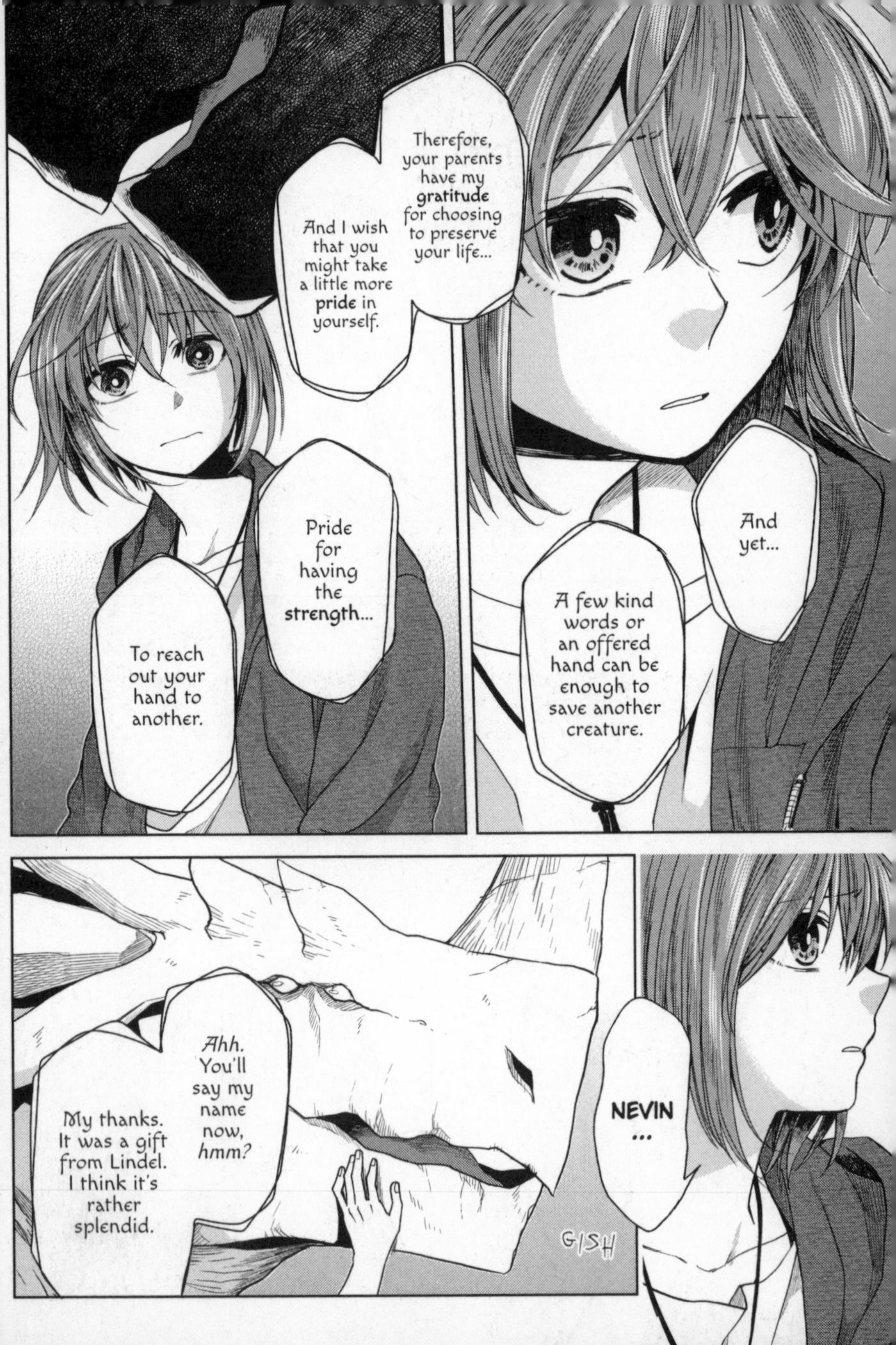
And yet...
A few kind words or an offered hand can be enough to save another creature.
Therefore, your parents have my **gratitude** for choosing to preserve your life...
And I wish that you might take a little more **pride** in yourself.
Pride for having the **strength**...
To reach out your hand to another.
NEVIN...
GISH
Ahh. You'll say my name now, *hmm?*
My thanks. It was a gift from Lindel. I think it's rather splendid.

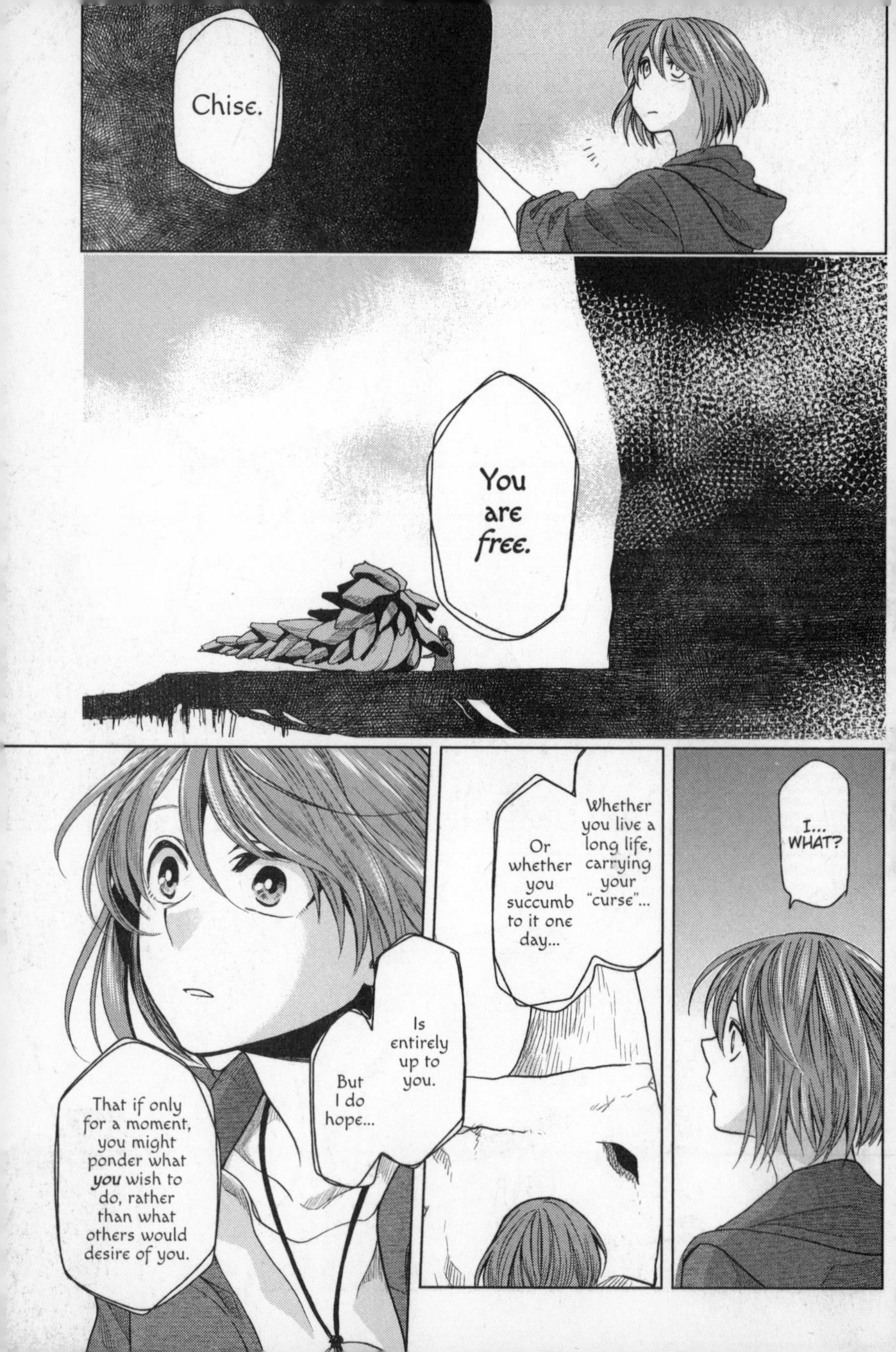
Chise.
You are *free.*
I... WHAT?
Whether you live a long life, carrying your "curse"...
Or whether you succumb to it one day...
Is entirely up to you.
But I do hope...
That if only for a moment, you might ponder what ***you*** wish to do, rather than what others would desire of you.

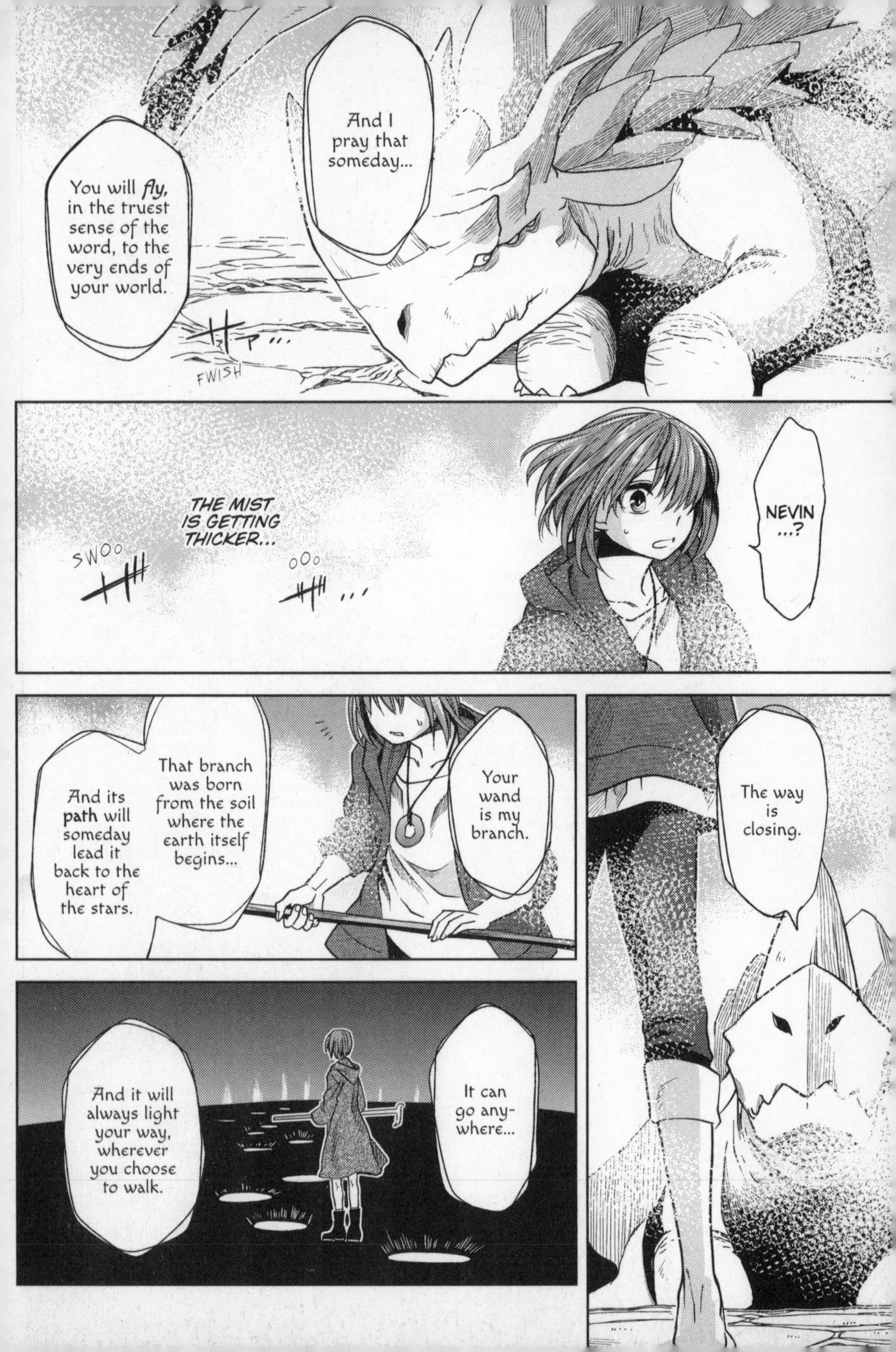
And I pray that someday...
You will *fly*, in the truest sense of the word, to the very ends of your world.
FWISH
NEVIN ...?
THE MIST IS GETTING THICKER...
SWOO
OOO
The way is closing.
Your wand is my branch.
That branch was born from the soil where the earth itself begins...
And its **path** will someday lead it back to the heart of the stars.
It can go any-where...
And it will always light your way, wherever you choose to walk.

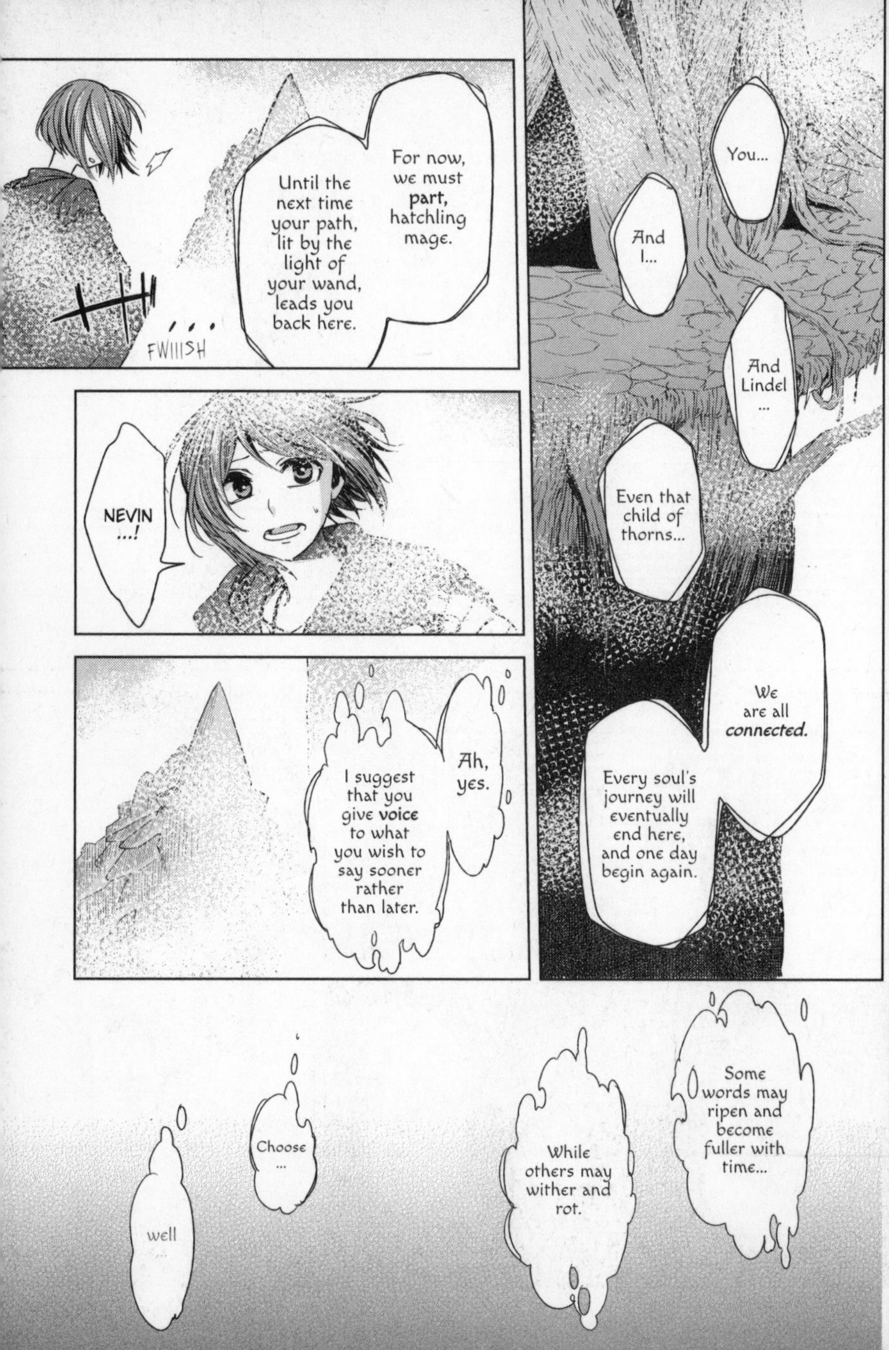
You...
And I...
And Lindel...
Even that child of thorns...
We are all **connected.**
Every soul's journey will eventually end here, and one day begin again.
For now, we must **part,** hatchling mage.
Until the next time your path, lit by the light of your wand, leads you back here.
...
FWIIISH
NEVIN ...!
Ah, yes.
I suggest that you give **voice** to what you wish to say sooner rather than later.
Some words may ripen and become fuller with time...
While others may wither and rot.
Choose ...
well ...

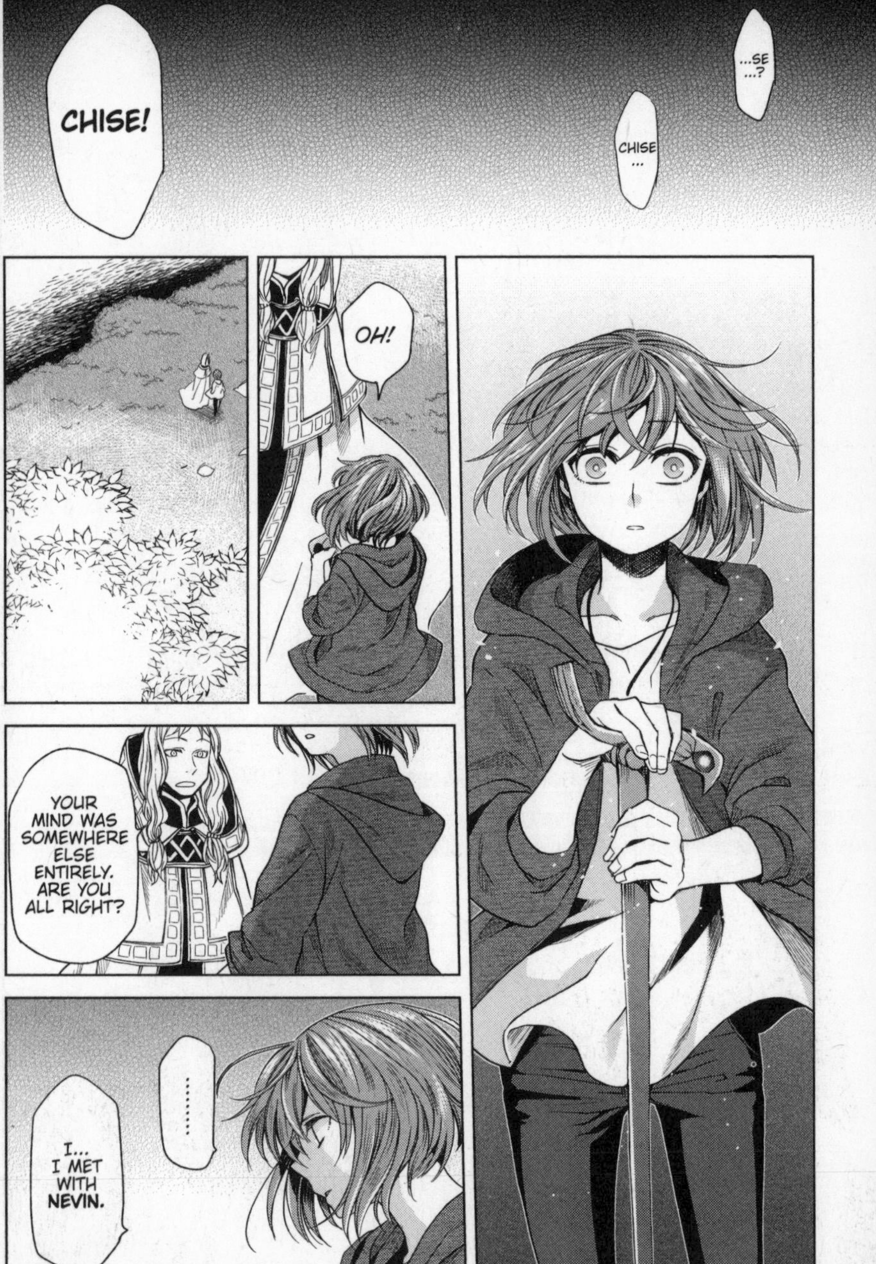
...SE ...?
CHISE ...
CHISE!
OH!
YOUR MIND WAS SOMEWHERE ELSE ENTIRELY. ARE YOU ALL RIGHT?
......
I... I MET WITH NEVIN.

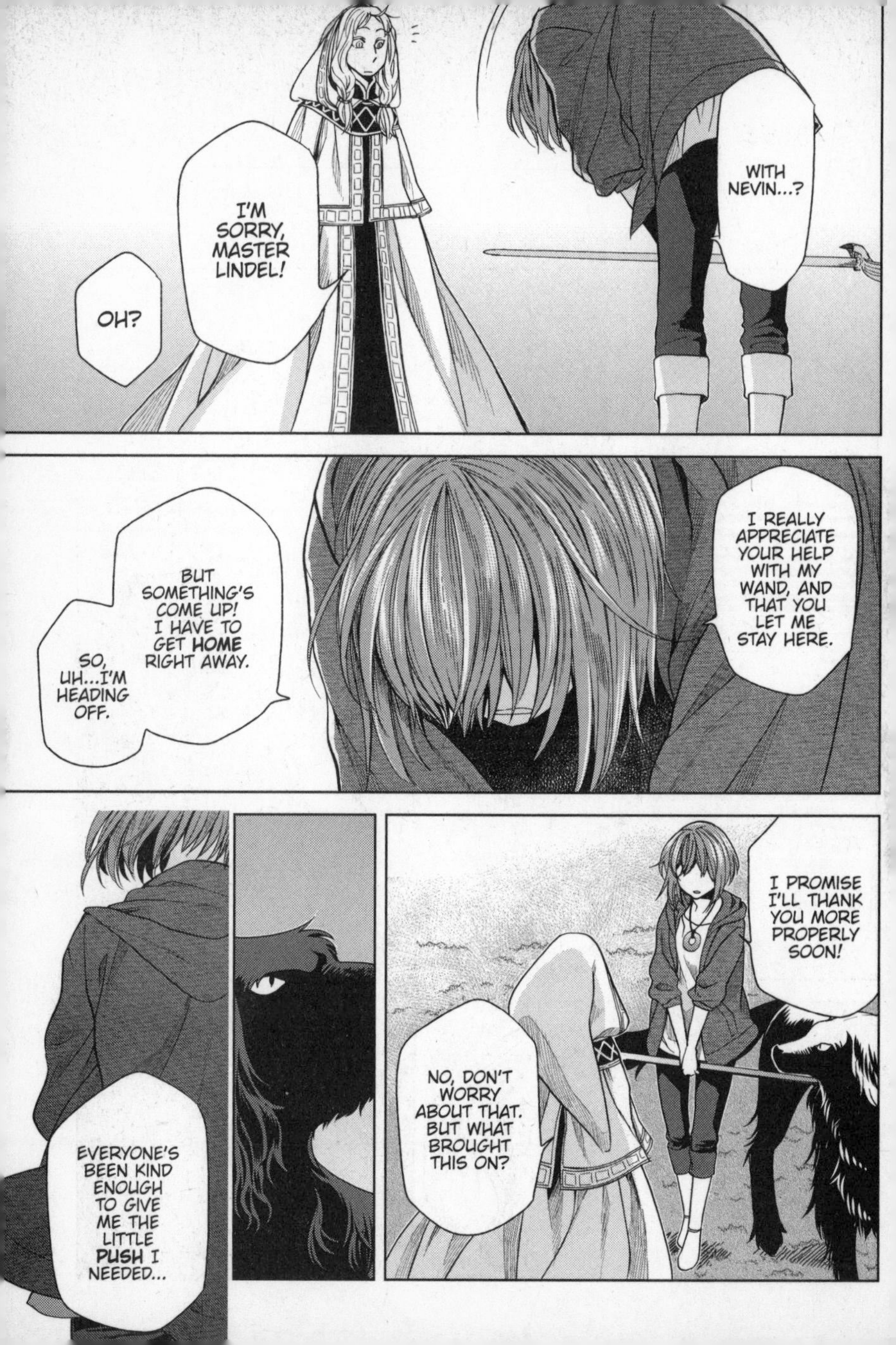
WITH NEVIN...?
I'M SORRY, MASTER LINDEL!
OH?
I REALLY APPRECIATE YOUR HELP WITH MY WAND, AND THAT YOU LET ME STAY HERE.
BUT SOMETHING'S COME UP! I HAVE TO GET **HOME** RIGHT AWAY.
SO, UH...I'M HEADING OFF.
I PROMISE I'LL THANK YOU MORE PROPERLY SOON!
NO, DON'T WORRY ABOUT THAT. BUT WHAT BROUGHT THIS ON?
EVERYONE'S BEEN KIND ENOUGH TO GIVE ME THE LITTLE **PUSH** I NEEDED...

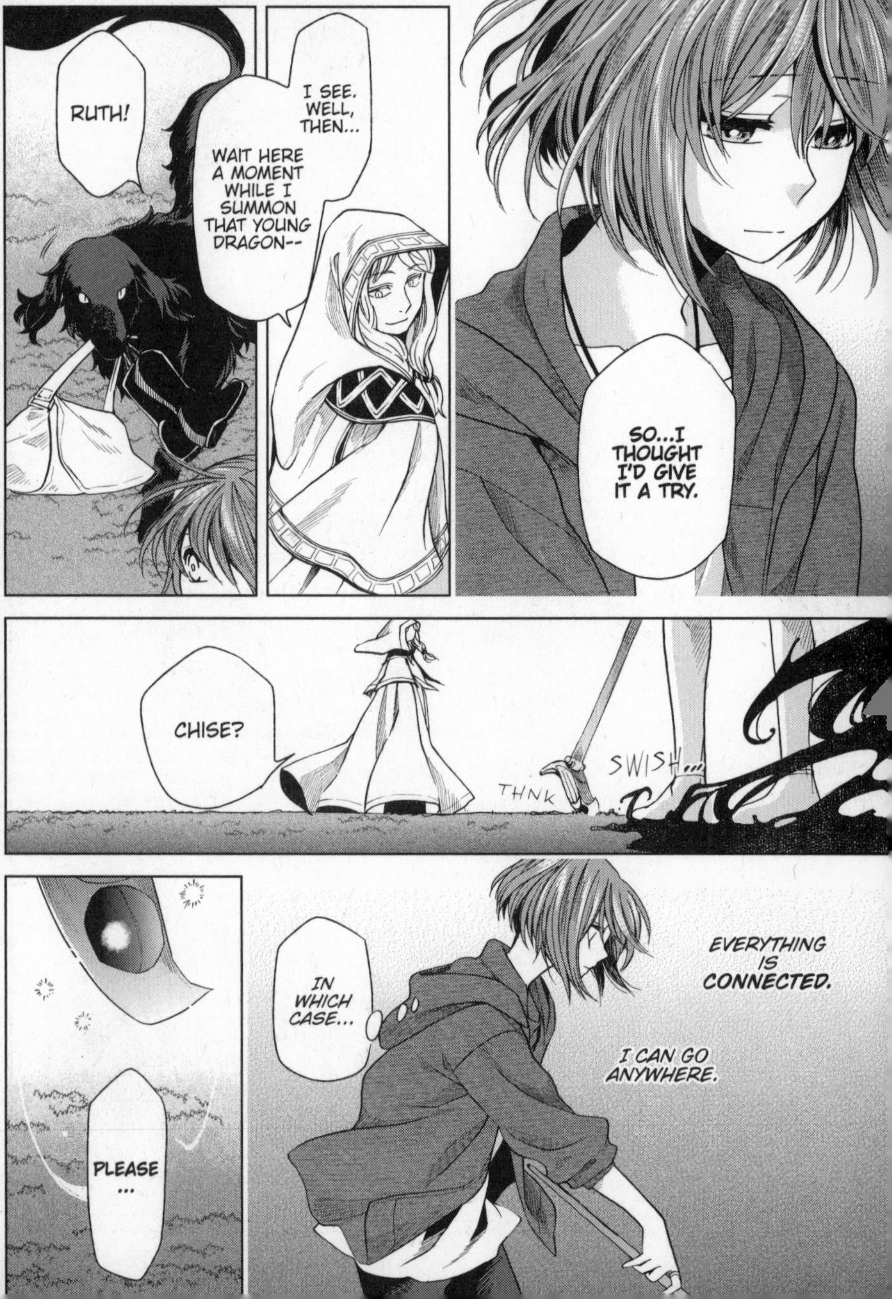
SO...I THOUGHT I'D GIVE IT A TRY.
I SEE. WELL, THEN...
WAIT HERE A MOMENT WHILE I SUMMON THAT YOUNG DRAGON--
RUTH!
SWISH...
THNK
CHISE?
EVERYTHING IS CONNECTED.
I CAN GO ANYWHERE.
IN WHICH CASE...
PLEASE ...

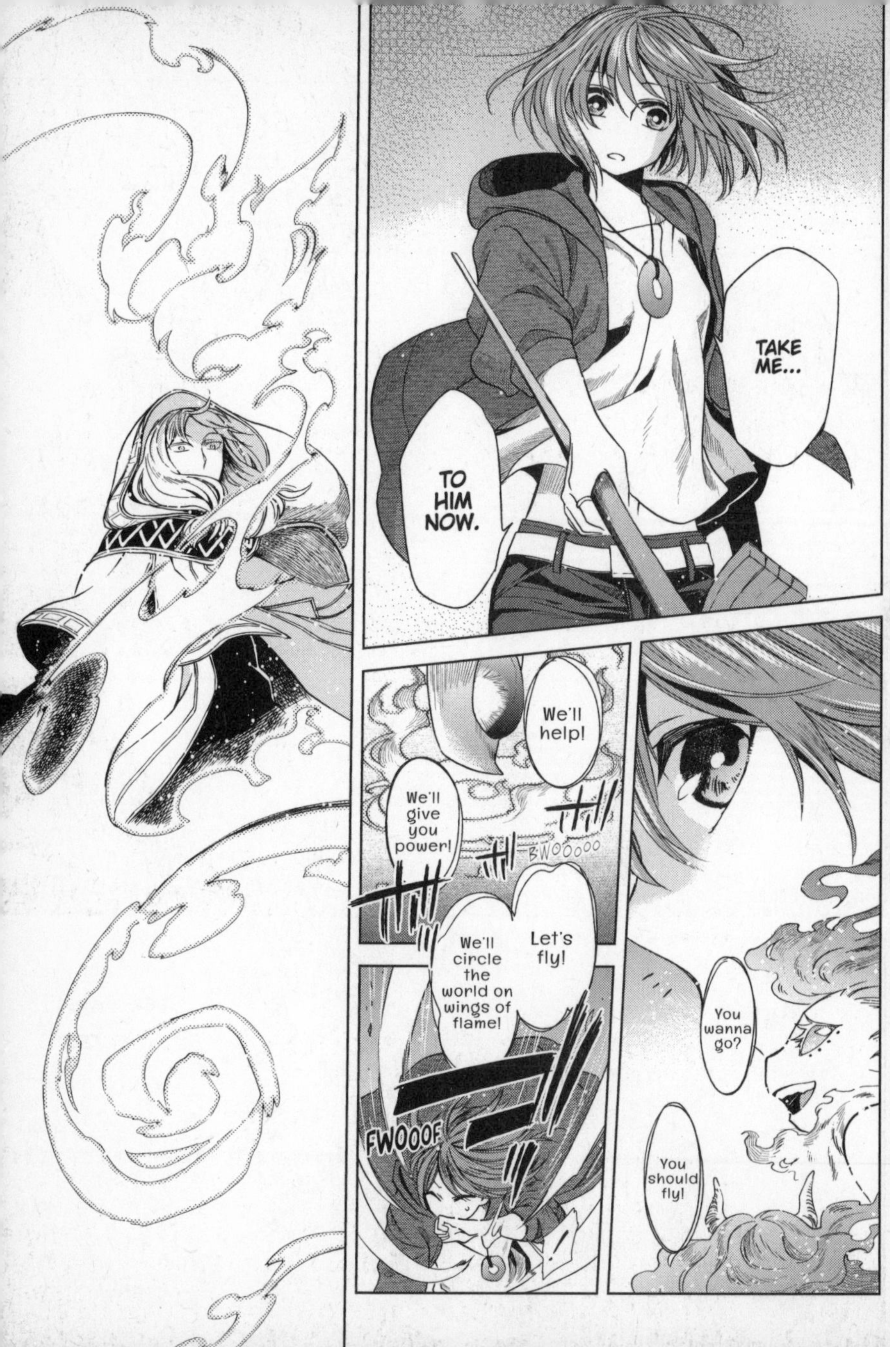
TAKE ME...
TO HIM NOW.
You wanna go?
You should fly!
We'll help!
We'll give you power!
BWOOOOO
Let's fly!
We'll circle the world on wings of flame!
FWOOOF

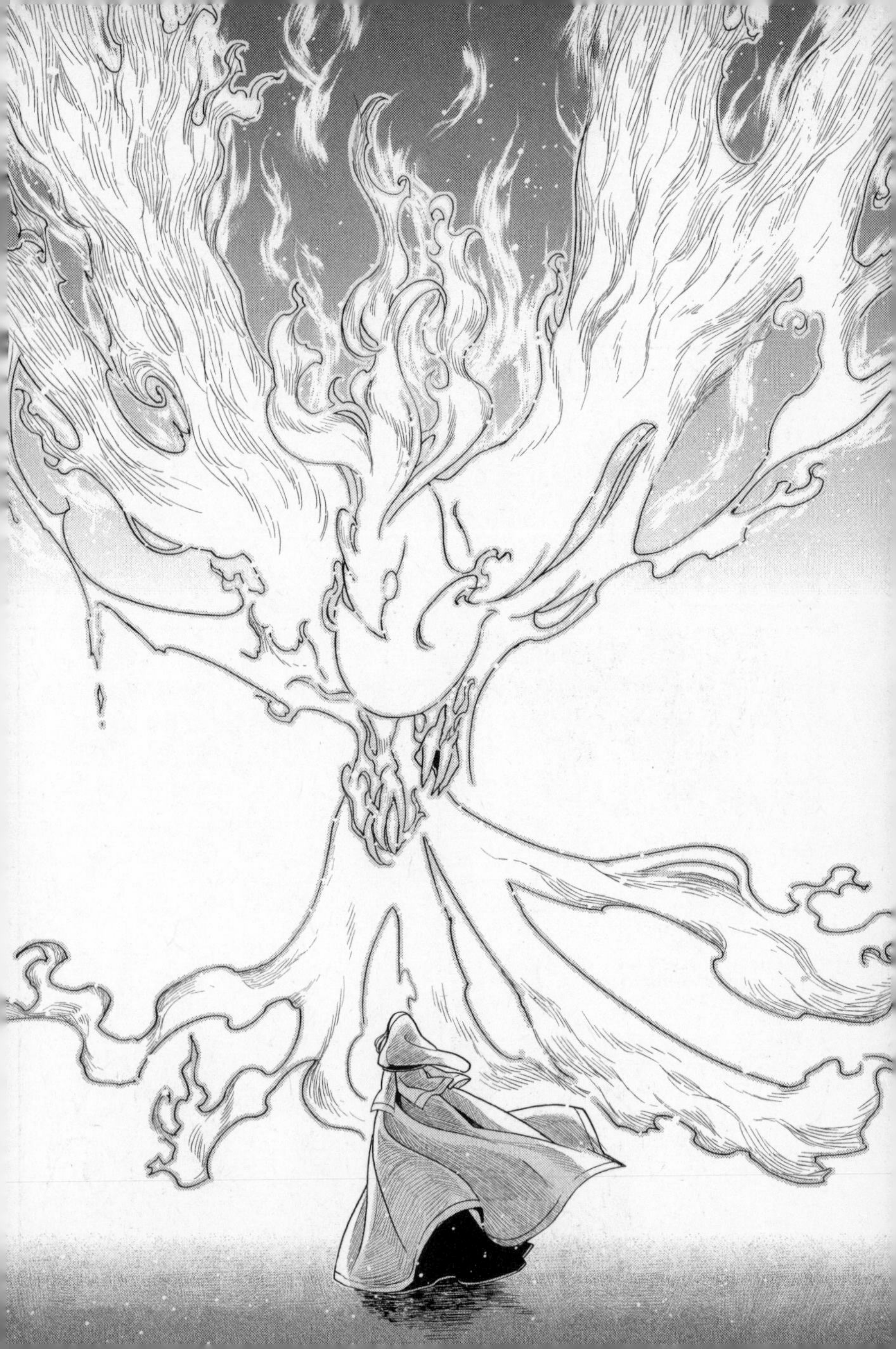

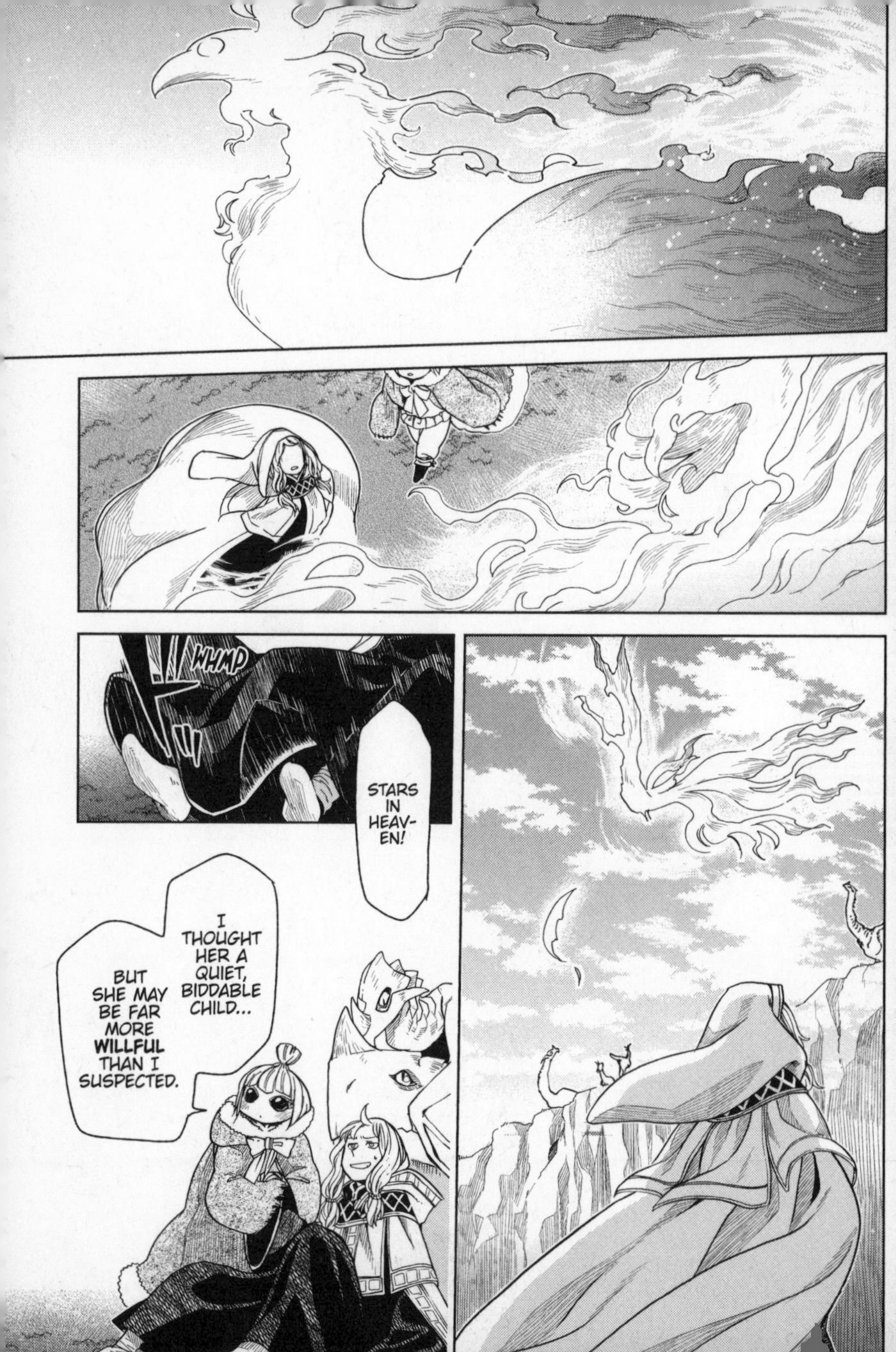
WHMP
STARS IN HEAV-EN!
I THOUGHT HER A QUIET, BIDDABLE CHILD... BUT SHE MAY BE FAR MORE WILLFUL THAN I SUSPECTED.

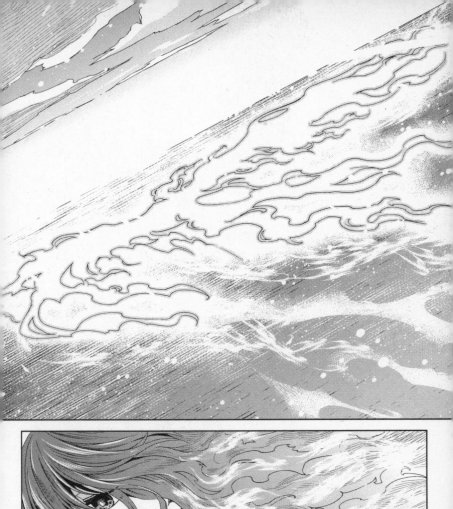

I THINK NEVIN WAS BEING LITERAL...

WHEN HE SAID...

THAT I COULD GO **ANYWHERE.**

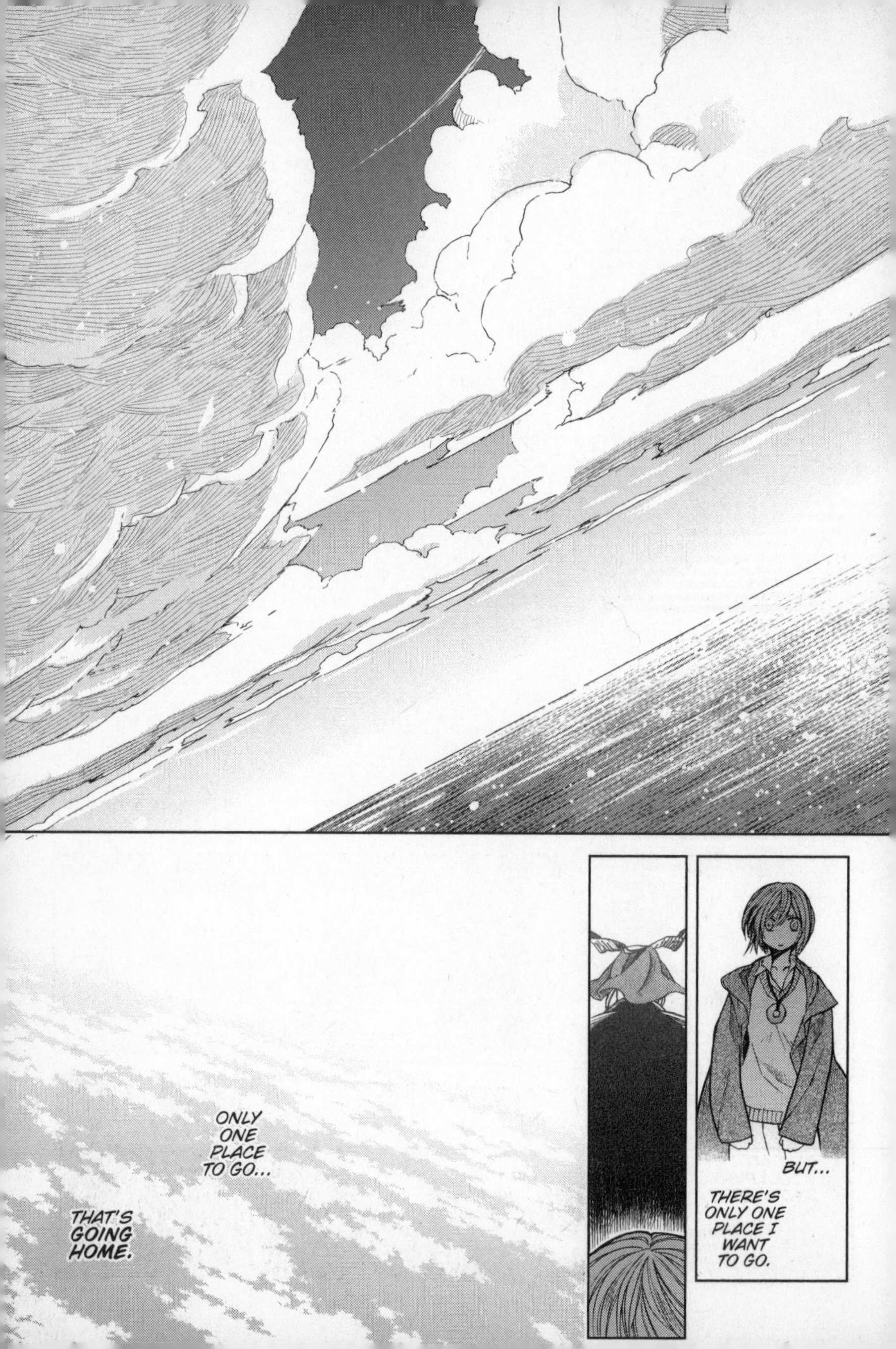
BUT...
THERE'S ONLY ONE PLACE I WANT TO GO.
ONLY ONE PLACE TO GO...
THAT'S GOING HOME.

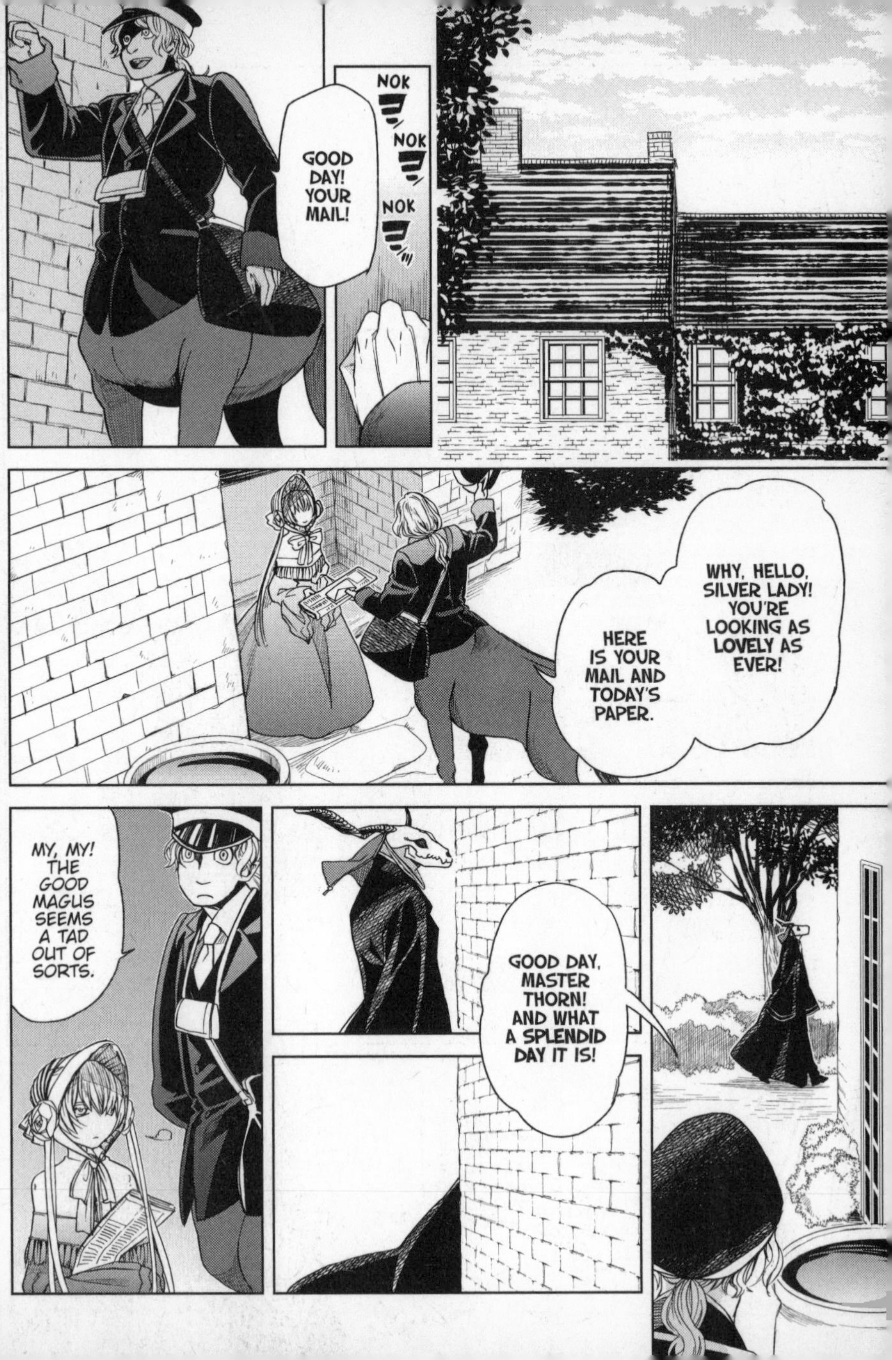
NOK NOK NOK
GOOD DAY! YOUR MAIL!
WHY, HELLO, SILVER LADY! YOU'RE LOOKING AS LOVELY AS EVER!
HERE IS YOUR MAIL AND TODAY'S PAPER.
GOOD DAY, MASTER THORN! AND WHAT A SPLENDID DAY IT IS!
MY, MY! THE GOOD MAGUS SEEMS A TAD OUT OF SORTS.

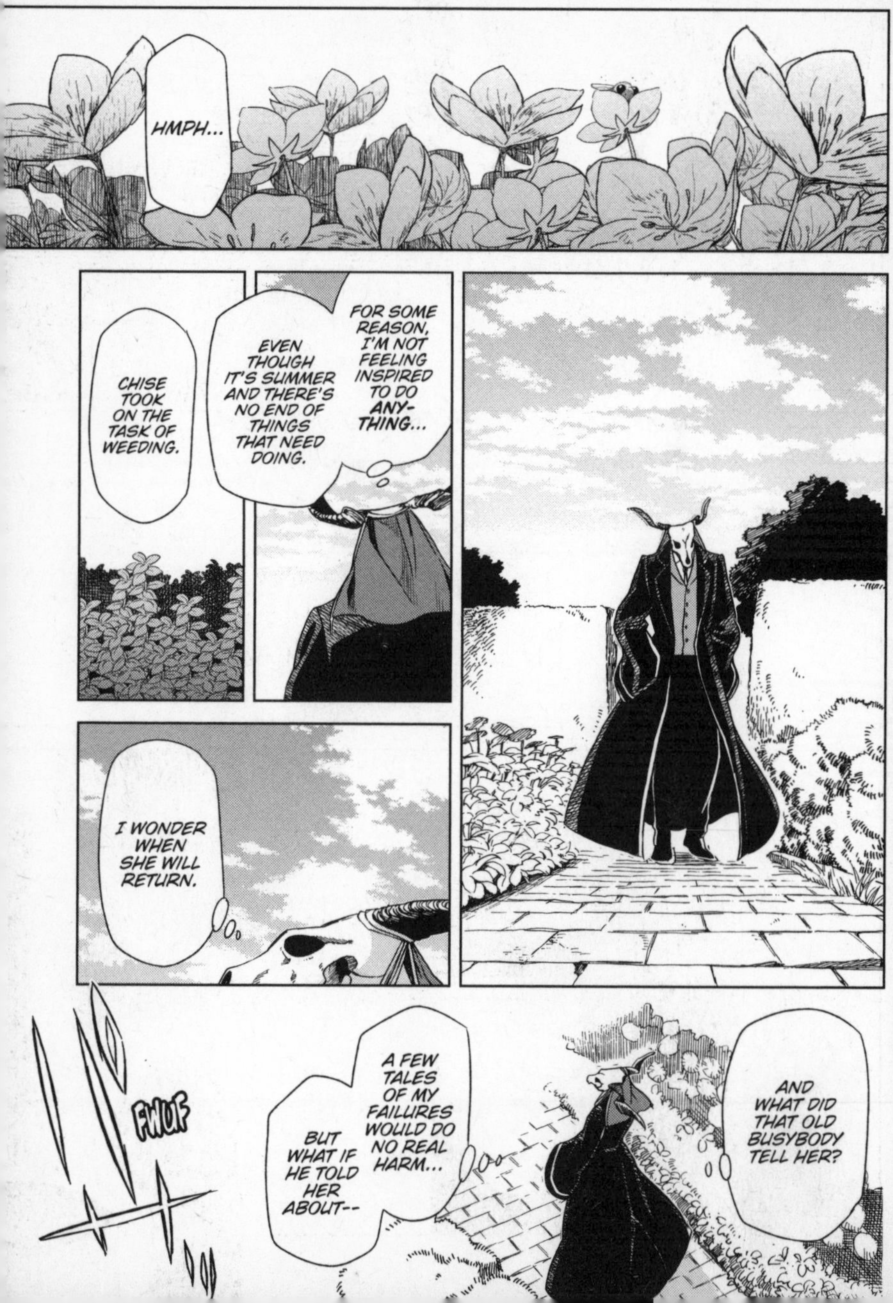
HMPH...
FOR SOME REASON, I'M NOT FEELING INSPIRED TO DO ANYTHING...
EVEN THOUGH IT'S SUMMER AND THERE'S NO END OF THINGS THAT NEED DOING.
CHISE TOOK ON THE TASK OF WEEDING.
I WONDER WHEN SHE WILL RETURN.
AND WHAT DID THAT OLD BUSYBODY TELL HER?
A FEW TALES OF MY FAILURES WOULD DO NO REAL HARM...
BUT WHAT IF HE TOLD HER ABOUT--
FWUF

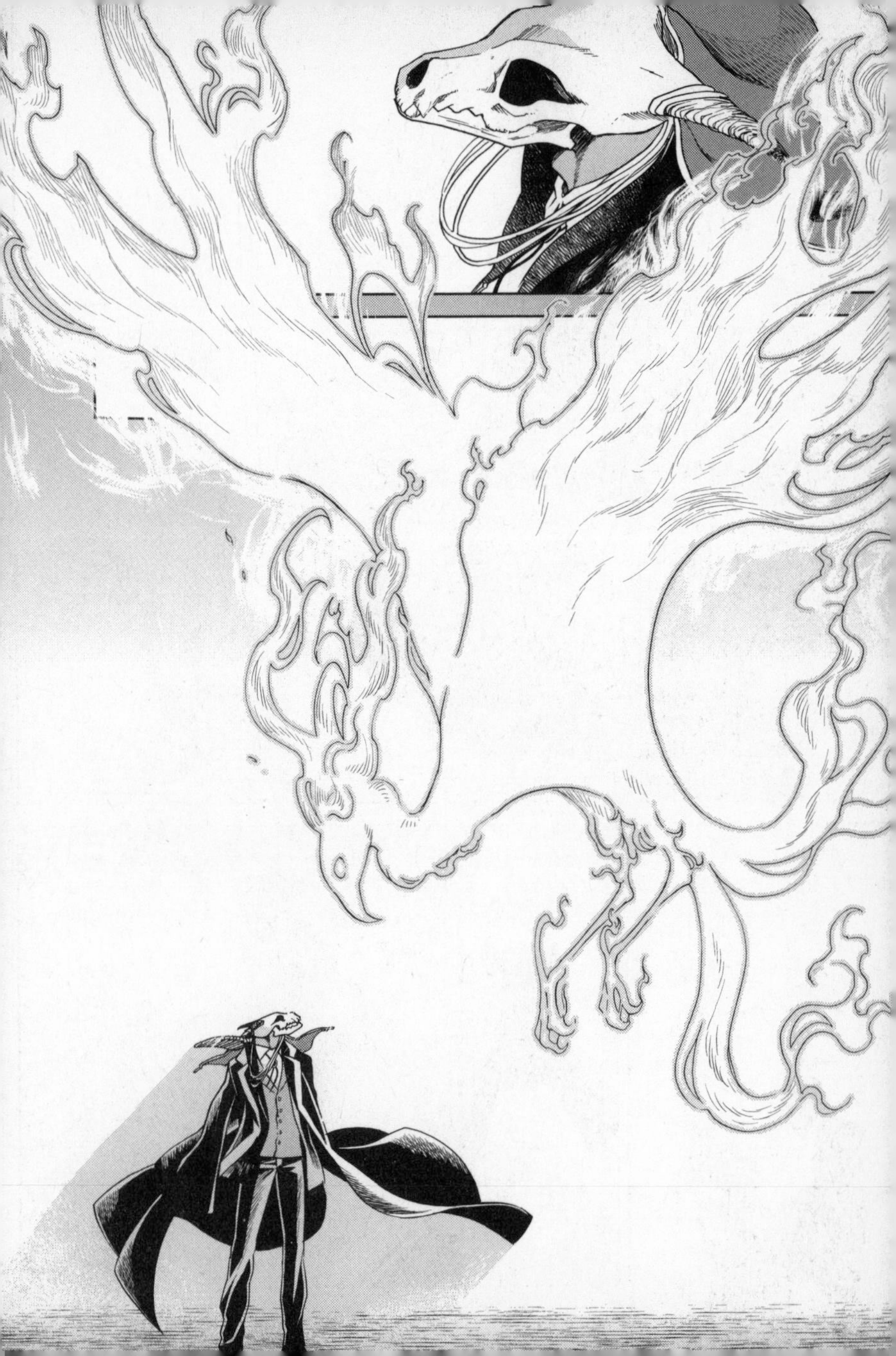

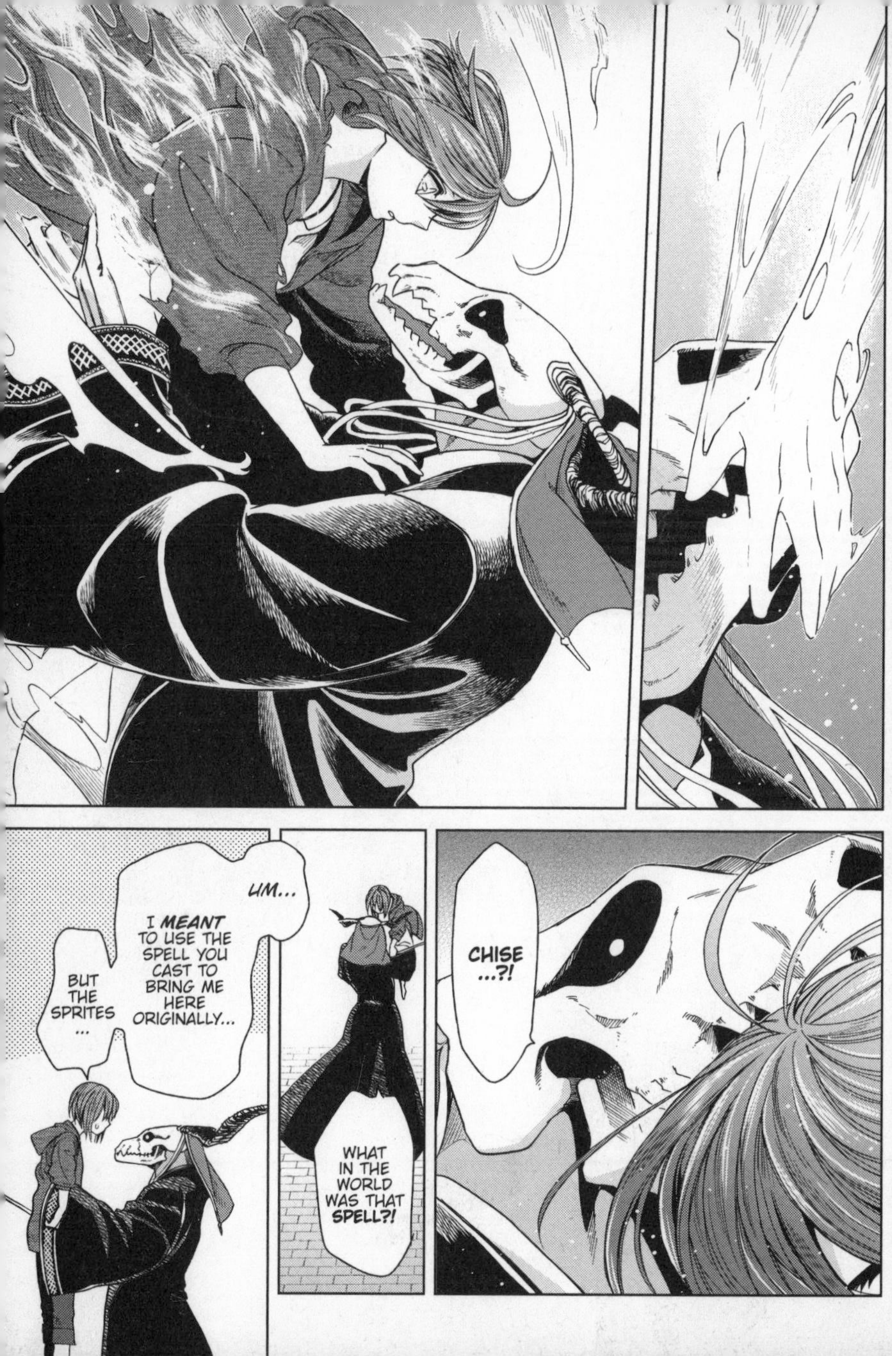
CHISE ...?!
WHAT IN THE WORLD WAS THAT SPELL?!
UM...
I MEANT TO USE THE SPELL YOU CAST TO BRING ME HERE ORIGINALLY...
BUT THE SPRITES ...

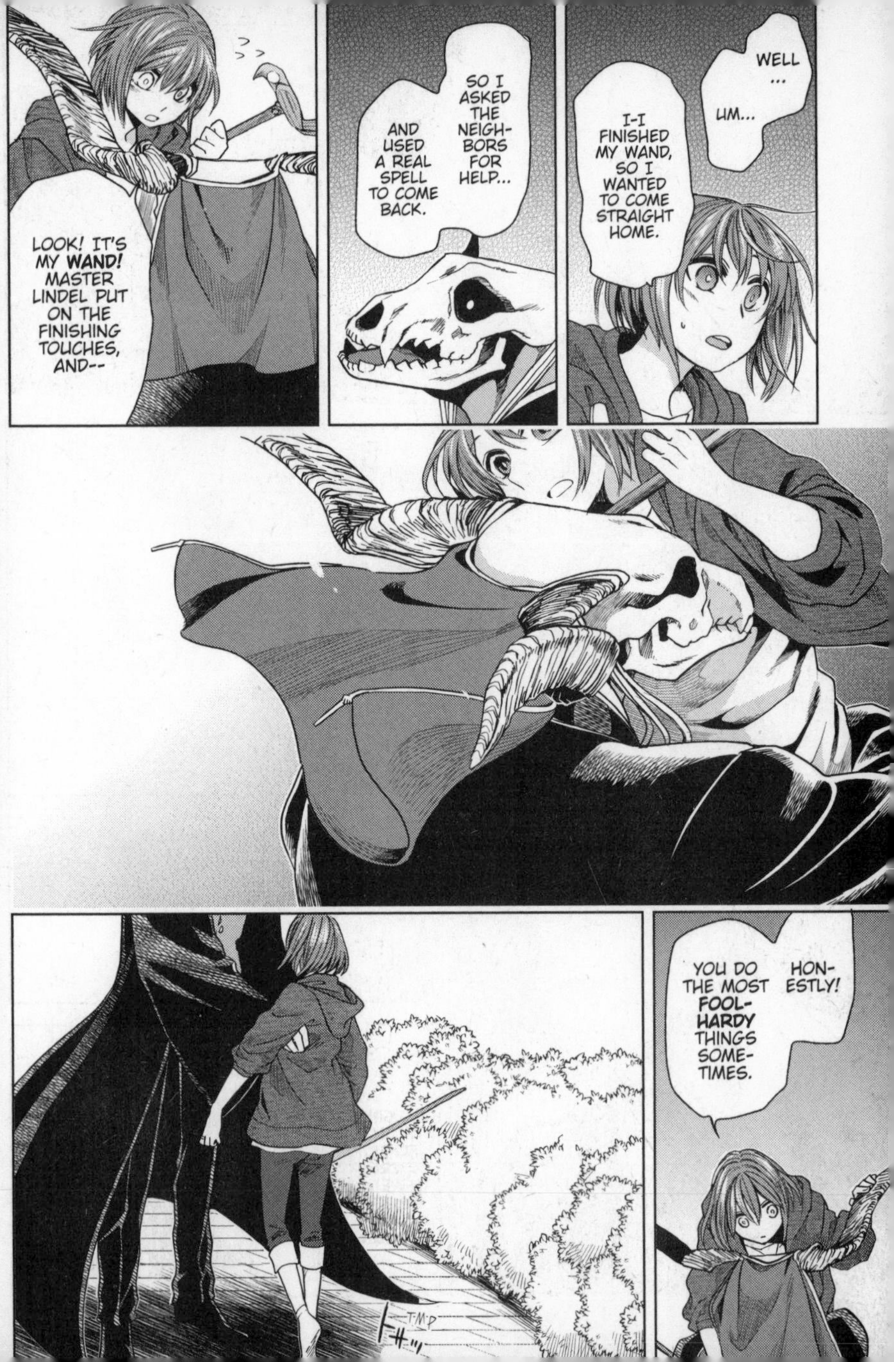
WELL... UM...
I-I FINISHED MY WAND, SO I WANTED TO COME STRAIGHT HOME.
SO I ASKED THE NEIGHBORS FOR HELP...
AND USED A REAL SPELL TO COME BACK.
LOOK! IT'S MY **WAND!** MASTER LINDEL PUT ON THE FINISHING TOUCHES, AND--
HONESTLY!
YOU DO THE MOST **FOOLHARDY** THINGS SOMETIMES.
T·M·D

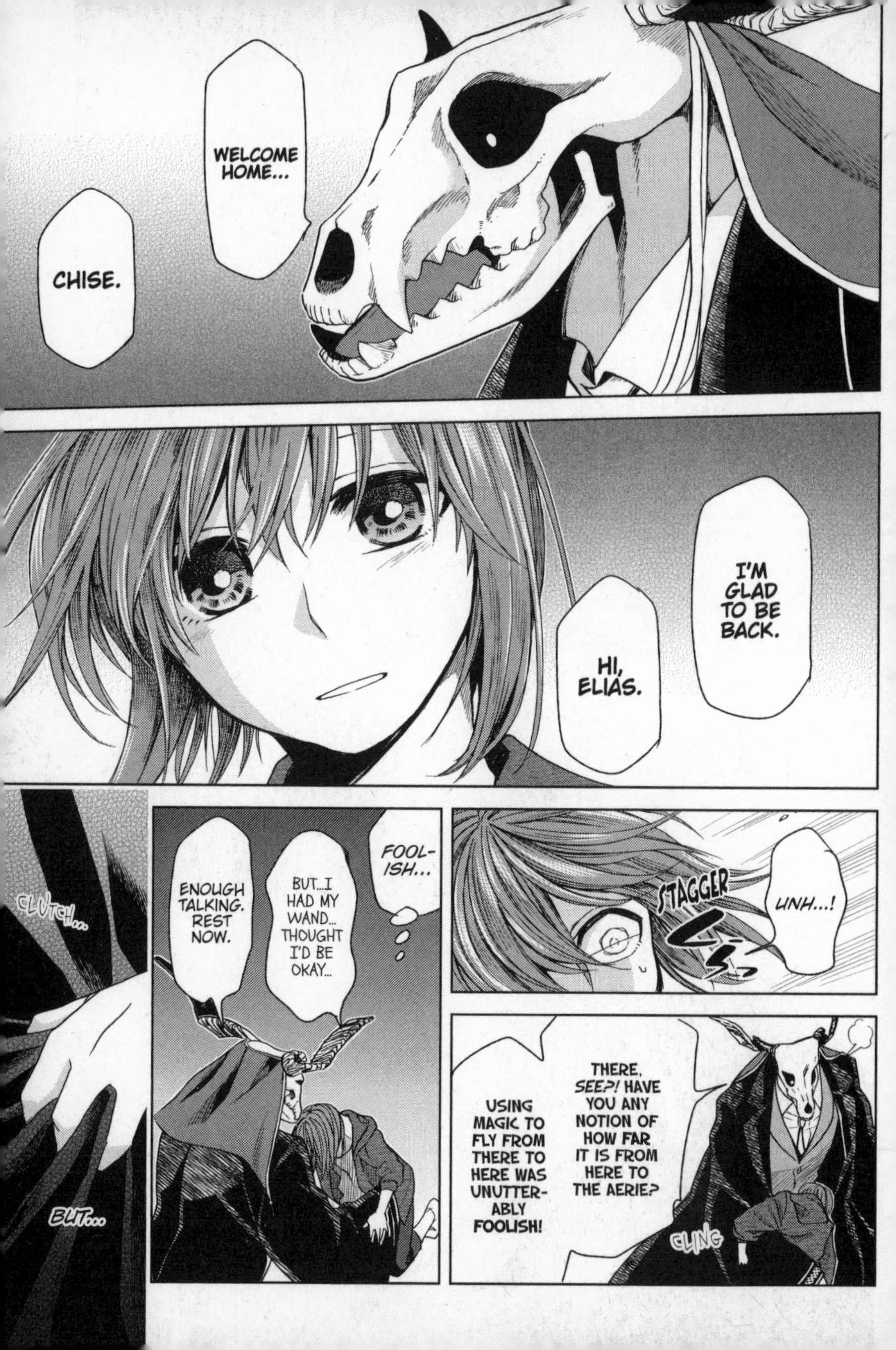
WELCOME HOME...
CHISE.
I'M GLAD TO BE BACK.
HI, ELIAS.
UNH...!
STAGGER
THERE, SEE?! HAVE YOU ANY NOTION OF HOW FAR IT IS FROM HERE TO THE AERIE?
USING MAGIC TO FLY FROM THERE TO HERE WAS UNUTTER-ABLY FOOLISH!
CLING
FOOL-ISH...
BUT...I HAD MY WAND... THOUGHT I'D BE OKAY...
ENOUGH TALKING. REST NOW.
CLUTCH...
BUT...

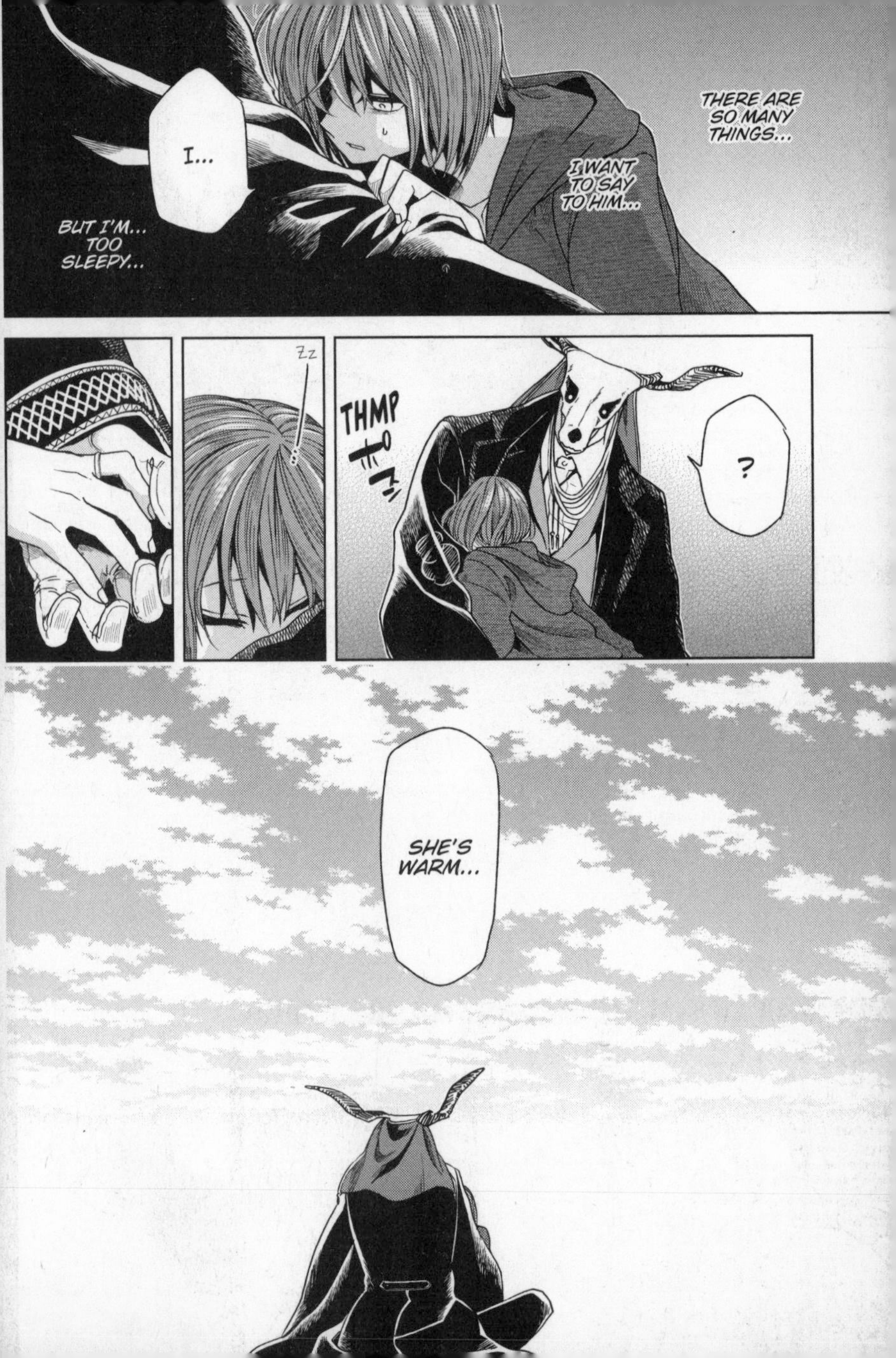
THERE ARE SO MANY THINGS...
I WANT TO SAY TO HIM...
I...
BUT I'M... TOO SLEEPY...
?
THMP
Zz
SHE'S WARM...

Chapter 19: It is a long lane that has no turning.

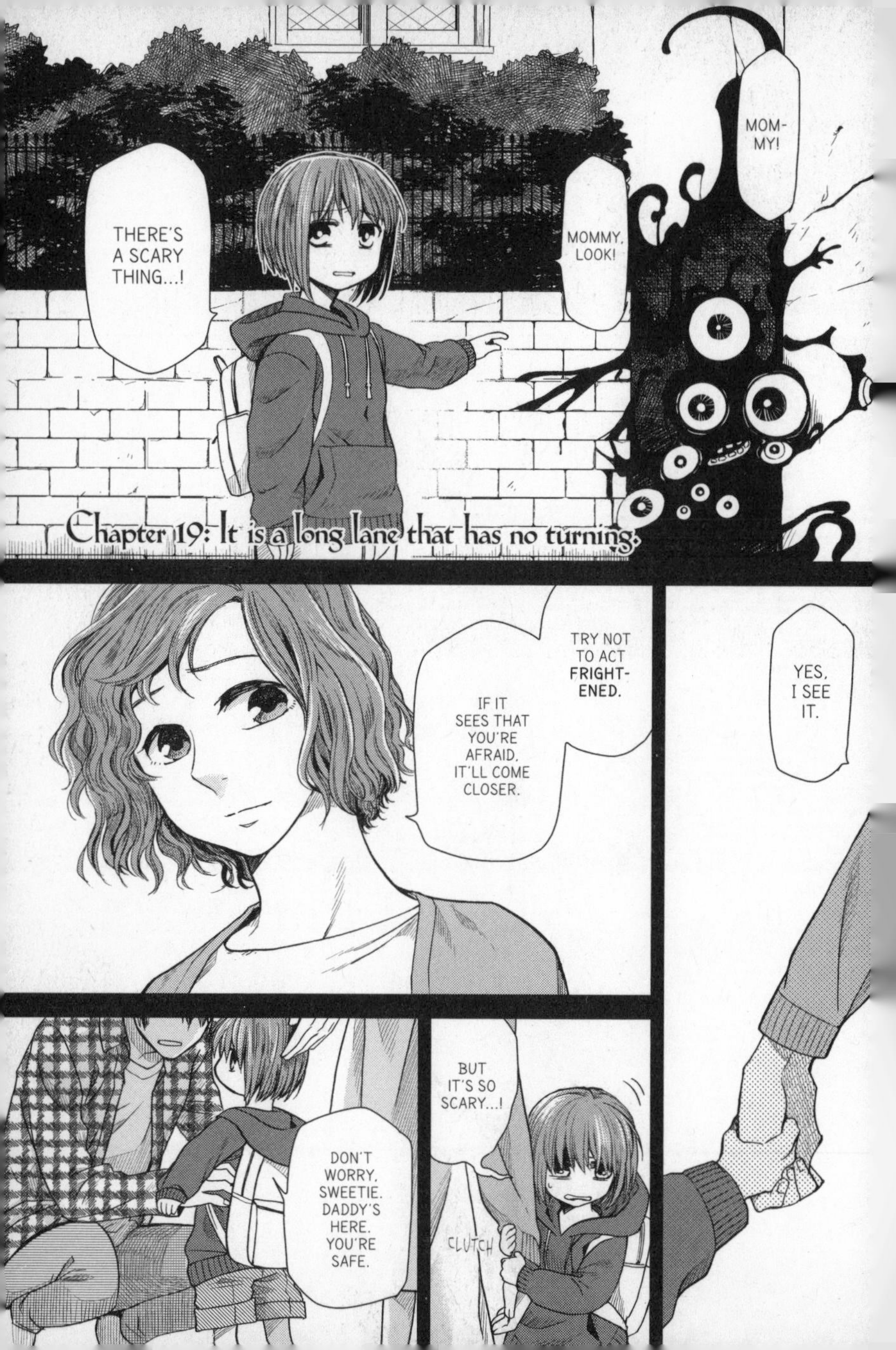
MOM-MY!
MOMMY, LOOK!
THERE'S A SCARY THING...!
YES, I SEE IT.
TRY NOT TO ACT FRIGHT-ENED.
IF IT SEES THAT YOU'RE AFRAID, IT'LL COME CLOSER.
BUT IT'S SO SCARY...!
CLUTCH
DON'T WORRY, SWEETIE. DADDY'S HERE. YOU'RE SAFE.

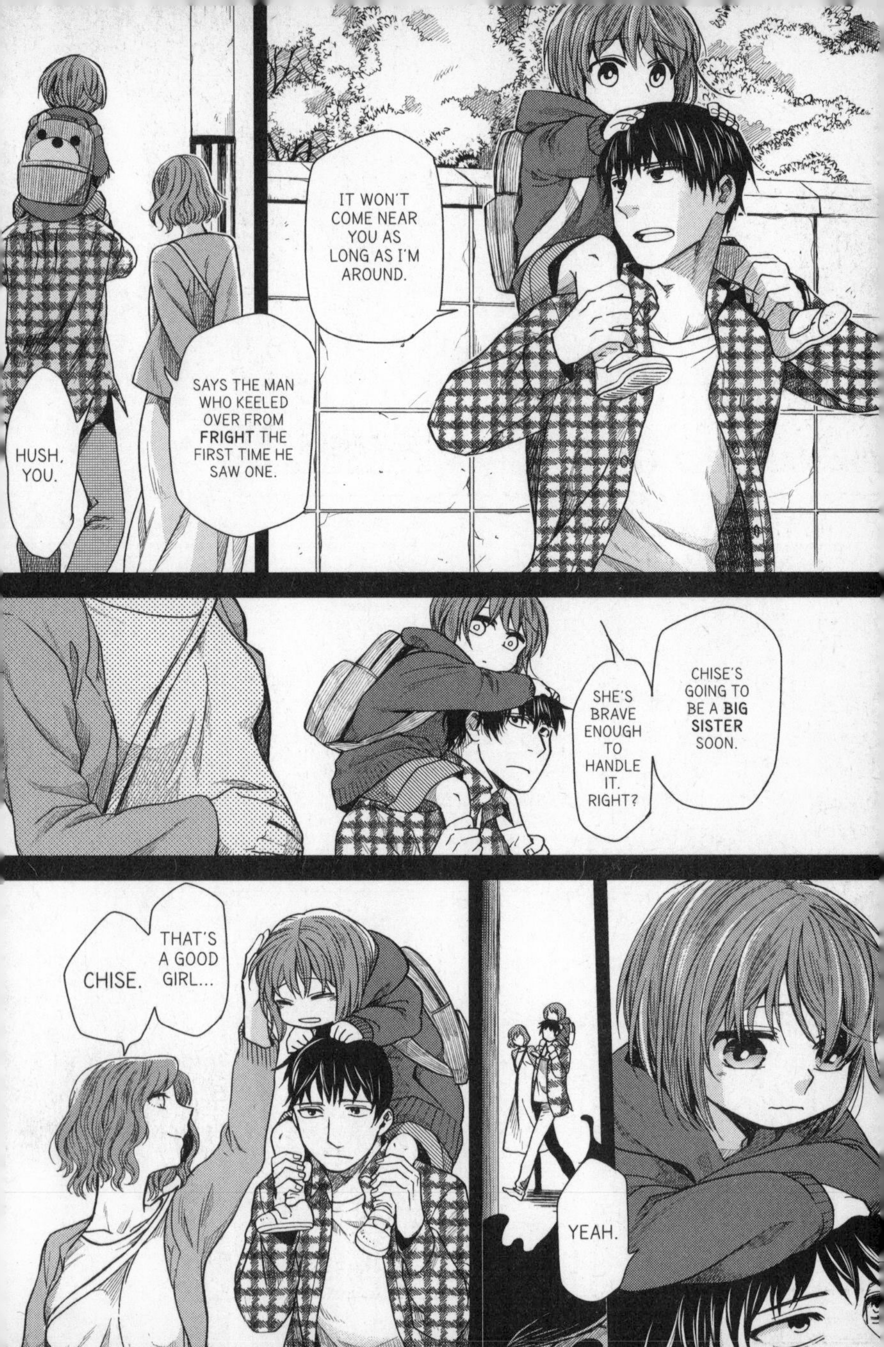
IT WON'T COME NEAR YOU AS LONG AS I'M AROUND.
SAYS THE MAN WHO KEELED OVER FROM **FRIGHT** THE FIRST TIME HE SAW ONE.
HUSH, YOU.
CHISE'S GOING TO BE A **BIG SISTER** SOON.
SHE'S BRAVE ENOUGH TO HANDLE IT. RIGHT?
YEAH.
THAT'S A GOOD GIRL...
CHISE.

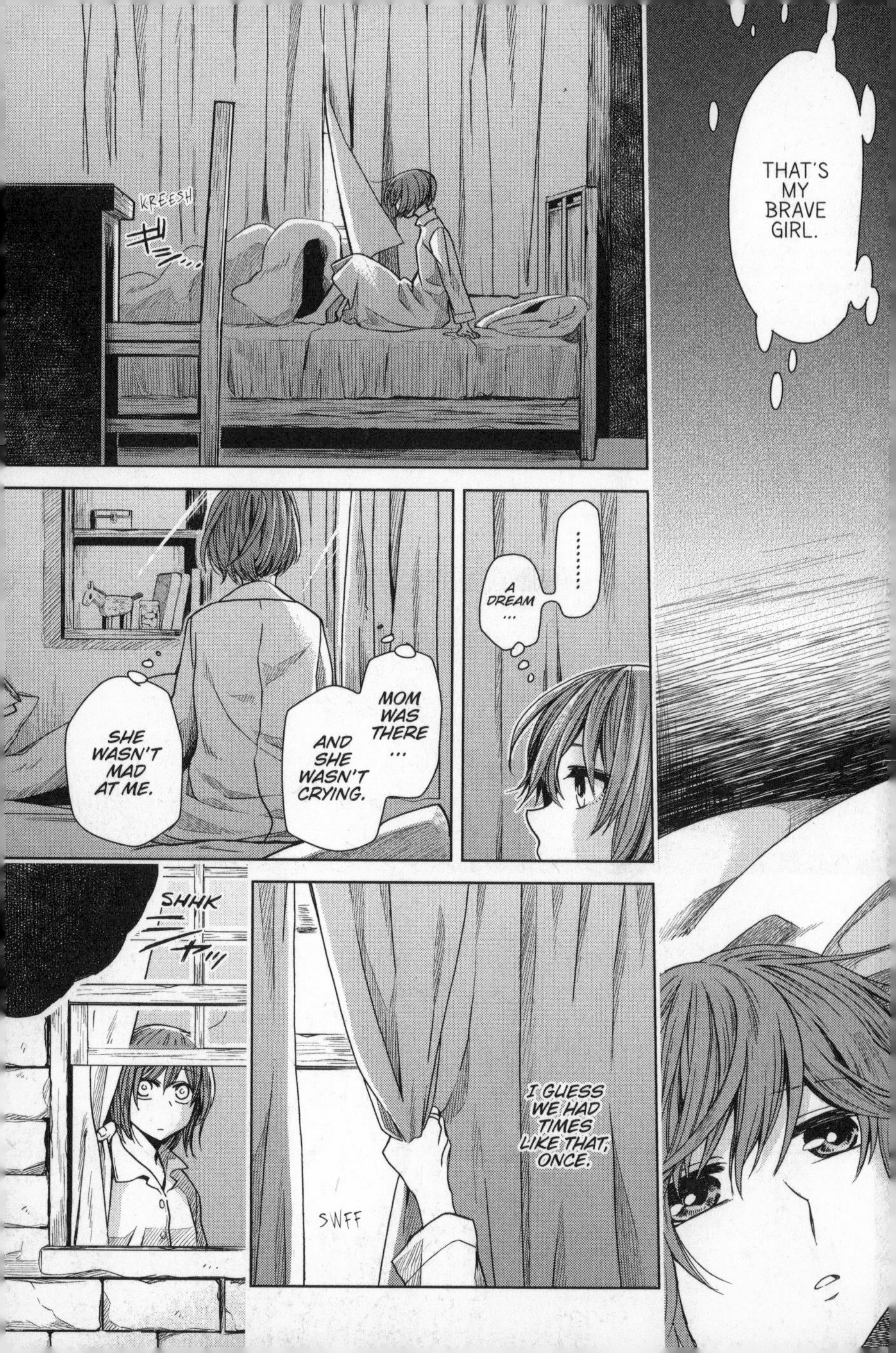
THAT'S MY BRAVE GIRL.
KREESH
......
A DREAM ...
MOM WAS THERE ...
AND SHE WASN'T CRYING.
SHE WASN'T MAD AT ME.
I GUESS WE HAD TIMES LIKE THAT, ONCE.
SWFF
SHHK

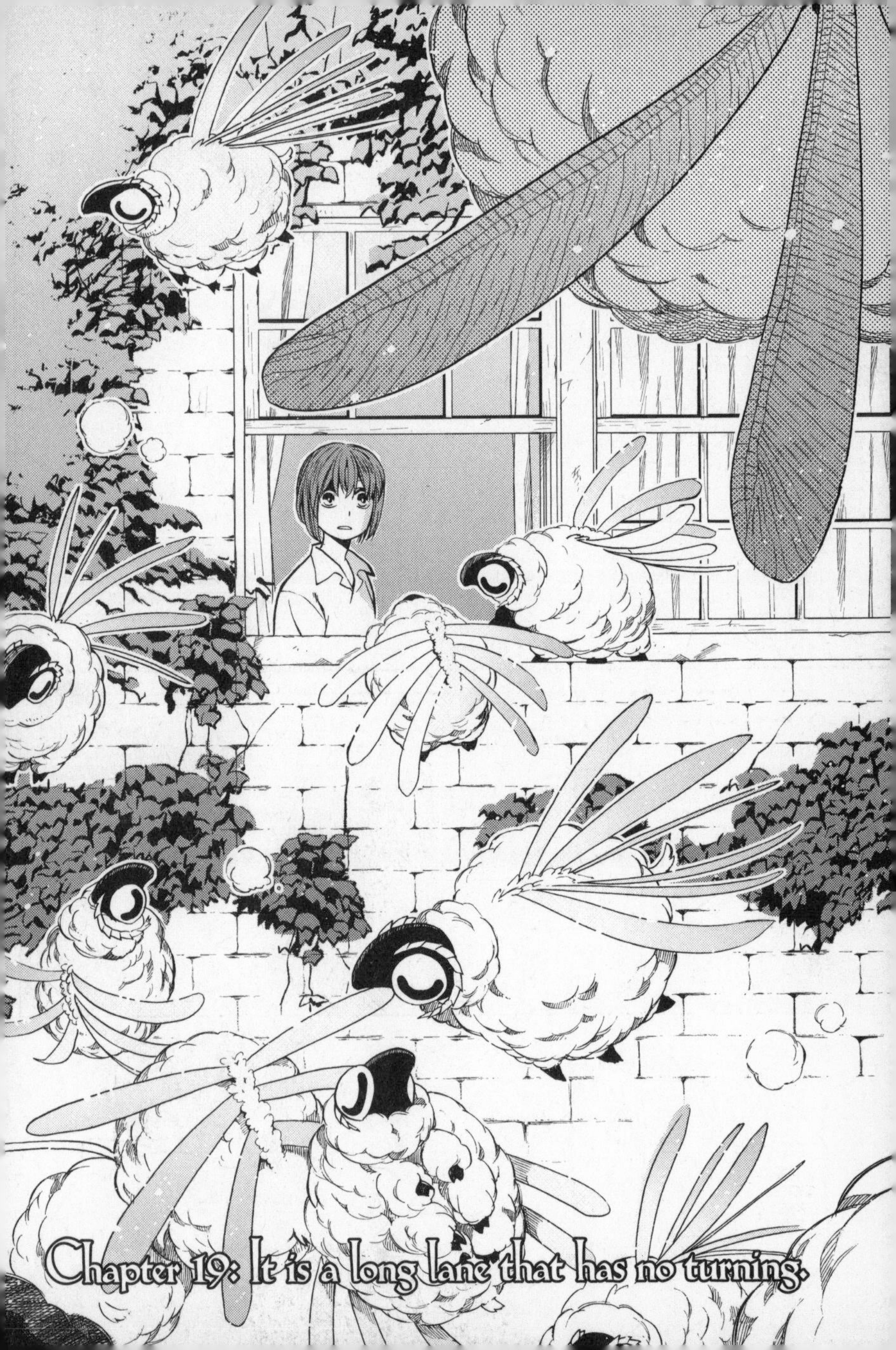
Chapter 19: It is a long lane that has no turning.

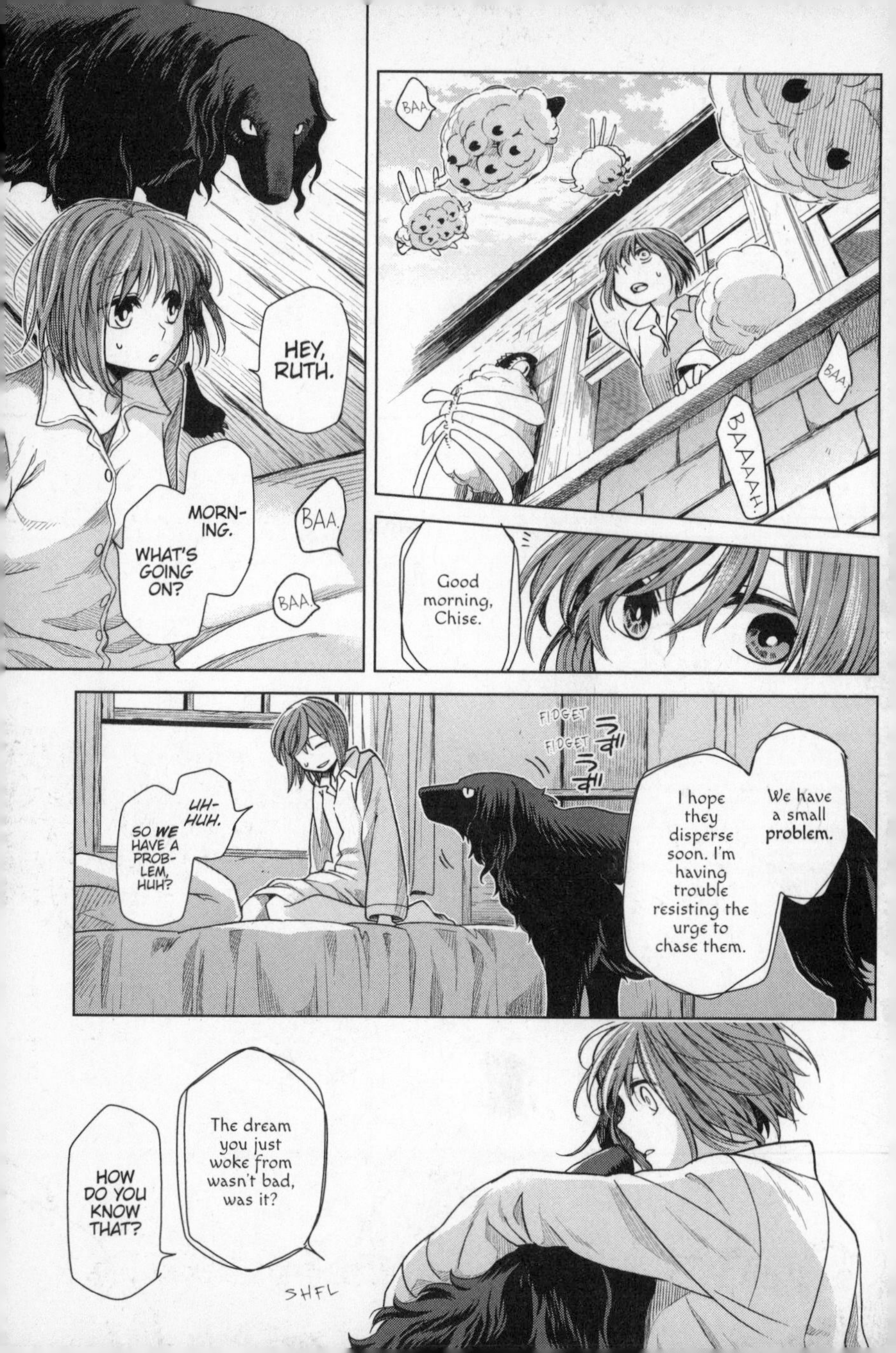
BAA.
BAA.
BAAAAH.
Good morning, Chise.
HEY, RUTH.
MORNING. WHAT'S GOING ON?
BAA.
BAA.
We have a small problem.
I hope they disperse soon. I'm having trouble resisting the urge to chase them.
FIDGET
FIDGET
UH-HUH. SO WE HAVE A PROBLEM, HUH?
The dream you just woke from wasn't bad, was it?
HOW DO YOU KNOW THAT?
SHFL

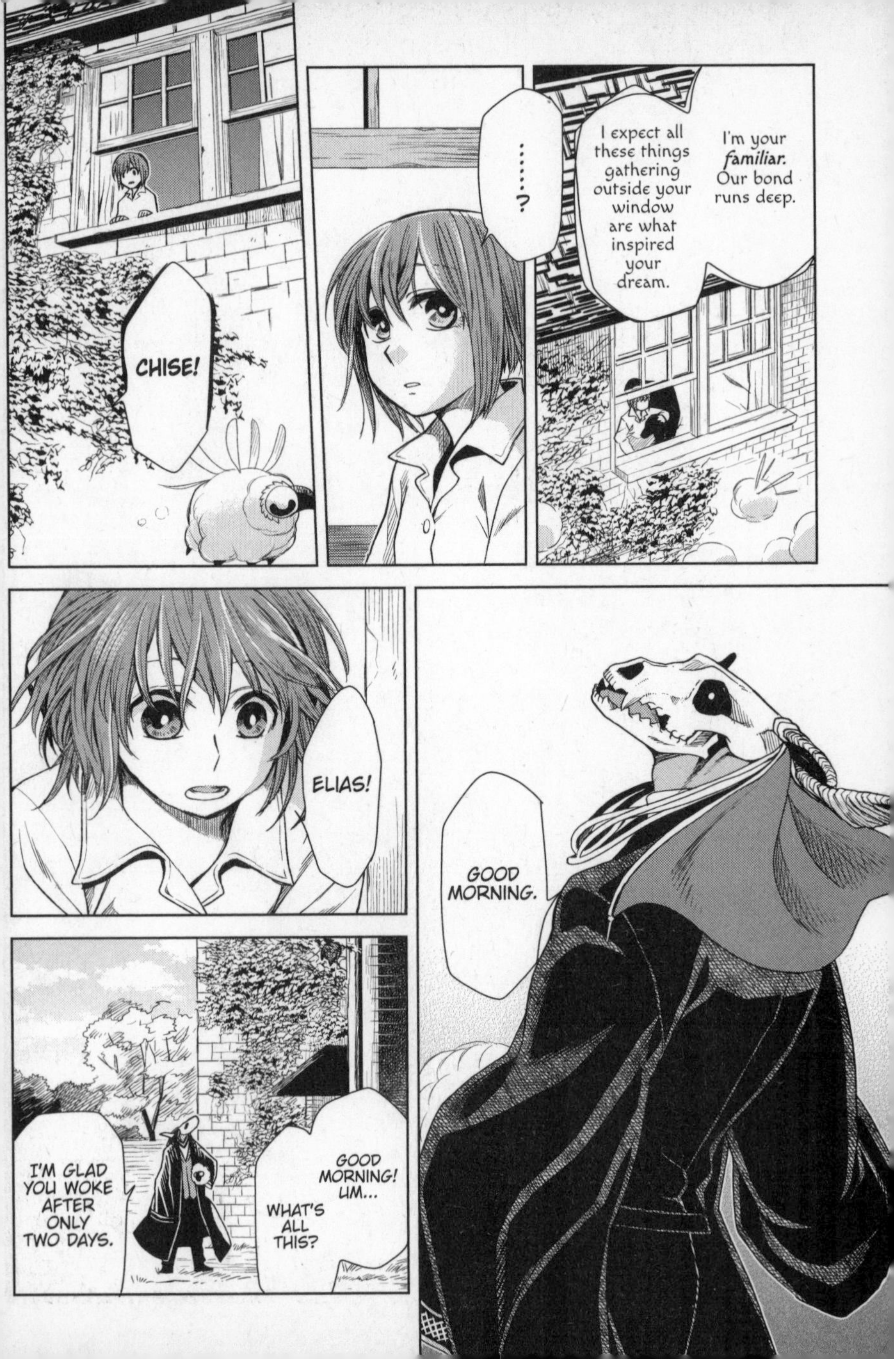
I'm your familiar. Our bond runs deep.
I expect all these things gathering outside your window are what inspired your dream.
......?
CHISE!
GOOD MORNING.
ELIAS!
GOOD MORNING! UM...
WHAT'S ALL THIS?
I'M GLAD YOU WOKE AFTER ONLY TWO DAYS.

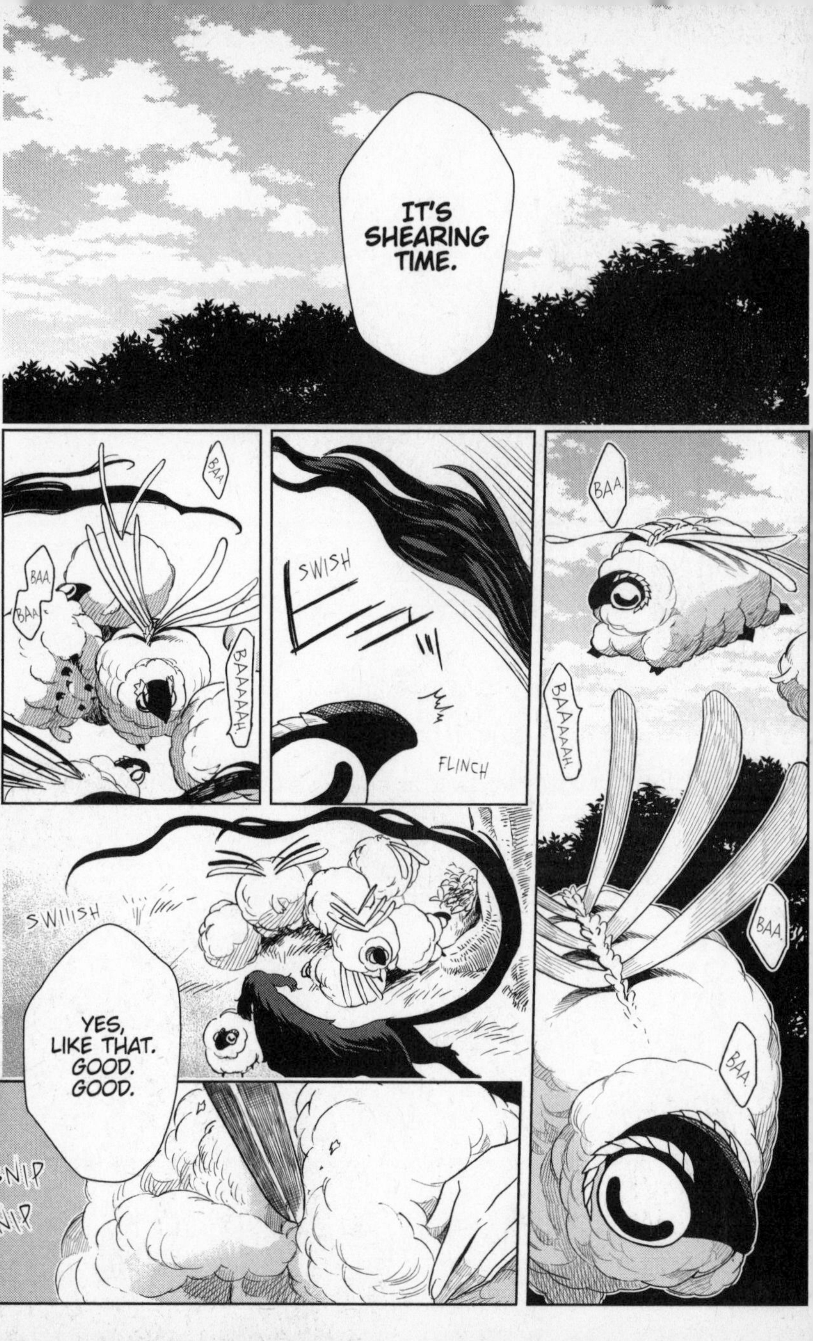
IT'S SHEARING TIME.
BAA.
BAAAAAH.
BAA.
BAA.
SWISH
FLINCH
BAA.
BAA.
BAA.
BAAAAAH.
SWIIISH
YES, LIKE THAT. GOOD. GOOD.
SNIP
SNIP

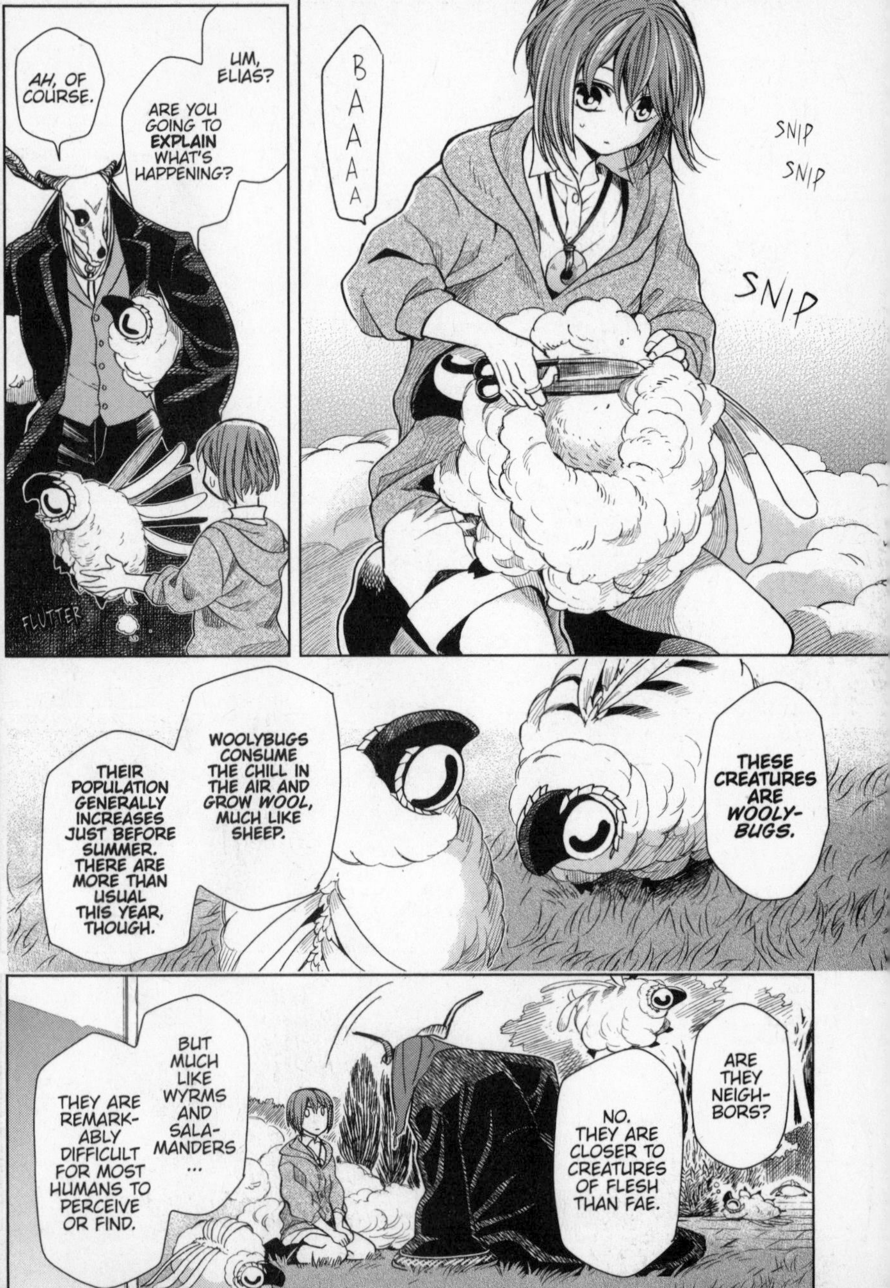
BAAAAA
SNIP
SNIP
SNIP
UM, ELIAS?
ARE YOU GOING TO EXPLAIN WHAT'S HAPPENING?
AH, OF COURSE.
FLUTTER
THESE CREATURES ARE WOOLY-BUGS.
WOOLYBUGS CONSUME THE CHILL IN THE AIR AND GROW WOOL, MUCH LIKE SHEEP.
THEIR POPULATION GENERALLY INCREASES JUST BEFORE SUMMER. THERE ARE MORE THAN USUAL THIS YEAR, THOUGH.
ARE THEY NEIGH-BORS?
NO. THEY ARE CLOSER TO CREATURES OF FLESH THAN FAE.
BUT MUCH LIKE WYRMS AND SALA-MANDERS...
THEY ARE REMARK-ABLY DIFFICULT FOR MOST HUMANS TO PERCEIVE OR FIND.

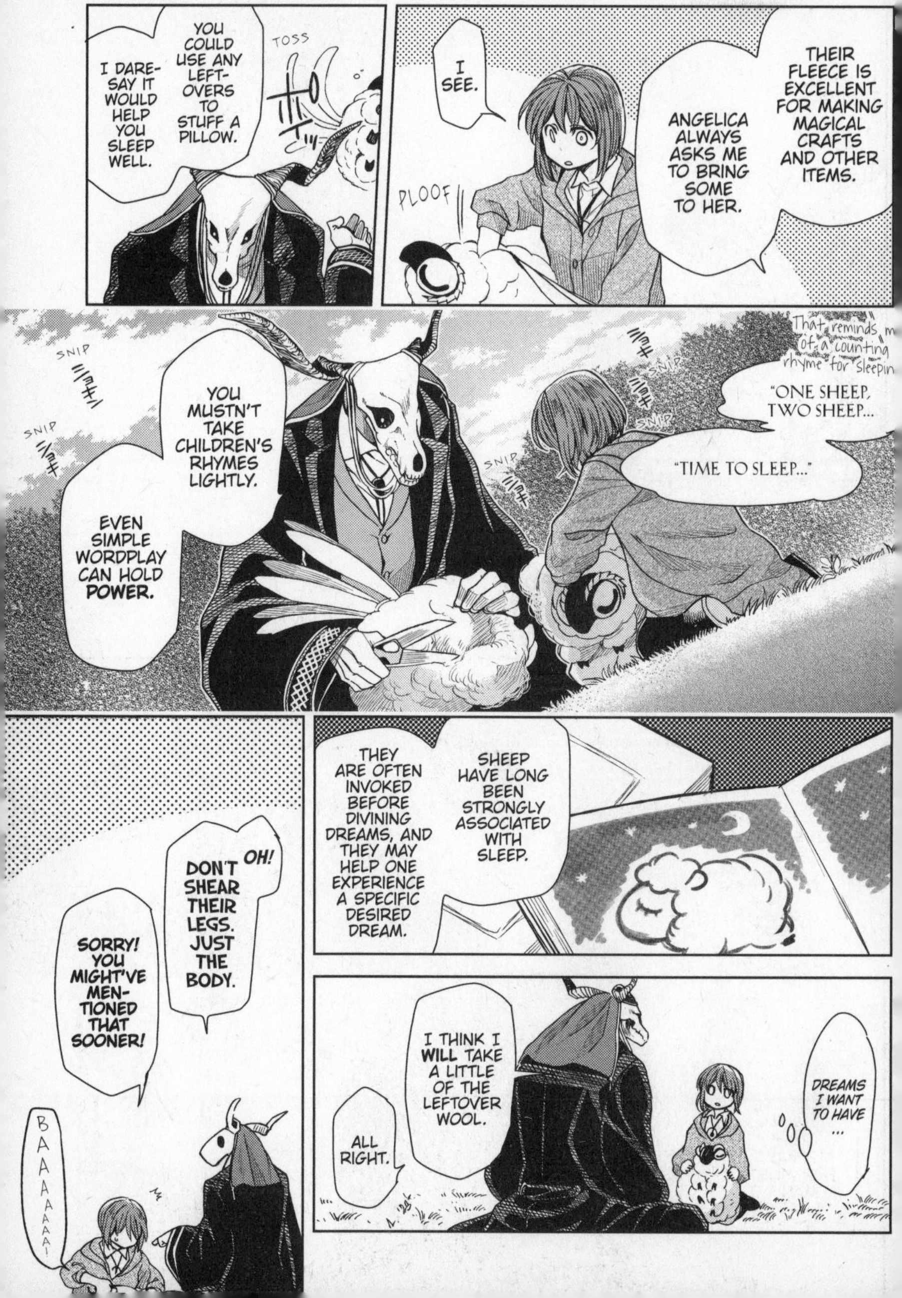
THEIR FLEECE IS EXCELLENT FOR MAKING MAGICAL CRAFTS AND OTHER ITEMS.
ANGELICA ALWAYS ASKS ME TO BRING SOME TO HER.
I SEE.
PLOOF
YOU COULD USE ANY LEFT-OVERS TO STUFF A PILLOW.
I DARE-SAY IT WOULD HELP YOU SLEEP WELL.
TOSS
That reminds m of a counting rhyme for sleepin
"ONE SHEEP, TWO SHEEP...
"TIME TO SLEEP..."
SNIP
SNIP
SNIP
SNIP
SNIP
YOU MUSTN'T TAKE CHILDREN'S RHYMES LIGHTLY.
EVEN SIMPLE WORDPLAY CAN HOLD POWER.
SHEEP HAVE LONG BEEN STRONGLY ASSOCIATED WITH SLEEP.
THEY ARE OFTEN INVOKED BEFORE DIVINING DREAMS, AND THEY MAY HELP ONE EXPERIENCE A SPECIFIC DESIRED DREAM.
DREAMS I WANT TO HAVE ...
I THINK I WILL TAKE A LITTLE OF THE LEFTOVER WOOL.
ALL RIGHT.
OH!
DON'T SHEAR THEIR LEGS. JUST THE BODY.
SORRY! YOU MIGHT'VE MEN-TIONED THAT SOONER!
BAAAAAA!

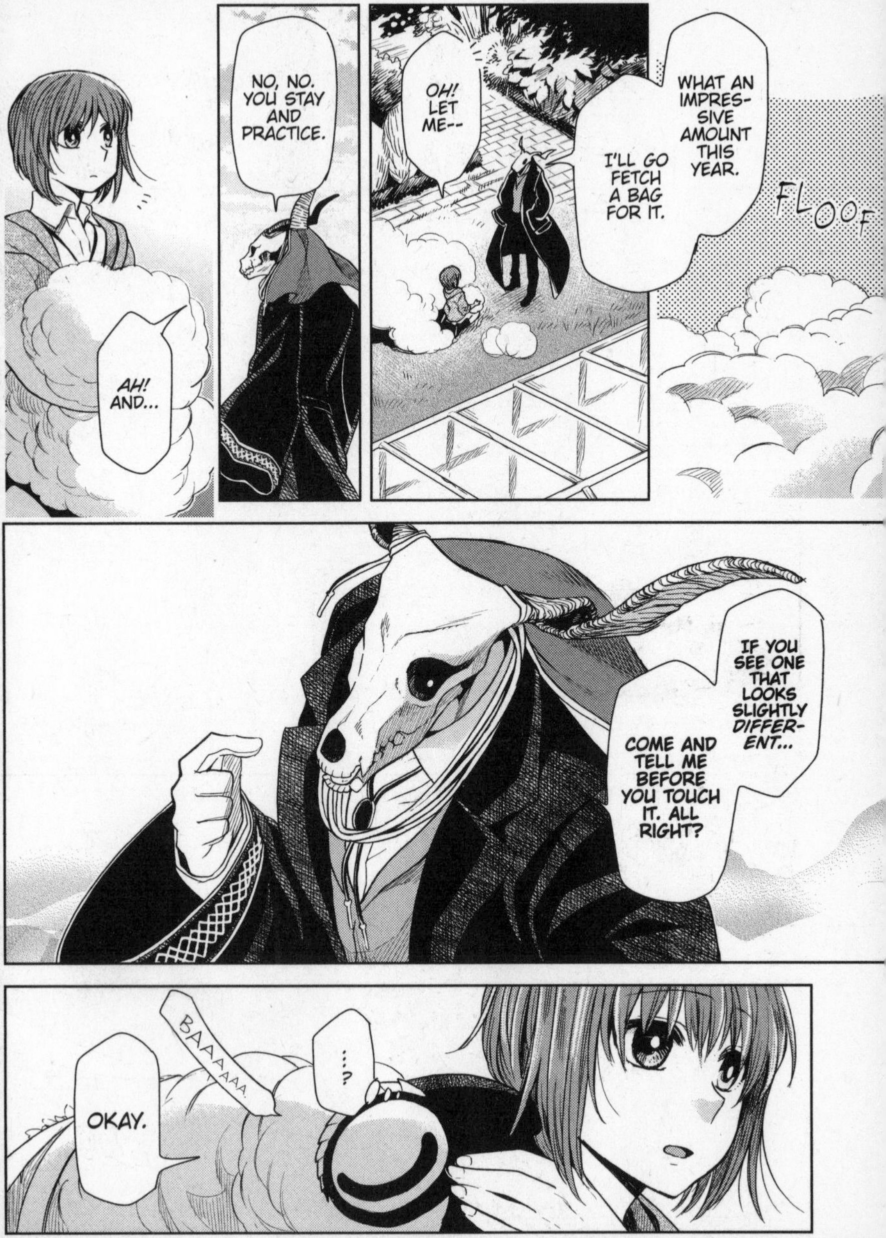
FLOOF
WHAT AN IMPRESSIVE AMOUNT THIS YEAR.
I'LL GO FETCH A BAG FOR IT.
OH! LET ME--
NO, NO. YOU STAY AND PRACTICE.
AH! AND...
IF YOU SEE ONE THAT LOOKS SLIGHTLY DIFFERENT...
COME AND TELL ME BEFORE YOU TOUCH IT. ALL RIGHT?
...?
BAAAAAAA
OKAY.

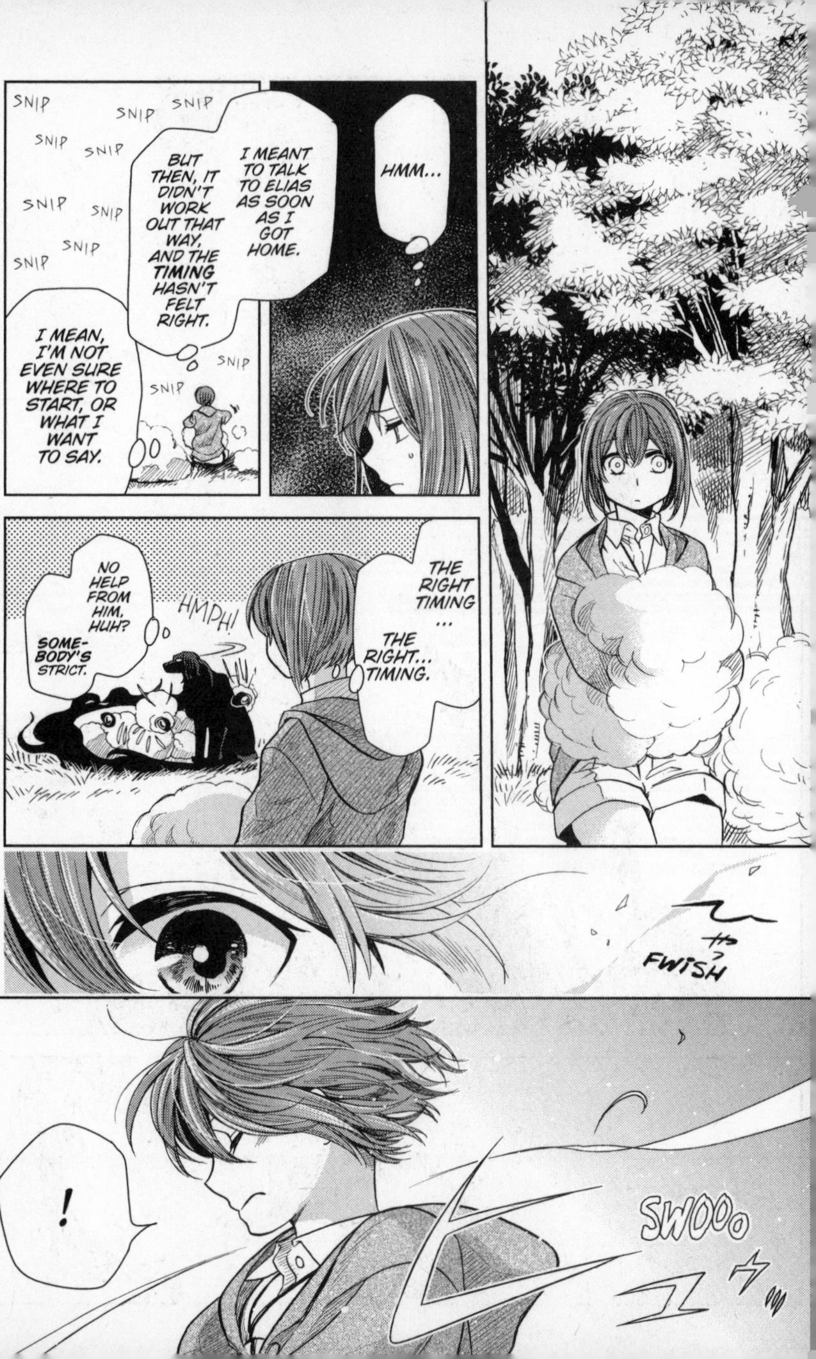
HMM...
I MEANT TO TALK TO ELIAS AS SOON AS I GOT HOME.
BUT THEN, IT DIDN'T WORK OUT THAT WAY, AND THE TIMING HASN'T FELT RIGHT.
SNIP SNIP SNIP SNIP SNIP SNIP SNIP SNIP SNIP
I MEAN, I'M NOT EVEN SURE WHERE TO START, OR WHAT I WANT TO SAY.
SNIP SNIP
THE RIGHT TIMING...
THE RIGHT... TIMING.
HMPH!
NO HELP FROM HIM, HUH? SOMEBODY'S STRICT.
FWISH
!
SWOOo

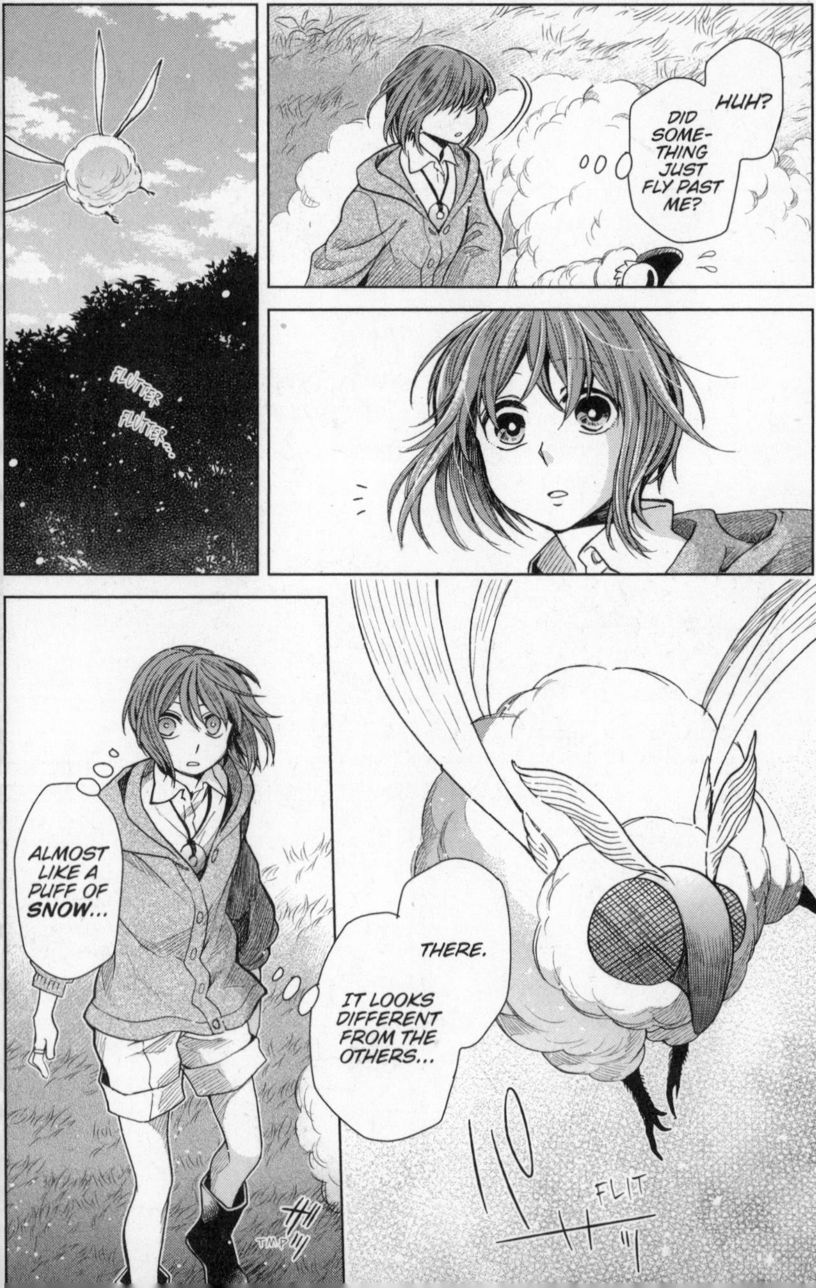
HUH?
DID SOMETHING JUST FLY PAST ME?
FLUTTER
FLUTTER...
THERE.
IT LOOKS DIFFERENT FROM THE OTHERS...
FLIT
ALMOST LIKE A PUFF OF SNOW...
TMP

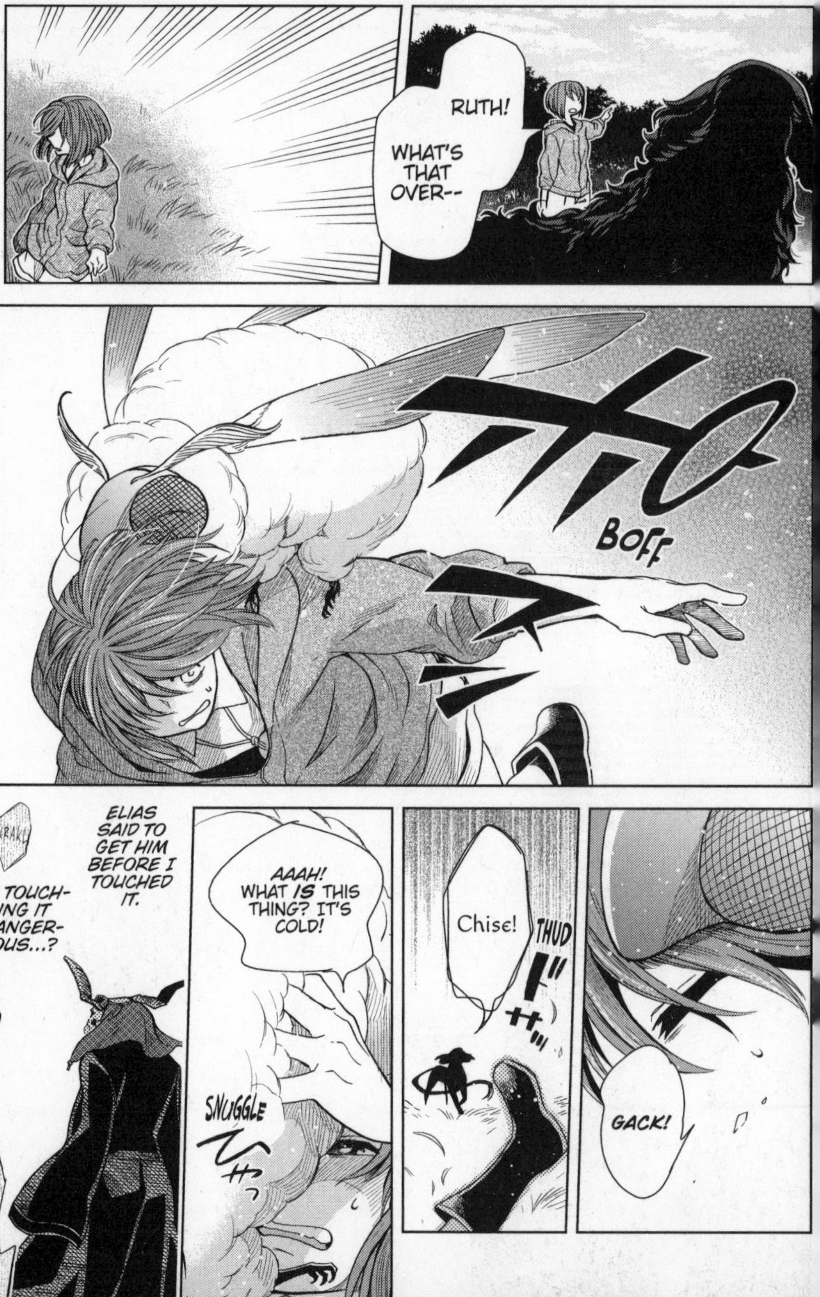
RUTH!
WHAT'S THAT OVER--
BOFF
GACK!
Chise!
THUD
AAAH! WHAT *IS* THIS THING? IT'S COLD!
SNUGGLE
ELIAS SAID TO GET HIM BEFORE I TOUCHED IT.
IS TOUCHING IT DANGEROUS...?
KRAK
KRAK
KRIK
KRAK

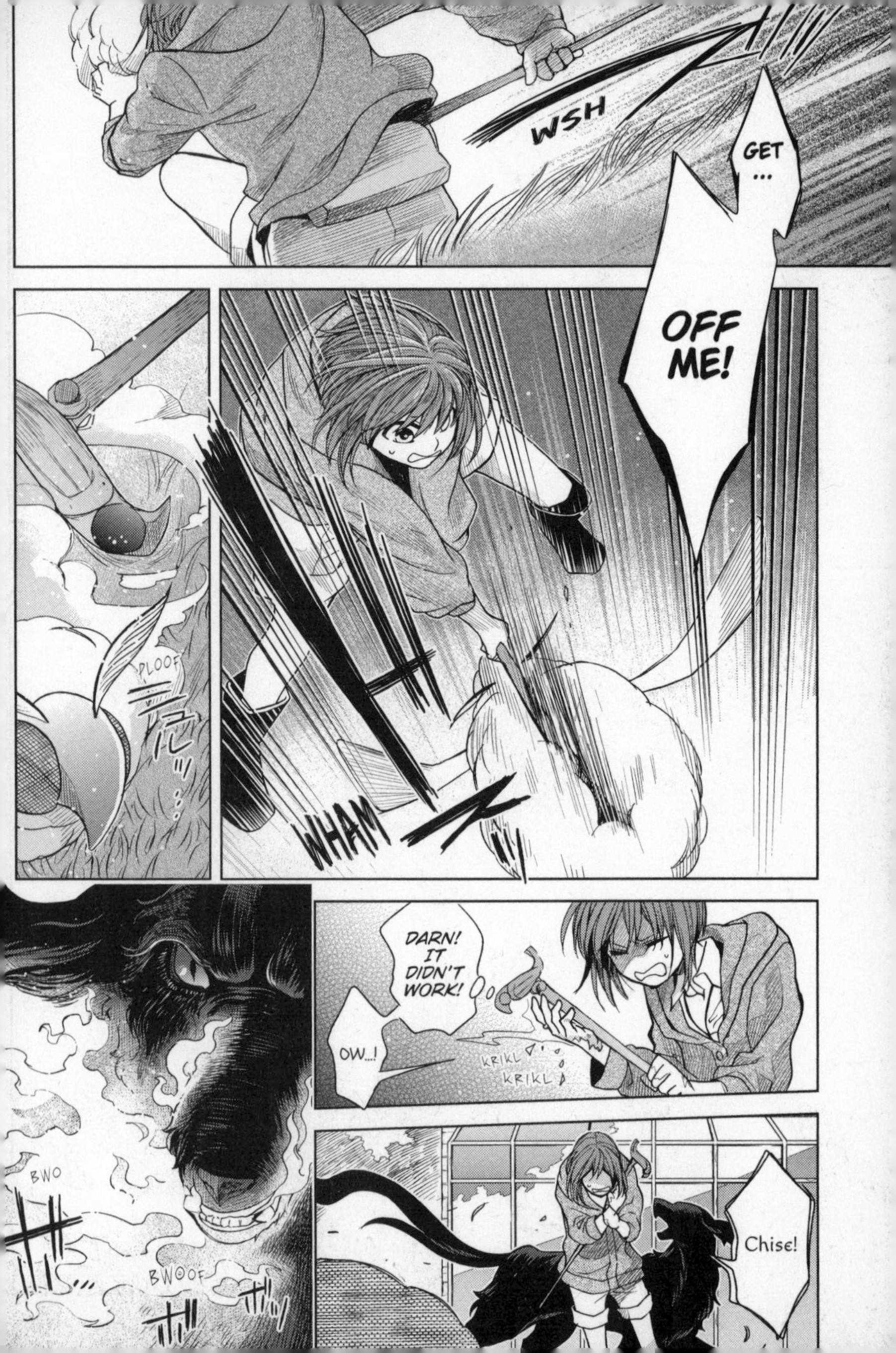
WSH
GET...
OFF ME!
WHAM
PLOOF
DARN! IT DIDN'T WORK!
OW...!
KRIKL
KRIKL
Chise!
BWO
BWOOF

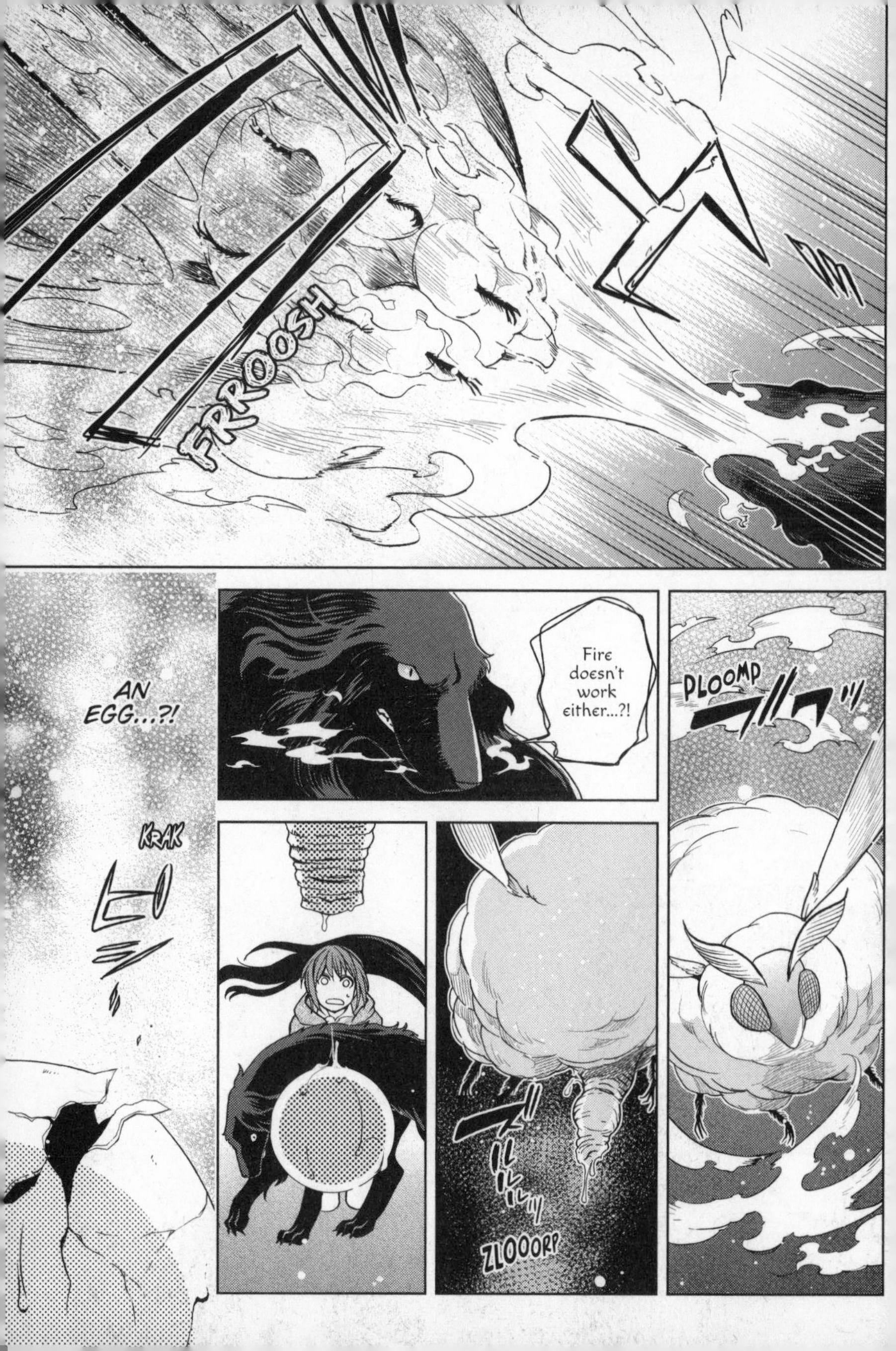
FRROOSH
PLOOMP
Fire doesn't work either...?!
ZLOOORP
AN EGG...?!
KRAK

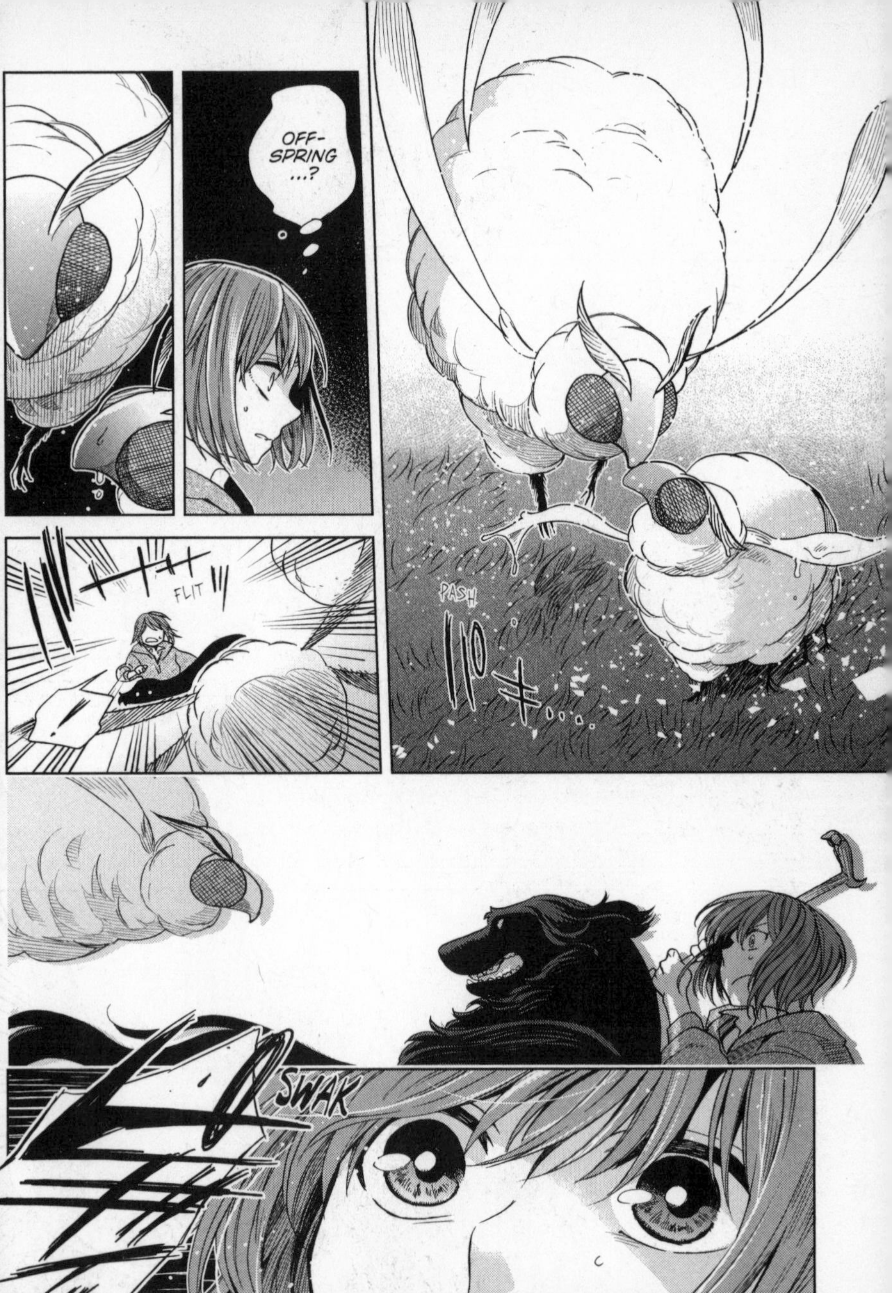
PASH
OFF-SPRING ...?
FLIT
SWAK

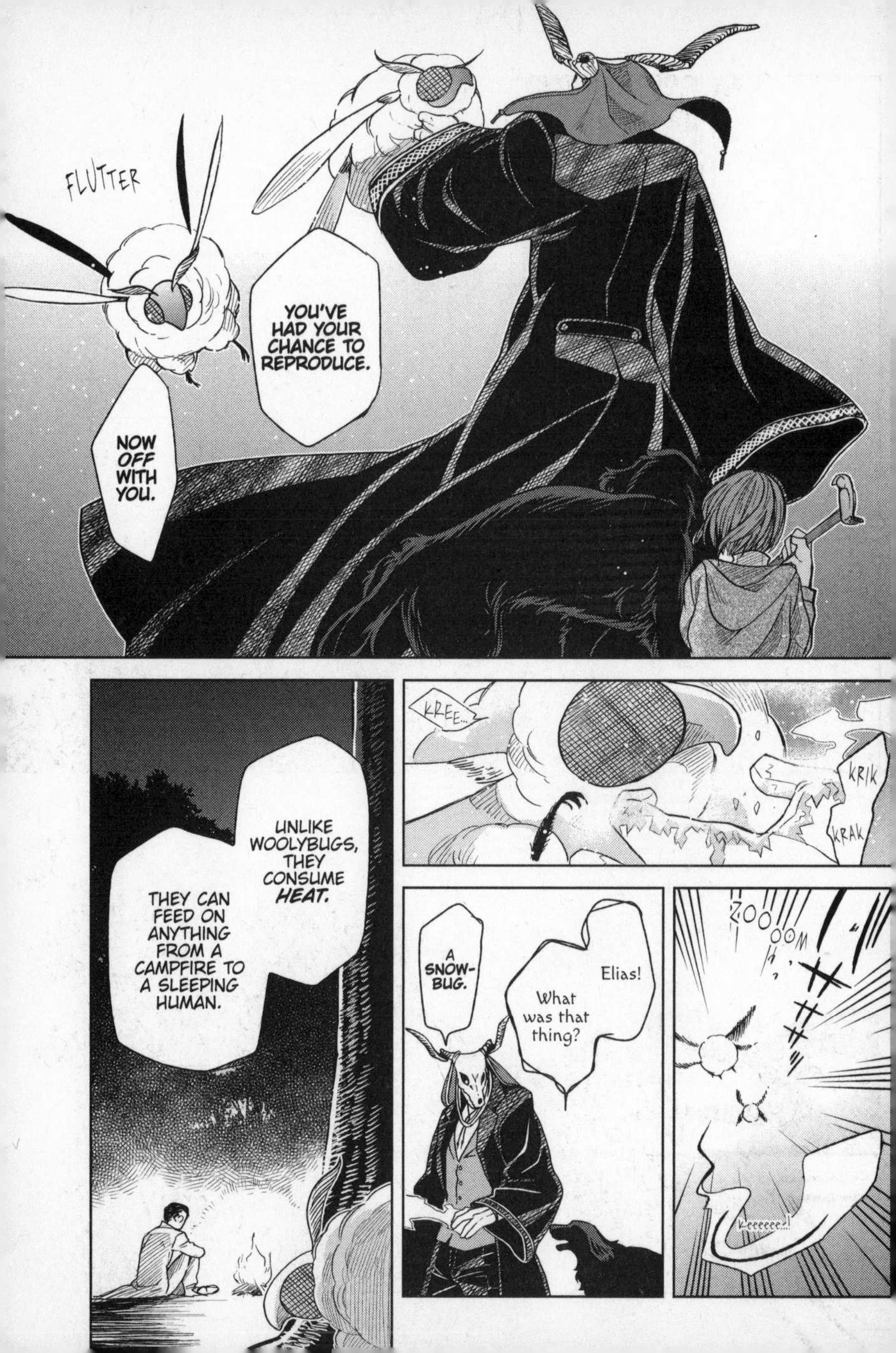
FLUTTER
YOU'VE HAD YOUR CHANCE TO REPRODUCE.
NOW OFF WITH YOU.
KRIK
KRAK
KREE...
ZOOOOM
Keeeeee..!
Elias! What was that thing?
A SNOWBUG.
UNLIKE WOOLYBUGS, THEY CONSUME *HEAT.*
THEY CAN FEED ON ANYTHING FROM A CAMPFIRE TO A SLEEPING HUMAN.

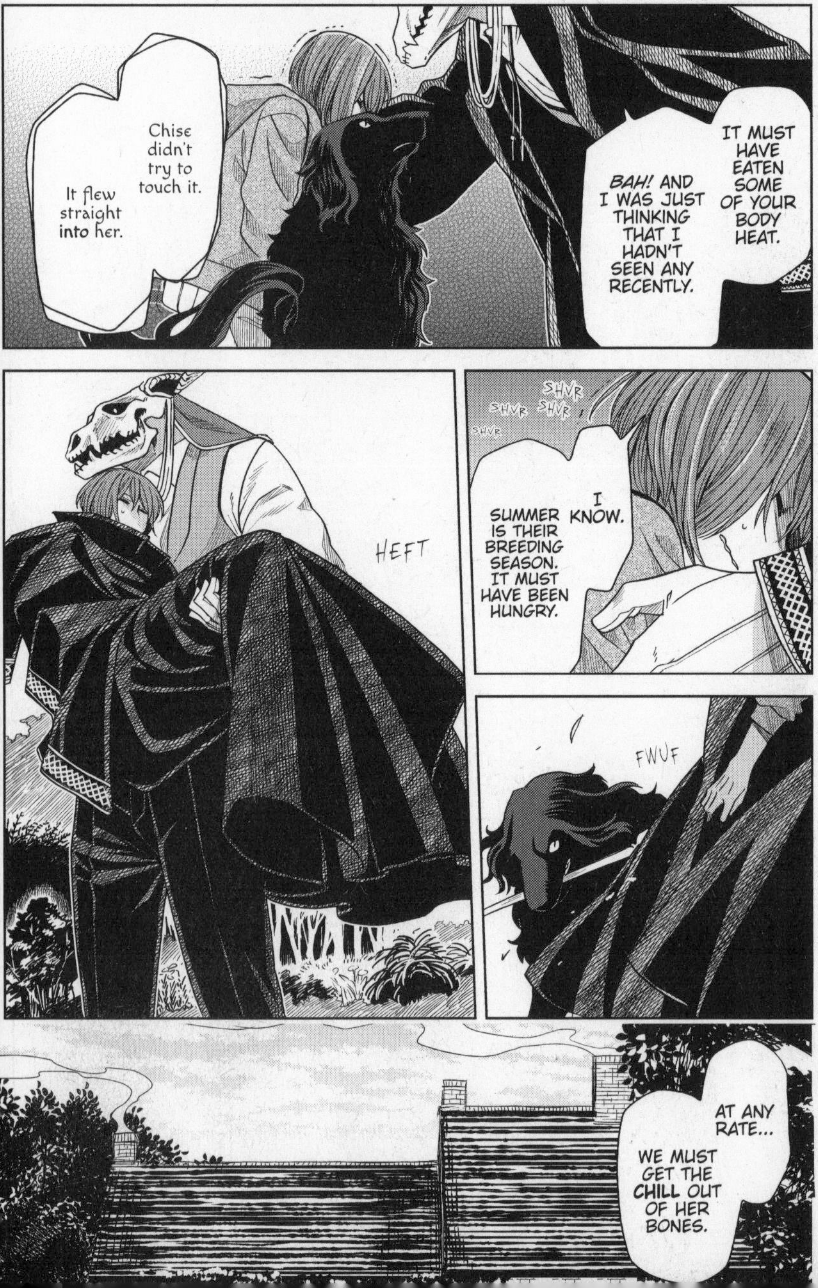
IT MUST HAVE EATEN SOME OF YOUR BODY HEAT.
BAH! AND I WAS JUST THINKING THAT I HADN'T SEEN ANY RECENTLY.
Chise didn't try to touch it.
It flew straight into her.
SHVR SHVR SHVR SHVR
I KNOW.
SUMMER IS THEIR BREEDING SEASON. IT MUST HAVE BEEN HUNGRY.
FWUF
HEFT
AT ANY RATE...
WE MUST GET THE CHILL OUT OF HER BONES.

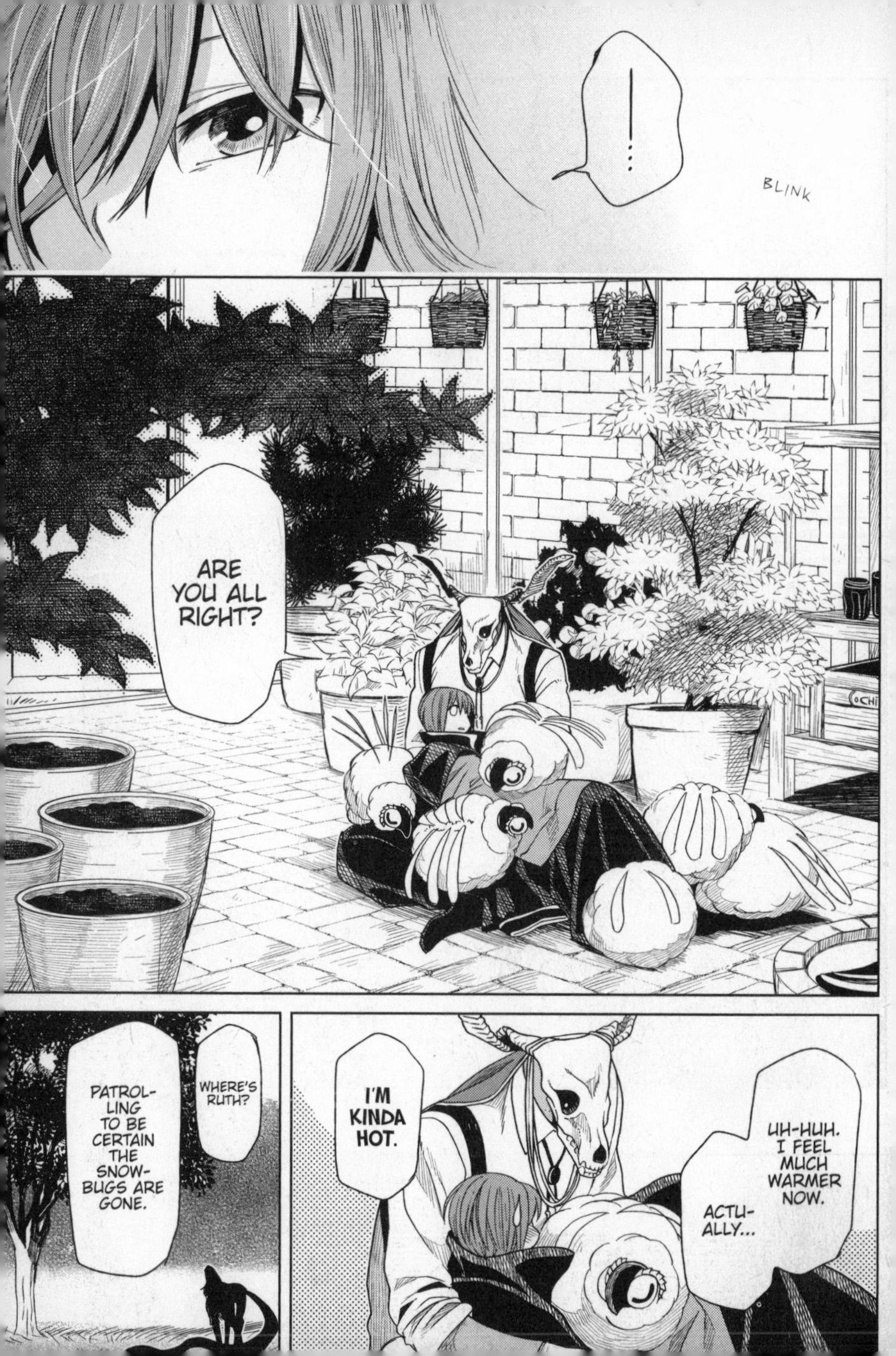
...!
BLINK
ARE YOU ALL RIGHT?
UH-HUH. I FEEL MUCH WARMER NOW.
ACTU-ALLY...
I'M KINDA HOT.
WHERE'S RUTH?
PATROL-LING TO BE CERTAIN THE SNOW-BUGS ARE GONE.

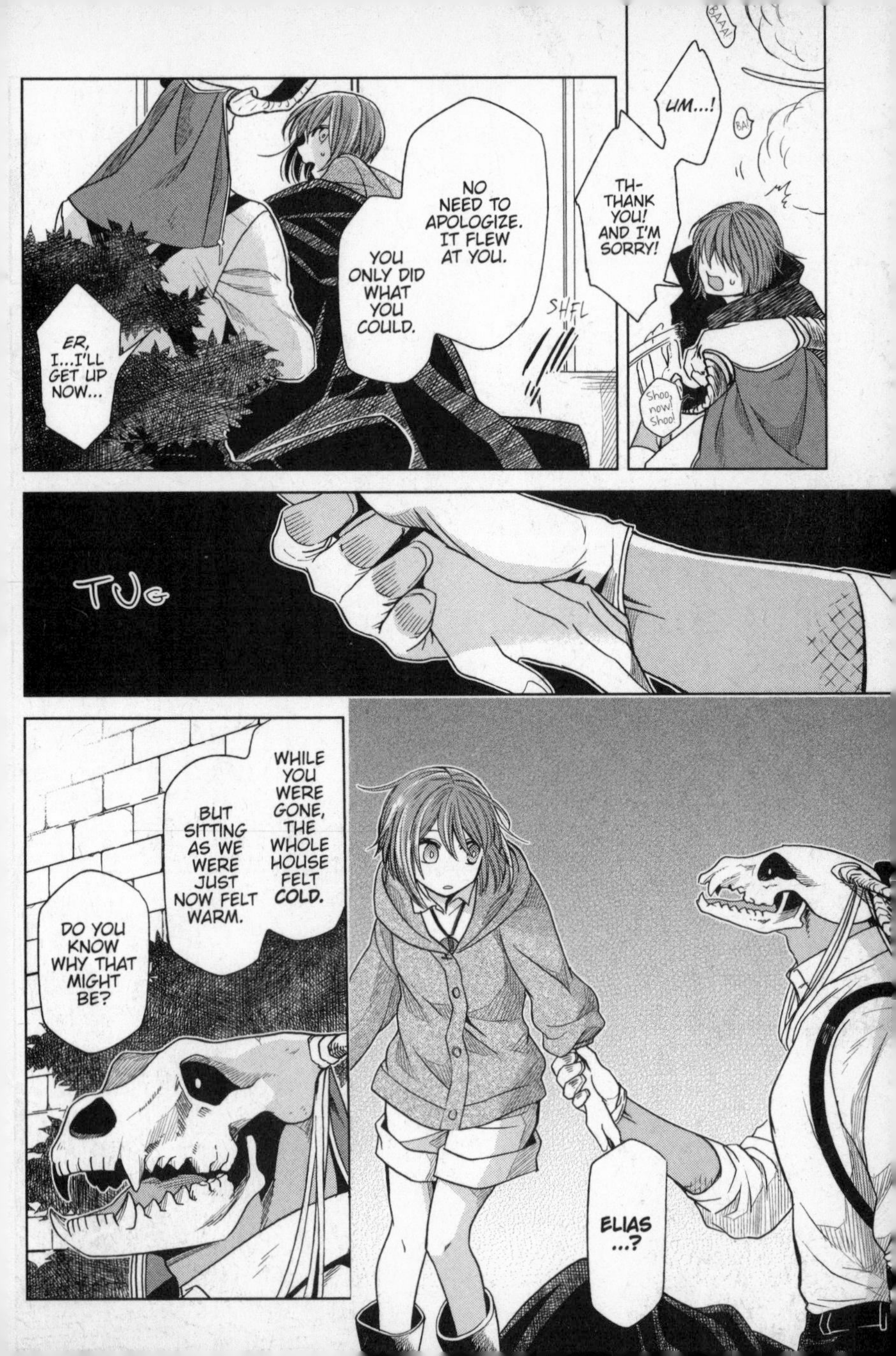
BAAA!
UM...!
BA!
TH-THANK YOU! AND I'M SORRY!
Shoo, now! Shoo!
NO NEED TO APOLOGIZE. IT FLEW AT YOU.
YOU ONLY DID WHAT YOU COULD.
SHFL
ER, I...I'LL GET UP NOW...
TUG
ELIAS ...?
WHILE YOU WERE GONE, THE WHOLE HOUSE FELT COLD.
BUT SITTING AS WE WERE JUST NOW FELT WARM.
DO YOU KNOW WHY THAT MIGHT BE?

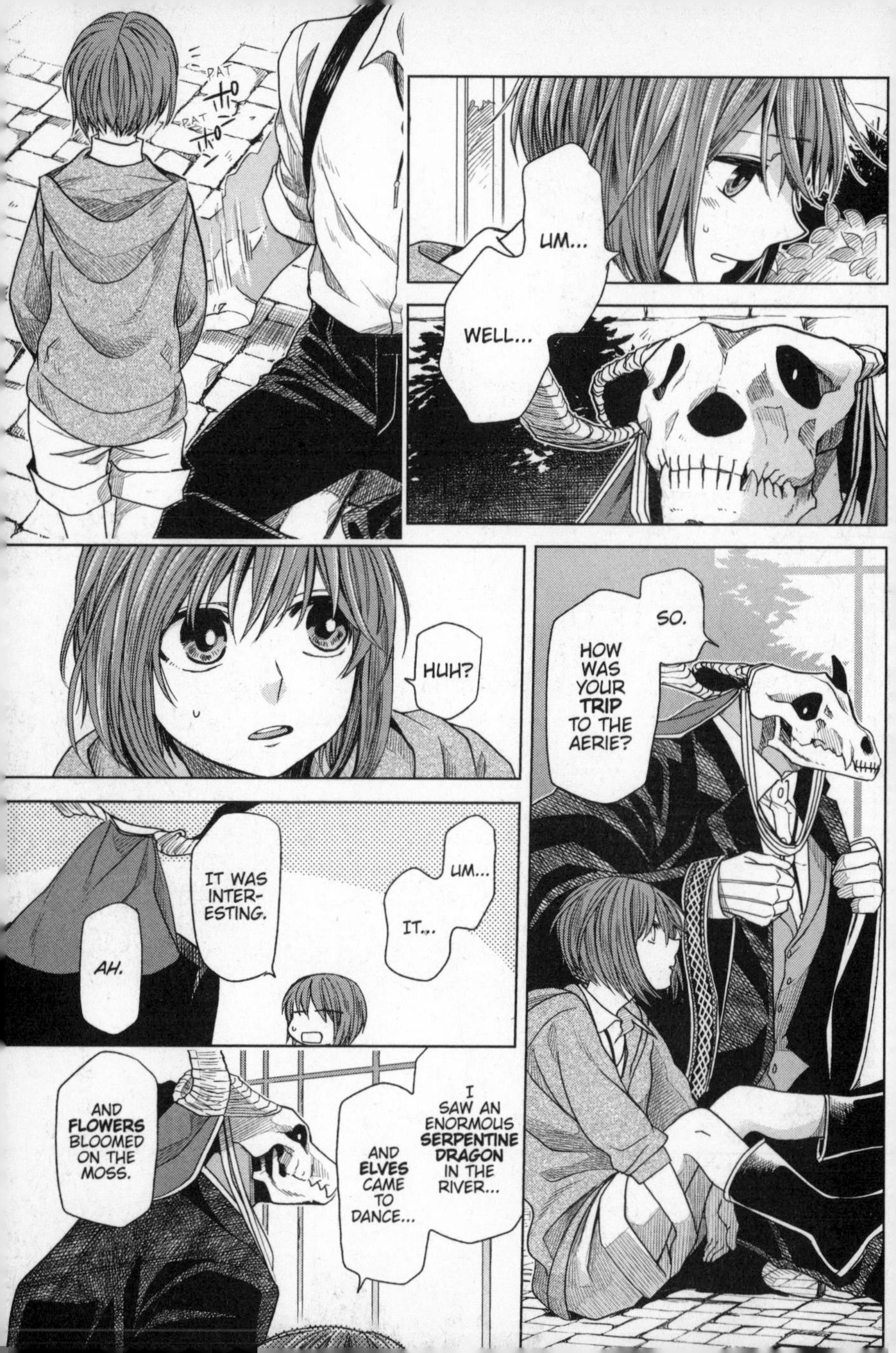
UM...
WELL...
PAT
PAT
SO.
HOW WAS YOUR TRIP TO THE AERIE?
HUH?
UM...
IT...
IT WAS INTER-ESTING.
AH.
I SAW AN ENORMOUS SERPENTINE DRAGON IN THE RIVER...
AND ELVES CAME TO DANCE...
AND FLOWERS BLOOMED ON THE MOSS.

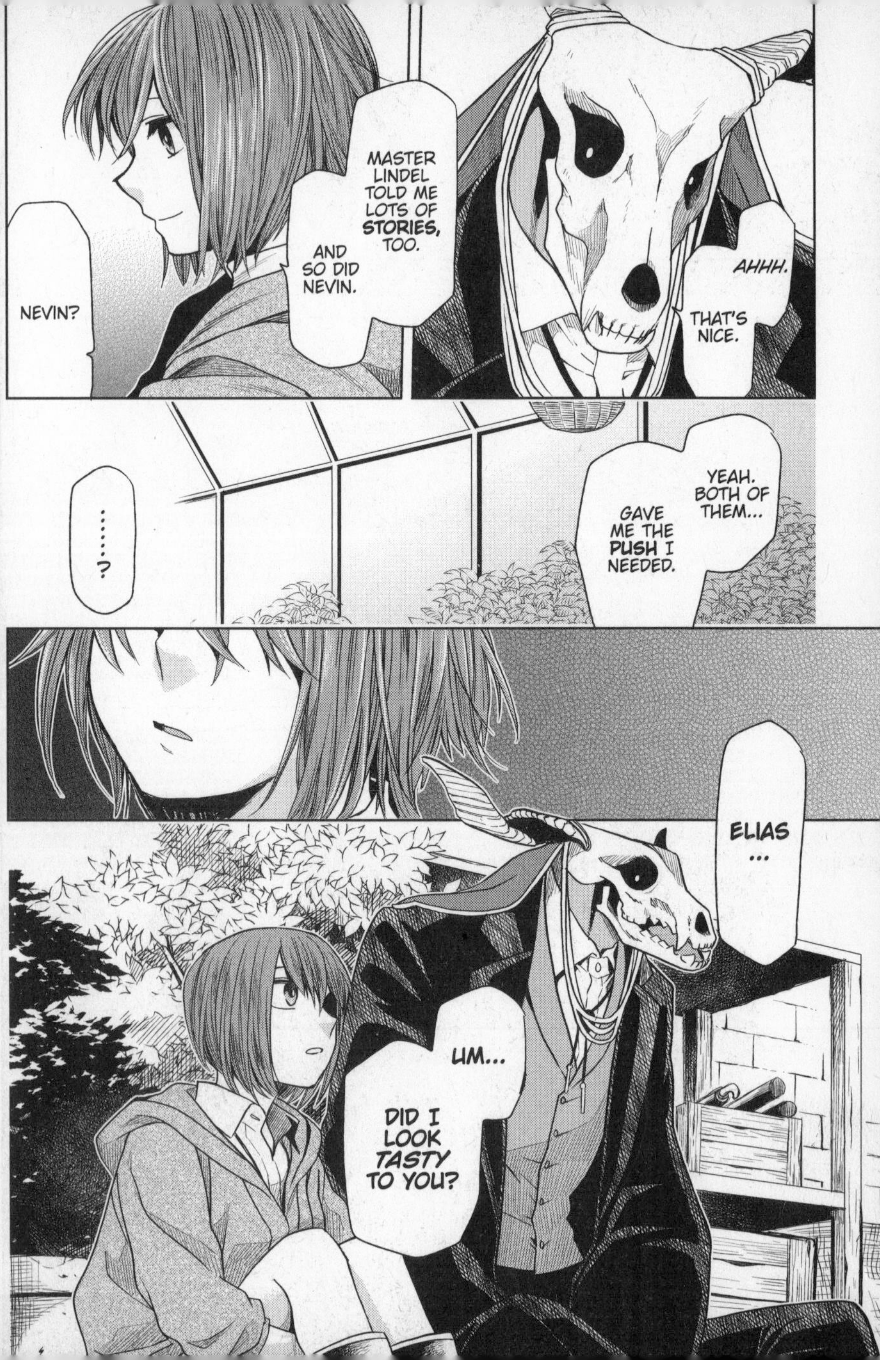
MASTER LINDEL TOLD ME LOTS OF STORIES, TOO.
AHHH. THAT'S NICE.
AND SO DID NEVIN.
NEVIN?
YEAH. BOTH OF THEM... GAVE ME THE PUSH I NEEDED.
......?
ELIAS ...
UM...
DID I LOOK TASTY TO YOU?

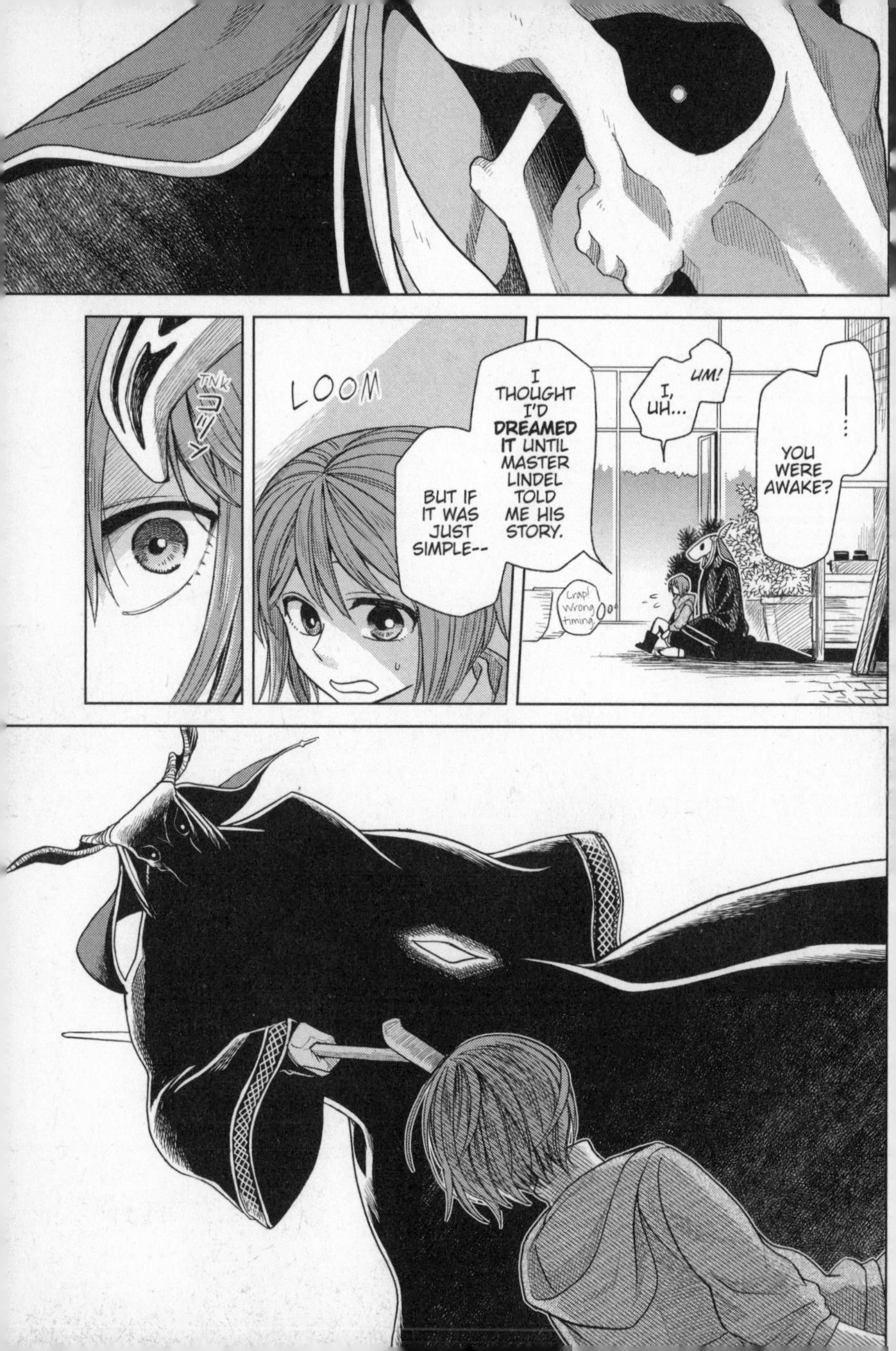

...!
YOU WERE AWAKE?
UM! I, UH...
Crap! Wrong timing.
I THOUGHT I'D **DREAMED IT** UNTIL MASTER LINDEL TOLD ME HIS STORY.
BUT IF IT WAS JUST SIMPLE--
LOOM
TNK

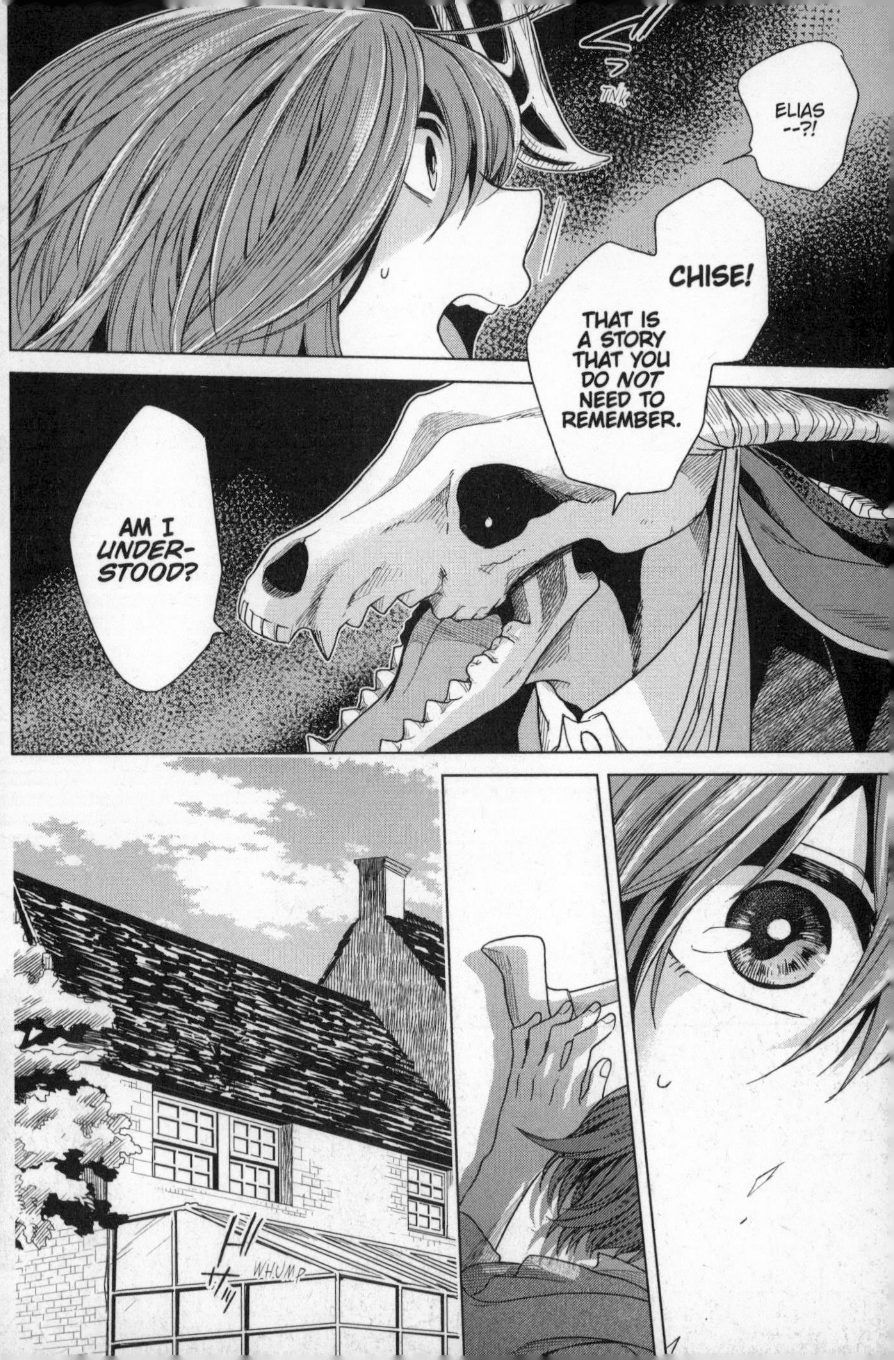
ELIAS --?!
TNK
CHISE!
THAT IS A STORY THAT YOU DO *NOT* NEED TO REMEMBER.
AM I UNDER-STOOD?
WHUMP

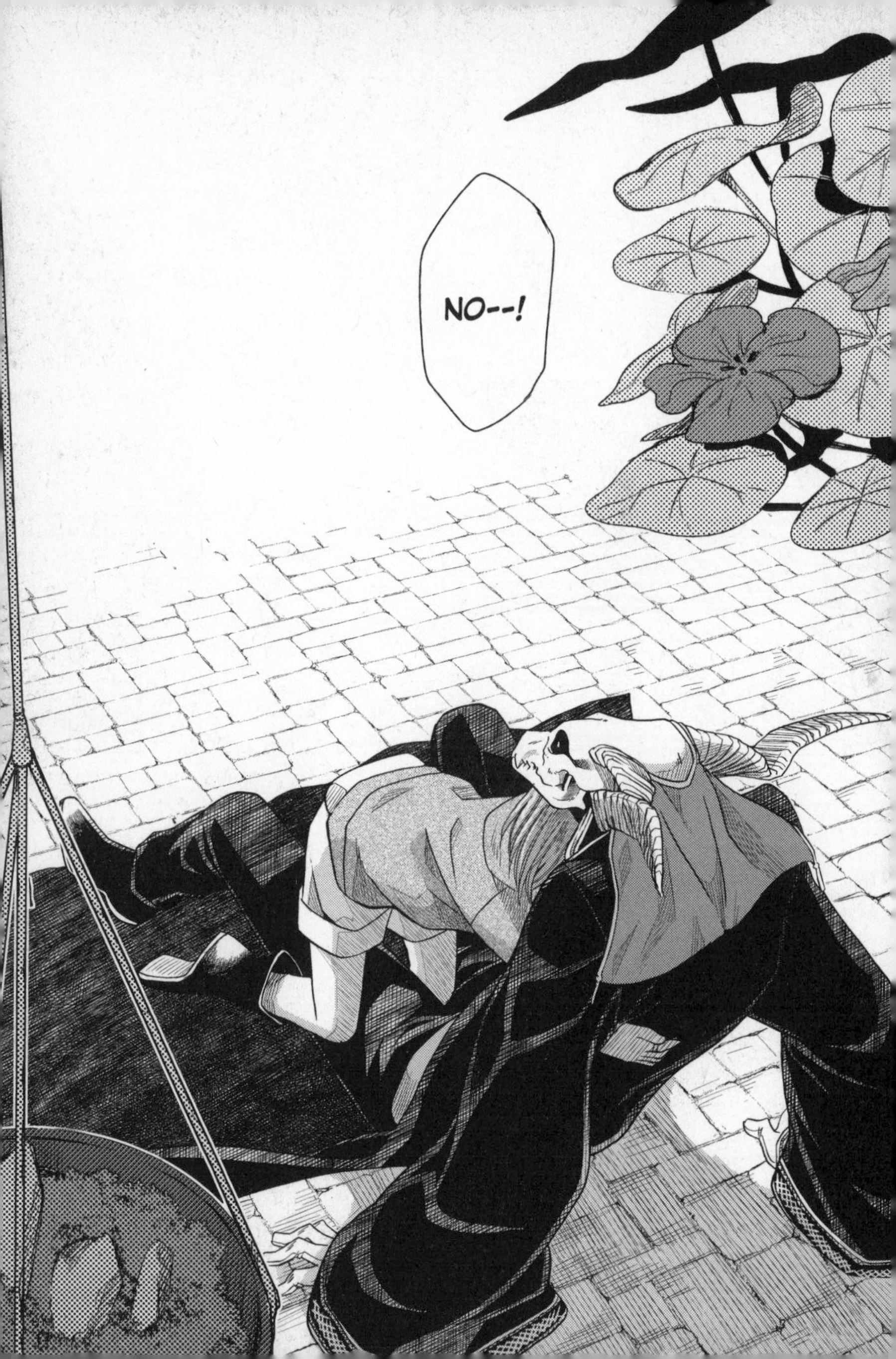
NO--!

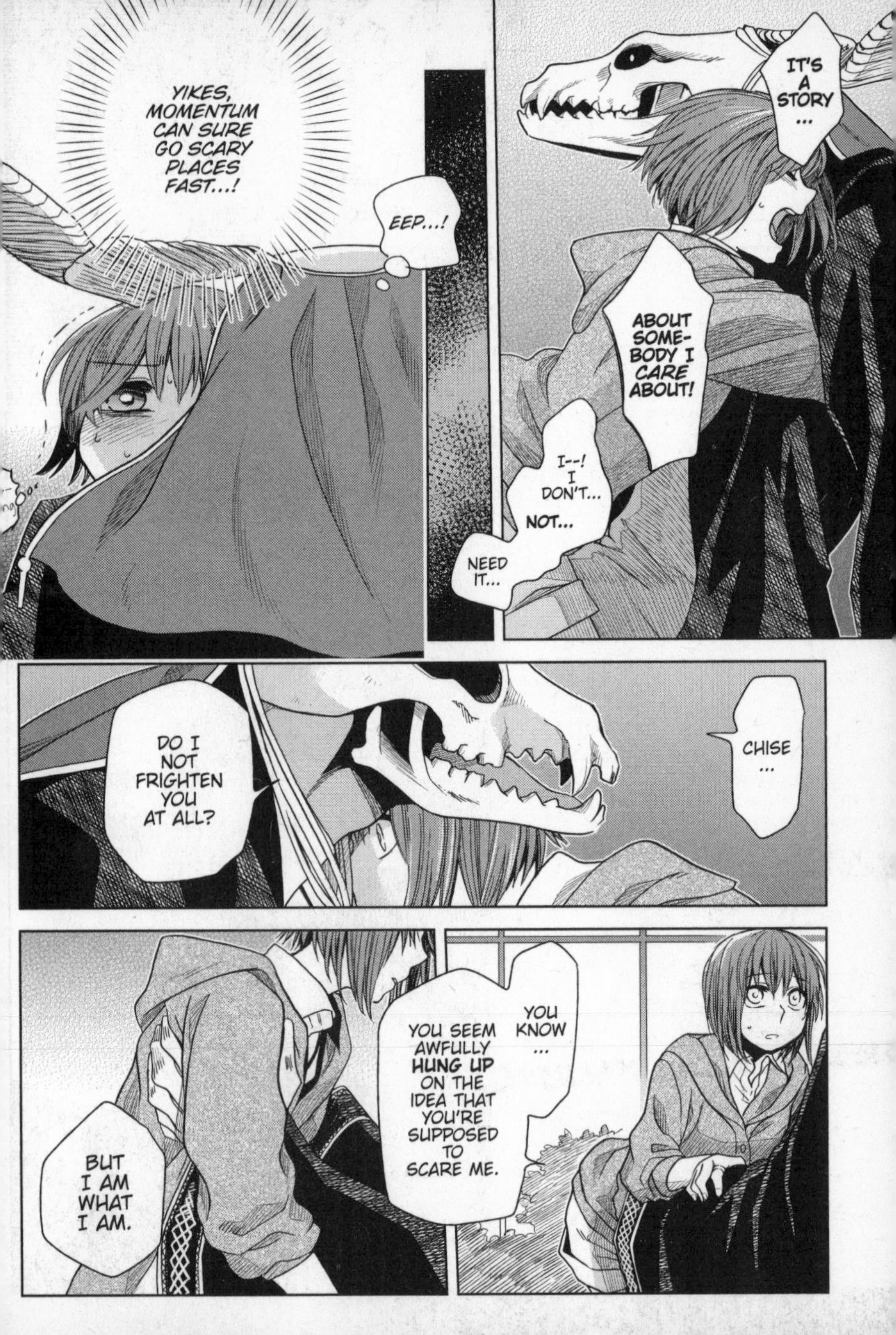
IT'S A STORY...
ABOUT SOMEBODY I CARE ABOUT!
I--! I DON'T...
NOT...
NEED IT...
YIKES, MOMENTUM CAN SURE GO SCARY PLACES FAST...!
EEP...!
CHISE...
DO I NOT FRIGHTEN YOU AT ALL?
YOU KNOW...
YOU SEEM AWFULLY HUNG UP ON THE IDEA THAT YOU'RE SUPPOSED TO SCARE ME.
BUT I AM WHAT I AM.

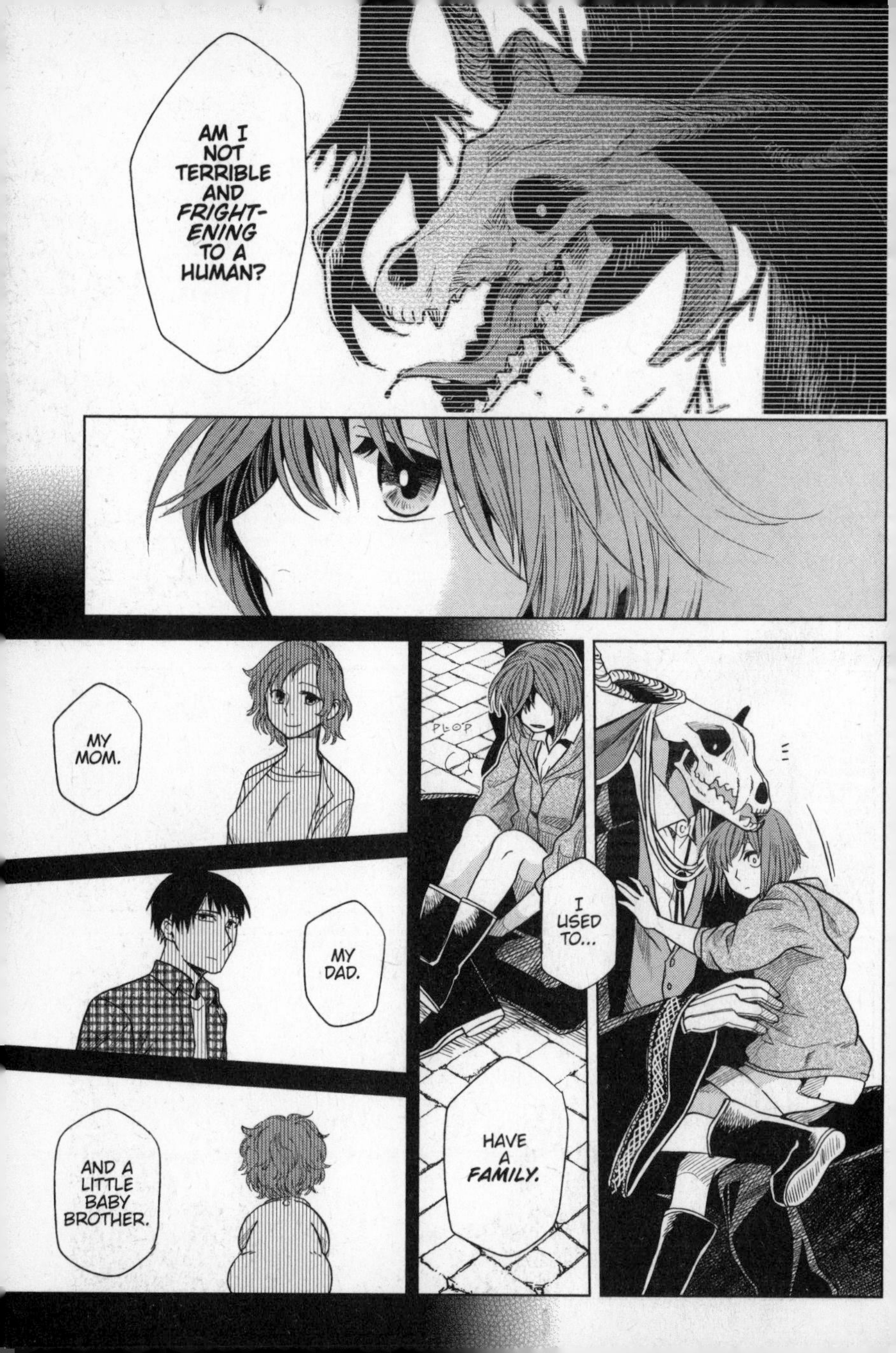

AM I NOT TERRIBLE AND FRIGHTENING TO A HUMAN?
I USED TO...
PLOP
HAVE A FAMILY.
MY MOM.
MY DAD.
AND A LITTLE BABY BROTHER.

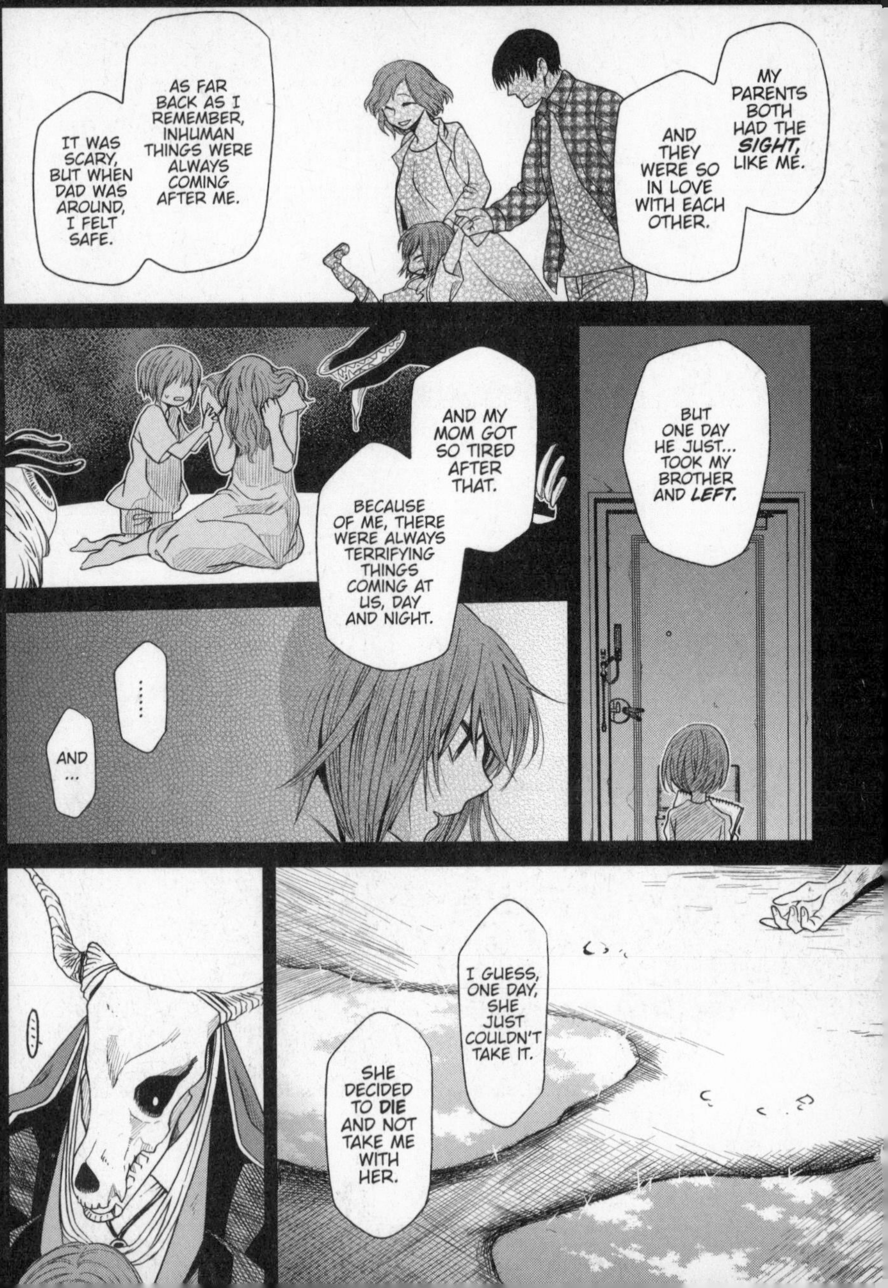
MY PARENTS BOTH HAD THE **SIGHT,** LIKE ME.
AND THEY WERE SO IN LOVE WITH EACH OTHER.
AS FAR BACK AS I REMEMBER, INHUMAN THINGS WERE ALWAYS COMING AFTER ME.
IT WAS SCARY, BUT WHEN DAD WAS AROUND, I FELT SAFE.
BUT ONE DAY HE JUST... TOOK MY BROTHER AND **LEFT.**
AND MY MOM GOT SO TIRED AFTER THAT.
BECAUSE OF ME, THERE WERE ALWAYS TERRIFYING THINGS COMING AT US, DAY AND NIGHT.
......
AND ...
I GUESS, ONE DAY, SHE JUST COULDN'T TAKE IT.
SHE DECIDED TO **DIE** AND NOT TAKE ME WITH HER.

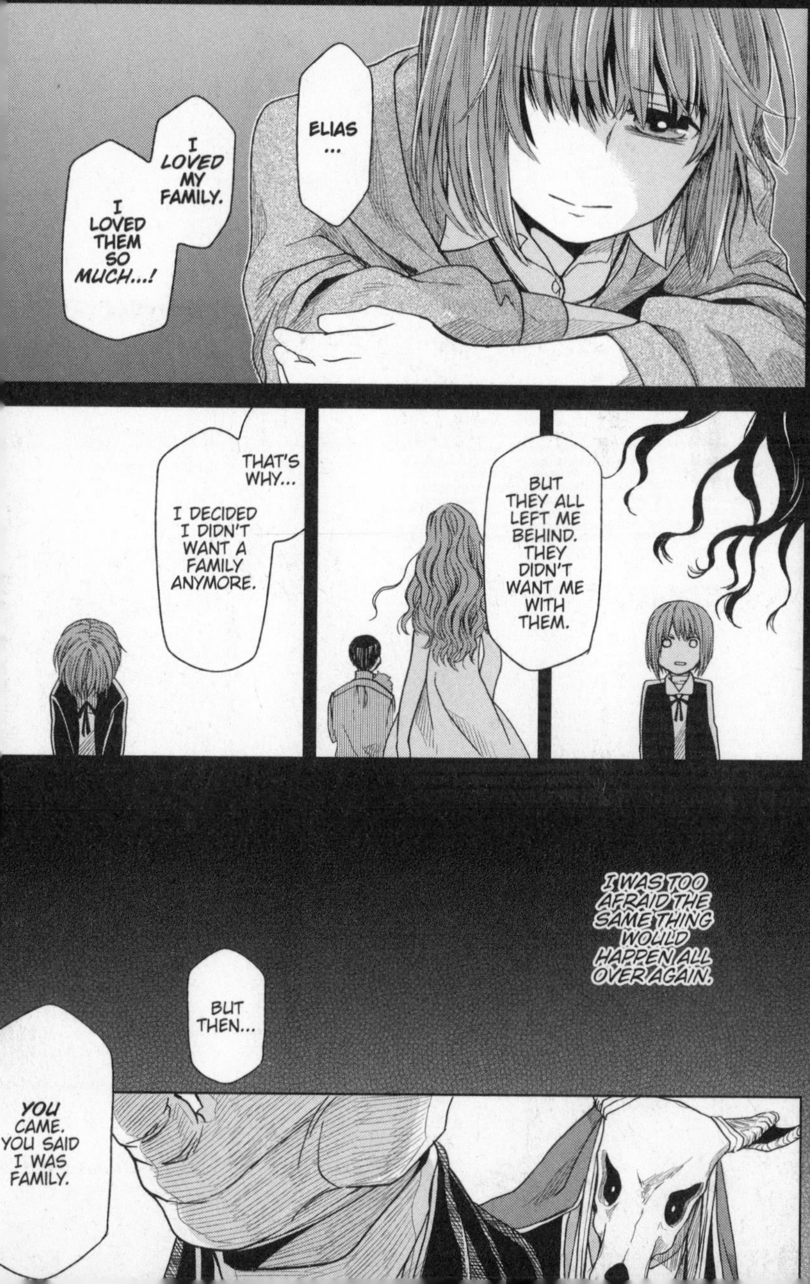
ELIAS...
I LOVED MY FAMILY.
I LOVED THEM SO MUCH...!
BUT THEY ALL LEFT ME BEHIND. THEY DIDN'T WANT ME WITH THEM.
THAT'S WHY...
I DECIDED I DIDN'T WANT A FAMILY ANYMORE.
I WAS TOO AFRAID THE SAME THING WOULD HAPPEN ALL OVER AGAIN.
BUT THEN...
YOU CAME. YOU SAID I WAS FAMILY.

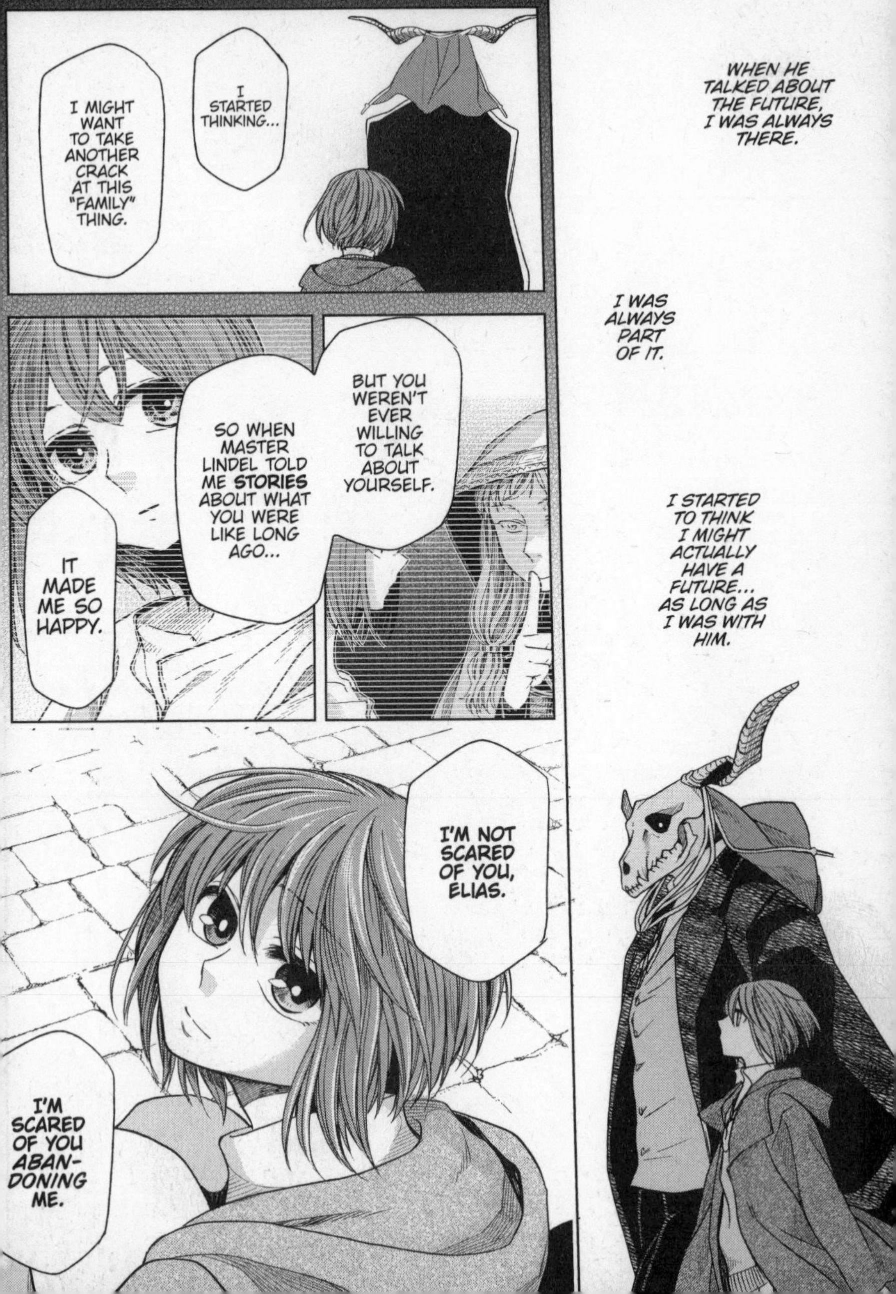
WHEN HE TALKED ABOUT THE FUTURE, I WAS ALWAYS THERE.
I WAS ALWAYS PART OF IT.
I STARTED TO THINK I MIGHT ACTUALLY HAVE A FUTURE... AS LONG AS I WAS WITH HIM.
I STARTED THINKING...
I MIGHT WANT TO TAKE ANOTHER CRACK AT THIS "FAMILY" THING.
BUT YOU WEREN'T EVER WILLING TO TALK ABOUT YOURSELF.
SO WHEN MASTER LINDEL TOLD ME **STORIES** ABOUT WHAT YOU WERE LIKE LONG AGO...
IT MADE ME SO HAPPY.
I'M NOT SCARED OF YOU, ELIAS.
I'M SCARED OF YOU ABAN-DONING ME.

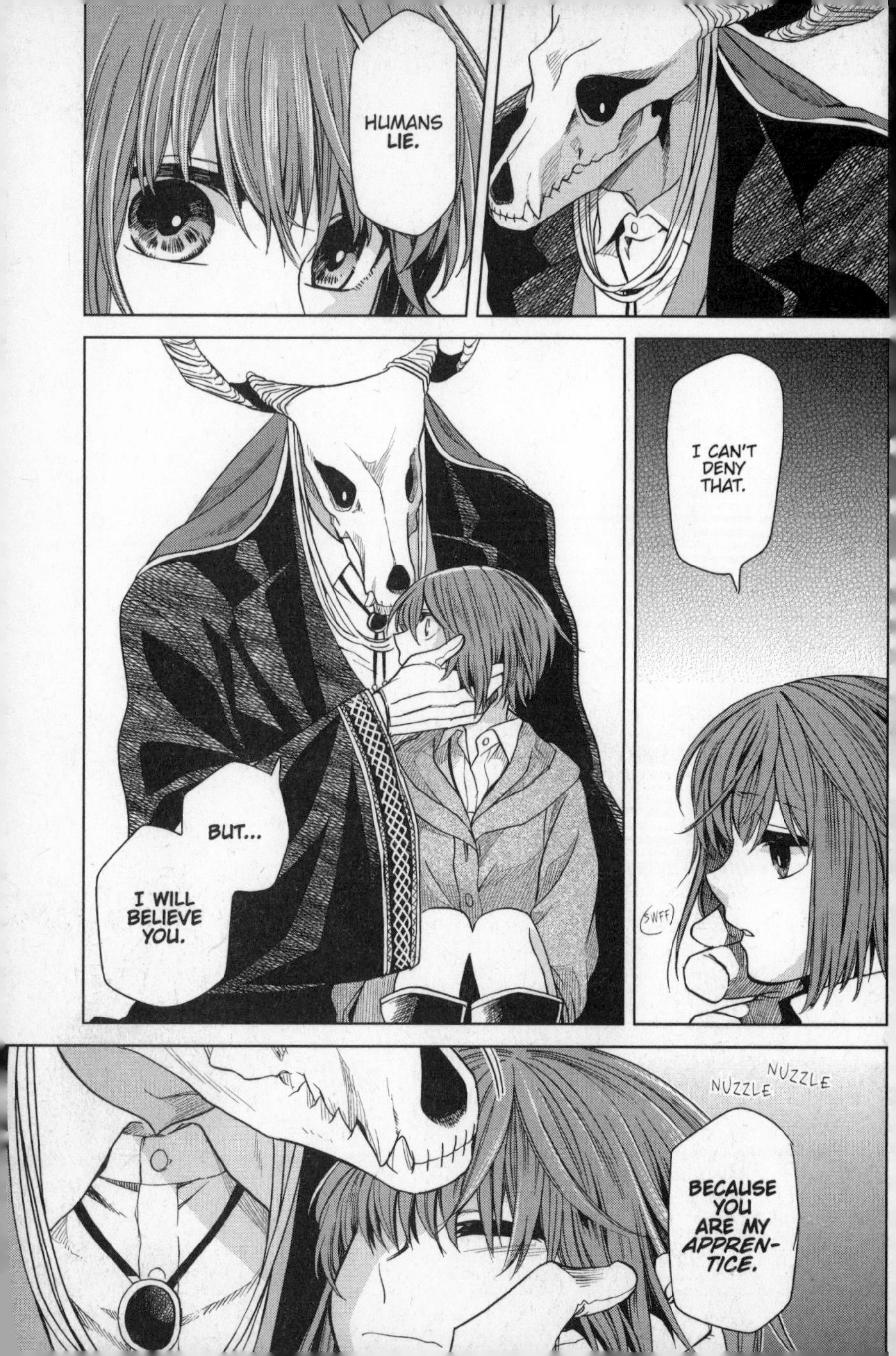
HUMANS LIE.
I CAN'T DENY THAT.
(SWFF)
BUT...
I WILL BELIEVE YOU.
NUZZLE NUZZLE
BECAUSE YOU ARE MY APPREN-TICE.

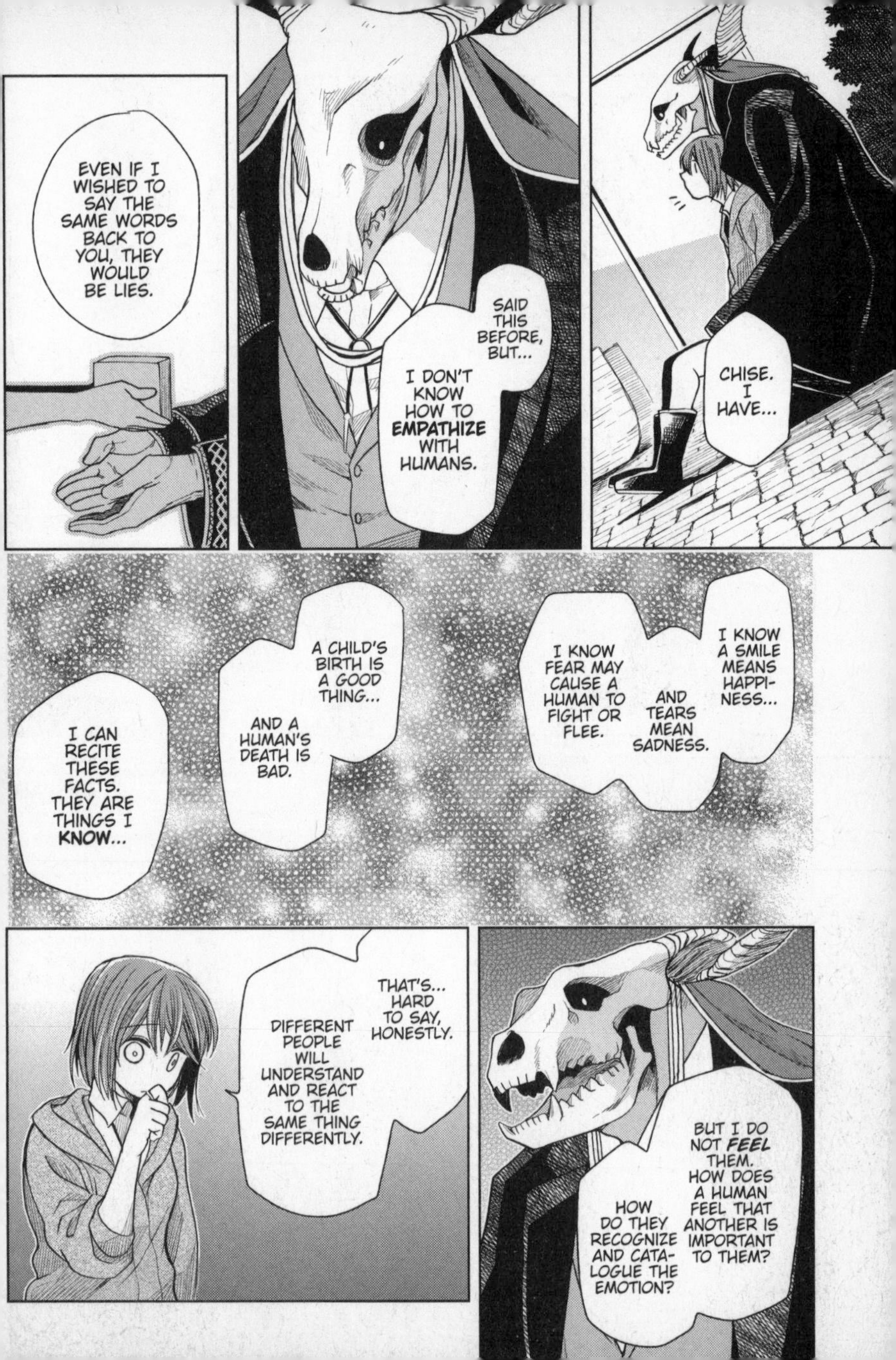
CHISE. I HAVE...
SAID THIS BEFORE, BUT...
I DON'T KNOW HOW TO **EMPATHIZE** WITH HUMANS.
EVEN IF I WISHED TO SAY THE SAME WORDS BACK TO YOU, THEY WOULD BE LIES.
I KNOW A SMILE MEANS HAPPI-NESS...
AND TEARS MEAN SADNESS.
I KNOW FEAR MAY CAUSE A HUMAN TO FIGHT OR FLEE.
A CHILD'S BIRTH IS A GOOD THING...
AND A HUMAN'S DEATH IS BAD.
I CAN RECITE THESE FACTS. THEY ARE THINGS I **KNOW**...
BUT I DO NOT ***FEEL*** THEM. HOW DOES A HUMAN FEEL THAT ANOTHER IS IMPORTANT TO THEM?
HOW DO THEY RECOGNIZE AND CATA-LOGUE THE EMOTION?
THAT'S... HARD TO SAY, HONESTLY.
DIFFERENT PEOPLE WILL UNDERSTAND AND REACT TO THE SAME THING DIFFERENTLY.

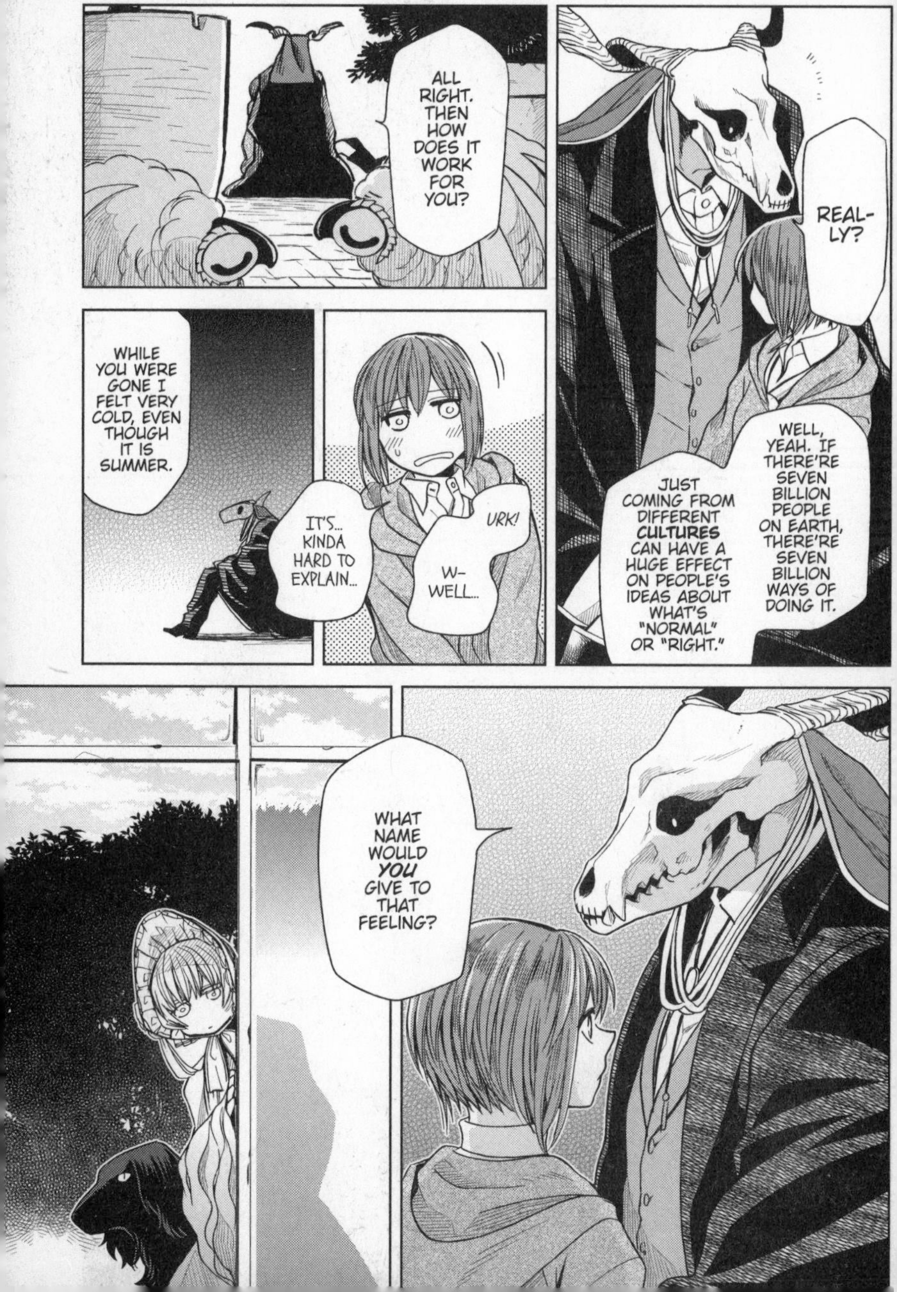
REAL-LY?
WELL, YEAH. IF THERE'RE SEVEN BILLION PEOPLE ON EARTH, THERE'RE SEVEN BILLION WAYS OF DOING IT.
JUST COMING FROM DIFFERENT **CULTURES** CAN HAVE A HUGE EFFECT ON PEOPLE'S IDEAS ABOUT WHAT'S "NORMAL" OR "RIGHT."
ALL RIGHT. THEN HOW DOES IT WORK FOR YOU?
URK!
W-WELL...
IT'S... KINDA HARD TO EXPLAIN...
WHILE YOU WERE GONE I FELT VERY COLD, EVEN THOUGH IT IS SUMMER.
WHAT NAME WOULD ***YOU*** GIVE TO THAT FEELING?

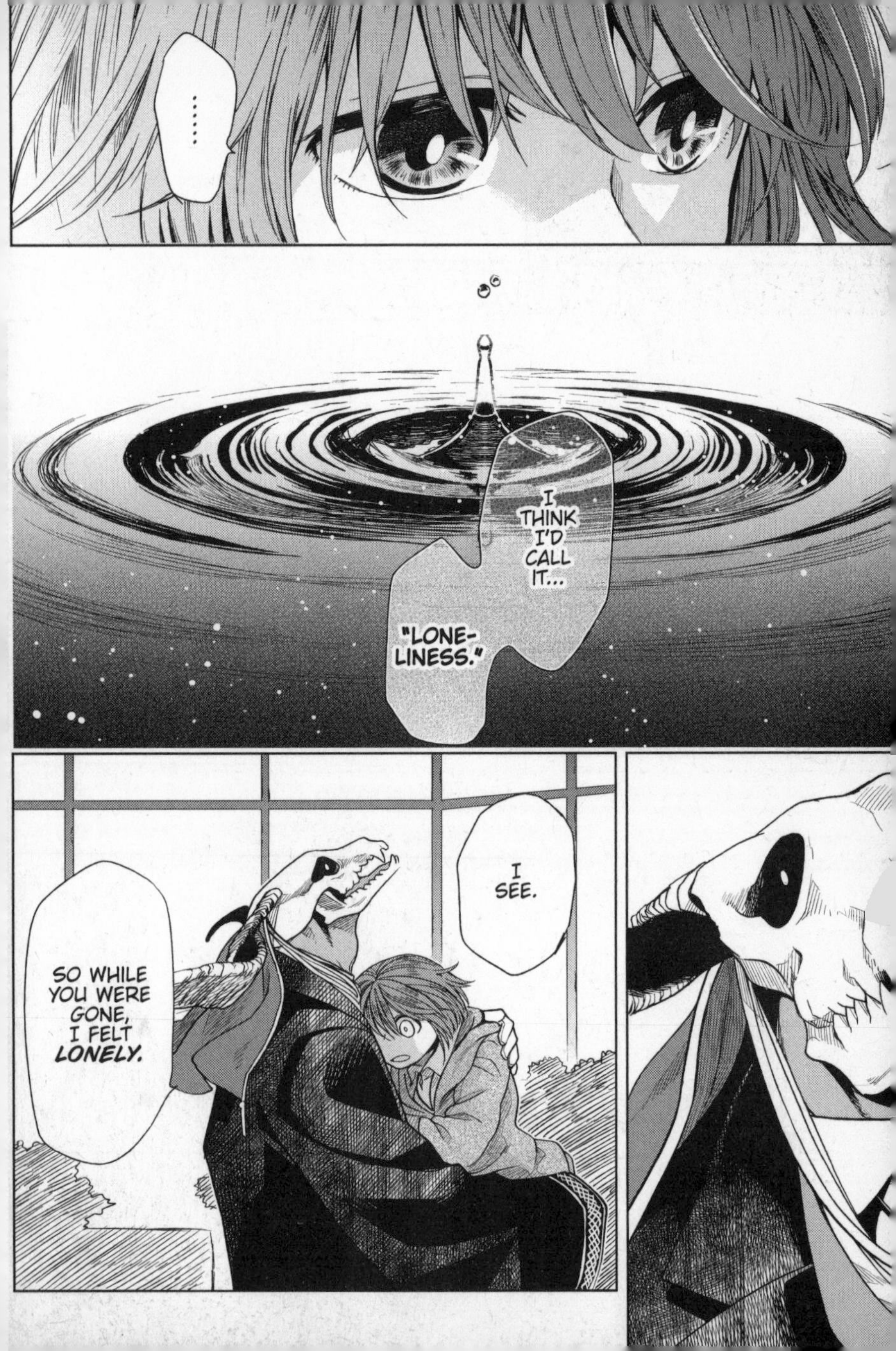
……
I THINK I'D CALL IT...
"LONELINESS."
I SEE.
SO WHILE YOU WERE GONE, I FELT LONELY.

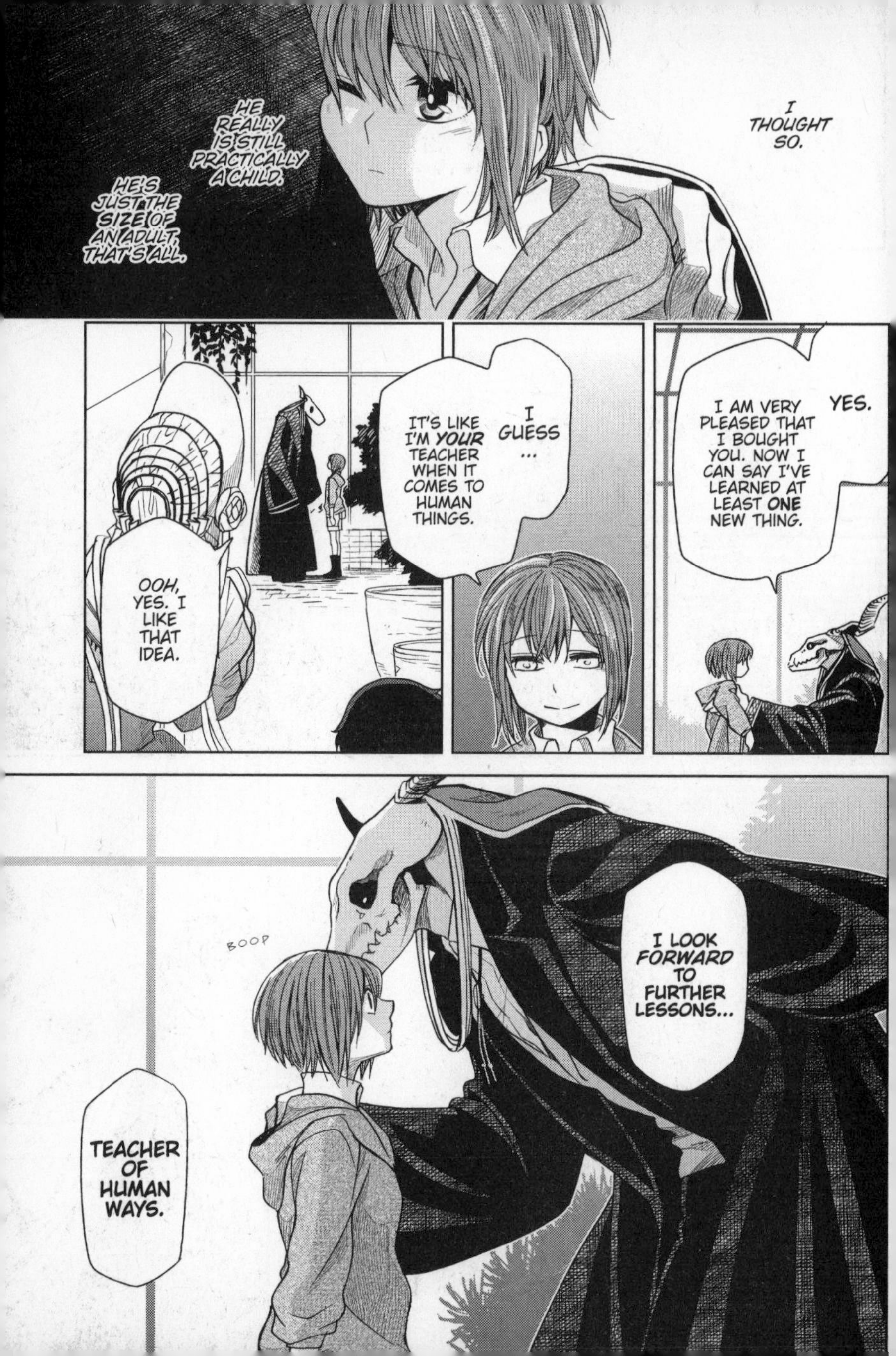
I THOUGHT SO.
HE REALLY IS STILL PRACTICALLY A CHILD.
HE'S JUST THE SIZE OF AN ADULT, THAT'S ALL.
YES.
I AM VERY PLEASED THAT I BOUGHT YOU. NOW I CAN SAY I'VE LEARNED AT LEAST ONE NEW THING.
I GUESS...
IT'S LIKE I'M YOUR TEACHER WHEN IT COMES TO HUMAN THINGS.
OOH, YES. I LIKE THAT IDEA.
I LOOK FORWARD TO FURTHER LESSONS...
BOOP
TEACHER OF HUMAN WAYS.

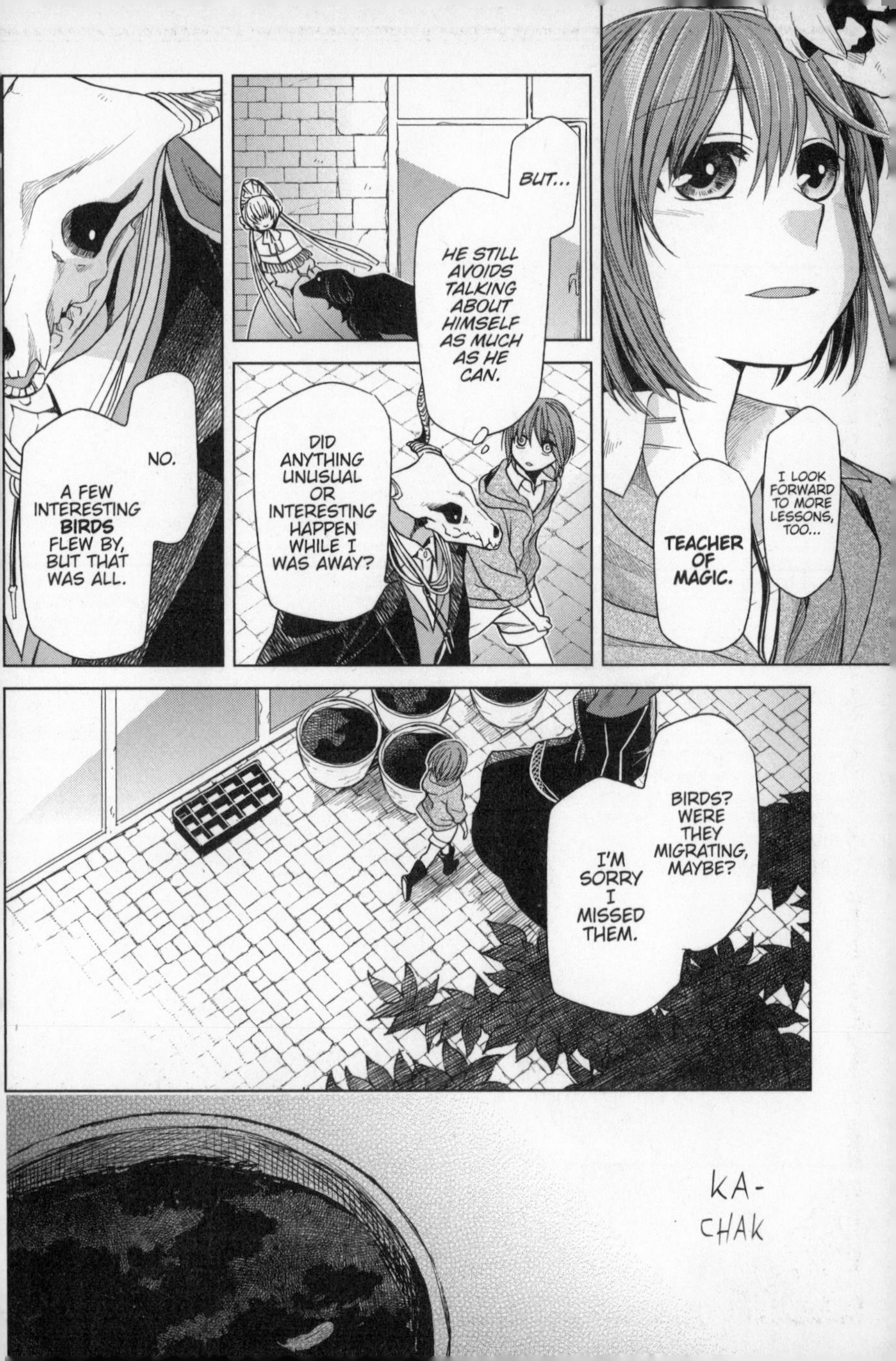

I LOOK FORWARD TO MORE LESSONS, TOO...
TEACHER OF MAGIC.
BUT...
HE STILL AVOIDS TALKING ABOUT HIMSELF AS MUCH AS HE CAN.
DID ANYTHING UNUSUAL OR INTERESTING HAPPEN WHILE I WAS AWAY?
NO.
A FEW INTERESTING BIRDS FLEW BY, BUT THAT WAS ALL.
BIRDS? WERE THEY MIGRATING, MAYBE?
I'M SORRY I MISSED THEM.
KA-CHAK

The Ancient Magus' Bride

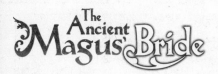

The Ancient Magus' Bride

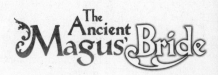

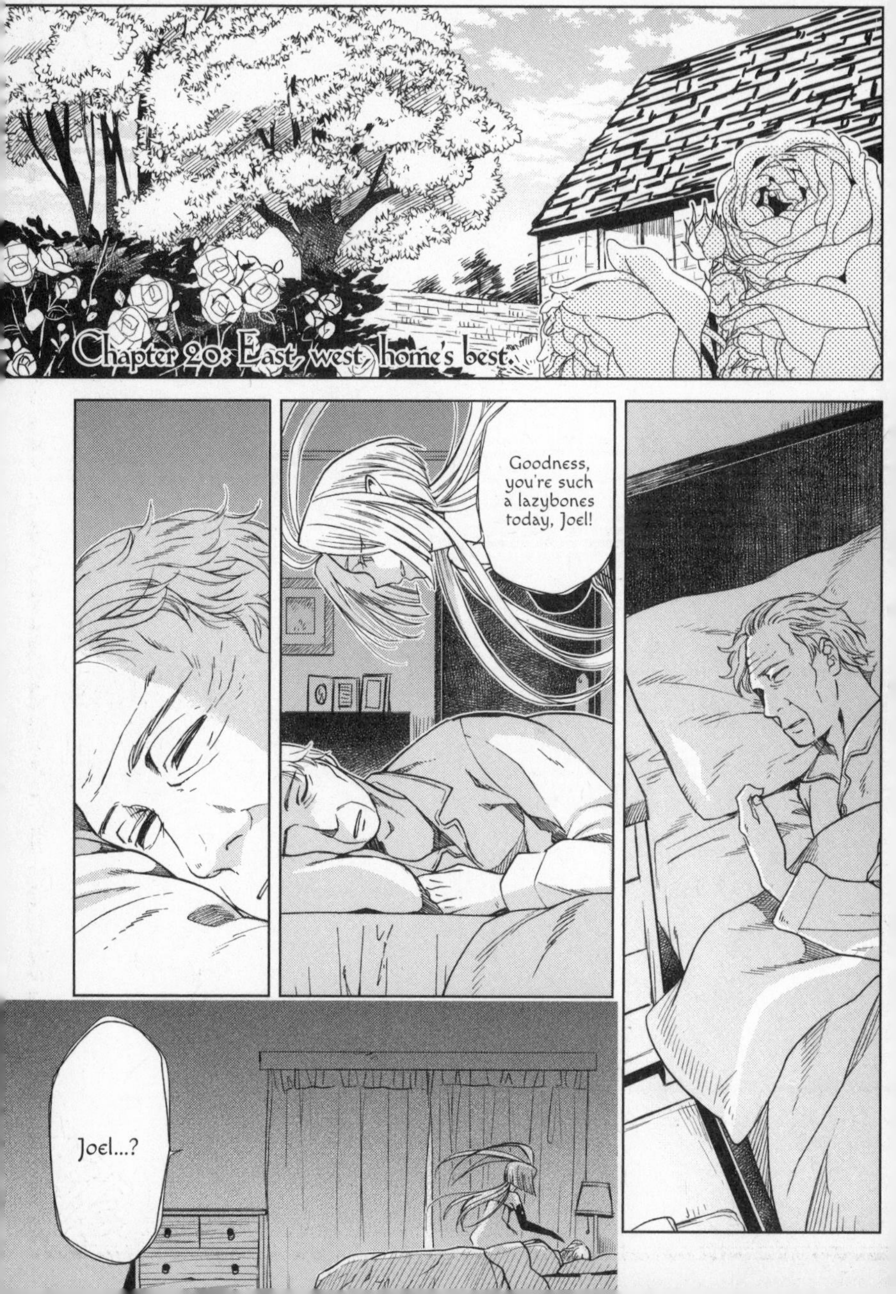
Chapter 20: East, west, home's best.
Goodness, you're such a lazybones today, Joel!
Joel...?

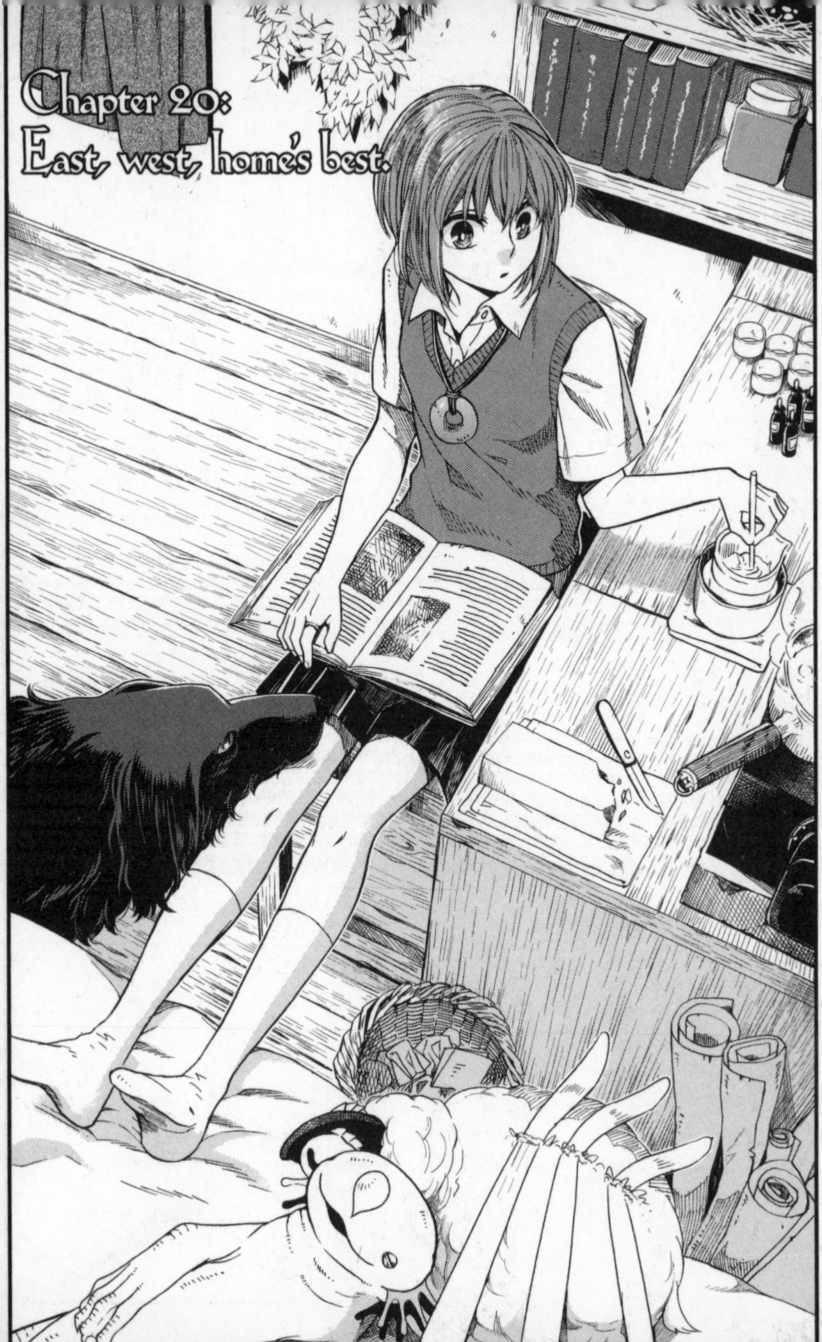
Chapter 20:
East, west, home's best.

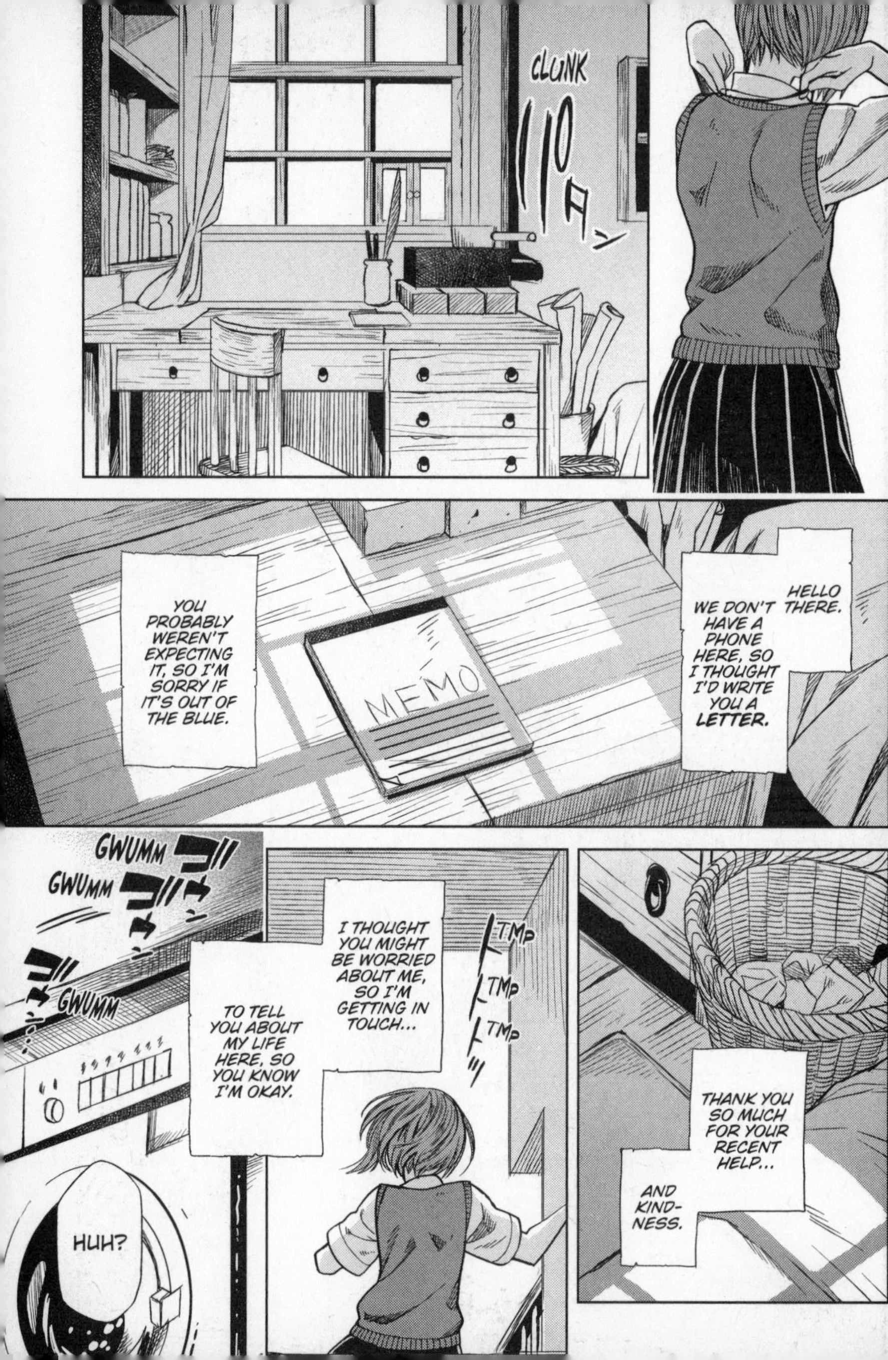
CLUNK
HELLO THERE. WE DON'T HAVE A PHONE HERE, SO I THOUGHT I'D WRITE YOU A LETTER.
YOU PROBABLY WEREN'T EXPECTING IT, SO I'M SORRY IF IT'S OUT OF THE BLUE.
THANK YOU SO MUCH FOR YOUR RECENT HELP...
AND KIND-NESS.
I THOUGHT YOU MIGHT BE WORRIED ABOUT ME, SO I'M GETTING IN TOUCH...
TMP
TMP
TMP
TO TELL YOU ABOUT MY LIFE HERE, SO YOU KNOW I'M OKAY.
GWUMM
GWUMM
GWUMM
HUH?

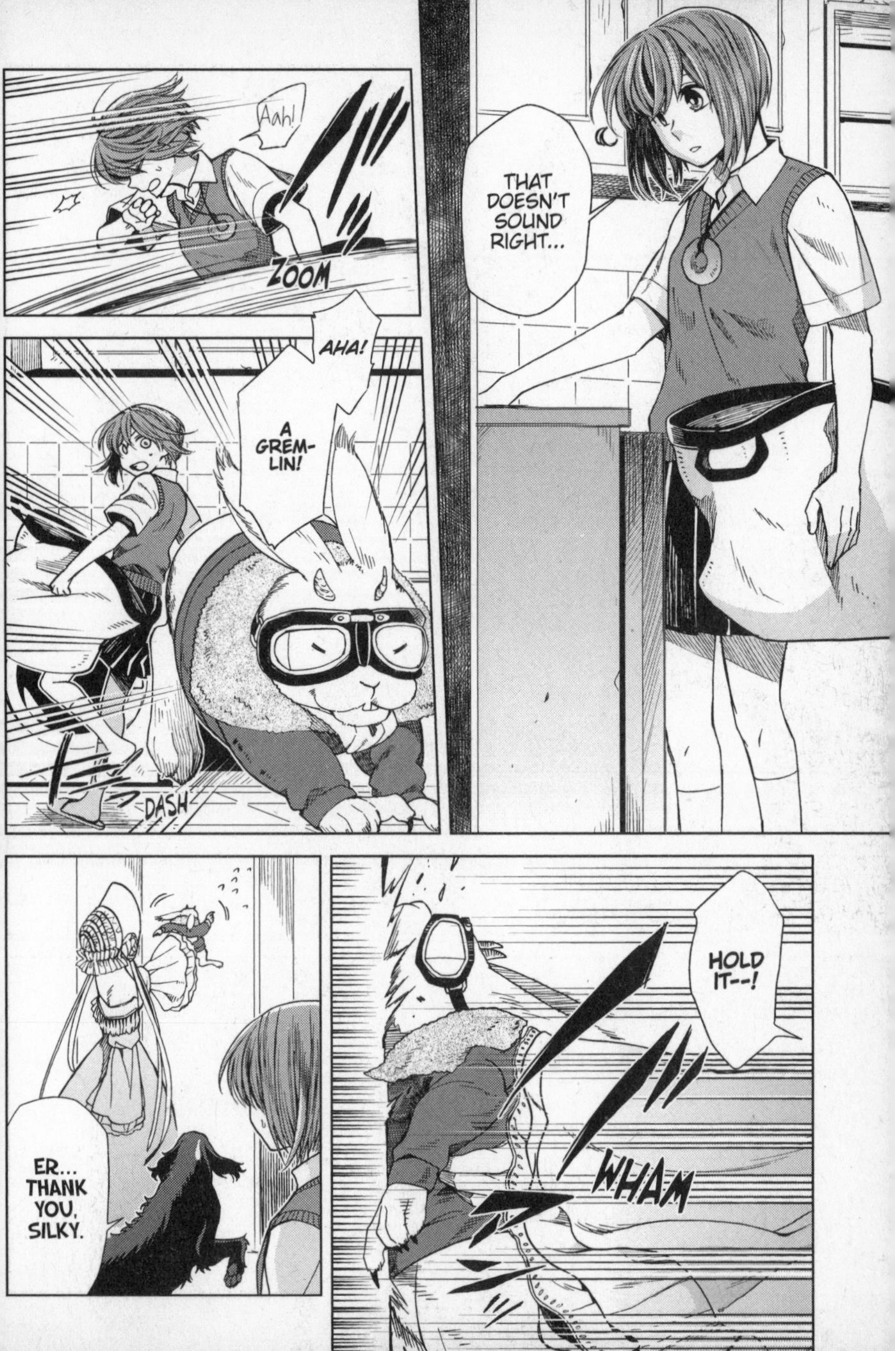
THAT DOESN'T SOUND RIGHT...
Aah!
ZOOM
AHA!
A GREM-LIN!
DASH
HOLD IT--!
WHAM
ER... THANK YOU, SILKY.

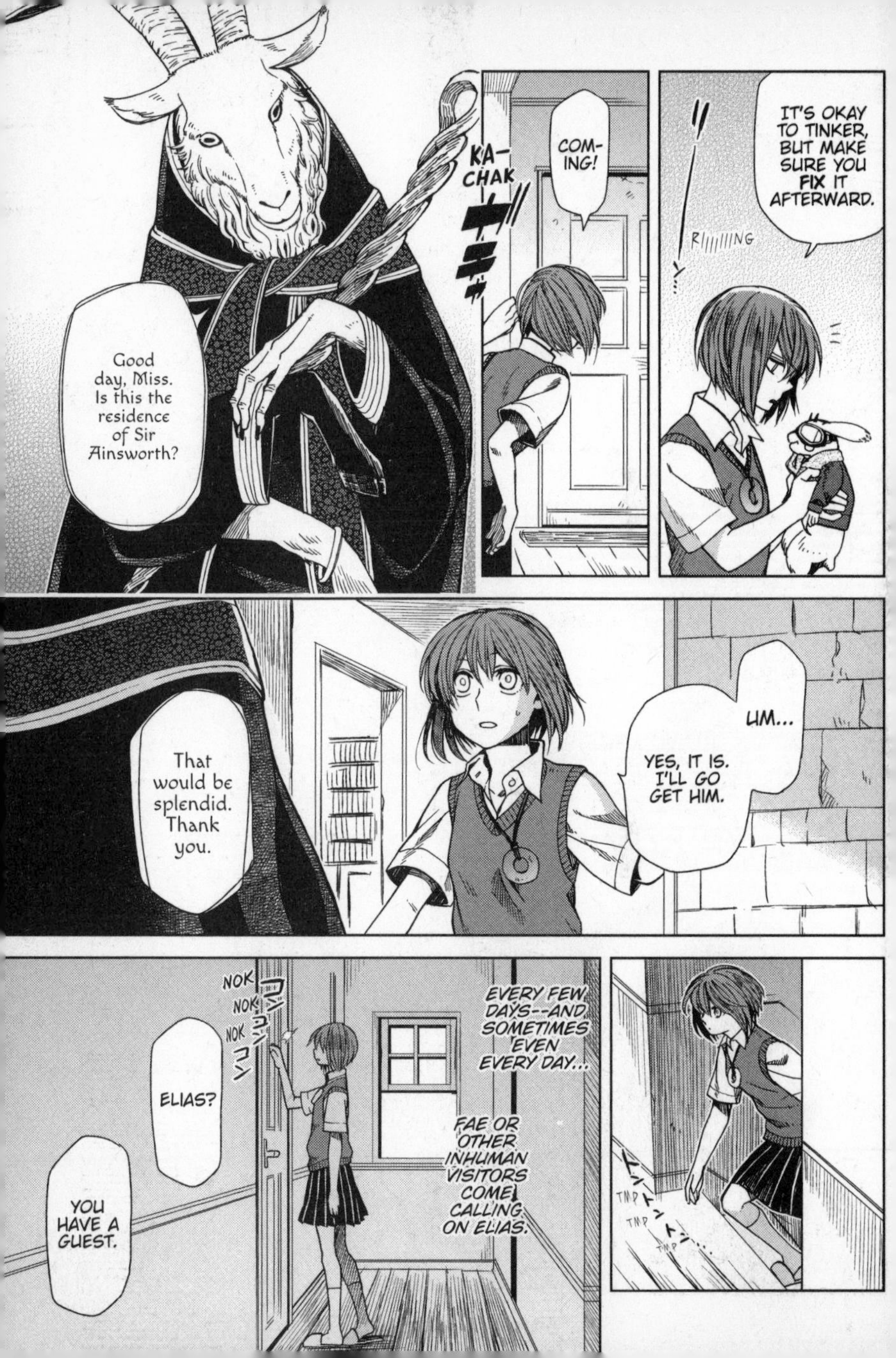
IT'S OKAY TO TINKER, BUT MAKE SURE YOU FIX IT AFTERWARD.
RIIIIIING
COM-ING!
KA-CHAK
Good day, Miss. Is this the residence of Sir Ainsworth?
UM...
YES, IT IS. I'LL GO GET HIM.
That would be splendid. Thank you.
TMP TMP TMP...
EVERY FEW DAYS--AND SOMETIMES EVEN EVERY DAY...
FAE OR OTHER INHUMAN VISITORS COME CALLING ON ELIAS.
NOK NOK NOK
ELIAS?
YOU HAVE A GUEST.

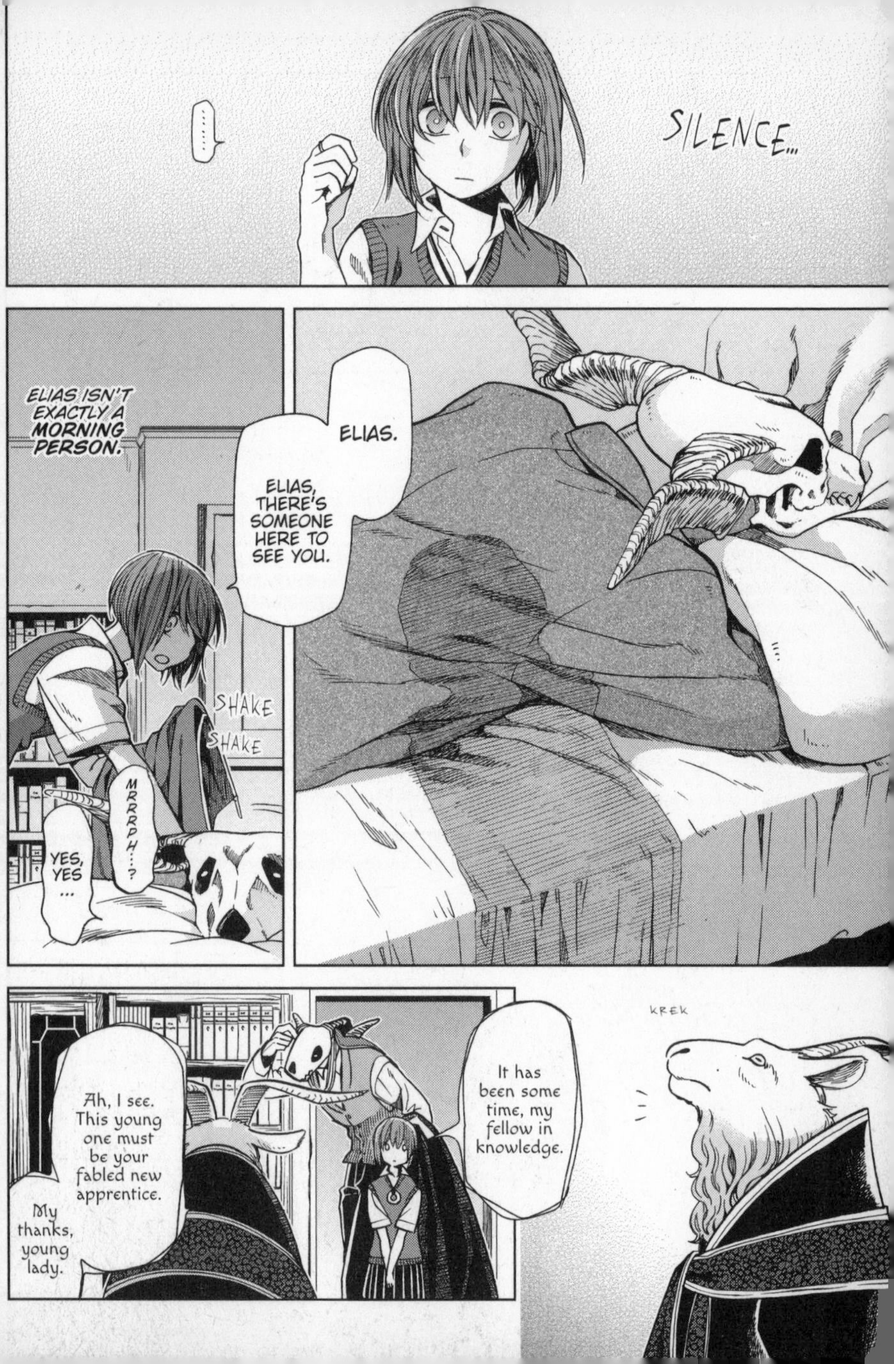
SILENCE...
......
ELIAS.
ELIAS, THERE'S SOMEONE HERE TO SEE YOU.
ELIAS ISN'T EXACTLY A MORNING PERSON.
SHAKE
SHAKE
MRRRPH...?
YES, YES ...
KREK
It has been some time, my fellow in knowledge.
Ah, I see. This young one must be your fabled new apprentice.
My thanks, young lady.

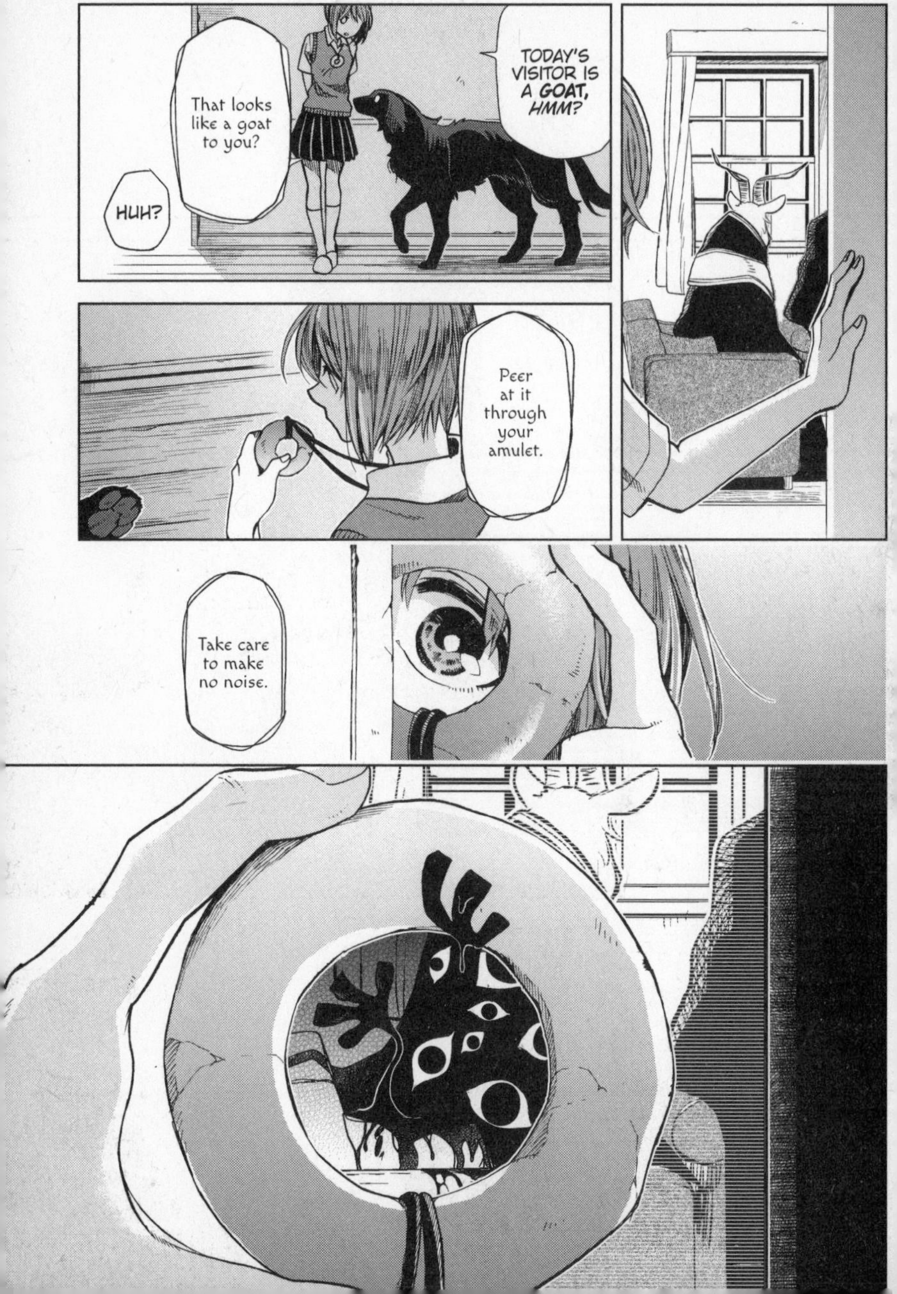
TODAY'S VISITOR IS A GOAT, HMM?
That looks like a goat to you?
HUH?
Peer at it through your amulet.
Take care to make no noise.

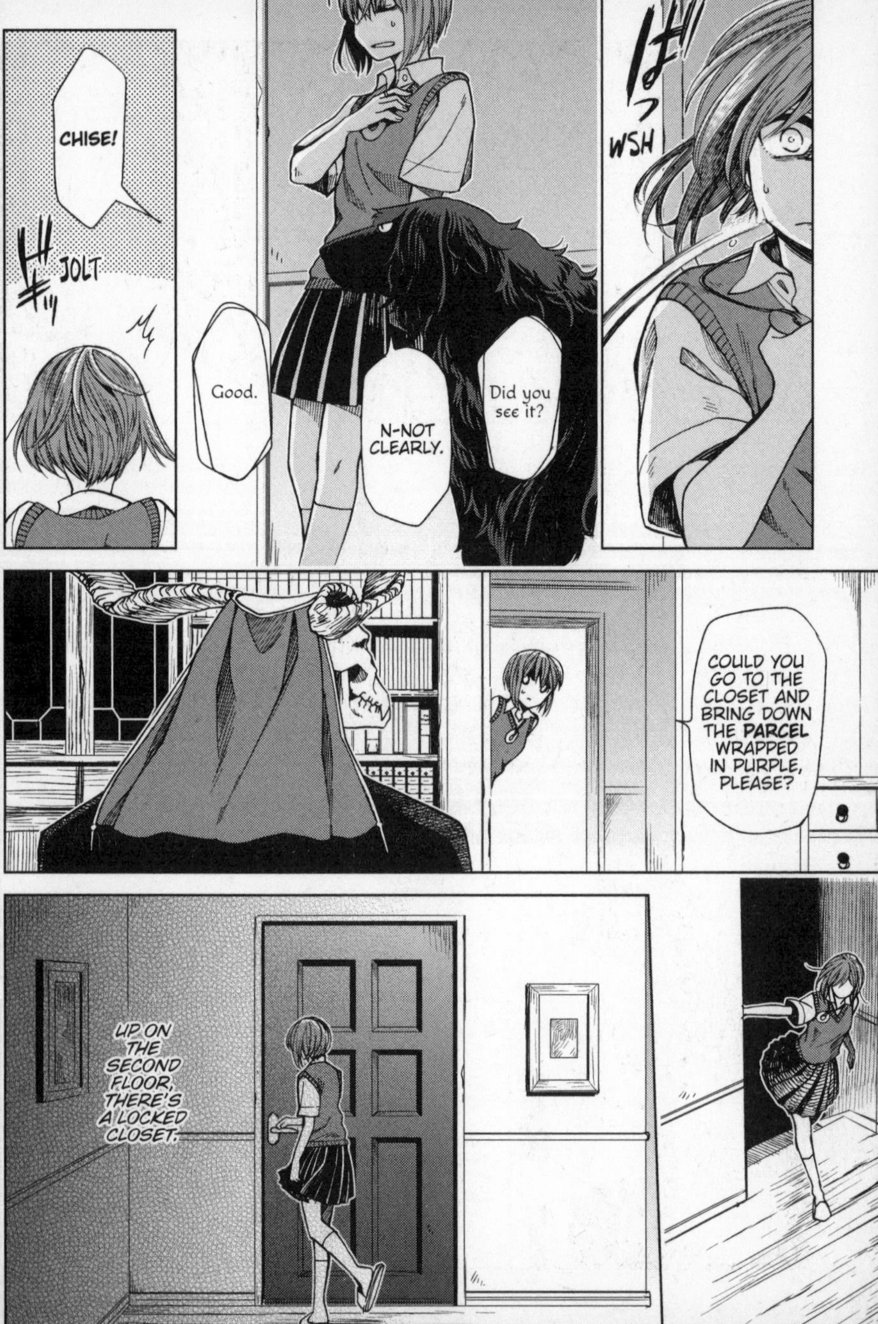
ばっ
WSH
Did you see it?
N-NOT CLEARLY.
Good.
CHISE!
JOLT
COULD YOU GO TO THE CLOSET AND BRING DOWN THE PARCEL WRAPPED IN PURPLE, PLEASE?
UP ON THE SECOND FLOOR, THERE'S A LOCKED CLOSET.

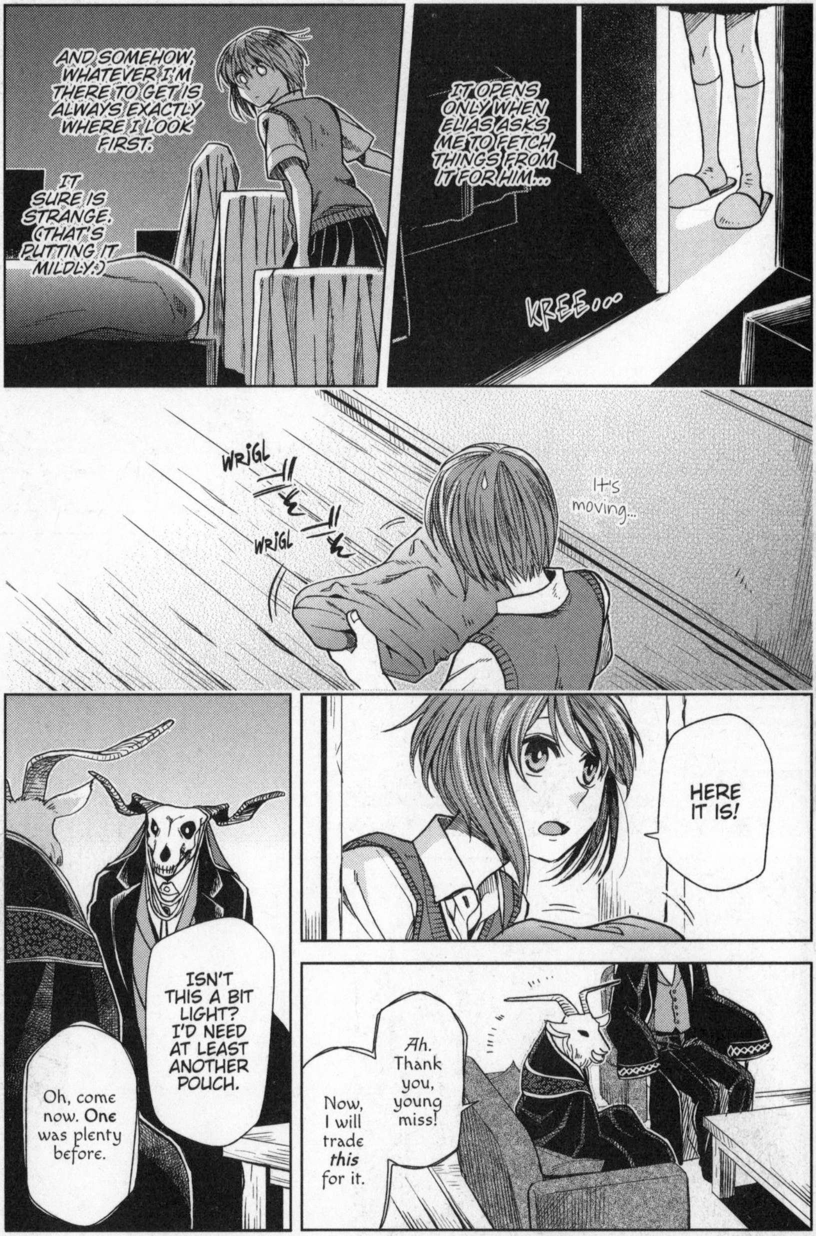
IT OPENS ONLY WHEN ELIAS ASKS ME TO FETCH THINGS FROM IT FOR HIM...
KREE...
AND SOMEHOW, WHATEVER I'M THERE TO GET IS ALWAYS EXACTLY WHERE I LOOK FIRST.
IT SURE IS STRANGE. (THAT'S PUTTING IT MILDLY.)
It's moving...
WRIGL
WRIGL
HERE IT IS!
Ah. Thank you, young miss!
Now, I will trade *this* for it.
ISN'T THIS A BIT LIGHT? I'D NEED AT LEAST ANOTHER POUCH.
Oh, come now. **One** was plenty before.

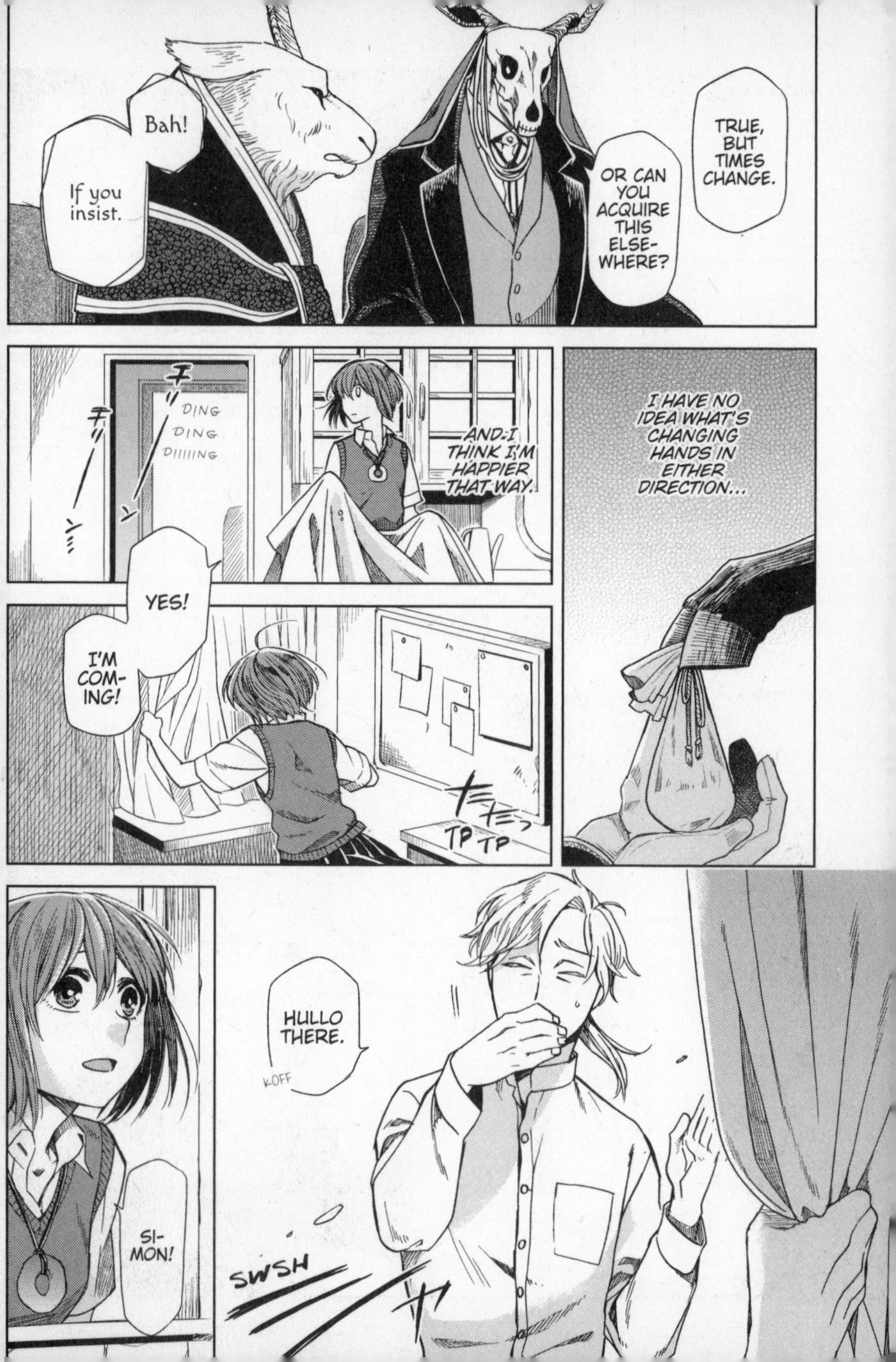
TRUE, BUT TIMES CHANGE.
OR CAN YOU ACQUIRE THIS ELSEWHERE?
Bah!
If you insist.
I HAVE NO IDEA WHAT'S CHANGING HANDS IN EITHER DIRECTION...
AND I THINK I'M HAPPIER THAT WAY.
DING
DING
DIIIIING
YES!
I'M COMING!
TP TP
HULLO THERE.
KOFF
SWSH
SI-MON!

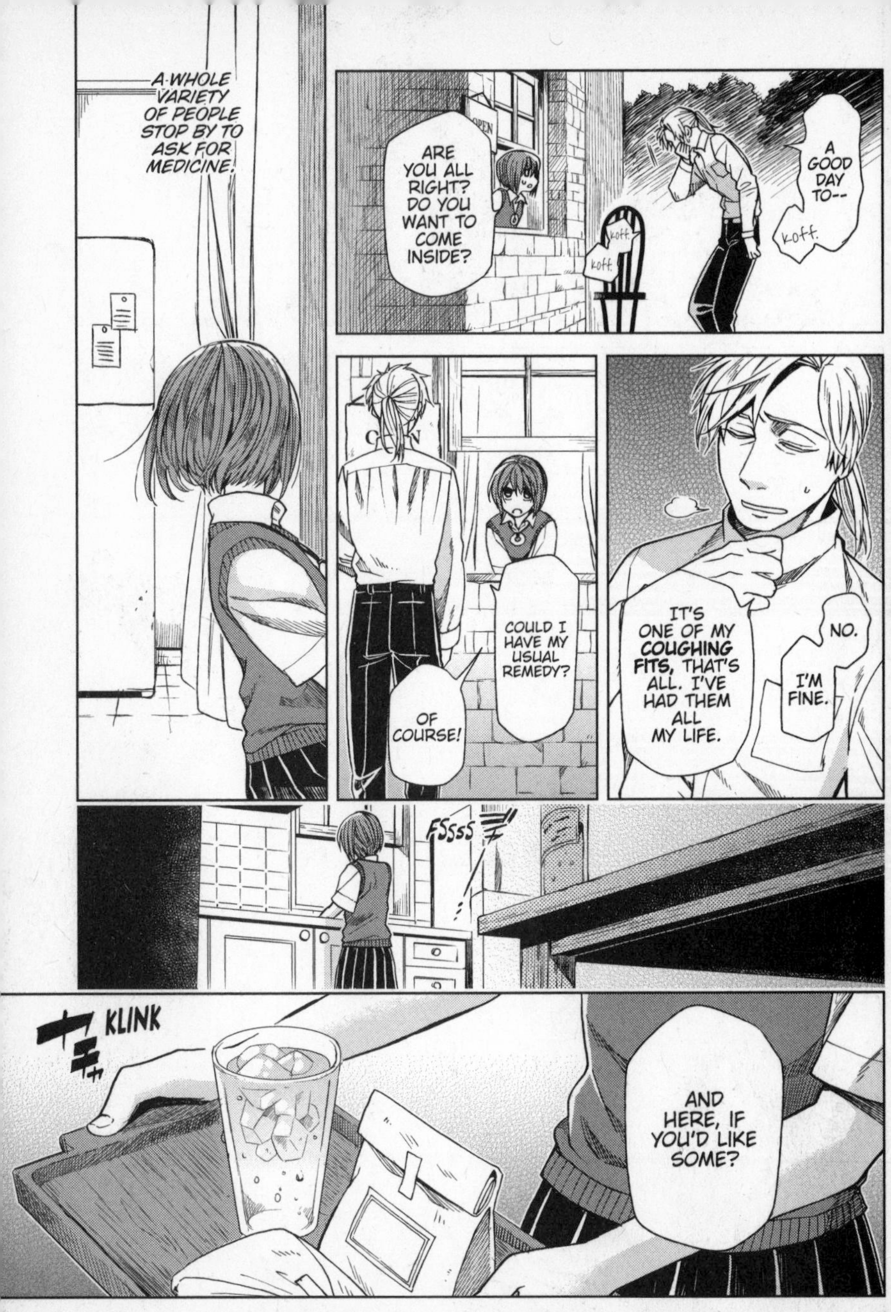
A GOOD DAY TO--
koff.
ARE YOU ALL RIGHT? DO YOU WANT TO COME INSIDE?
koff.
koff.
OPEN
NO.
I'M FINE.
IT'S ONE OF MY **COUGHING FITS,** THAT'S ALL. I'VE HAD THEM ALL MY LIFE.
COULD I HAVE MY USUAL REMEDY?
OF COURSE!
A WHOLE VARIETY OF PEOPLE STOP BY TO ASK FOR MEDICINE.
FSSSS
AND HERE, IF YOU'D LIKE SOME?
KLINK

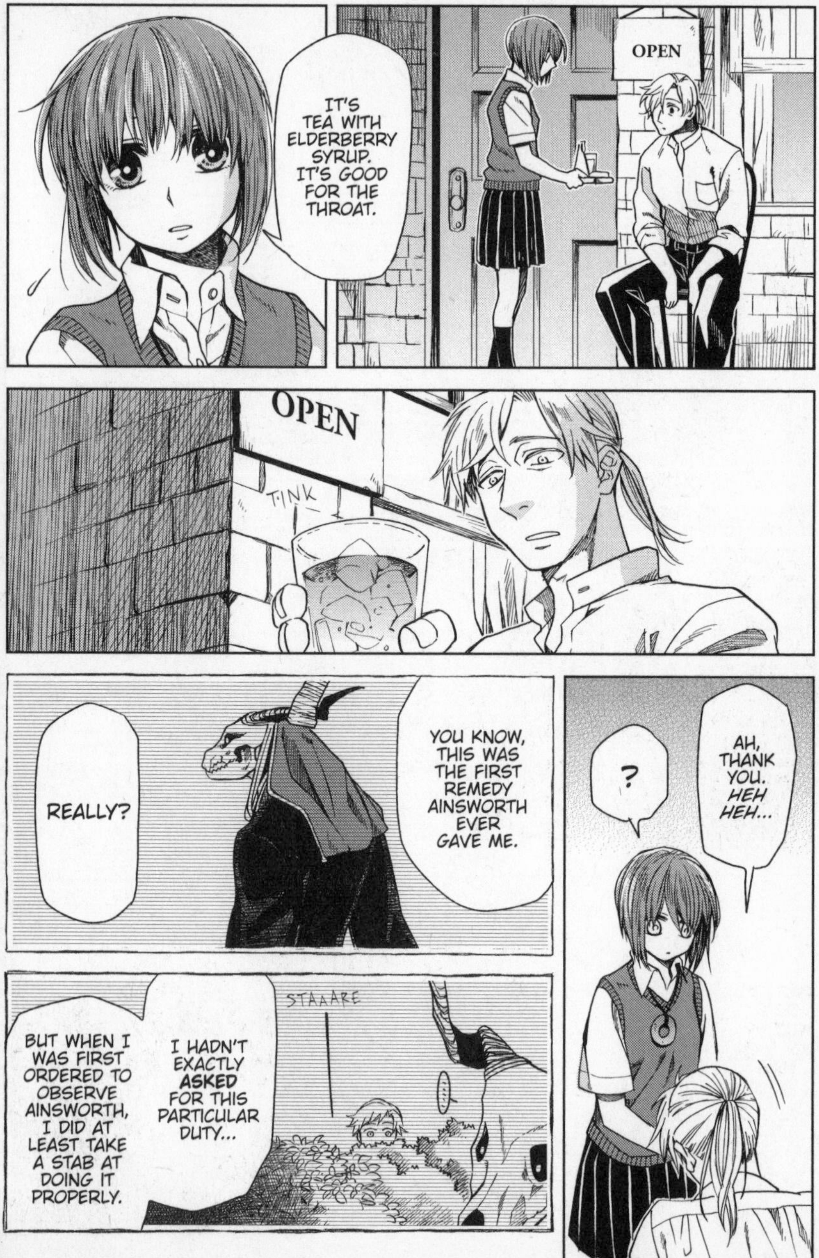
OPEN
IT'S TEA WITH ELDERBERRY SYRUP. IT'S GOOD FOR THE THROAT.
OPEN
TINK
AH, THANK YOU. *HEH HEH...*
?
YOU KNOW, THIS WAS THE FIRST REMEDY AINSWORTH EVER GAVE ME.
REALLY?
STAAARE
I HADN'T EXACTLY **ASKED** FOR THIS PARTICULAR DUTY...
BUT WHEN I WAS FIRST ORDERED TO OBSERVE AINSWORTH, I DID AT LEAST TAKE A STAB AT DOING IT PROPERLY.

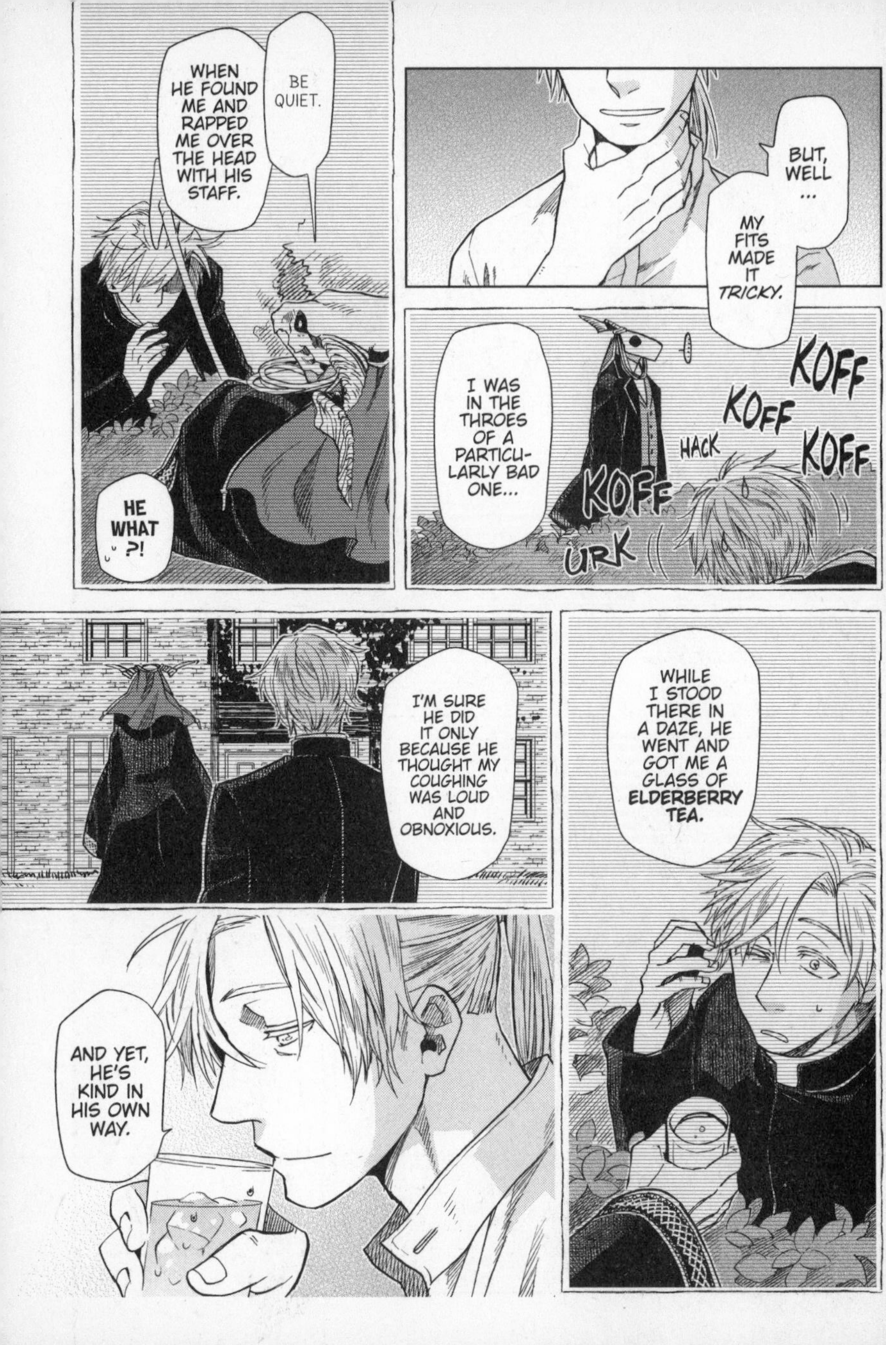

BUT, WELL...
MY FITS MADE IT *TRICKY.*
I WAS IN THE THROES OF A PARTICU-LARLY BAD ONE...
KOFF
KOFF
KOFF
HACK
KOFF
URK
WHEN HE FOUND ME AND RAPPED ME OVER THE HEAD WITH HIS STAFF.
BE QUIET.
HE WHAT ?!
WHILE I STOOD THERE IN A DAZE, HE WENT AND GOT ME A GLASS OF **ELDERBERRY TEA.**
I'M SURE HE DID IT ONLY BECAUSE HE THOUGHT MY COUGHING WAS LOUD AND OBNOXIOUS.
AND YET, HE'S KIND IN HIS OWN WAY.

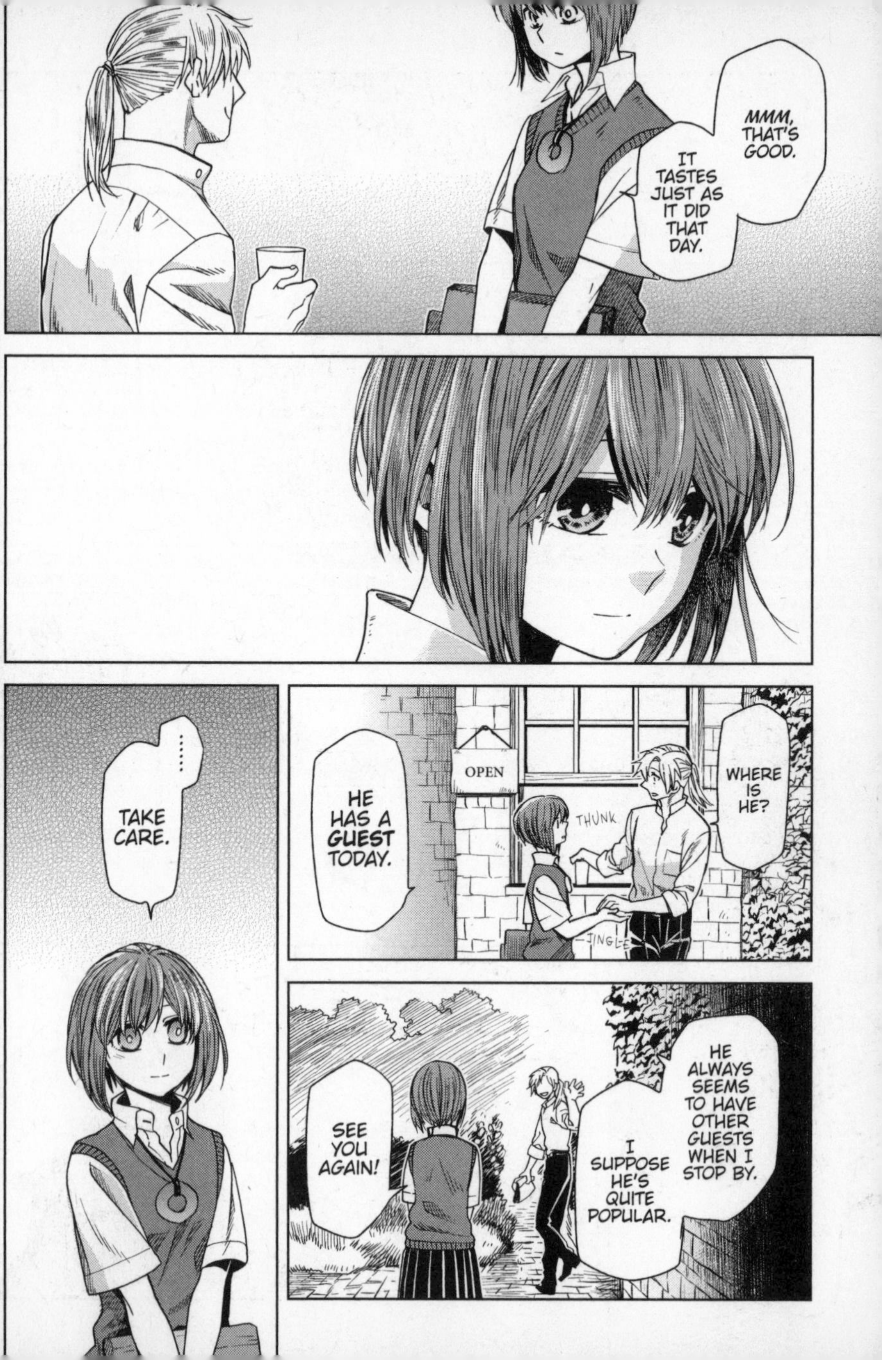
MMM, THAT'S GOOD.
IT TASTES JUST AS IT DID THAT DAY.
WHERE IS HE?
HE HAS A GUEST TODAY.
THUNK
JINGLE
HE ALWAYS SEEMS TO HAVE OTHER GUESTS WHEN I STOP BY.
I SUPPOSE HE'S QUITE POPULAR.
SEE YOU AGAIN!
......
TAKE CARE.

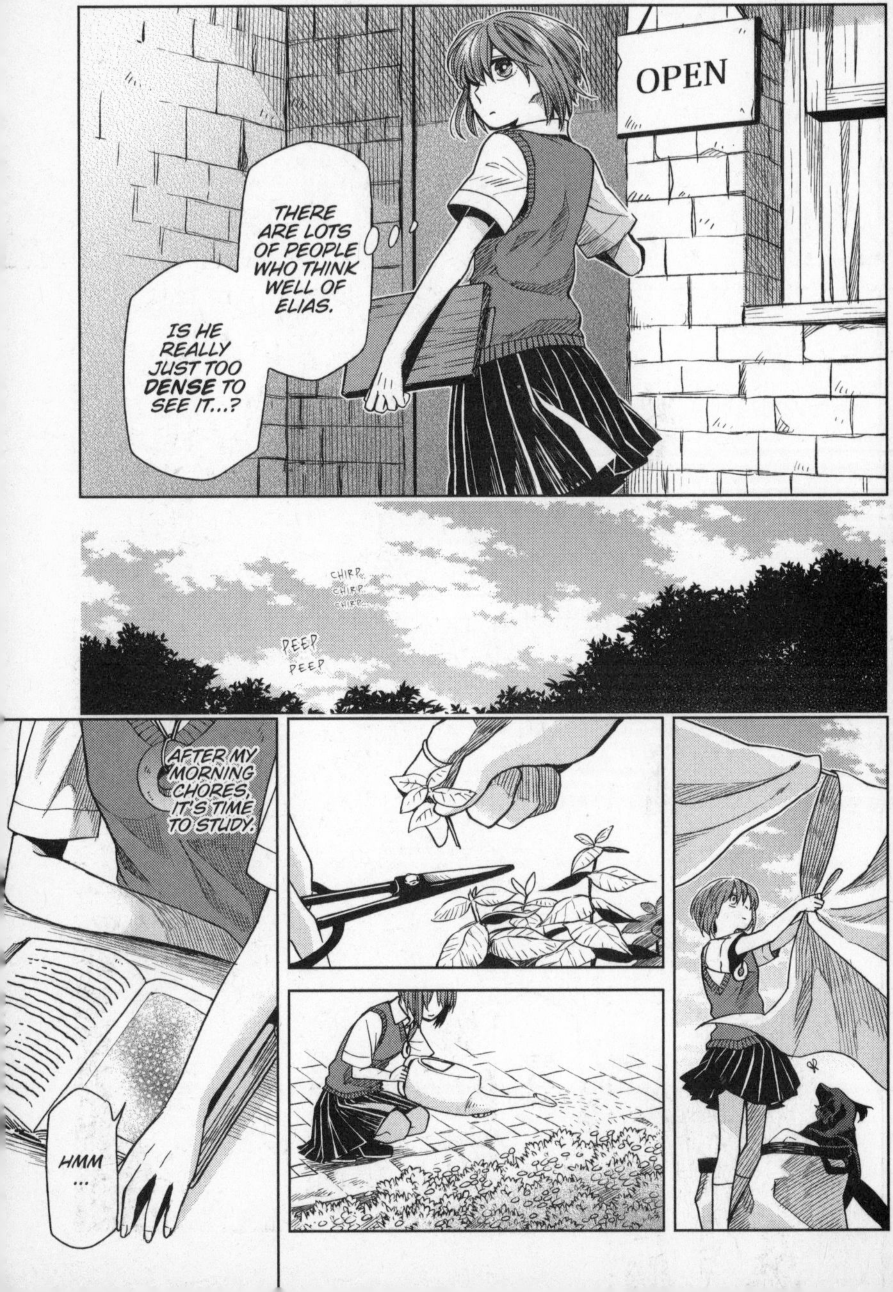
OPEN
THERE ARE LOTS OF PEOPLE WHO THINK WELL OF ELIAS.
IS HE REALLY JUST TOO DENSE TO SEE IT...?
CHIRP CHIRP CHIRP
PEEP PEEP
AFTER MY MORNING CHORES, IT'S TIME TO STUDY.
HMM ...

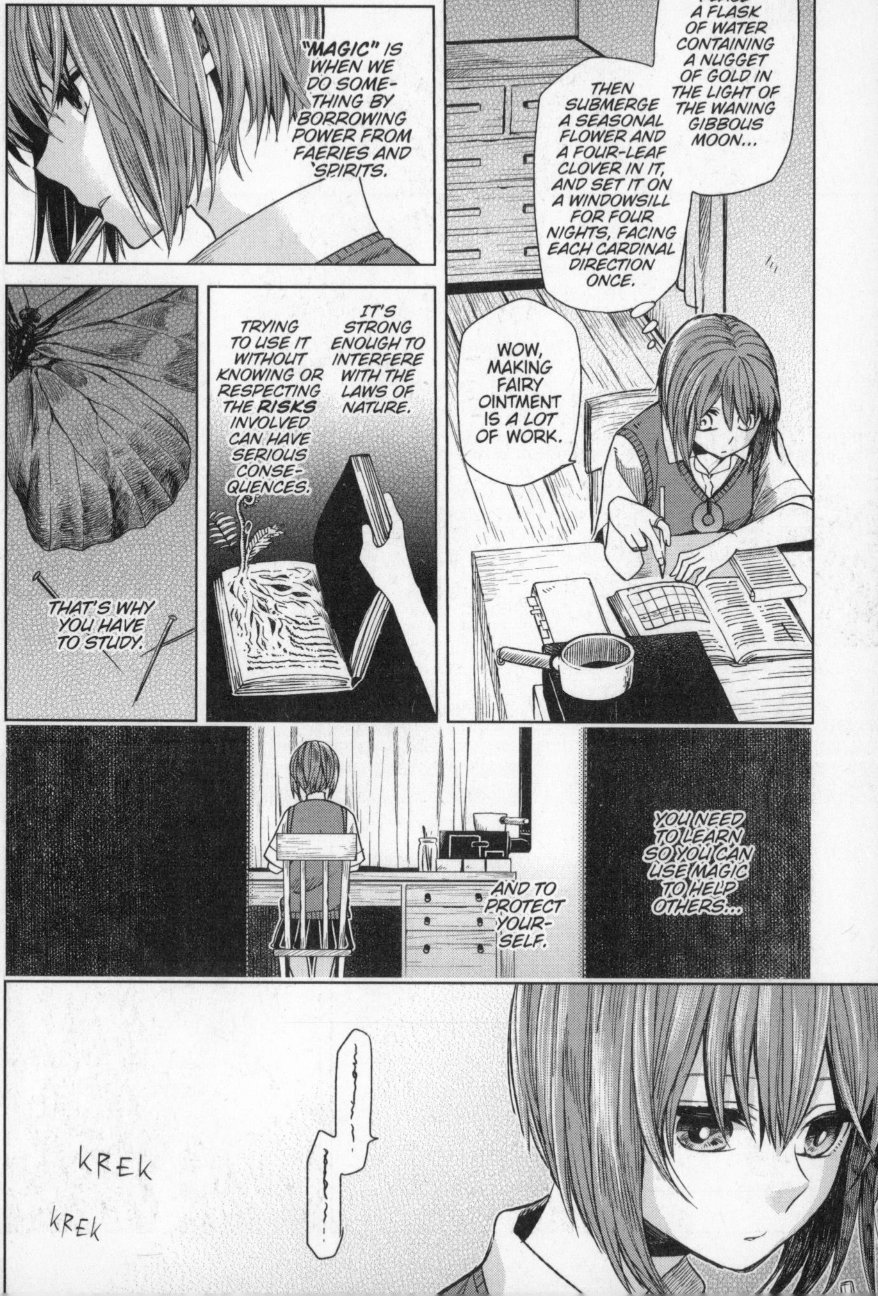
PLACE A FLASK OF WATER CONTAINING A NUGGET OF GOLD IN THE LIGHT OF THE WANING GIBBOUS MOON...
THEN SUBMERGE A SEASONAL FLOWER AND A FOUR-LEAF CLOVER IN IT, AND SET IT ON A WINDOWSILL FOR FOUR NIGHTS, FACING EACH CARDINAL DIRECTION ONCE.
WOW, MAKING FAIRY OINTMENT IS A LOT OF WORK.
"MAGIC" IS WHEN WE DO SOME-THING BY BORROWING POWER FROM FAERIES AND SPIRITS.
IT'S STRONG ENOUGH TO INTERFERE WITH THE LAWS OF NATURE.
TRYING TO USE IT WITHOUT KNOWING OR RESPECTING THE RISKS INVOLVED CAN HAVE SERIOUS CONSE-QUENCES.
THAT'S WHY YOU HAVE TO STUDY.
YOU NEED TO LEARN SO YOU CAN USE MAGIC TO HELP OTHERS...
AND TO PROTECT YOUR-SELF.
KREK
KREK

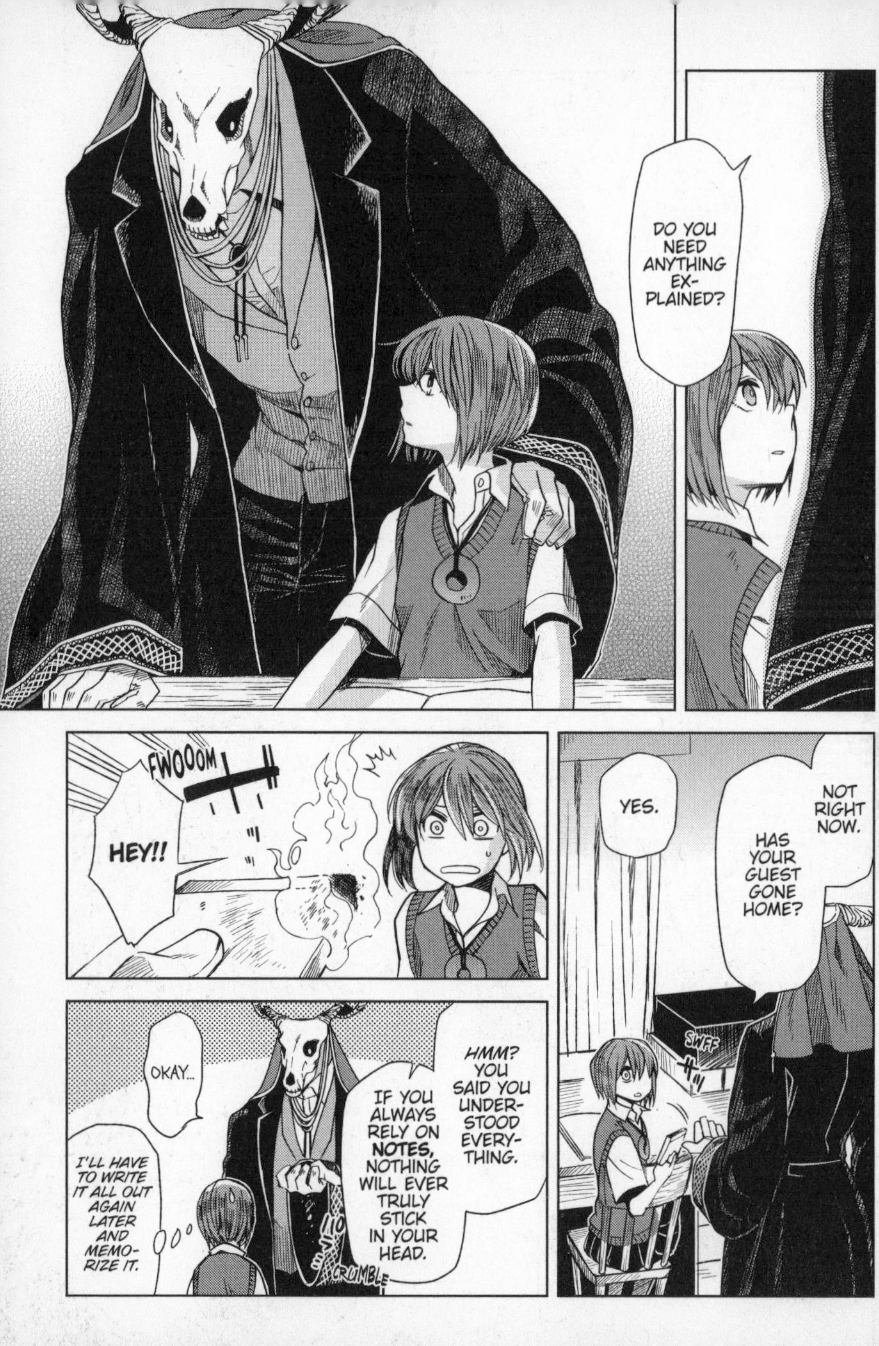
DO YOU NEED ANYTHING EX-PLAINED?
NOT RIGHT NOW.
HAS YOUR GUEST GONE HOME?
YES.
SWFF
FWOOOM
HEY!!
HMM? YOU SAID YOU UNDER-STOOD EVERY-THING.
IF YOU ALWAYS RELY ON **NOTES,** NOTHING WILL EVER TRULY STICK IN YOUR HEAD.
OKAY...
I'LL HAVE TO WRITE IT ALL OUT AGAIN LATER AND MEMO-RIZE IT.
CRUMBLE

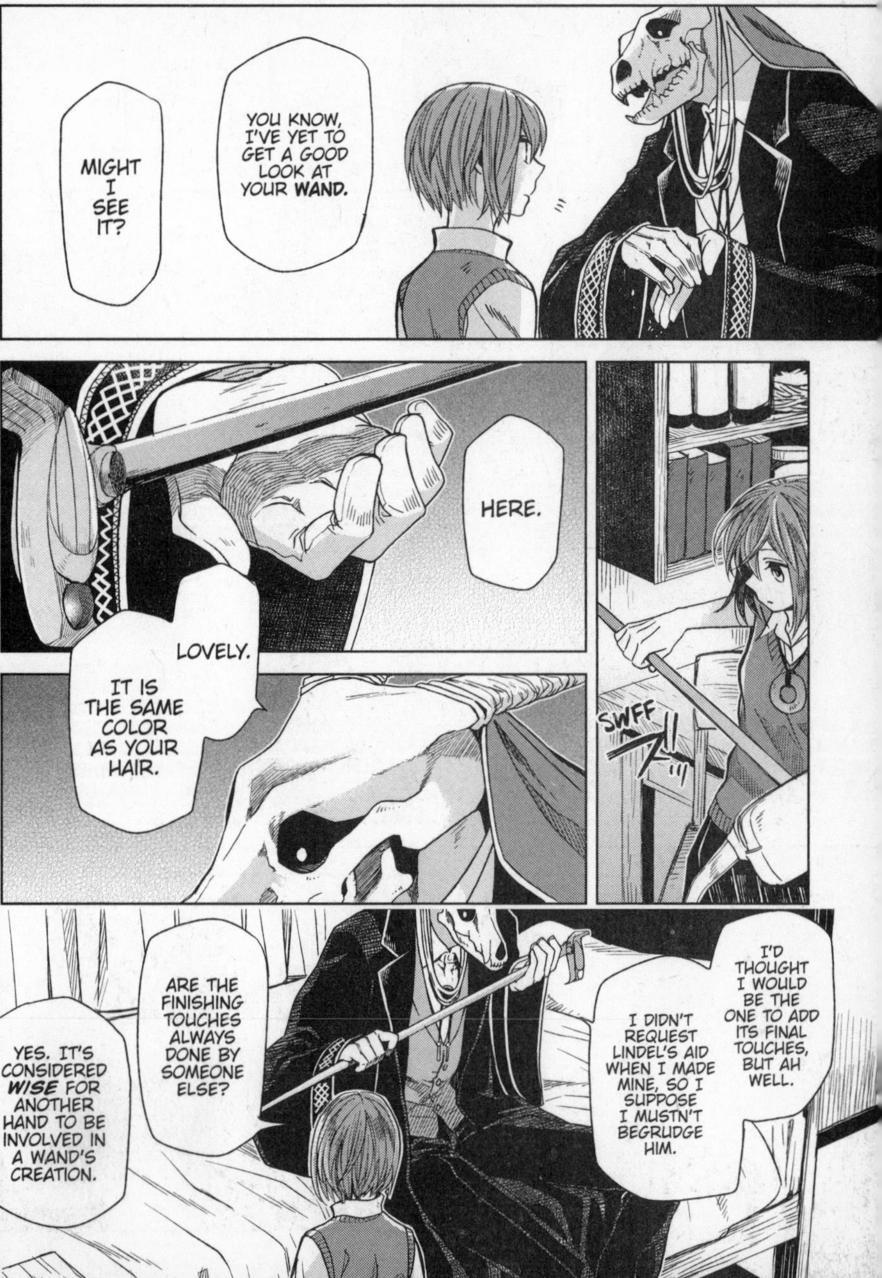
YOU KNOW, I'VE YET TO GET A GOOD LOOK AT YOUR WAND.
MIGHT I SEE IT?
SWFF
HERE.
LOVELY.
IT IS THE SAME COLOR AS YOUR HAIR.
I'D THOUGHT I WOULD BE THE ONE TO ADD ITS FINAL TOUCHES, BUT AH WELL.
I DIDN'T REQUEST LINDEL'S AID WHEN I MADE MINE, SO I SUPPOSE I MUSTN'T BEGRUDGE HIM.
ARE THE FINISHING TOUCHES ALWAYS DONE BY SOMEONE ELSE?
YES. IT'S CONSIDERED WISE FOR ANOTHER HAND TO BE INVOLVED IN A WAND'S CREATION.

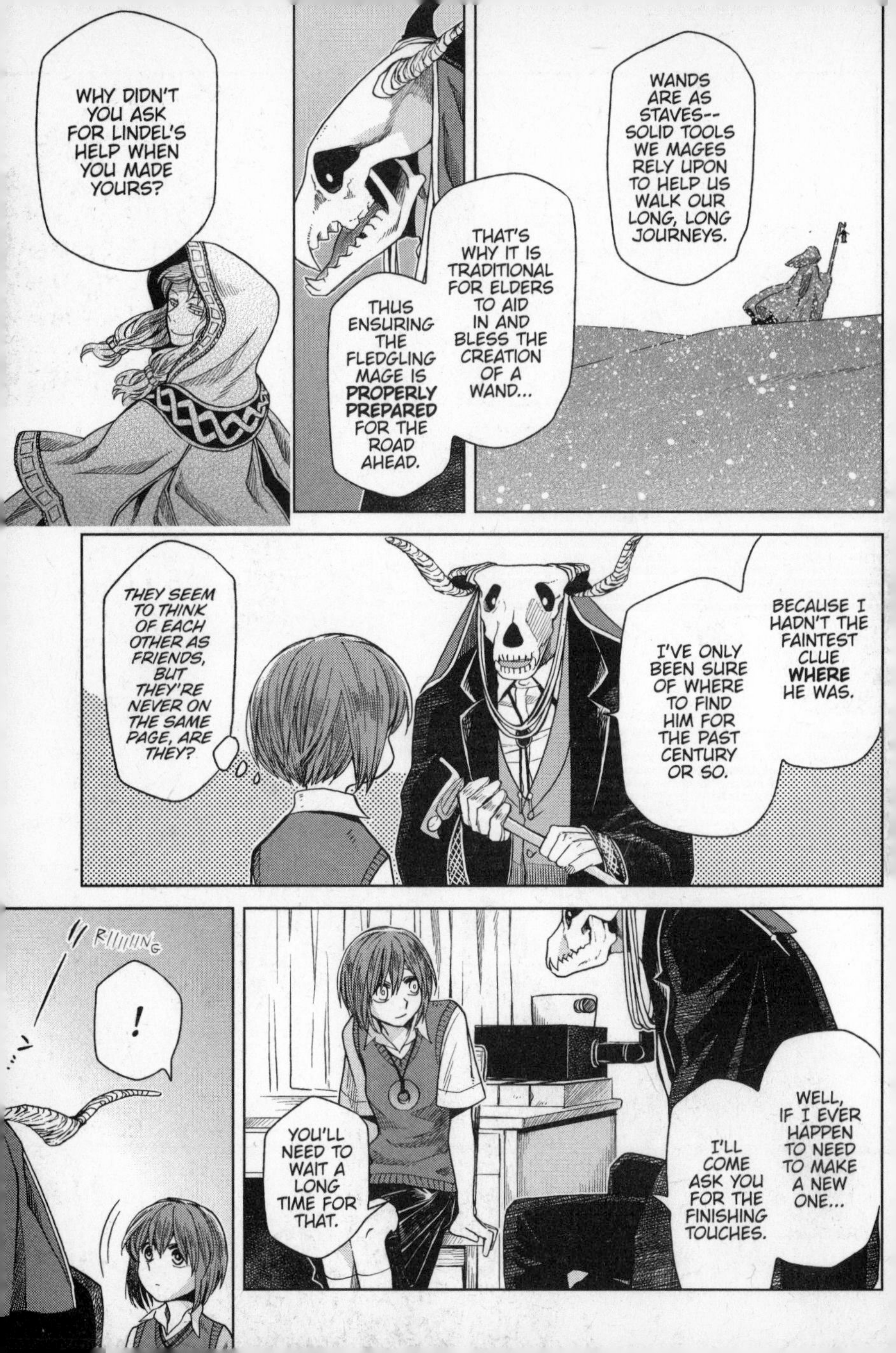
WANDS ARE AS STAVES-- SOLID TOOLS WE MAGES RELY UPON TO HELP US WALK OUR LONG, LONG JOURNEYS.
THAT'S WHY IT IS TRADITIONAL FOR ELDERS TO AID IN AND BLESS THE CREATION OF A WAND...
THUS ENSURING THE FLEDGLING MAGE IS PROPERLY PREPARED FOR THE ROAD AHEAD.
WHY DIDN'T YOU ASK FOR LINDEL'S HELP WHEN YOU MADE YOURS?
BECAUSE I HADN'T THE FAINTEST CLUE WHERE HE WAS.
I'VE ONLY BEEN SURE OF WHERE TO FIND HIM FOR THE PAST CENTURY OR SO.
THEY SEEM TO THINK OF EACH OTHER AS FRIENDS, BUT THEY'RE NEVER ON THE SAME PAGE, ARE THEY?
WELL, IF I EVER HAPPEN TO NEED TO MAKE A NEW ONE...
I'LL COME ASK YOU FOR THE FINISHING TOUCHES.
YOU'LL NEED TO WAIT A LONG TIME FOR THAT.
RIIIIING
!

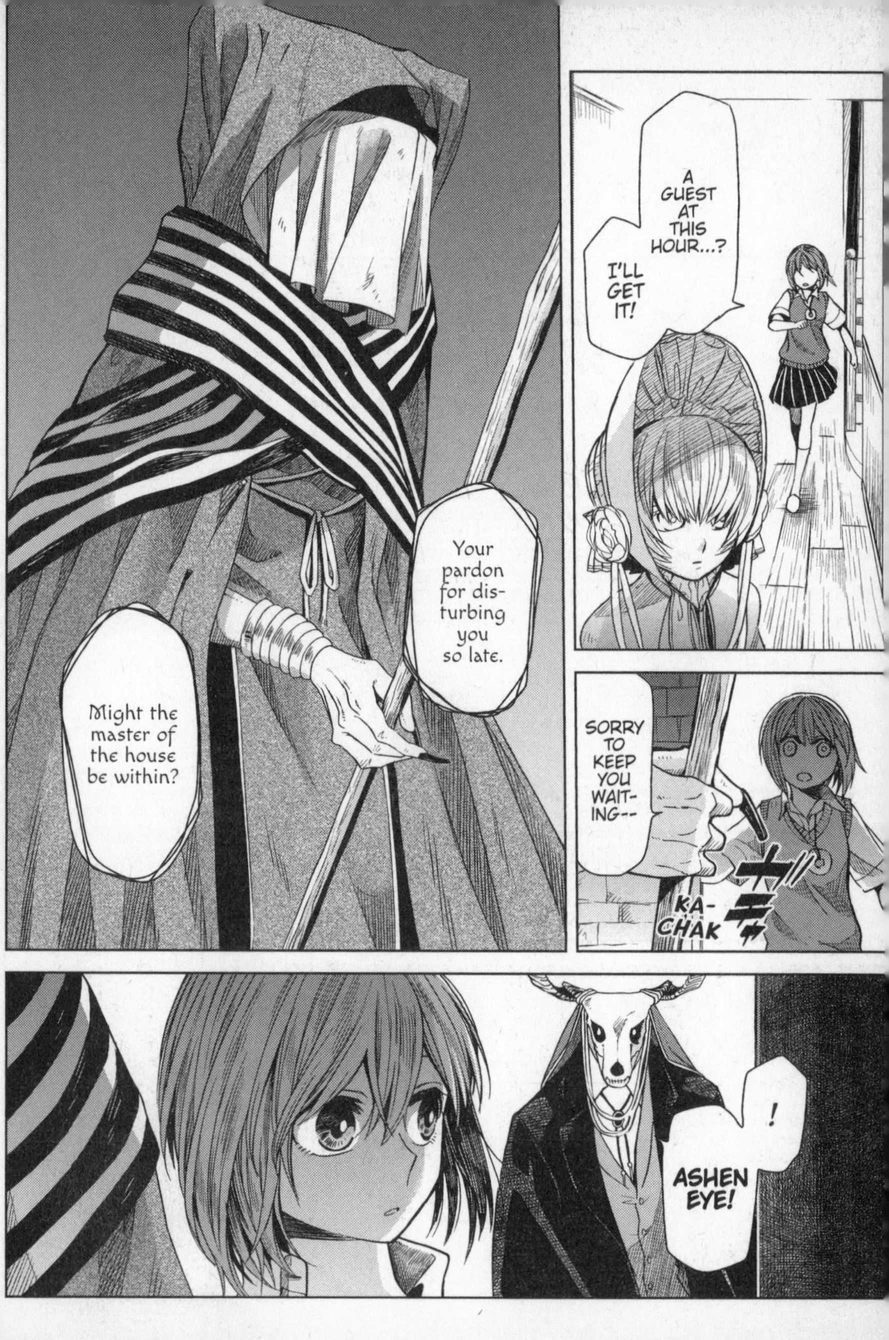
A GUEST AT THIS HOUR...?
I'LL GET IT!
SORRY TO KEEP YOU WAITING--
KA-CHAK
Your pardon for disturbing you so late.
Might the master of the house be within?
!
ASHEN EYE!

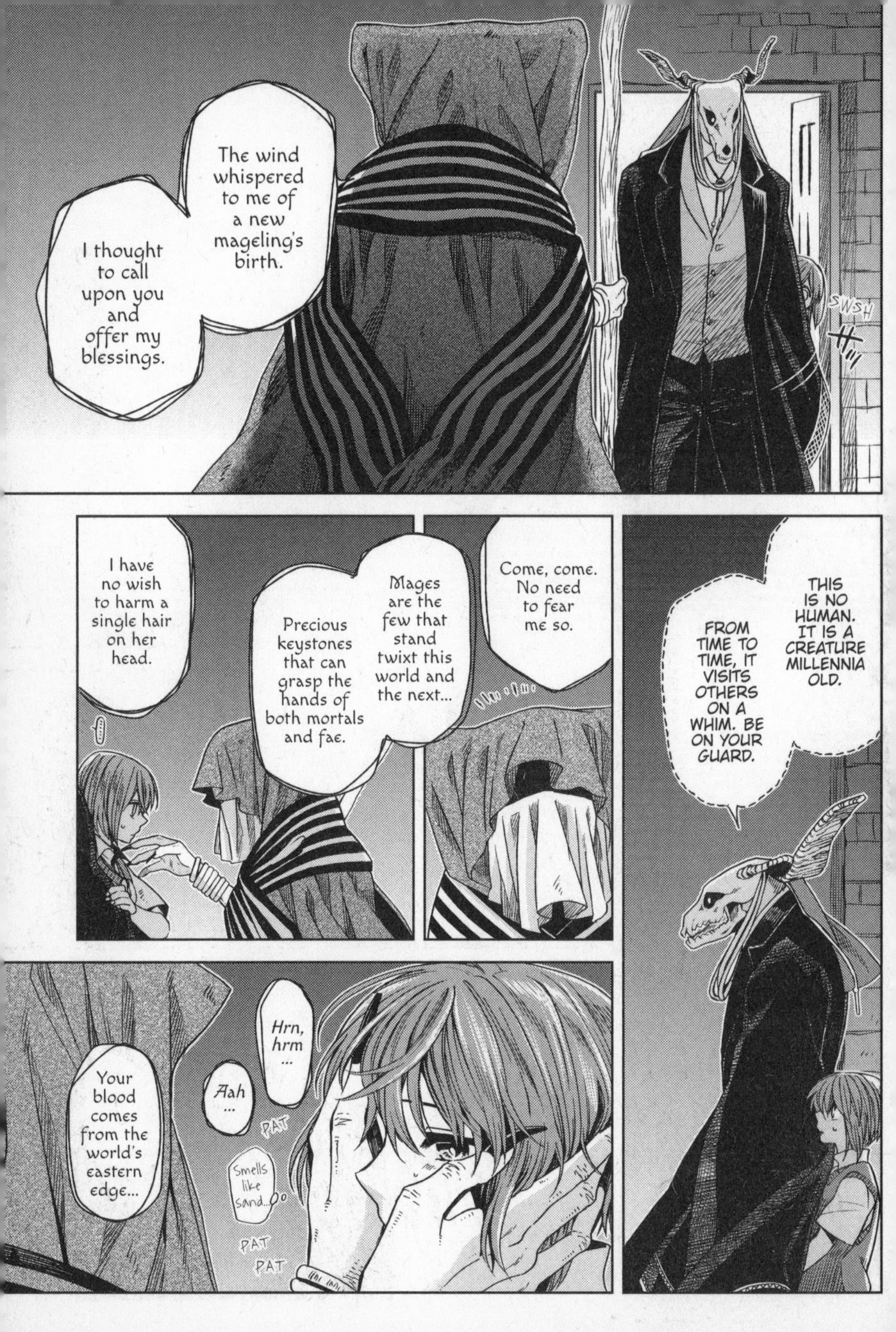
The wind whispered to me of a new mageling's birth.
I thought to call upon you and offer my blessings.
SWSH
THIS IS NO HUMAN. IT IS A CREATURE MILLENNIA OLD.
FROM TIME TO TIME, IT VISITS OTHERS ON A WHIM. BE ON YOUR GUARD.
Come, come. No need to fear me so.
Mages are the few that stand twixt this world and the next...
Precious keystones that can grasp the hands of both mortals and fae.
I have no wish to harm a single hair on her head.
......
Hrn, hrm ...
Aah ...
Your blood comes from the world's eastern edge...
PAT
Smells like sand...
PAT
PAT

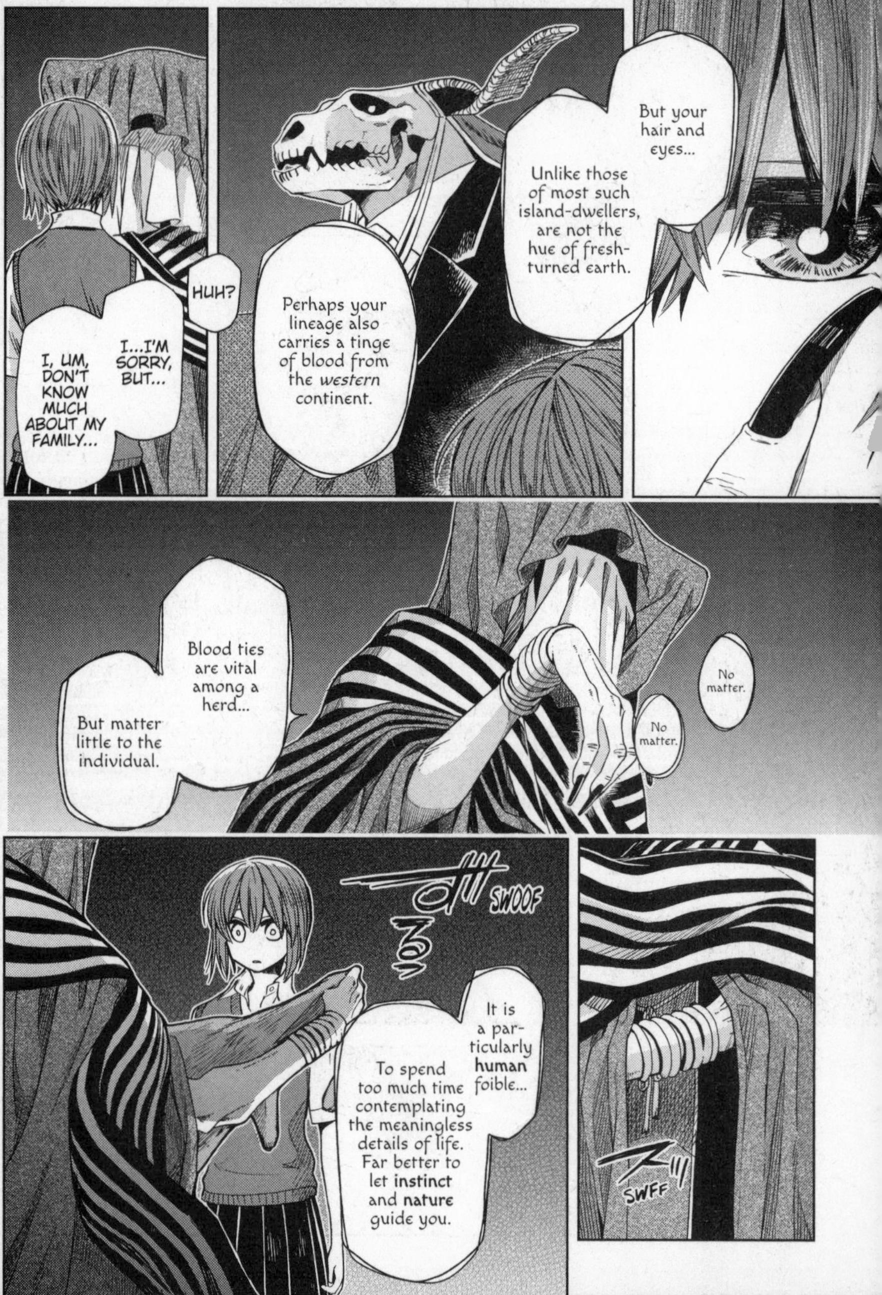

But your hair and eyes...
Unlike those of most such island-dwellers, are not the hue of fresh-turned earth.
Perhaps your lineage also carries a tinge of blood from the *western* continent.
HUH?
I...I'M SORRY, BUT...
I, UM, DON'T KNOW MUCH ABOUT MY FAMILY...
No matter.
No matter.
Blood ties are vital among a herd...
But matter little to the individual.
SWFF
SWOOF
It is a particularly **human** foible...
To spend too much time contemplating the meaningless details of life. Far better to let **instinct** and **nature** guide you.

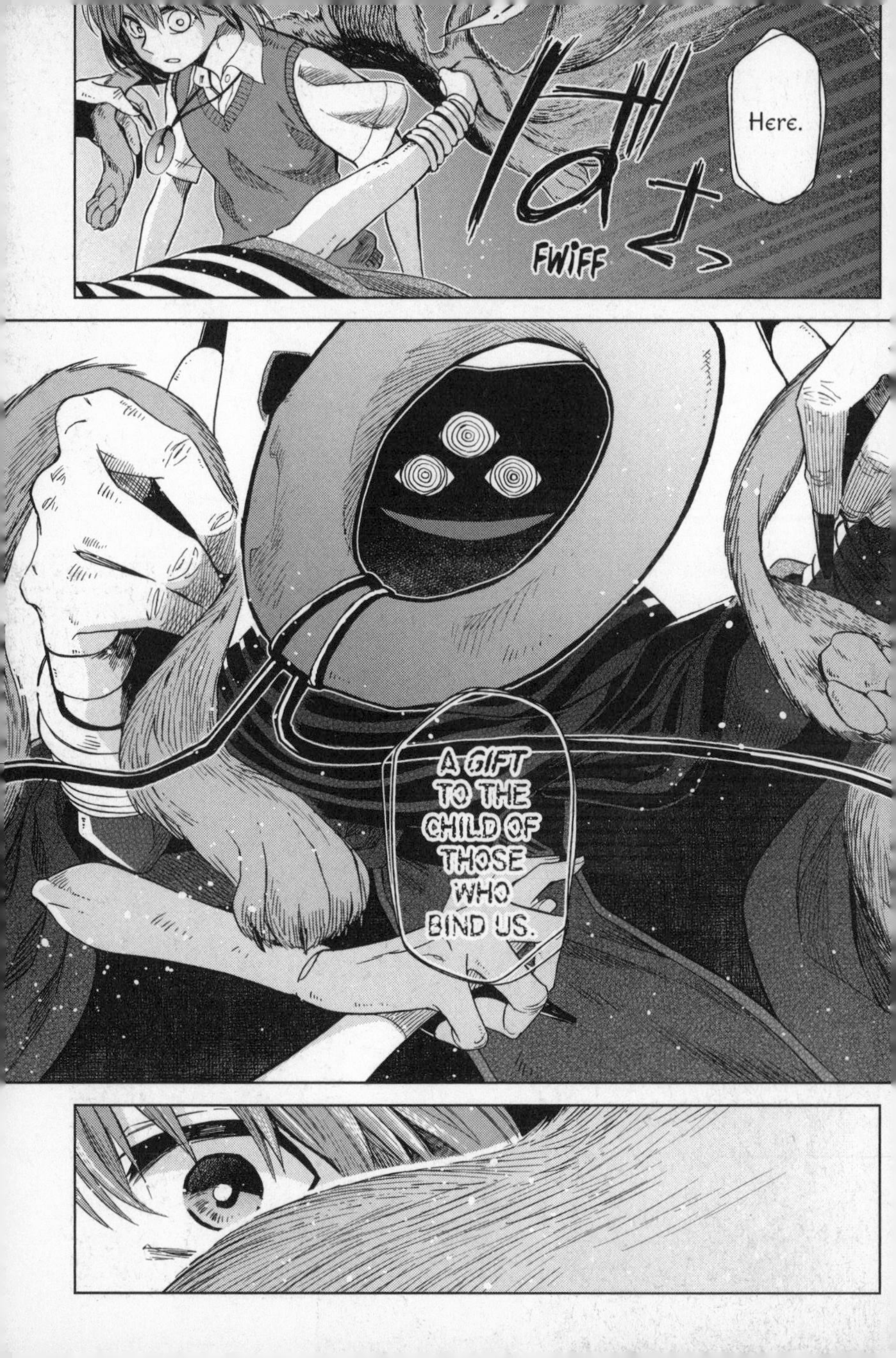
Here.
はさっ
FWIFF
A GIFT TO THE CHILD OF THOSE WHO BIND US.

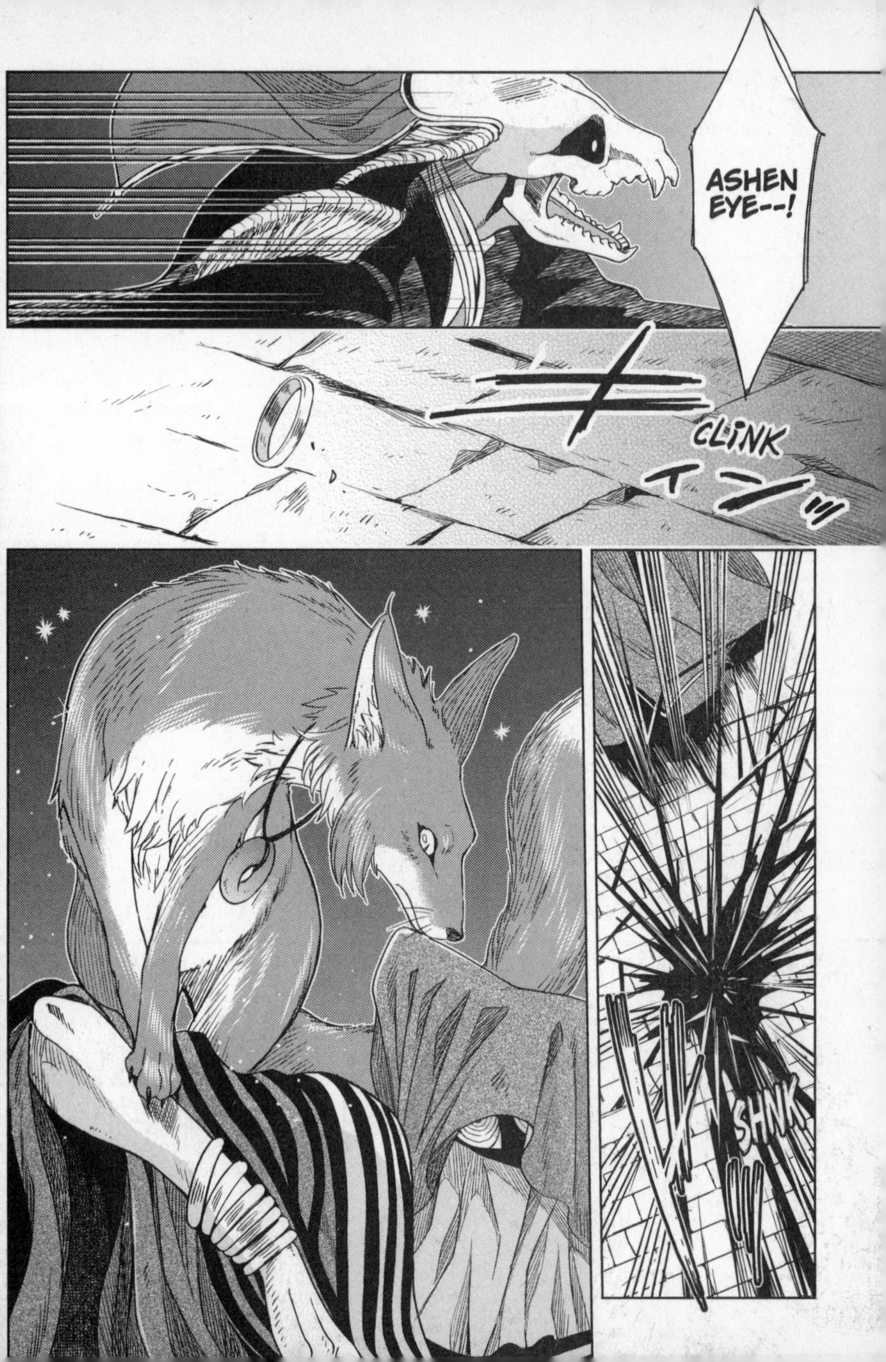
ASHEN EYE--!
CLINK
イン
SHNK

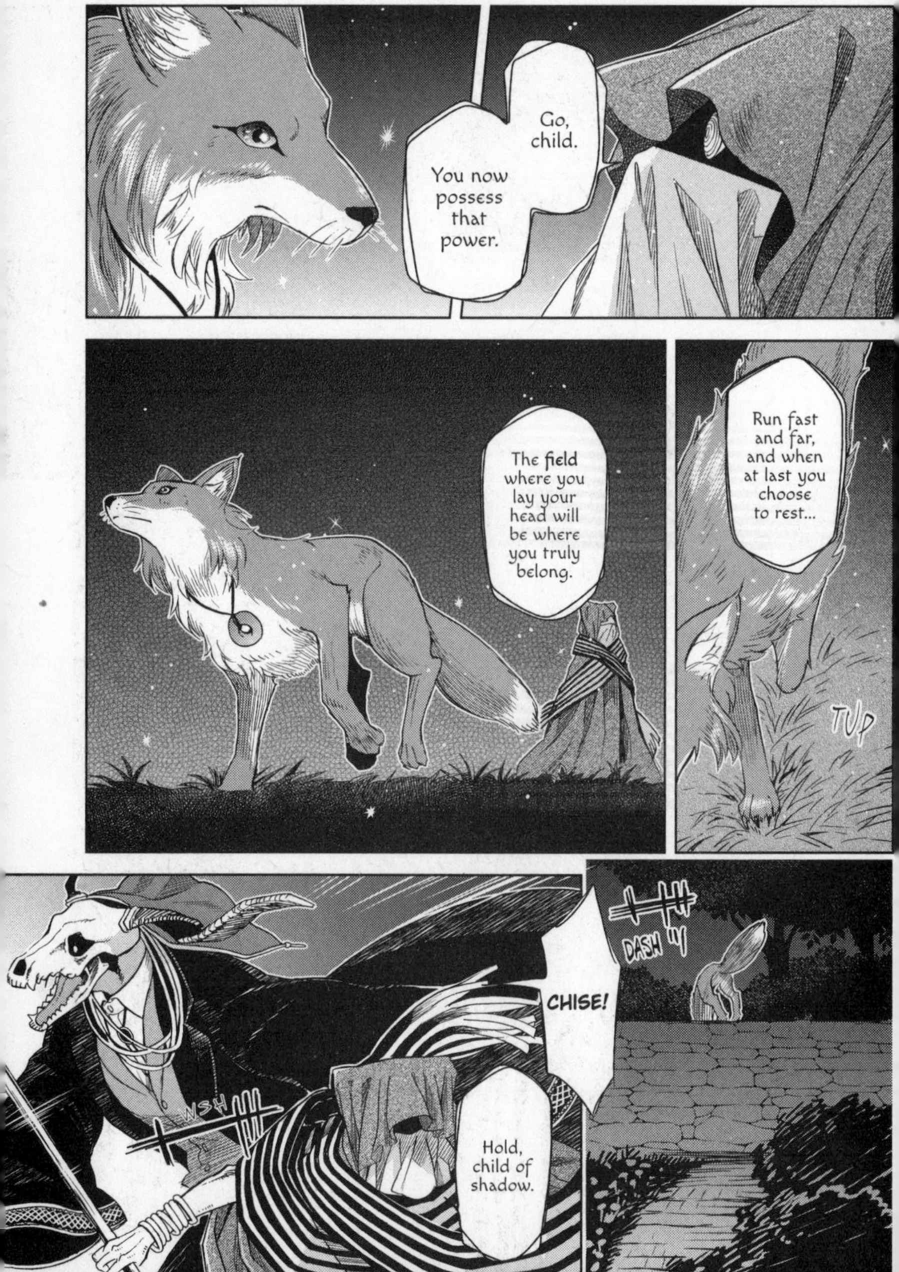
Go, child.
You now possess that power.
Run fast and far, and when at last you choose to rest...
TUP
The field where you lay your head will be where you truly belong.
DASH
CHISE!
WSH
Hold, child of shadow.

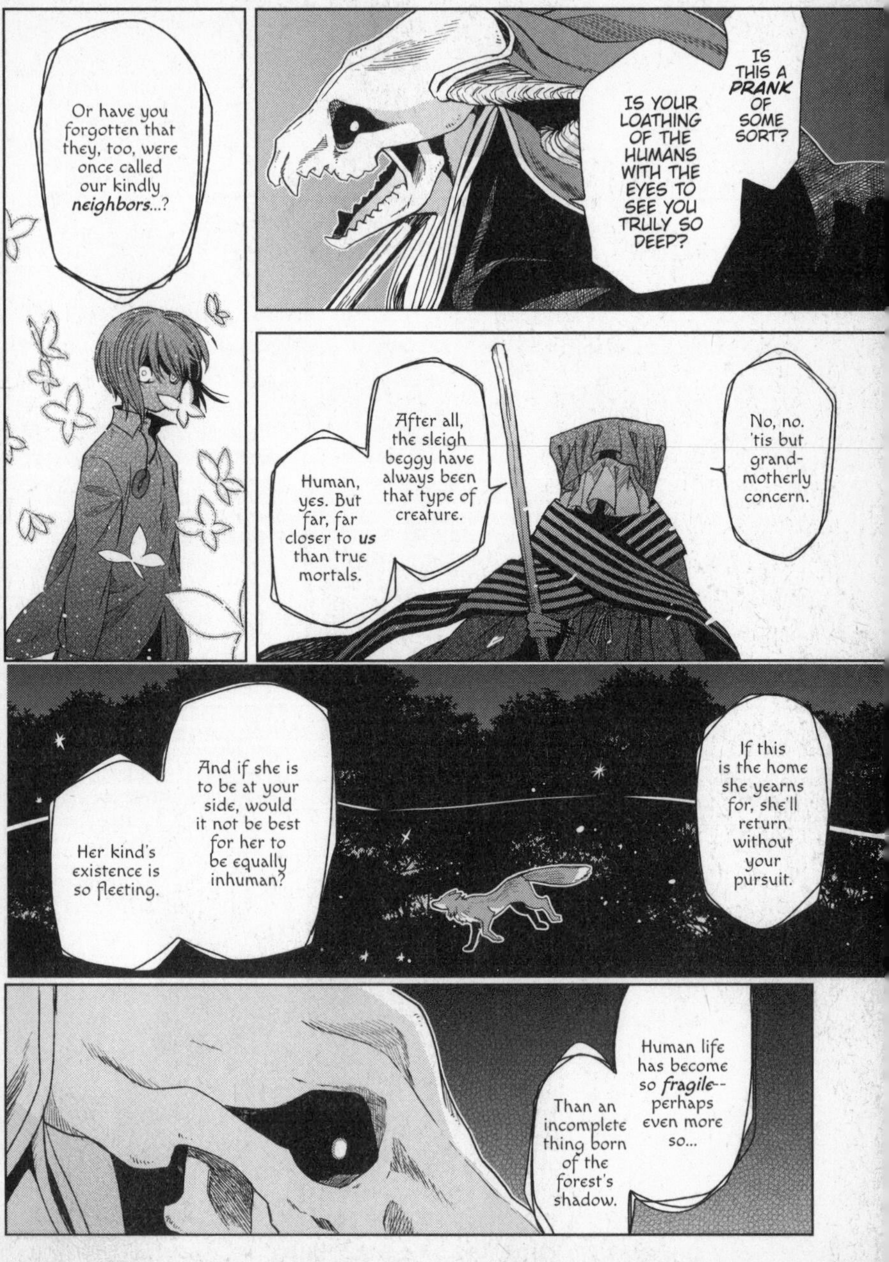
IS THIS A PRANK OF SOME SORT?
IS YOUR LOATHING OF THE HUMANS WITH THE EYES TO SEE YOU TRULY SO DEEP?
No, no. 'tis but grand-motherly concern.
After all, the sleigh beggy have always been that type of creature.
Human, yes. But far, far closer to us than true mortals.
Or have you forgotten that they, too, were once called our kindly neighbors...?
If this is the home she yearns for, she'll return without your pursuit.
And if she is to be at your side, would it not be best for her to be equally inhuman?
Her kind's existence is so fleeting.
Human life has become so fragile-- perhaps even more so...
Than an incomplete thing born of the forest's shadow.

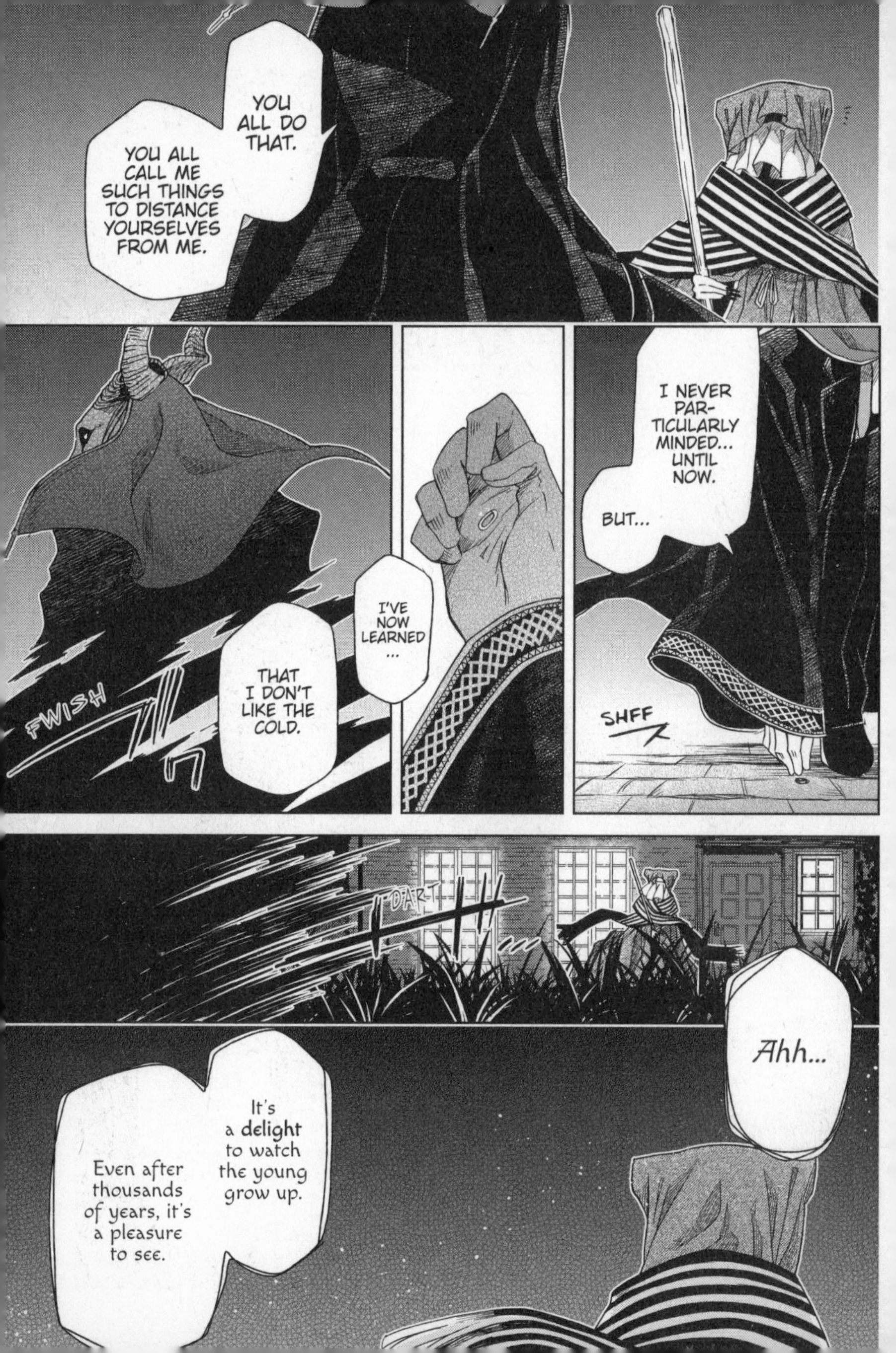
YOU ALL DO THAT.
YOU ALL CALL ME SUCH THINGS TO DISTANCE YOURSELVES FROM ME.
I NEVER PAR-TICULARLY MINDED... UNTIL NOW.
BUT...
SHFF
I'VE NOW LEARNED ...
THAT I DON'T LIKE THE COLD.
FWISH
DART
Ahh...
It's a delight to watch the young grow up.
Even after thousands of years, it's a pleasure to see.

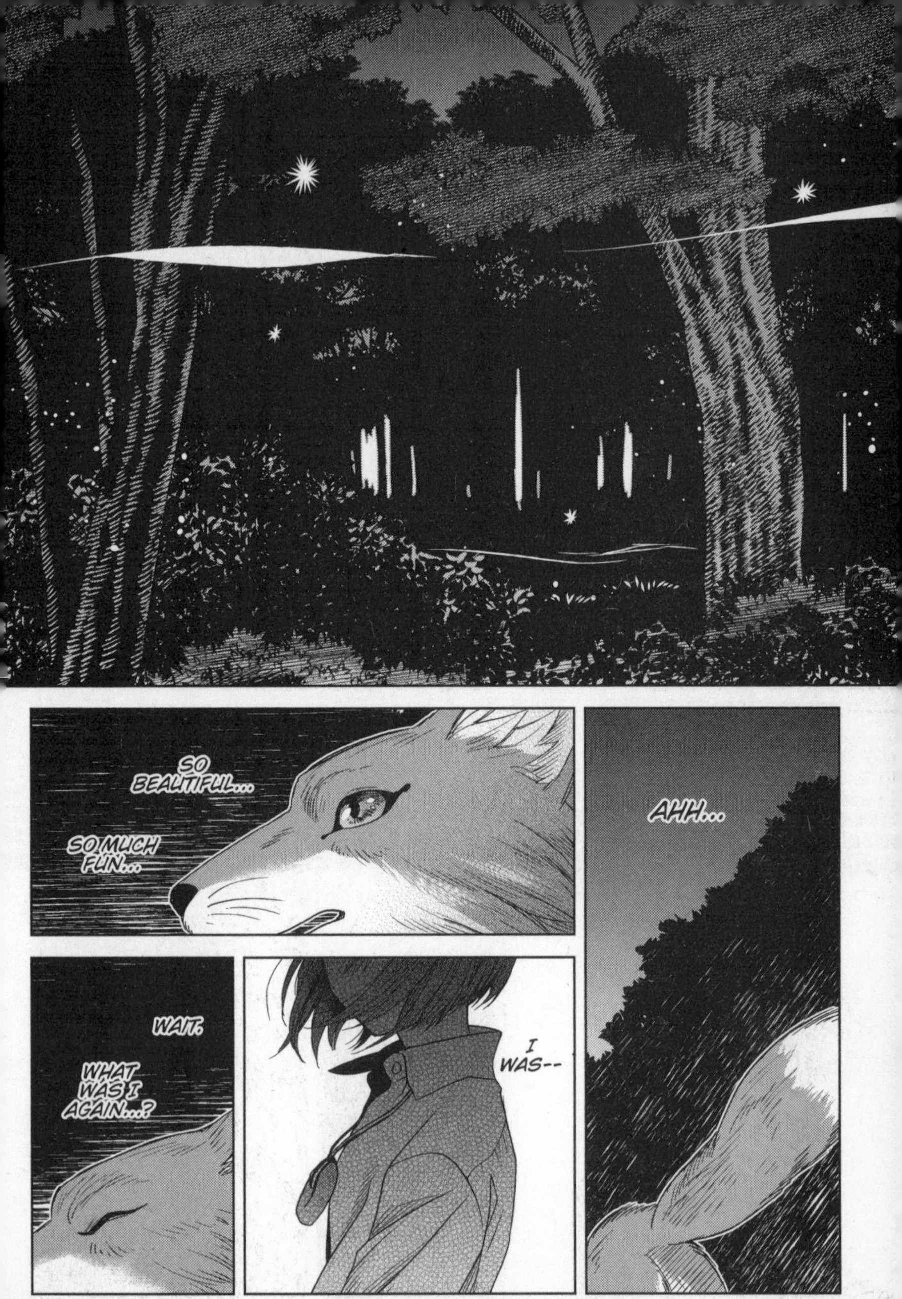
AHH...
SO BEAUTIFUL...
SO MUCH FUN...
I WAS--
WAIT.
WHAT WAS I AGAIN...?

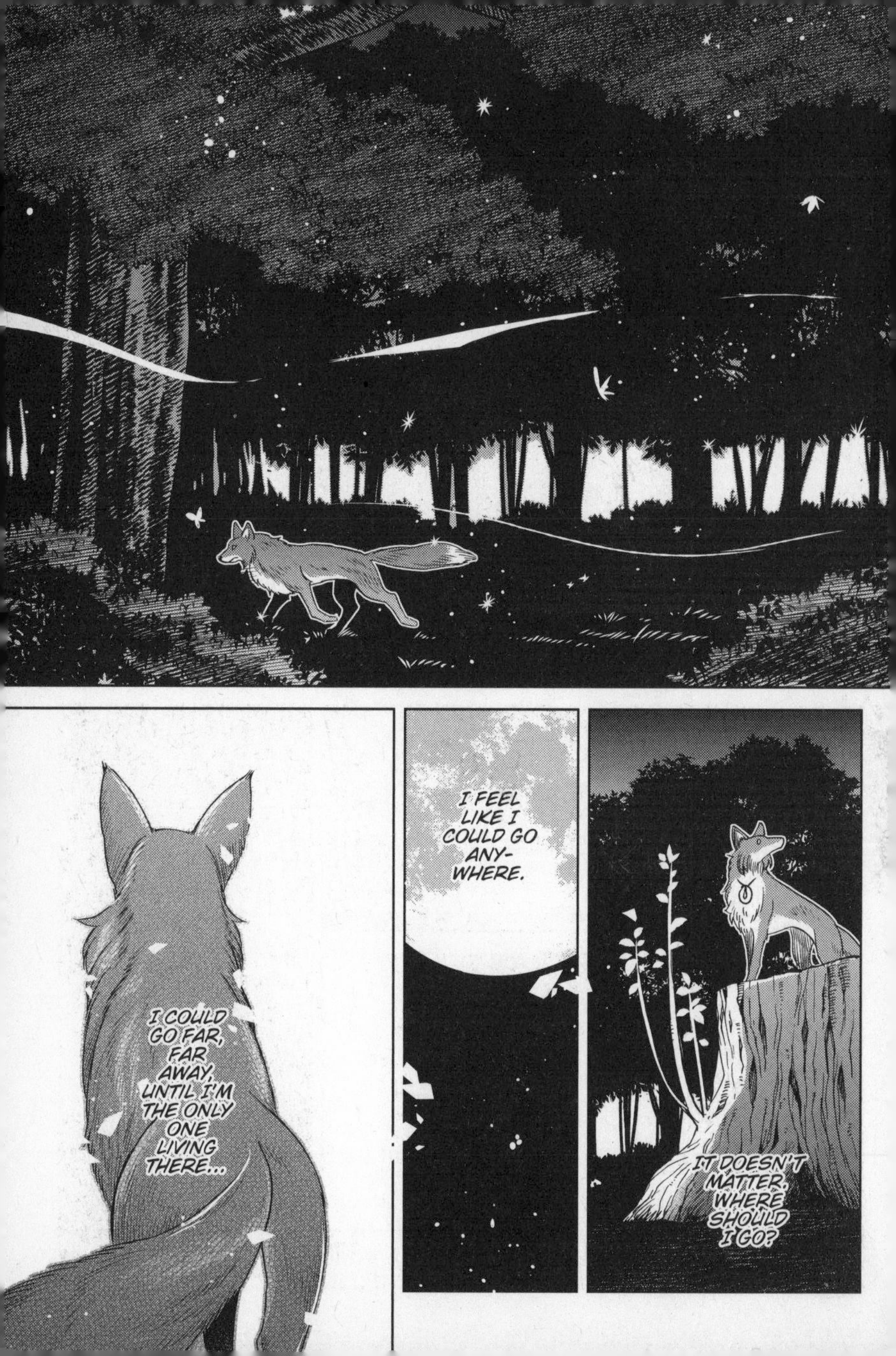
IT DOESN'T MATTER. WHERE SHOULD I GO?
I FEEL LIKE I COULD GO ANYWHERE.
I COULD GO FAR, FAR AWAY, UNTIL I'M THE ONLY ONE LIVING THERE...

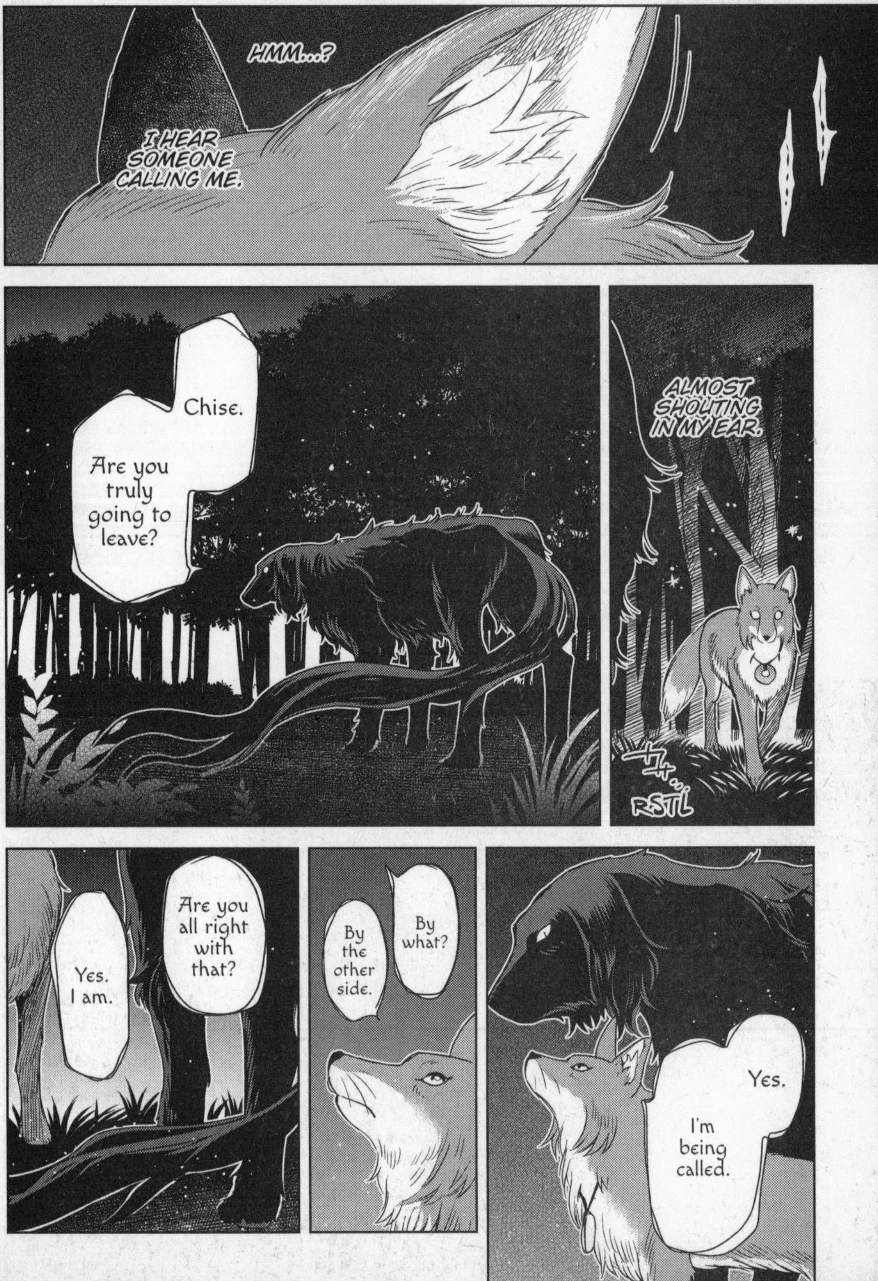
HMM...?
I HEAR SOMEONE CALLING ME.
ALMOST SHOUTING IN MY EAR.
RSTL
Chise.
Are you truly going to leave?
Yes.
I'm being called.
By what?
By the other side.
Are you all right with that?
Yes. I am.

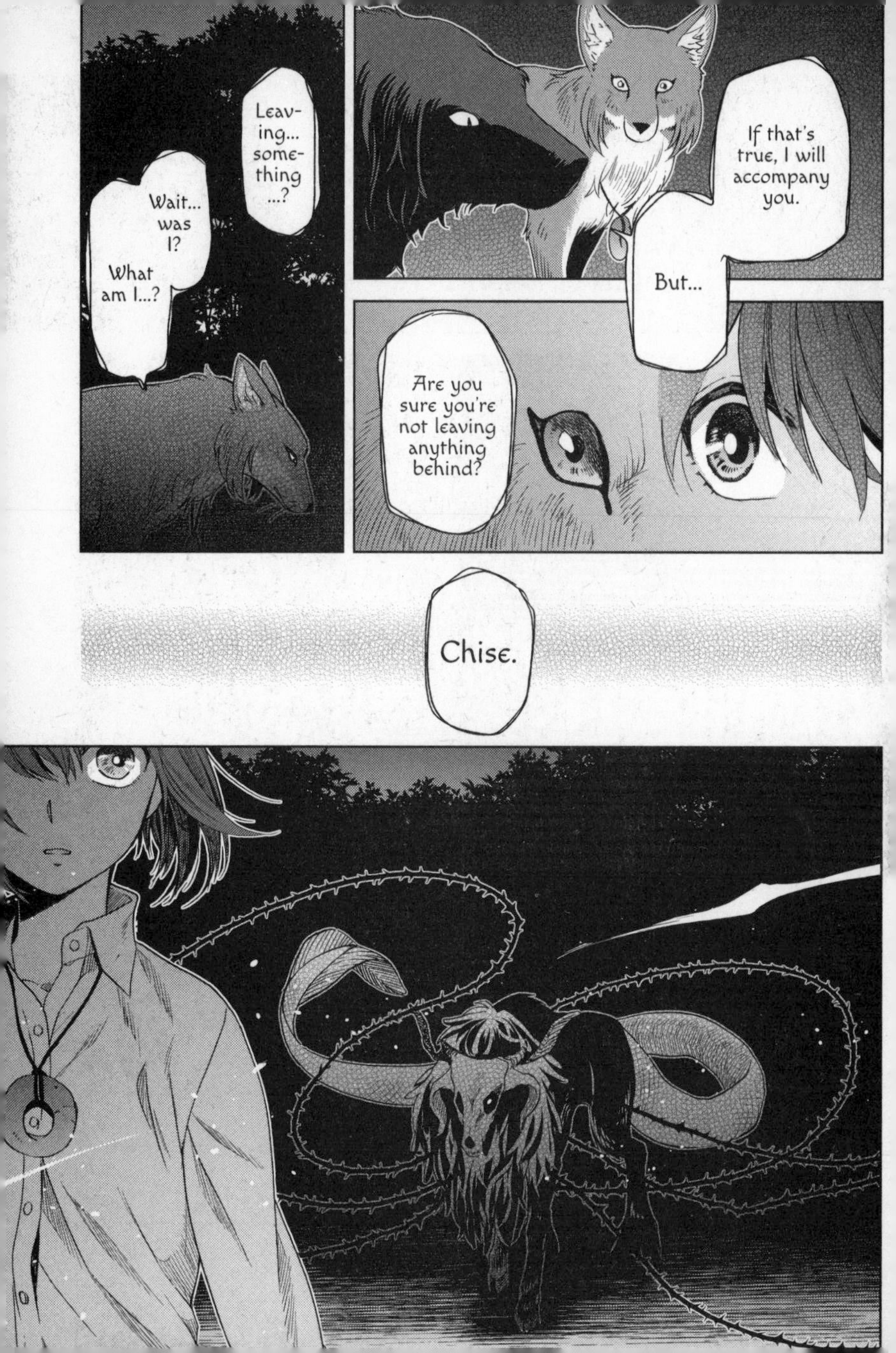

If that's true, I will accompany you.
But...
Are you sure you're not leaving anything behind?
Leaving... something...?
Wait... was I?
What am I...?
Chise.

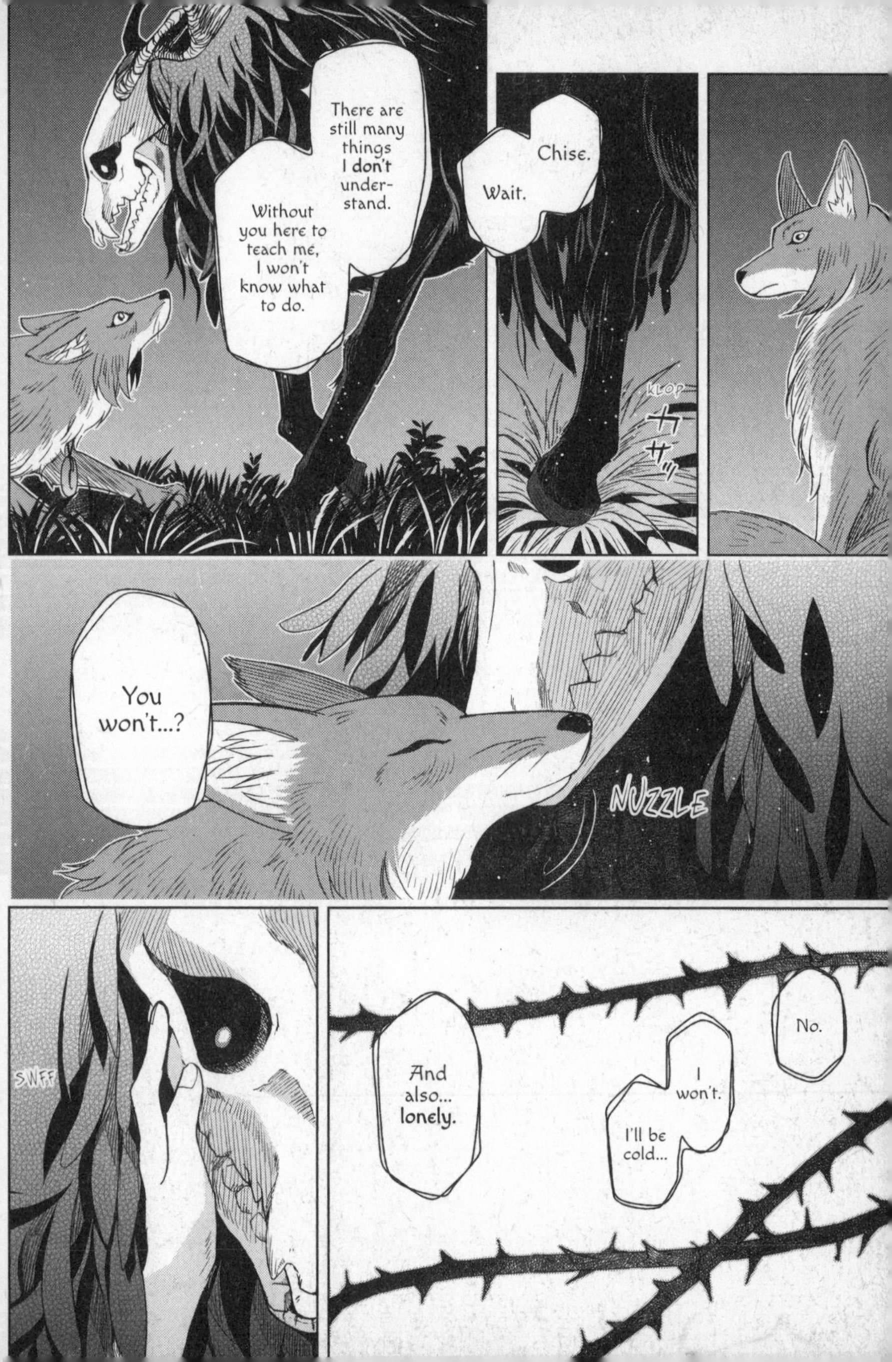

Chise.
Wait.
KLOP
There are still many things I **don't** understand.
Without you here to teach me, I won't know what to do.
You won't...?
NUZZLE
No.
I won't.
I'll be cold...
And also... **lonely.**
SWFF

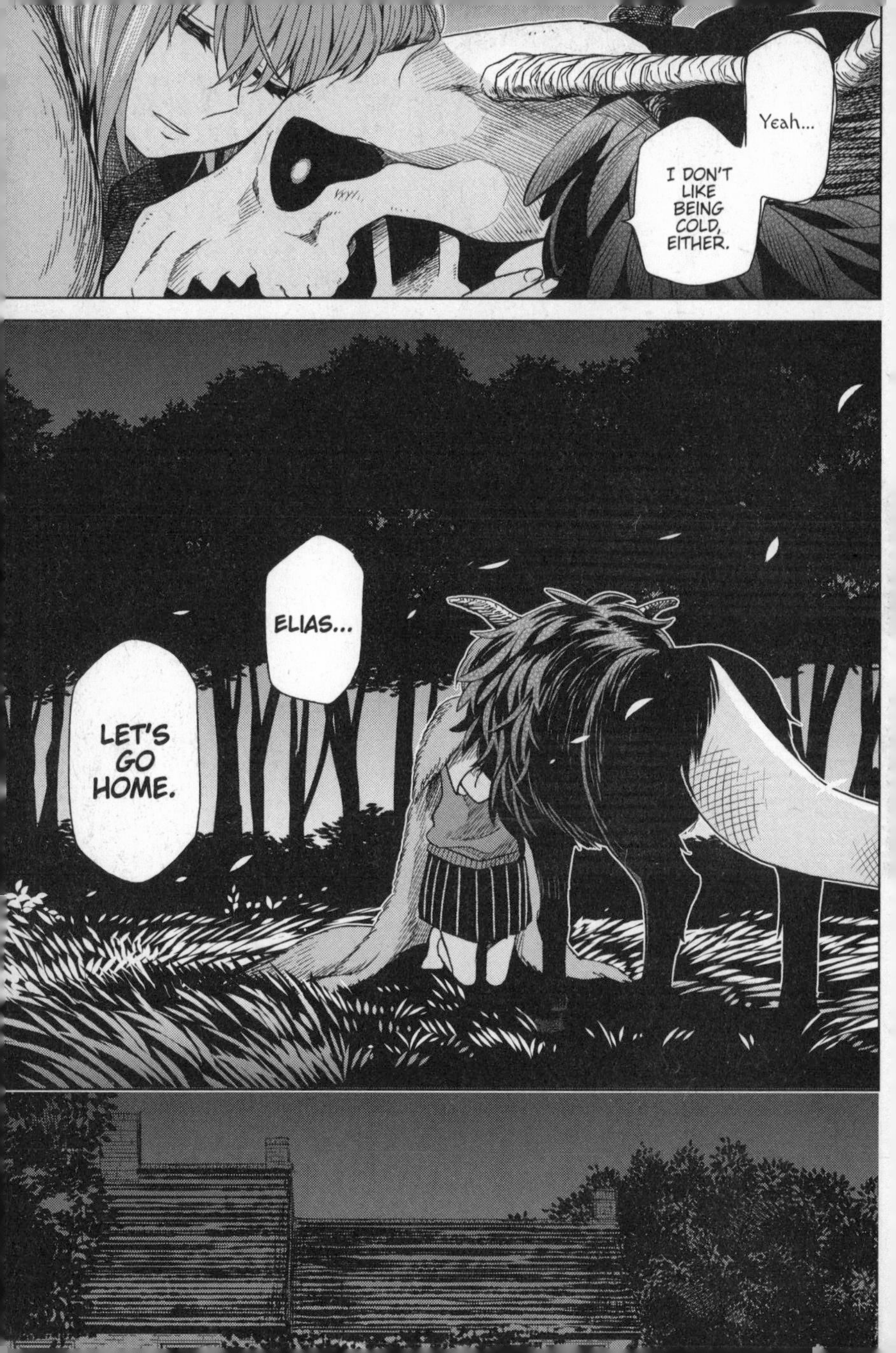
Yeah...
I DON'T LIKE BEING COLD, EITHER.
ELIAS...
LET'S GO HOME.

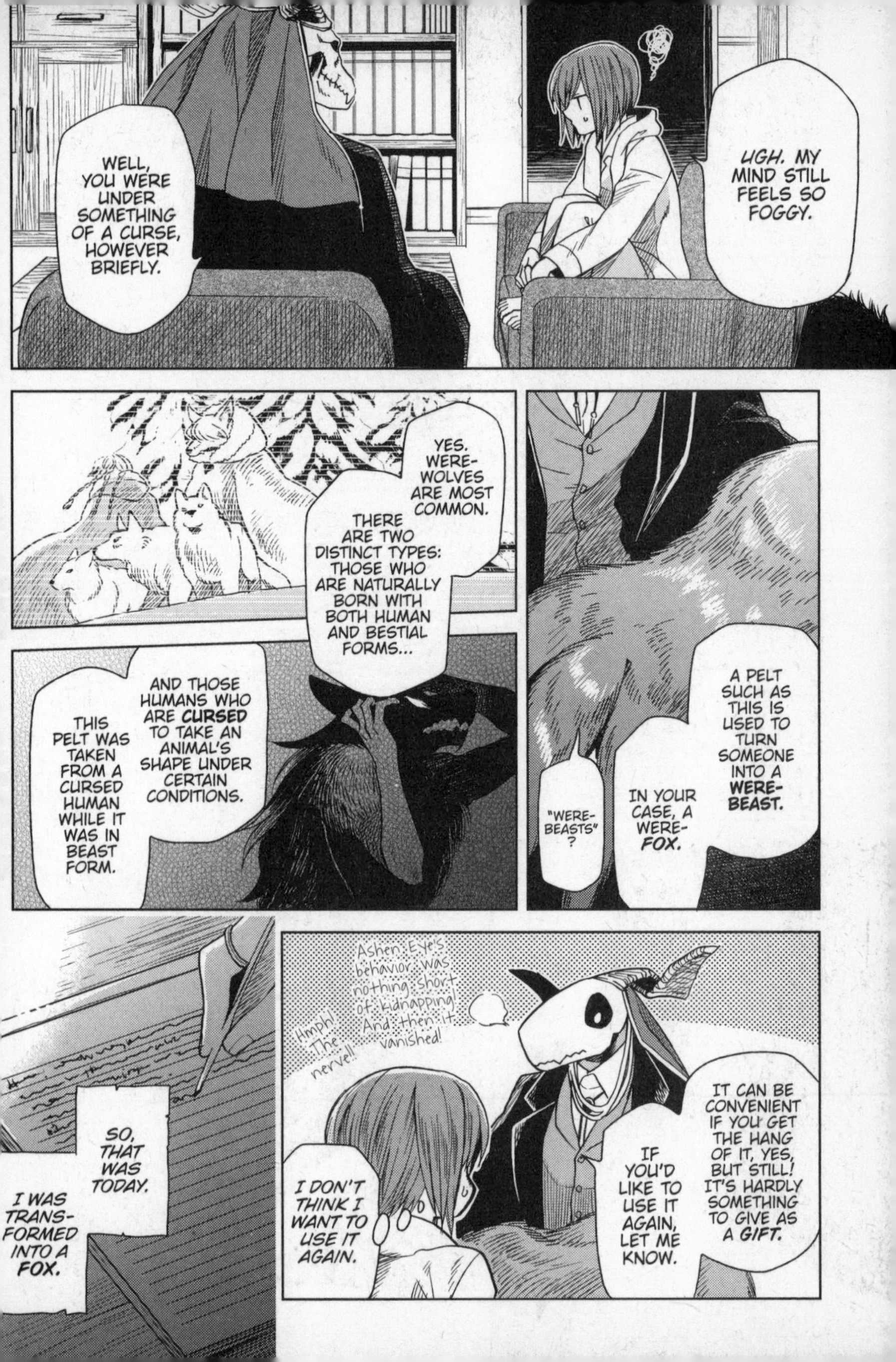
UGH. MY MIND STILL FEELS SO FOGGY.
WELL, YOU WERE UNDER SOMETHING OF A CURSE, HOWEVER BRIEFLY.
A PELT SUCH AS THIS IS USED TO TURN SOMEONE INTO A WERE-BEAST.
IN YOUR CASE, A WERE-FOX.
"WERE-BEASTS"?
YES. WERE-WOLVES ARE MOST COMMON.
THERE ARE TWO DISTINCT TYPES: THOSE WHO ARE NATURALLY BORN WITH BOTH HUMAN AND BESTIAL FORMS...
AND THOSE HUMANS WHO ARE CURSED TO TAKE AN ANIMAL'S SHAPE UNDER CERTAIN CONDITIONS.
THIS PELT WAS TAKEN FROM A CURSED HUMAN WHILE IT WAS IN BEAST FORM.
IT CAN BE CONVENIENT IF YOU GET THE HANG OF IT, YES, BUT STILL! IT'S HARDLY SOMETHING TO GIVE AS A GIFT.
Ashen Eye's behavior was nothing short of kidnapping! And then it vanished!
Hmph! The nerve!!
IF YOU'D LIKE TO USE IT AGAIN, LET ME KNOW.
I DON'T THINK I WANT TO USE IT AGAIN.
SO, THAT WAS TODAY.
I WAS TRANS-FORMED INTO A FOX.

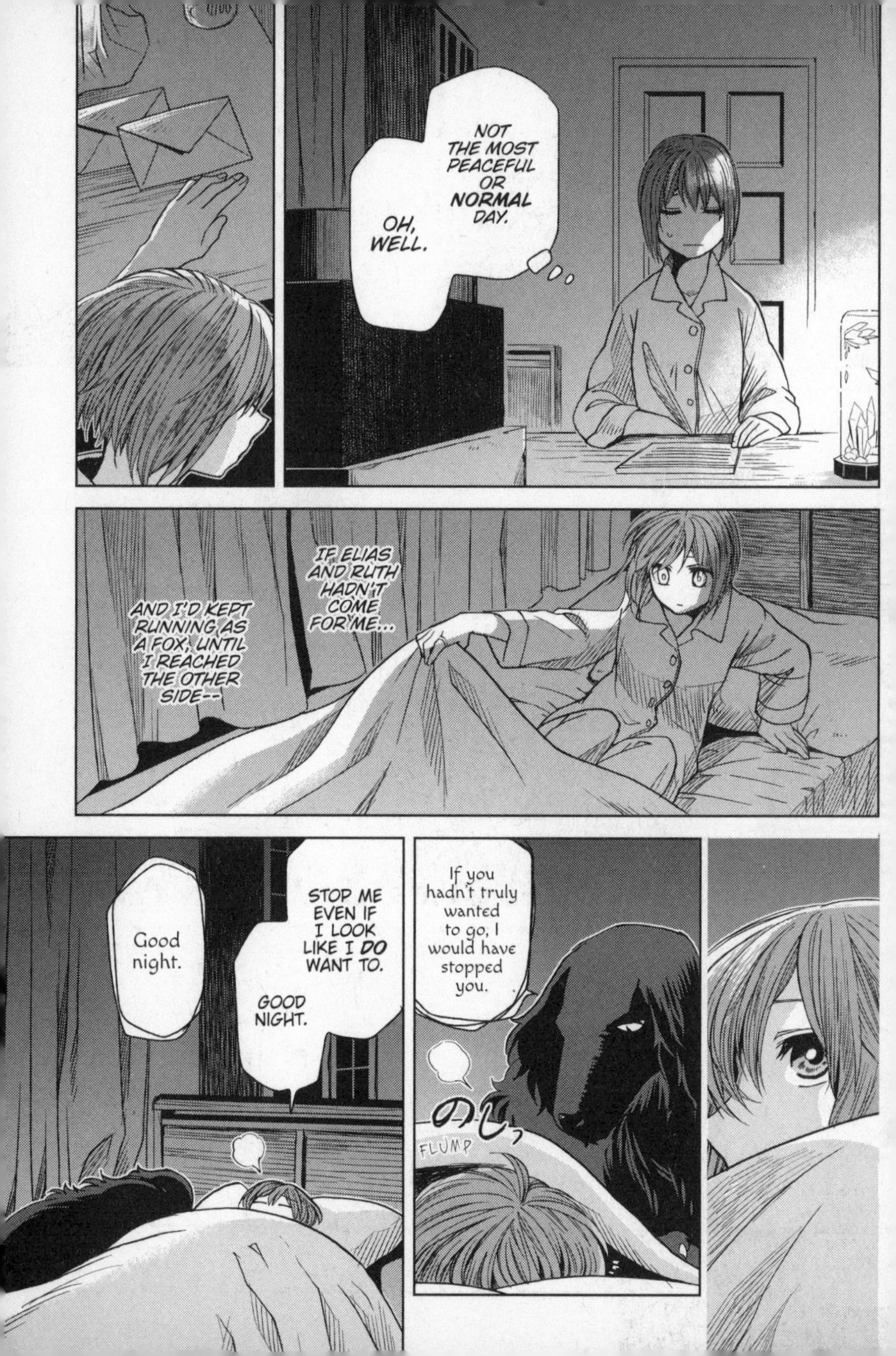
NOT THE MOST PEACEFUL OR NORMAL DAY.
OH, WELL.
IF ELIAS AND RUTH HADN'T COME FOR ME...
AND I'D KEPT RUNNING AS A FOX, UNTIL I REACHED THE OTHER SIDE--
If you hadn't truly wanted to go, I would have stopped you.
のしっ
FLUMP
STOP ME EVEN IF I LOOK LIKE I DO WANT TO.
GOOD NIGHT.
Good night.

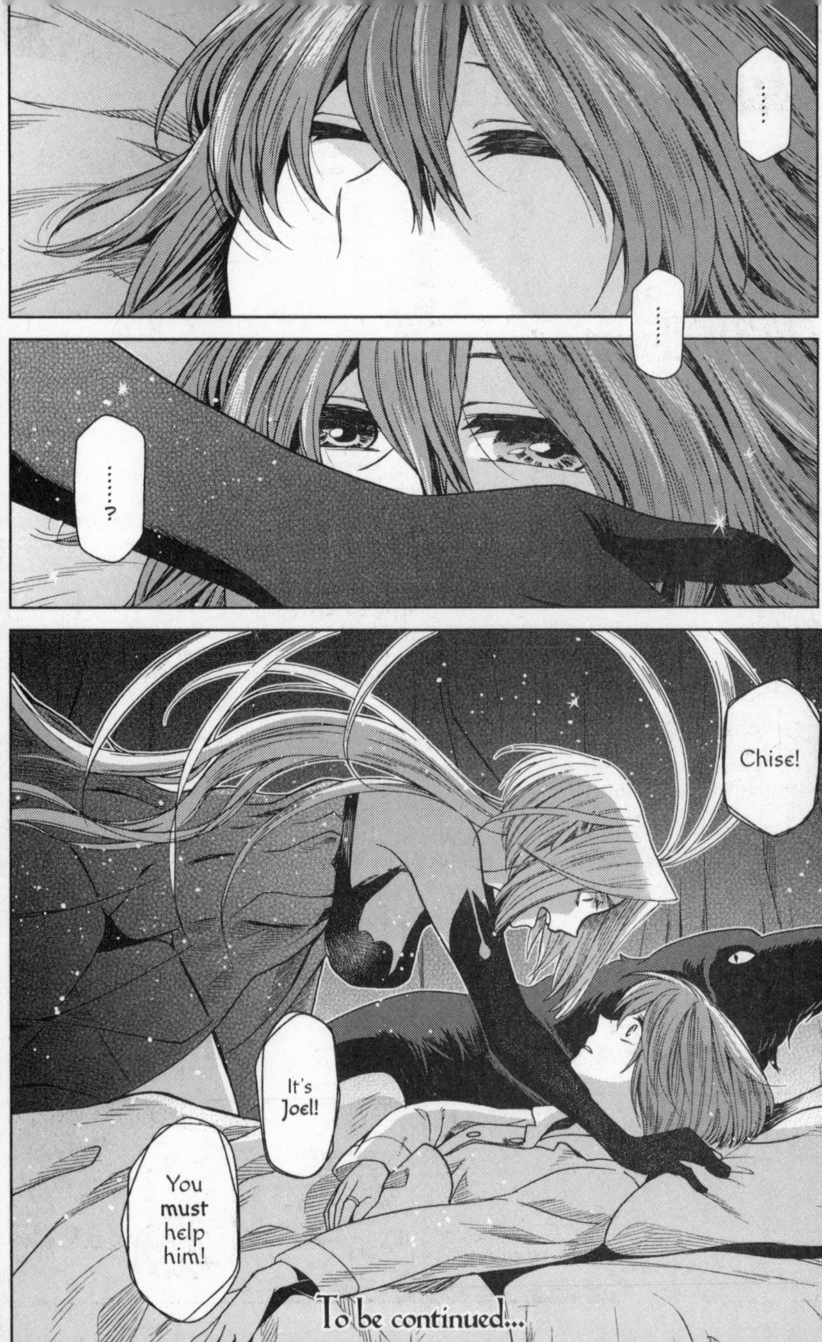
……
……
……?
Chise!
It's Joel!
You **must** help him!
To be continued…

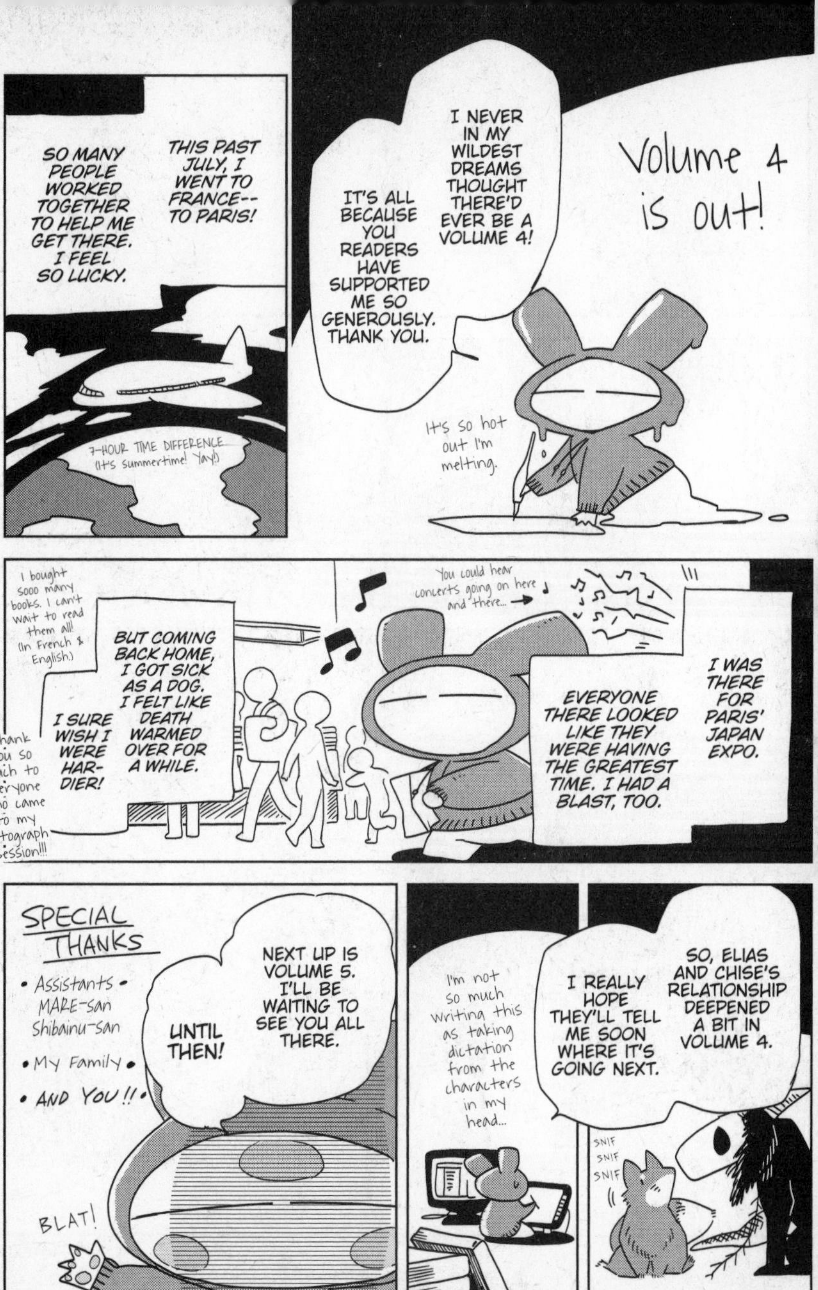
Volume 4 is out!
I NEVER IN MY WILDEST DREAMS THOUGHT THERE'D EVER BE A VOLUME 4!
IT'S ALL BECAUSE YOU READERS HAVE SUPPORTED ME SO GENEROUSLY. THANK YOU.
It's so hot out I'm melting.
THIS PAST JULY, I WENT TO FRANCE-- TO PARIS!
SO MANY PEOPLE WORKED TOGETHER TO HELP ME GET THERE. I FEEL SO LUCKY.
7-HOUR TIME DIFFERENCE (It's summertime! Yay!)
I WAS THERE FOR PARIS' JAPAN EXPO.
EVERYONE THERE LOOKED LIKE THEY WERE HAVING THE GREATEST TIME. I HAD A BLAST, TOO.
You could hear concerts going on here and there...
I bought sooo many books. I can't wait to read them all! (In French & English.)
BUT COMING BACK HOME, I GOT SICK AS A DOG. I FELT LIKE DEATH WARMED OVER FOR A WHILE.
I SURE WISH I WERE HAR-DIER!
Thank you so much to everyone who came to my autograph session!!!
SO, ELIAS AND CHISE'S RELATIONSHIP DEEPENED A BIT IN VOLUME 4.
I REALLY HOPE THEY'LL TELL ME SOON WHERE IT'S GOING NEXT.
SNIF SNIF SNIF
I'm not so much writing this as taking dictation from the characters in my head...
SPECIAL THANKS
• Assistants •
MARE-san
Shibainu-san
• My Family •
• AND YOU!! •
NEXT UP IS VOLUME 5. I'LL BE WAITING TO SEE YOU ALL THERE.
UNTIL THEN!
BLAT!

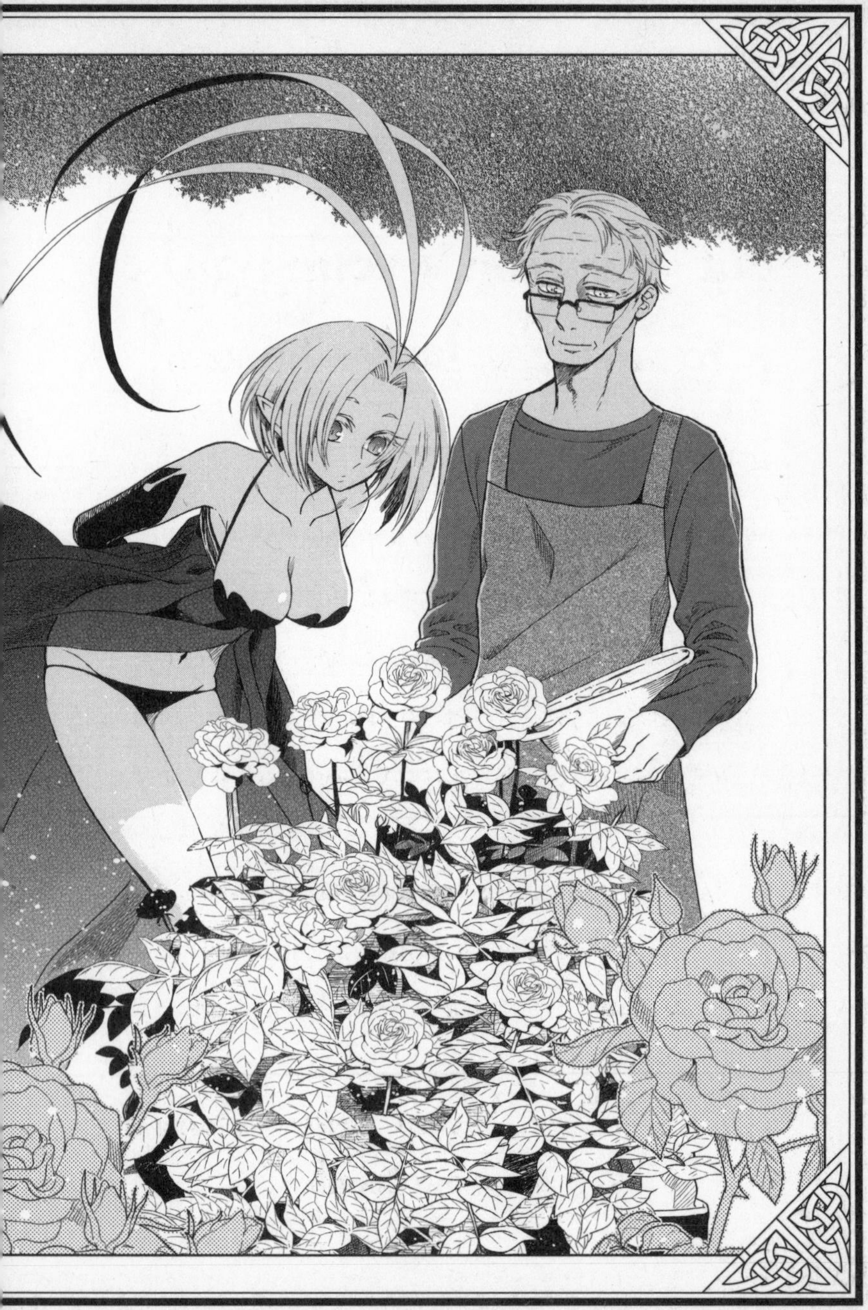

A fae begs for help, but what can a young girl do to save the fairy's lover...?

Thanks to her time living with Elias, Chise has finally begun to move past the fear and loneliness she struggled with in her past. And thanks to Chise, Elias has finally learned to put a name to one of his emotions, and the world seems more beautiful to him.

But one day a leannán sídhe comes to Chise begging for help. What--if anything--can Chise do...?

The Ancient Magus' Bride Volume 5 Coming Soon!

VEN SEAS ENTERTAI...

The Ancient Magus' Bride
VOLUME 4

story and art by **KORE YAMAZAKI**

TRANSLATION
Adrienne Beck

ADAPTATION
Ysabet Reinhardt MacFarlane

LETTERING AND LAYOUT
Lys Blakeslee

COVER DESIGN
Nicky Lim

PROOFREADER
Shanti Whitesides

PRODUCTION MANAGER
Lissa Pattillo

EDITOR-IN-CHIEF
Adam Arnold

PUBLISHER
Jason DeAngelis

THE ANCIENT MAGUS' BRIDE VOL. 4
© Kore Yamazaki 2015
Originally published in Japan in 2015 by MAG Garden Corporation, Tokyo.
English translation rights arranged through TOHAN CORPORATION, Tokyo.

Seven Seas books may be purchased in bulk for educational, business, or promotional use. For information on bulk purchases, please contact Macmillan Corporate & Premium Sales Department at 1-800-221-7945 (ext 5442) or write specialmarkets@macmillan.com.

Seven Seas and the Seven Seas logo are trademarks of Seven Seas Entertainment, LLC. All rights reserved.

ISBN: 978-1-626922-55-6

Printed in Canada
First Printing: April 2016

10 9 8 7 6 5 4 3 2 1

FOLLOW US ONLINE: *www.gomanga.com*

READING DIRECTIONS

This book reads from ***right to left***, Japanese style. If this is your first time reading manga, you start reading from the top right panel on each page and take it from there. If you get lost, just follow the numbered diagram here. It may seem backwards at first, but you'll get the hang of it! Have fun!!

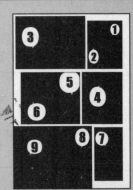